G·L·O·B·A·L S·T·U·D·I·E·S

LATIN AMERICA

NINTH EDITION

Dr. Paul B. Goodwin Jr.
University of Connecticut, Storrs

OTHER BOOKS IN THE GLOBAL STUDIES SERIES

- Africa
- China
- India and South Asia
- Japan and the Pacific Rim
- The Middle East
- Russia, the Eurasian Republics, and Central/Eastern Europe
- Western Europe

Dushkin/McGraw-Hill
Sluice Dock, Guilford, Connecticut 06437
Visit us on the Internet—http://www.dushkin.com

STAFF

Ian A. Nielsen	Publisher
Brenda S. Filley	Production Manager
Lisa M. Clyde	Developmental Editor
Roberta Monaco	Editor
Charles Vitelli	Designer
Cheryl Greenleaf	Permissions Coordinator
Lisa Holmes-Doebrick	Administrative Coordinator
Lara M. Johnson	Design/Advertising Coordinator
Laura Levine	Graphics
Michael Campbell	Graphics
Tom Goddard	Graphics
Eldis Lima	Graphics
Juliana Arbo	Typesetting Supervisor

Cataloging in Publication Data
Main Entry under title: Global Studies: Latin America. 9/E.
    1. Latin America—History. 2. Central America—History. 3. South America—History. I.
Title: Latin America. II. Goodwin, Paul, Jr., *comp.*
ISBN 0–07-236586-2   954   94-71536   ISSN 1061-2831

Ninth Edition

We would like to thank Digital Wisdom Incorporated for allowing us to use their Mountain High Maps cartography software. This
software was used to create the relief maps in this edition.

Printed in the United States of America   234567890BAHBAH54321   Printed on Recycled Paper

Latin America

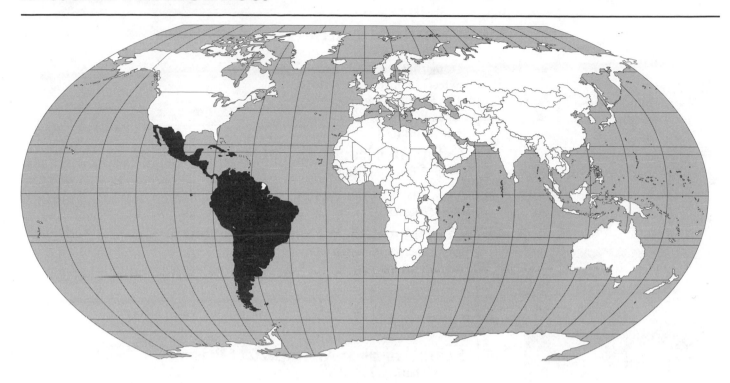

AUTHOR/EDITOR

Dr. Paul B. Goodwin Jr.

The author/editor of *Global Studies: Latin America* is Associate Dean of Arts and Sciences at the University of Connecticut at Storrs. Dr. Goodwin has written, reviewed, and lectured extensively at universities in the United States and many other countries. His particular area of interest is modern Argentina and Anglo–Latin American relations. Dr. Goodwin has lectured frequently for the Smithsonian Institution, and he has authored or edited three books and numerous articles.

SERIES CONSULTANT

H. Thomas Collins
PROJECT LINKS
George Washington University

Contents

Global Studies: Latin America

Latin America   Page 5

Mexico   Page 10

Central America   Page 23

South America   Page 51

South America   Page 95

Caribbean   Page 101

Using Global Studies: Latin America

THE GLOBAL STUDIES SERIES

The Global Studies series was created to help readers acquire a basic knowledge and understanding of the regions and countries in the world. Each volume provides a foundation of information—geographic, cultural, economic, political, historical, artistic, and religious—that will allow readers to better assess the current and future problems within these countries and regions and to comprehend how events there might affect their own well-being. In short, these volumes present the background information necessary to respond to the realities of our global age.

Each of the volumes in the Global Studies series is crafted under the careful direction of an authors/editor—an expert in the area under study. The author/editors teach and conduct research and have traveled extensively through the regions about which they are writing.

In this *Global Studies: Latin America* edition, the author/editor has written an introductory essay on Latin America as a whole, several subregional essays, and country reports for each of the countries included.

MAJOR FEATURES OF THE GLOBAL STUDIES SERIES

The Global Studies volumes are organized to provide concise information on the regions and countries within those areas under study. The major sections and features of the books are described here.

Regional Essays

For *Global Studies: Latin America,* the author/editor has written several essays focusing on the religious, cultural, sociopolitical, and economic differences and similarities of the countries and peoples in the various subregions of Latin America. Regional maps accompany the essays.

Country Reports

Concise reports are written for each of the countries within the region under study. These reports are the heart of each Global Studies volume. *Global Studies: Latin America, Ninth Edition,* contains 33 country reports, including a Mexico report, seven reports for Central America, 12 for South America, and 13 for the Caribbean. The reports cover each *independent country* in Latin America.

The country reports are composed of five standard elements. Each report contains a detailed map visually positioning the country among its neighboring states; a summary of statistical information; a current essay providing important historical, geographical, political, cultural, and economic information; a historical timeline, offering a convenient visual survey of a few key historical events; and four "graphic indicators," with summary statements about the country in terms of development, freedom, health/welfare, and achievements.

A Note on the Statistical Reports

The statistical information provided for each country has been drawn from a wide range of sources. (The most frequently referenced are listed on page 206.) Every effort has been made to provide the most current and accurate information available. However, sometimes the information cited by these sources differs to some extent; and, all too often, the most current information available for some countries is somewhat dated. Aside from these occasional difficulties, the statistical summary of each country is generally quite complete and up to date. Care should be taken, however, in using these statistics (or, for that matter, any published statistics) in making hard comparisons among countries. We have also provided comparable statistics for the United States and Canada, which can be found on pages viii and ix.

World Press Articles

Within each Global Studies volume is reprinted a number of articles carefully selected by our editorial staff and the author/editor from a broad range of international periodicals and newspapers. The articles have been chosen for currency, interest, and their differing perspectives on the subject countries. There are 20 articles in *Global Studies: Latin America, Ninth Edition.*

The articles section is preceded by an annotated table of contents as well as a topic guide. The annotated table of contents offers a brief summary of each article, while the topic guide indicates the main theme(s) of each article. Thus, readers desiring to focus on articles dealing with a particular theme, say, the environment, may refer to the topic guide to find those articles.

WWW Sites

An extensive annotated list of selected World Wide Web sites can be found on the facing page (vii) in this edition of *Global Studies: Latin America.* In addition, the URL addresses for country-specific Web sites are provided on the statistics page of most countries. All of the Web site addresses were correct and operational at press time. Instructors and students alike are urged to refer to those sites often to enhance their understanding of the region and to keep up with current events.

Glossary, Bibliography, Index

At the back of each Global Studies volume, readers will find a glossary of terms and abbreviations, which provides a quick reference to the specialized vocabulary of the area under study and to the standard abbreviations used throughout the volume.

Following the glossary is a bibliography, which lists general works, national histories, and current-events publications and periodicals that provide regular coverage on Latin America.

The index at the end of the volume is an accurate reference to the contents of the volume. Readers seeking specific information and citations should consult this standard index.

Currency and Usefulness

Global Studies: Latin America, like the other Global Studies volumes, is intended to provide the most current and useful information available necessary to understand the events that are shaping the cultures of the region today.

This volume is revised on a regular basis. The statistics are updated, regional essays and country reports revised, and world press articles replaced. In order to accomplish this task, we turn to our author/editor, our advisory boards, and—hopefully—to you, the users of this volume. Your comments are more than welcome. If you have an idea that you think will make the next edition more useful, an article or bit of information that will make it more current, or a general comment on its organization, content, or features that you would like to share with us, please send it in for serious consideration.

Selected World Wide Web Sites for Latin America

All of these Web sites are hot-linked through the *Global Studies* home page:
http://www.dushkin.com/globalstudies (just click on a book).

Some Web sites are continually changing their structure and content, so the information listed may not always be available.

General Sites

1. CNN Online Page—**http://www.cnn.com**—U.S. 24-hour video news channel. News is updated every few hours.

2. C-SPAN Online—**http://www.c-span.org**—See especially C-SPAN International on the Web for International Programming Highlights and archived C-SPAN programs.

3. International Network Information Center at University of Texas—**http://inic.utexas.edu**—Gateway has pointers to international sites, including all Latin American countries.

4. International Business Resources on the WWW—**http://ciber.bus.msu.edu/busres/inttrade.htm**—Connect to several international business links from this site. Included are links to a glossary of international trade terms, exporting data, international trade, current laws, and data on GATT, NAFTA, and MERCOSUR.

5. The Latino Connection—**http://home.tampabay.rr.com/latinoconnect/**—Individual Latino/Hispanic countries data include country information, government, history and culture, economy, business, travel, arts, higher education, and related Web pages.

6. Library of Congress Country Studies—**http://lcweb2.loc.gov/frd/cs/cshome.html#toc**—An invaluable resource for facts and analysis of 100 countries' political, economic, social, and national-security systems and installations.

7. Political Science Resources—**http://www.psr.keele.ac.uk**—Dynamic gateway to sources available via European addresses. Listed by country name, this site includes official government pages, official documents, speeches, election information, and political events.

8. ReliefWeb—**http://www.reliefweb.int**—UN's Department of Humanitarian Affairs clearinghouse for international humanitarian emergencies. It has daily updates, including Reuters, VOA, and PANA.

9. Social Science Information Gateway (SOSIG)—**http://sosig.esrc.bris.ac.uk**—Project of the Economic and Social Research Council (ESRC). It catalogs 22 subjects and lists developing countries' URL addresses.

10. United Nations System—**http://www.unsystem.org**—The official Web site for the United Nations system of organizations. Everything is listed alphabetically, and data on UNICC and Food and Agriculture Organization are available.

11. UN Development Programme (UNDP)—**http://www.undp.org**—Publications and current information on world poverty, Mission Statement, UN Development Fund for Women, and much more. Be sure to see the Poverty Clock.

12. UN Environmental Programme (UNEP)—**http://www.unep.org**—Official site of UNEP. Information on UN environmental programs, products, services, events, and a search engine.

13. U.S. Agency for International Development (USAID)—**http://www.info.usaid.gov**—Graphically presented U.S. trade statistics with Latin America and the Caribbean.

14. U.S. Central Intelligence Agency Home Page—**http://www.odci.gov/cia/publications/factbook/index.html**—This site includes publications of the CIA, such as the World Fact Book, Fact Book on Intelligence, Handbook of International Economic Statistics, CIA Maps and Publications, and much more.

15. U.S. Department of State Home Page—**http://www.state.gov/www/ind.html**—Organized alphabetically Hot Topics (i.e., Country Reports, Human Rights, International Organizations, and much more).

16. World Bank Group—**http://www.worldbank.org**—News (press releases, summary of new projects, speeches), publications, topics in development, and countries and regions. Links to other financial organizations are available.

17. World Health Organizations (WHO)—**http://www.who.ch**—Maintained by WHO's headquarters in Geneva, Switzerland, the site uses Excite search engine to conduct keyword searches.

18. World Trade Organization—**http://www.wto.org**—Topics include foundation of world trade systems, data on textiles, intellectual property rights, legal frameworks, trade and environmental policies, and recent agreements.

Mexico

19. The Mexican Government—**http://world.presidencia.gob.mx**—This site offers a brief overview of the organization of the Mexican Republic, including the Executive, Legislative, and Judicial Branches of the federal government.

20. Documents on Mexican Politics—**http://www.cs.unb.ca/~alopez-o/polind.html**—An archive of a large number of articles on Mexican democracy, freedom of the press, political parties, NAFTA, the economy, Chiapas, and so forth can be found on this Web site.

Central America

21. Central America News—**http://www.centralamericanews.com**—Access to data that includes individual country reports, politics, economic news, travel, media coverage, and links to other sites are available here.

22. Latin World—**http://www.latinworld.com/centro/index.html**—Connecting links to data on the economy and finance, businesses, culture, government, and other areas of interest are available on this site.

South America

23. South America Daily—**http://www.southamericadaily.com**—Everything you want to know about South America is available from this site—from arts and culture, to government data, to environment issues, to individual countries.

Caribbean

24. Caribbean Studies—**http://www.hist.unt.edu/09w-blk4.htm**—A complete site for information about the Caribbean. Topics include general information, Caribbean religions, English Caribbean Islands, Dutch Caribbean Islands, French Caribbean Islands, Hispanic Caribbean Islands, and the U.S. Virgin Islands.

25. Library of Congress Report on the Islands of the Commonwealth Carribbean—**http://lcweb2.loc.gov/frd/cs/cxtoc.html**—An extended study of the Caribbean is possible from this site.

We highly recommend that you review our Web site for expanded information and our other product lines. We are continually updating and adding links to our Web site in order to offer you the most usable and useful information that will support and expand the value of your book. You can reach us at: *http://www.dushkin.com/*

The United States (United States of America)

GEOGRAPHY

Area in Square Miles (Kilometers): 3,618,770 (9,578,626) (slightly larger than China)

Capital (Population): Washington, D.C. (567,100)

Environmental Concerns: air pollution resulting in acid rain; water pollution from runoff of pesticides and fertilizers; desertification; habitat loss; other concerns

Geographical Features: vast central plain, mountains in the west; hills and low mountains in the east; rugged mountains and broad river valleys in Alaska; volcanic topography in Hawaii

Climate: mostly temperate; wide regional variations

PEOPLE

Population

Total: 270,312,000

Annual Growth Rate: 0.87%

Rural/Urban Population Ratio: 24/76

Major Languages: predominantly English; a sizable Spanish-speaking minority; many others

Ethnic Makeup: 83% white; 12% black; 5% Asian, Amerindian, and others

Religions: 56% Protestant; 28% Roman Catholic; 2% Jewish; 14% others or no affiliation

Health

Life Expectancy at Birth: 73 years (male); 80 years (female)

Infant Mortality Rate (Ratio): 6.44/1,000

Average Caloric Intake: 138% of FAO minimum

Physicians Available (Ratio): 1/381

Education

Adult Literacy Rate: 97.9% (official) (estimates vary widely)

Compulsory (Ages): 7–16; free

COMMUNICATION

Telephones: 1 per 1.6 people

Daily Newspaper Circulation: 228 per 1,000 people; approximately 63,000,000 circulation

Televisions: 1 per 1.2 people

TRANSPORTATION

Highways in Miles (Kilometers): 3,906,960 (6,261,154)

Railroads in Miles (Kilometers): 149,161 (240,000)

Usable Airfields: 13,387

Motor Vehicles in Use: 200,500,000

GOVERNMENT

Type: federal republic

Independence Date: July 4, 1776 (from the United Kingdom)

Head of State: President William ("Bill") Jefferson Clinton

Political Parties: Democratic Party; Republican Party; others of minor political significance

Suffrage: universal at 18

MILITARY

Military Expenditures (% of GDP): 3.8%

Current Disputes: none

ECONOMY

Per Capita Income/GDP: $30,200/$8.08 trillion

GDP Growth Rate: 3.8%

Inflation Rate: 2%

Unemployment Rate: 4.9%

Labor Force: 136,300,000

Natural Resources: metallic and non-metallic minerals; petroleum; natural gas; timber

Agriculture: food grains; feed crops; oil-bearing crops; livestock; dairy products

Industry: diversified in both capital- and consumer-goods industries

Exports: $625.1 billion (primary partners Canada, Western Europe, Japan, Mexico)

Imports: $822 billion (primary partners Canada, Western Europe, Japan, Mexico)

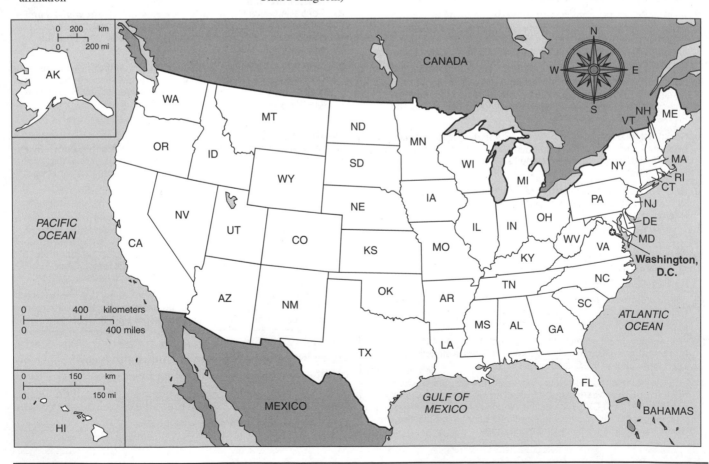

Canada

GEOGRAPHY

Area in Square Miles (Kilometers): 3,850,790 (9,976,140) (slightly larger than the United States)

Capital (Population): Ottawa (1,000,000)

Environmental Concerns: air pollution and resulting acid rain severely affecting lakes and damaging forests; water pollution

Geographical Features: permafrost in the north; mountains in the west; central plains

Climate: from temperate in south to subarctic and arctic in north

PEOPLE

Population

Total: 30,676,000

Annual Growth Rate: 1.09%

Rural/Urban Population Ratio: 23/77

Major Languages: both English and French are official

Ethnic Makeup: 40% British Isles origin; 27% French origin; 20% other European; 1.5% indigenous Indian and Eskimo; 11.5% others, mostly Asian

Religions: 46% Roman Catholic; 16% United Church; 10% Anglican; 28% others

Health

Life Expectancy at Birth: 76 years (male); 83 years (female)

Infant Mortality Rate (Ratio): 5.59/1,000

Average Caloric Intake: 127% of FAO minimum

Physicians Available (Ratio): 1/464

Education

Adult Literacy Rate: 97%

Compulsory (Ages): primary school

COMMUNICATION

Telephones: 1 per 1.7 people

Daily Newspaper Circulation: 189 per 1,000 people

Televisions: 1 per 1.5 people

TRANSPORTATION

Highways in Miles (Kilometers): 637,104 (1,021,000)

Railroads in Miles (Kilometers): 48,764 (78,148)

Usable Airfields: 1,139

Motor Vehicles in Use: 16,700,000

GOVERNMENT

Type: confederation with parliamentary democracy

Independence Date: July 1, 1867 (from United Kingdom)

Head of State/Government: Queen Elizabeth II; Prime Minister Jean Chrétien

Political Parties: Progressive Conservative Party; Liberal Party; New Democratic Party; Reform Party; Bloc Québécois

Suffrage: universal at 18

MILITARY

Military Expenditures (% of GDP): 1.53%

Current Disputes: none

ECONOMY

Currency ($U.S. Equivalent): 1.53 Canadian dollars = $1

Per Capita Income/GDP: $21,700/$658 billion

GDP Growth Rate: 3.5%

Inflation Rate: 1.8%

Unemployment Rate: 8.6%

Labor Force: 15,300,000

Natural Resources: petroleum; coal; natural gas; fish and other wildlife; minerals; cement; forestry products

Agriculture: grains; livestock; dairy products; potatoes; hogs; poultry and eggs; tobacco

Industry: oil production and refining; natural-gas development; fish products; wood and paper products; chemicals; transportation equipment

Exports: $208.6 billion (primary partners United States, Japan, United Kingdom)

Imports: $194.4 billion (primary partners United States, Japan, United Kingdom)

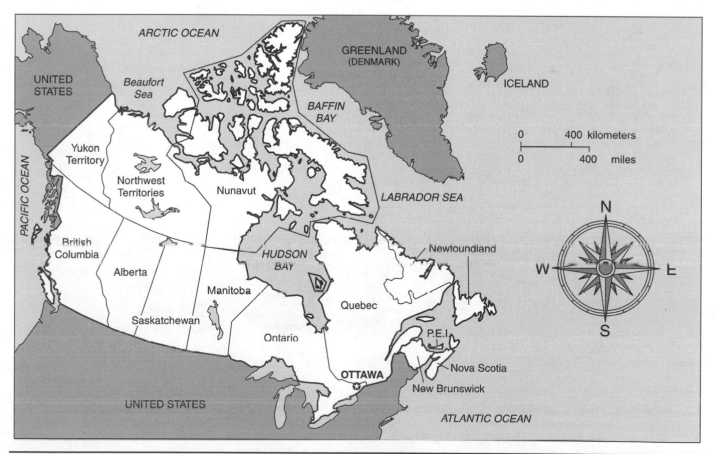

GLOBAL STUDIES

This map is provided to give you a graphic picture of where the countries of the world are located, the relationships they have with their region and neighbors, and their positions relative to the superpowers and power blocs. We have focused on certain areas to illustrate these crowded regions more clearly.

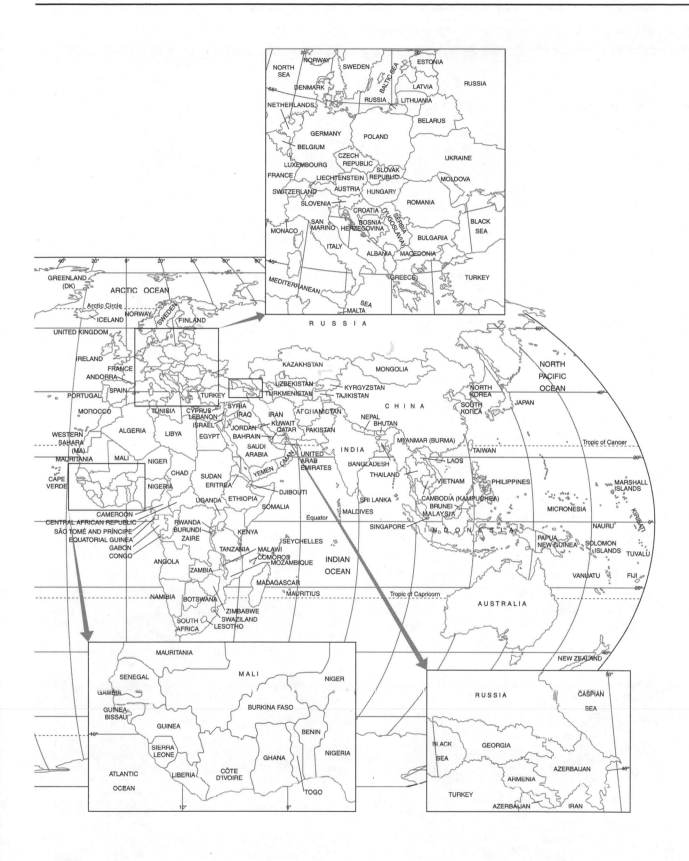

Latin America

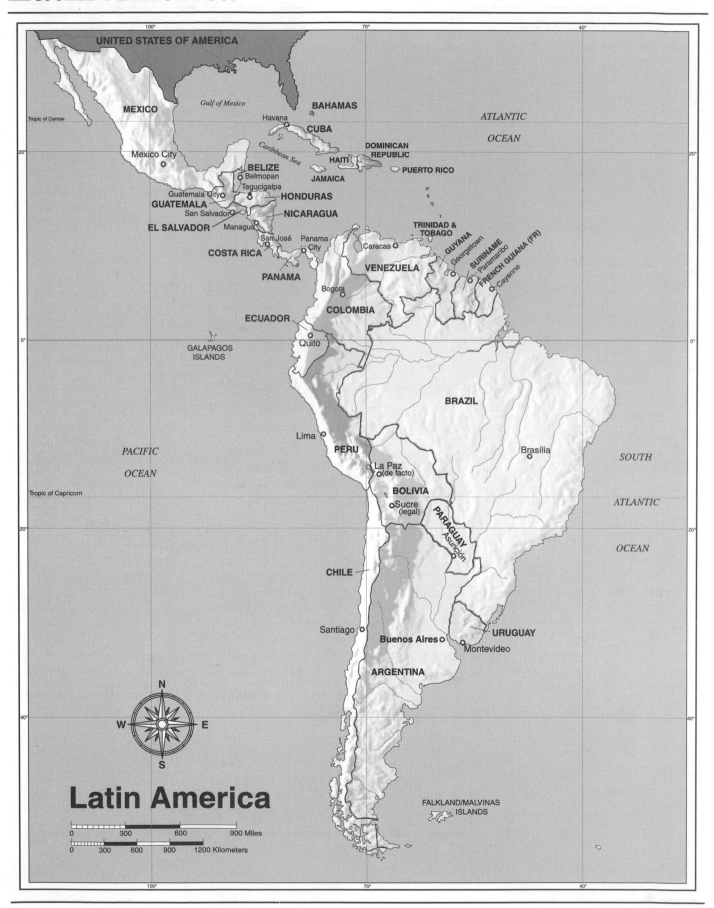

UNITED STATES OF AMERICA

MEXICO

Gulf of Mexico

Tropic of Cancer

Mexico City

BAHAMAS

Havana

CUBA

Caribbean Sea

BELIZE

Belmopan

Tegucigalpa

Guatemala City

GUATEMALA

San Salvador

HONDURAS

EL SALVADOR

Managua

NICARAGUA

San José

Panama City

COSTA RICA

PANAMA

HAITI

JAMAICA

DOMINICAN REPUBLIC

PUERTO RICO

ATLANTIC

OCEAN

TRINIDAD & TOBAGO

Caracas

VENEZUELA

Bogota

COLOMBIA

ECUADOR

GUYANA

Georgetown

SURINAME

Paramaribo

FRENCH GUIANA (FR)

Cayenne

PACIFIC

OCEAN

GALAPAGOS ISLANDS

Quito

Lima

PERU

La Paz (de facto)

BOLIVIA

Sucre (legal)

Tropic of Capricorn

BRAZIL

Brasília

SOUTH

ATLANTIC

OCEAN

PARAGUAY

Asunción

CHILE

Santiago

Buenos Aires

URUGUAY

Montevideo

ARGENTINA

N
W   E
S

Latin America

0   300   600   900 Miles

0   300   600   900   1200 Kilometers

FALKLAND/MALVINAS ISLANDS

Latin America: Myth and Reality

Much of the world still tends to view Latin Americans in terms of stereotypes. The popular image of the mustachioed bandit sporting a large sombrero and draped with cartridge belts has been replaced by the figure of the modern-day guerrilla, but the same essential image, of lawlessness and violence, persists. Another common stereotype is that of the lazy Latin American who constantly puts things off until *mañana* ("tomorrow"). The implied message here is that Latin Americans lack industry and do not know how to make the best use of their time. A third widespread image is that of the Latin lover and the cult of *machismo* (manliness).

Many of those outside the culture find it difficult to conceive of Latin America as a mixture of peoples and cultures, each one distinct from the others. Indeed, it was not so long ago that then–U.S. president Ronald Reagan, after a tour of the region, remarked with some surprise that all of the countries were "different." Stereotypes spring from ignorance and bias; images are not necessarily a reflection of reality. In the words of Spanish philosopher José Ortega y Gasset: "In politics and history, if one takes accepted statements at face value, one will be sadly misled."

THE LATIN AMERICAN REALITY

The reality of Latin America's multiplicity of cultures is, in a word, complexity. Europeans, Africans, and the indigenous people of Latin America have all contributed substantially to these cultures. If one sets aside non-Hispanic influences for a moment, is it possible to argue, as does historian Claudio Veliz, that "the Iberian [Spanish and Portuguese] inheritance is an essential part of our lives and customs; Brazil and Spanish America [i.e., Spanish-speaking] have derived their personality from Iberia"?

Many scholars would disagree. For example, political scientist Lawrence S. Graham argues that "what is clear is that generalizations about Latin American cultural unity are no longer tenable." And that "one of the effects of nationalism has been to . . . lead growing numbers of individuals within the region to identify with their own nation-state before they think in terms of a more amorphous land mass called Latin America."

Granted, Argentines speak of their Argentinity and Mexicans of their *mejicanidad.* It is true that there are profound differences that separate the nations of the region. But there exists a cultural bedrock that ties Latin America to Spain and Portugal, and beyond—to the Roman Empire and the great cultures of the Mediterranean world. African influence, too, is substantial in many parts of the region. Latin America's Indians, of course, trace their roots to indigenous sources.

To understand the nature of Latin American culture, one must remember that there exist many exceptions to the generalizations; the cultural mold is not rigid. Much of what has happened in Latin America, including the evolution of its cultures, is the result of a fortunate—and sometimes an unfortunate—combination of various factors.

THE FAMILY

Let us first consider the Latin American family. The family unit has survived even Latin America's uneven economic development and the pressures of modernization. Family ties are strong and dominant. These bonds are not confined to the nuclear family of father, mother, and children. The same close ties are found in the extended family (a network of second cousins, godparents, and close friends of blood relatives). In times of difficulty, the family can be counted on to help. It is a fortress against the misery of the outside world; it is the repository of dignity, honor, and respect.

AN URBAN CIVILIZATION

In a region where the interaction of networks of families is the rule and where frequent human contact is sought out, it is not surprising to find that Latin Americans are, above all, an

(United Nations photo)

In Latin America, the family is an important element in the cultural context. These loving children live in a poor section of Santiago, Chile.

urban people. There are more cities of more than half a million people in Latin America than in the United States.

Latin America's high urban population is unusual, for urbanization is usually associated with industrialization. In Latin America, urban culture was not created by industrial growth; it actually pre-dated it. As soon as the opportunity presented itself, the Spanish conquerors of the New World, in Veliz's words, "founded cities in which to take refuge from the barbaric, harsh, uncivilized, and rural world outside. . . . For those men civilization was strictly and uniquely a function of well-ordered city life."

The city, from the Spanish conquest until the present, has dominated the social and cultural horizon of Latin America. Opportunity is found in the city, not in the countryside. This cultural fact of life, in addition to economic motives, accounts for the continuing flow of population from rural to urban areas in Latin America.

A WORLD OF APPEARANCES

Because in their urban environment Latin Americans are in close contact with many other people, appearances are important to them. There is a constant quest for prestige, dignity, status, and honor. People are forever trying to impress one another with their public worth. Hence, it is not unusual to see a blue-collar worker traveling to work dressed in a suit, briefcase in hand. It is not uncommon to see jungles of television antennas over shantytowns, although many are not connected to anything.

It is a society that, in the opinion of writer Octavio Paz, hides behind masks. Latin Americans convey an impression of importance, no matter how menial their position. Glen Dealy, a political scientist, writes: "And those of the lower class who must wait on tables, wash cars, and do gardening for a living can help to gain back a measure of self-respect by having their shoes shined by someone else, buying a drink for a friend . . . , or concealing their occupation by wearing a tie to and from work."

MACHISMO

Closely related to appearances is *machismo*. The term is usually understood solely, and mistakenly, in terms of virility—the image of the Latin lover, for example. But machismo also connotes generosity, dignity, and honor. In many respects, macho behavior is indulged in because of social convention; it is expected of men. Machismo is also one of those cultural traits that cuts through class lines, for the macho is admired regardless of his social position.

THE ROLE OF WOMEN

If the complex nature of machismo is misunderstood by those outside the culture, so too is the role of women. The commonly held stereotype is that Latin American women are submissive and that the culture is dominated by males. Again, appearances mask a far more complex reality, for Latin

American cultures actually allow for strong female roles. Political scientist Evelyn Stevens, for example, has found that *marianismo*—the female counterpart of machismo—permeates all strata of Latin American society. Marianismo is the cult of feminine spiritual superiority that "teaches that women are semi-divine, morally superior to and spiritually stronger than men."

When Mexico's war for independence broke out in 1810, a religious symbol—the Virgin of Guadalupe—was identified with the rebels and became a rallying point for the first stirrings of Mexican nationalism. It was not uncommon in Argentine textbooks to portray Eva Perón (1919–1952), president Juan Perón's wife, in the image of the Virgin Mary, complete with a blue veil and halo. In less religious terms, one of Latin America's most popular novels, *Doña Barbara,* by Rómulo Gallegos, is the story of a female *caudillo* ("man on horseback") on the plains of Venezuela.

The Latin American woman dominates the family because of a deep-seated respect for motherhood. Personal identity is less of a problem for her because she retains her family name upon marriage and passes it on to her children. Women who work outside the home are also supposed to retain respect for their motherhood, which is sacred. In any conflict between a woman's job and the needs of her family, the employer, by custom, must grant her a leave to tend to the family's needs. Recent historical scholarship has also revealed that Latin

(United Nations photo/Bernard P. Wolff)

The role of the indigenous woman in Latin America has been defined by centuries of tradition. This woman is spinning wool, in Chimburaso, Ecuador, just as her ancestors did.

American women have long enjoyed rights denied to women in other, more "advanced" parts of the world. For example, Latin American women were allowed to own property and to sign for mortgages in their own names even in colonial days. In the 1920s, they won the right to vote in local elections in Yucatán, Mexico, and San Juan, Argentina.

Here again, though, appearances can be deceiving. Many Latin American constitutions guarantee equality of treatment, but reality is burdensome for women in many parts of the region. They do not have the same kinds of access to jobs that men enjoy; they seldom receive equal pay for equal work; and family life, at times, can be brutalizing.

WORK AND LEISURE

Work, leisure, and concepts of time in Latin America correspond to an entirely different cultural mind-set than exists in Northern Europe and North America. The essential difference was demonstrated in a North American television commercial for a wine, in which two starry-eyed people were portrayed giving the Spanish toast *Salud, amor, y pesetas* ("Health, love, and money"). For a North American audience, the message was appropriate. But the full Spanish toast includes the tag line *y el tiempo para gozarlos* ("and the time to enjoy them").

In Latin America, leisure is viewed as a perfectly rational goal. It has nothing to do with being lazy or indolent. Indeed, in *Ariel,* by writer José Enrique Rodó, leisure is described within the context of the culture: "To think, to dream, to admire—these are the ministrants that haunt my cell. The ancients ranked them under the word *otium,* well-employed leisure, which they deemed the highest use of being truly rational, liberty of thought emancipated of all ignoble chains. Such leisure meant that use of time which they opposed to mere economic activity as the expression of a higher life. Their concept of dignity was linked closely to this lofty conception of leisure." Work, by contrast, is often perceived as a necessary evil.

CONCEPTS OF TIME

Latin American attitudes toward time also reveal the inner workings of the culture. Exasperated North American businesspeople have for years complained about the *mañana, mañana* attitude of Latin Americans. People often are late for appointments; sometimes little *appears* to get done.

For the North American who believes that time is money, such behavior appears senseless. However, Glen Dealy, in his perceptive book *The Public Man,* argues that such behavior is perfectly rational. A Latin American man who spends hours over lunch or over coffee in a café is not wasting time. For here, with his friends and relatives, he is with the source of his power. Indeed, networks of friends and families are the glue of Latin American society. "Without spending time in this fashion he would, in fact, soon have fewer friends. Addi-

(United Nations photo/Jerry Frank)

Agriculture is the backbone of much of Latin America's cultures and economies. These workers are harvesting sugarcane on a plantation in the state of Pernambuco, Brazil.

tionally, he knows that to leave a café precipitously for an 'appointment' would signify to all that he must not keep someone else waiting—which further indicates his lack of importance. If he had power and position the other person would wait upon his arrival. It is the powerless who wait." Therefore, friends and power relationships are more important than rushing to keep an appointment. The North American who wants the business deal will wait. In a sense, then, the North American is the client and the Latin American is the *patrón* (the "patron," or wielder of power).

Perceptions of time in Latin America also have a broader meaning. North American students who have been exposed to Latin American literature are almost always confused by the absence of a "logical," chronological development of the story. Time, for Latin Americans, tends to be circular rather than linear. That is, the past and the present are perceived as equally relevant—both are points on a circle. The past is as important as the present.

MYTH AND REALITY

The past that is exposed in works of Latin American literature as well as scholarly writings reflects wholly different attitudes toward what people from other cultures identify as reality. For example, in Nobel Prize–winning writer Gabriél García Márquez's classic novel *One Hundred Years of Solitude*—a fictional history of the town of Macondo and its leading family—fantasy and tall tales abound. But García Márquez drew his inspiration from stories he heard on his grandmother's knee about Aracataca, Colombia, the real town in which he grew up. The point here is that the fanciful story of the town's origins constitutes that town's memory of its past. The stories give the town a common heritage and memory.

From a North American or Northern European perspective, the historical memory is faulty. From the Latin American perspective, however, it is the perception of the past that is important, regardless of its factual accuracy. Myth and reality, appearances and substance, merge.

POLITICAL CULTURE

The generalizations drawn here about Latin American society apply also to its political culture, which is essentially authoritarian and oriented toward power and power relationships. Ideology—be it liberalism, conservatism, or communism—is little more than window dressing. It is the means by which contenders for power can be separated. As Claudio Veliz has noted, regardless of the aims of revolutionary leaders, the great upheavals in Latin America in the twentieth century have without exception ended up by strengthening the political center, which is essentially authoritarian. This was true of the Mexican Revolution (1910), the Bolivian Revolution (1952), the Cuban Revolution (1958), and the Nicaraguan Revolution (1979).

Ideology has never been a decisive factor in the historical and social reality of Latin America. But charisma and the ability to lead are crucial ingredients. José Velasco Ibarra, five times the president of Ecuador in the twentieth century, once boasted: "Give me a balcony and I will be president!" He saw his personality, not his ideology, as the key to power.

In the realm of national and international relations, Latin America often appears to those outside the culture to be in a constant state of turmoil and chaos. It seems that every day there are reports that a prominent politician has fallen from power, border clashes have intensified, or guerrillas have taken over another section of a country. But the conclusion that chaos reigns in Latin America is most often based on the visible political and social violence, not on the general nature of a country. Political violence is often local in nature, and the social fabric of the country is bound together by the enduring social stability of the family. Again, there is the dualism of what *appears to be* and what *is*.

Much of this upheaval can be attributed to the division in Latin America between the people of Mediterranean background and the indigenous Indian populations. There may be several hundred minority groups within a single country. The problems that may arise from such intense internal differences, however, are not always necessarily detrimental, because they contribute to the texture and color of Latin American culture.

SEEING BEHIND THE MASK

In order to grasp the essence of Latin America, one must ignore the stereotypes, appreciate appearances for what they are, and attempt to see behind the mask. Latin America must be appreciated as a culture in its own right, as an essentially Mediterranean variant of Western civilization.

A Latin American world view tends to be dualistic. The family constitutes the basic unit; here one finds generosity, warmth, honor, and love. Beyond the walls of the home, in the world of business and politics, Latin Americans don their masks and enter "combat." It is a world of power relationships, of macho bravado, and of appearances. This dualism is deep-seated; scholars such as Richard Morse and Glen Dealy have traced its roots to the Middle Ages. For Latin Americans, one's activities are compartmentalized into those fitting for the City of God, which corresponds to religion, the home, and one's intimate circle of friends; and those appropriate for the City of Man, which is secular and often ruthless and corrupt. North Americans, who tend to measure their public and private lives by the same yardstick, often interpret Latin American dualism as hypocrisy. Nothing could be further from the truth.

For the Latin American, life exists on several planes, has purpose, and is perfectly rational. Indeed, one is tempted to suggest that many Latin American institutions—particularly the supportive network of families and friends—are more in tune with a world that can alienate and isolate than are our own. As you will see in the following reports, the social structure and cultural diversity of Latin America add greatly to its character and, paradoxically, to its stability.

Mexico (United Mexican States)

GEOGRAPHY

Area in Square Miles (Kilometers):
764,000 (1,978,000) (about 3
times the size of Texas)
Capital (Population): Mexico
City (18,000,000)
Environmental Concerns: scarce
freshwater reserves; water
pollution; deforestation; soil
erosion; serious air pollution
Geographical Features: high,
rugged mountains; low coastal
plains; high plateaus; desert
Climate: varies from tropical to desert

PEOPLE

Population
Total: 98,553,000
Annual Growth Rate: 1.77%
Rural/Urban Population Ratio:
26/74
Major Languages: Spanish;
various Maya, Nahuatl, and
other regional indigenous
languages
Ethnic Makeup: 60% Mestizo;
30% Amerindian; 9% white;
1% others
Religions: 89% Roman Catholic;
6% Protestant; 5% others

Health
Life Expectancy at Birth: 69
years (male); 75 years (female)
Infant Mortality Rate (Ratio):
25.8/1,000
Average Caloric Intake: 121% of
FAO minimum
Physicians Available (Ratio):
1/613

Education
Adult Literacy Rate: 89.6%
Compulsory (Ages): 6–12; free

COMMUNICATION
Telephones: 1 per 10 people
Daily Newspaper Circulation:
113 per 1,000 people
Televisions: 1 per 6.1 people

TRANSPORTATION
Highways in Miles (Kilometers): 156,492
(252,000)
Railroads in Miles (Kilometers): 12,772 (20,567)
Usable Airfields: 1,810
Motor Vehicles in Use: 1,835,000

GOVERNMENT
Type: federal republic
Independence Date: September 16, 1810
(from Spain)
Head of State/Government: President
Ernesto Zedillo Ponce de León is both
head of state and head of government
Political Parties: Institutional Revolutionary
Party; National Action Party; Party of the

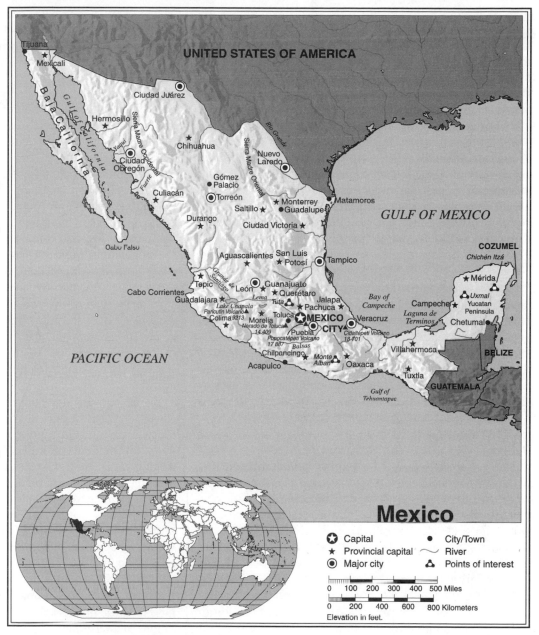

Mexico

- ✪ Capital
- ★ Provincial capital
- ◉ Major city
- • City/Town
- ∿ River
- ⬠ Points of interest

| 0 | 100 | 200 | 300 | 400 | 500 Miles |
| 0 | 200 | 400 | | 600 | 800 Kilometers |

Elevation in feet.

Democratic Revolution; Cardenist Front
for National Reconstruction Party;
Democratic Forum Party; Mexican Green
Ecologist Party; Workers Party
Suffrage: universal and compulsory at 18

MILITARY
Military Expenditures (% of GDP): 0.3%
Current Disputes: none

ECONOMY
Currency ($ U.S. Equivalent): 9.39 pesos = $1
Per Capita Income/GDP: $7,700/$694.3
billion
GDP Growth Rate: 7.3%
Inflation Rate: 15.7%
Unemployment Rate: 3.7%; considerable
underemployment

Labor Force: 36,600,000
Natural Resources: petroleum; silver; copper;
gold; lead; zinc; natural gas; timber
Agriculture: corn; wheat; soybeans; rice;
beans; cotton; coffee; fruit; tomatoes;
livestock products; wood products
Industry: food and beverages; tobacco;
chemicals; iron and steel; petroleum;
mining; textiles; clothing; motor vehicles;
consumer durables; tourism
Exports: $110.4 billion (primary partners
United States, Canada)
Imports: $109.8 billion (primary partners
United States, Japan, Germany)

 http://lcweb2.loc.gov/frd/cs/
mxtoc.html

Mexico: On the Verge of Change?

There is a story that Hernán Cortéz, the conqueror of the Aztec Empire in the sixteenth century, when asked to describe the landscape of New Spain (Mexico), took a piece of paper in his hands and crumpled it. The analogy is apt. Mexico is a tortured land of mountains and valleys, of deserts in the north and rain forests in the south. Geography has helped to create an intense regionalism in Mexico, and the existence of hundreds of *patrias chicas* ("little countries") has hindered national integration for decades.

Much of Mexico's territory is vulnerable to earthquakes and volcanic activity. In 1943, for example, a cornfield in one of Mexico's richest agricultural zones sprouted a volcano instead of maize. In 1982, a severe volcanic eruption in the south took several hundred lives, destroyed thousands of head of livestock, and buried crops under tons of ash. Thousands of people died when a series of earthquakes struck Mexico City in 1985.

Mexico is a nation of climatic extremes. Much-needed rains often fall so hard that most of the water runs off before it can be absorbed by the soil. When rains fail to materialize, crops die in the fields. The harsh face of the land, the unavailability of water, and erosion limit the agricultural potential of Mexico. Only 10 to 15 percent of Mexico's land can be planted with crops; but because of unpredictable weather or natural disasters, good harvests can be expected from only 6 to 8 percent of the land in any given year.

MEXICO CITY

Mexico's central region has the best cropland. It was here that the Aztecs built their capital city, the foundations of which lie beneath the current Mexican capital, Mexico City. Given their agricultural potential as well as its focus as the commercial and administrative center of the nation, Mexico City and the surrounding region have always supported a large population. For decades, Mexico City has acted as a magnet for rural poor who have given up attempts to eke out a living from the soil. In the 1940s and 1950s, the city experienced a great population surge. In that era, however, it had the capacity to absorb the tens of thousands of migrants, and so a myth of plentiful money and employment was created. Even today, that myth exercises a strong influence in the countryside; it partially accounts for the tremendous growth of the city and its metropolitan area, now home to approximately 18 million people.

The size and location of Mexico City have spawned awesome problems. Because it lies in a valley surrounded by mountains, air pollution is trapped. Mexico City has the worst smog in the Western Hemisphere. Traffic congestion is among the worst in the world. And essential services—including the provision of drinkable water, electricity, and sewers—have failed to keep pace with the city's growth in population.

Social and Cultural Changes

Dramatic social and cultural changes have accompanied Mexico's population growth. These are particularly evident in Mexico City, which daily becomes less Mexican and more cosmopolitan and international.

As Mexico City has become more worldly, English words have become more common in everyday vocabulary. "Okay," "coffee break," and "happy hour" are some examples of English idioms that have slipped into popular usage. In urban centers, quick lunches and coffee breaks have replaced the traditional large meal that was once served at noon. For most people, the afternoon *siesta* ("nap") is a fondly remembered custom of bygone days.

Mass communication has had an incalculable impact on culture. Television commercials primarily use models who are European or North American in appearance—preferably white, blue-eyed, and blonde. As if in defiance of the overwhelmingly Mestizo (mixed Indian and white) character of the population, Mexican newspapers and magazines carry advertisements for products guaranteed to lighten one's skin. Success has become associated with light skin.

Another symbol of success is ownership of a television. Antennas cover rooftops even in the poorest urban slums. Acute observers might note, however, that many of the antennas are not connected to anything; the residents of many hovels merely want to convey the impression that they can afford one.

Television, however, has helped to educate the illiterate. Some Mexican soap operas, for instance, incorporate educational materials. On a given day, a show's characters may attend an adult-education class that stresses basic reading and writing skills. Both the television characters and the home-viewing audience sit in on the class. Literacy is portrayed as being essential to one's success and well-being. Mexican *telenovelas*, or "soaps," have a special focus on teenagers and problems common to adolescents. Solutions are advanced within a traditional cultural context and reaffirm the central role of the family.

Cultural Survival: Compadrazgo

Despite these obvious signs of change, distinct Mexican traditions and customs have not only survived Mexico's transformation but have also flourished because of it. The chaos of city life, the hundreds of thousands of migrants uprooted from rural settings, and the sense of isolation and alienation common to city dwellers the world over are in part eased by the Hispanic institution of *compadrazgo* ("co-godparenthood" or "sponsorship").

Compadrazgo is found at all levels of Mexican society and in both rural and urban areas. It is a device for building economic and social alliances that are more enduring than simple friendship. Furthermore, it has a religious dimension as well as a secular, or everyday, application. In addition to basic religious occasions (such as baptism, confirmation, first communion, and marriage), Mexicans seek sponsors for minor religious occasions, such as the blessing of a business, and for events as common as a graduation or a boy's first haircut.

A man from the state of Puebla asks for money outside a jewelry store in Mexico City, hoping to raise enough funds to supply the peasants of his community with the water and electricity that the government has been unable to provide.

Anthropologist Robert V. Kemper observes that the institution of compadrazgo reaches across class lines and knits the various strands of Mexican society into a whole cloth. Compadrazgo performs many functions, including providing assistance from the more powerful to the less powerful and, reciprocally, providing homage from the less powerful to the more powerful. The most common choices for *compadres* are neighbors, relatives, fellow migrants, coworkers, and employers. A remarkably flexible institution, compadrazgo is perfectly compatible with the tensions and anxieties of urban life.

Yet even compadrazgo—a form of patron/client relationship—has its limitations. As Mexico City has sprawled ever wider across the landscape, multitudes of new neighborhoods have been created. Many are the result of well-planned land seizures, orchestrated by groups of people attracted by the promise of the city. Technically, such land seizures are illegal; and a primary goal of the *colonos* (inhabitants of these low-income communities) is legitimization and consequent community participation.

Beginning in the 1970s, colonos forcefully pursued their demands for legitimization through protest movements and demonstrations, some of which revealed a surprising degree of radicalism. In response, the Mexican government adopted a two-track policy: It selectively repressed the best-organized and most radical groups of colonos, and it tried to co-opt the remainder through negotiation. In the early 1980s, the government created "Citizen Representation" bodies, official channels within Mexico City through which colonos could participate, within the system, in the articulation of their demands.

From the perspective of the colonos, the establishment of the citizen organizations afforded them an additional means to advance their demands for garbage collection; street paving; provision of potable water; sewage removal; and, most critically, the regularization of land tenure—that is, legitimization. In the government's view, representation for the colonos served to win supporters for the Mexican political structure, particularly the authority of the official ruling party, at a time of outspoken challenge from other political sectors.

Citizens are encouraged to work within the system; potential dissidents are transformed through the process of co-optation into collaborators. In today's Mexico City, then, patronage and clientage have two faces: the traditional one of compadrazgo, the other a form of state paternalism that promotes community participation.

THE BORDER

In the past few decades, driven by poverty, unemployment, and underemployment, many Mexicans have chosen not Mexico City but the United States as the place to improve their lives. Mexican workers in the United States are not a new phenomenon. During World War II, the presidents of both nations agreed to allow Mexican workers, called *braceros*, to enter the United States as agricultural workers. They were strictly regulated. In contrast, the new wave of migrants is largely unregulated. Each year, hundreds of thousands of undocumented Mexicans illegally cross the border in search of work. It has been estimated that at any given time, between 4 million and 6 million Mexicans pursue an existence as illegal aliens in the United States.

Thousands of Mexicans are able to support families with the fruits of their labors, but, as undocumented workers, they are not protected by the law. Many are callously exploited by those who smuggle them across the border as well as by employers in the United States. For the Mexican government, however, such mass emigration has been a blessing in disguise. It has served as a kind of sociopolitical safety valve, and it has resulted in an inflow of dollars sent home by the workers.

In recent years, U.S. companies and the governments of Mexican states along the border have profited from the creation of assembly plants known as *maquiladoras*. Low wages and a docile labor force are attractive to employers, while the Mexican government reaps the benefits of employment and tax dollars. Despite the appearance of prosperity along the border, it must be emphasized that chronic unemployment in other parts of Mexico ensures the misery of millions of people. How these realities will be affected by the implementation of the North American Free Trade Agreement (NAFTA) remains to be seen.

THE INDIAN "PROBLEM"

During the 1900s, urbanization and racial mixing changed the demographic face of Mexico. A government official once commented: "A country predominately Mestizo, where Indian and white are now minorities, Mexico preserves the festivity and ceremonialism of the Indian civilizations and the religiosity and legalism of the Spanish Empire." The quotation is revealing, for it clearly identifies the Indian as a marginal member of society, as an object of curiosity.

In Mexico, as is the case with indigenous peoples in most of Latin America, Indians are viewed as obstacles to national integration and economic progress. There exist in Mexico more than 200 distinct Indian tribes or ethnic groups, who speak more than 50 languages or dialects. In the view of "progressive" Mexicans, the "sociocultural fragmentation" caused by the diversity of languages fosters political misunderstanding, insecurity, and regional incomprehension. Indians suffer from widespread discrimination. Language is not the only barrier to their economic progress. They have long endured the unequal practices of a ruling white and Mestizo elite. Indians may discover, for example, that they cannot expand a small industry, such as a furniture-making enterprise, because few financial institutions will lend a large amount of money to an Indian.

(United Nations photo)

In many ways, the Mexican people have two separate identities: one public and one private. This carved door by artist Diego Rivera, located in Chapingo, depicts the dual identity that is so much a part of Mexican culture.

NATIONAL IDENTITY

Mexico's Mestizo face has had a profound impact on the attempts of intellectuals to understand the meaning of the term "Mexican." The question of national identity has always been an important theme in Mexican history; it became a particularly burning issue in the aftermath of the Revolution of 1910. Octavio Paz believes that most Mexicans have denied their origins: They do not want to be either Indian or Spaniard, but they also refuse to see themselves as a mixture of both. One result of this essential denial of one's ethnic roots is a collective inferiority complex. The Mexican, Paz writes, is insecure. To hide that insecurity, which stems from his sense of "inferiority," the Mexican wears a "mask." Machismo (the cult of manliness) is one example of such a mask. In Paz's estimation, aggressive behavior at a sporting event, while driving a car, or in relationships with women reflects a deep-seated identity crisis.

Perhaps an analogy can be drawn from Mexican domestic architecture. Traditional Mexican homes are surrounded by high, solid walls, often topped with shards of glass and devoid of windows looking out onto the street. From the outside, these abodes appear cold and inhospitable. Once inside (once behind the mask), however, the Mexican home is warm and comfortable. Here, appearances are set aside and Mexicans can relax and be themselves. By contrast, many homes in the United States have vast expanses of glass that allow every passerby to see within. That whole style of open architecture, at least for homes, is jolting for many Mexicans (as well as other Latin Americans).

THE FAILURE OF THE 1910 REVOLUTION

In addition to the elusive search for Mexican identity, one of Mexican intellectuals' favorite themes is the Revolution of 1910 and what they perceive as its shortcomings. That momentous struggle (1910–1917) cost more than 1 million lives, but it offered Mexico the promise of a new society, free from the abuses of past centuries. It began with a search for truth and honesty in government; it ended with an assertion of the dignity and equality of all men and women.

The goals of the 1910 Revolution were set forth in the Constitution of 1917, a remarkable document—not only in its own era, but also today. Article 123, for example, which concerns labor, includes the following provisions: an eight-hour workday, a general minimum wage, and a six-week leave with pay for pregnant women before the approximate birth date plus a six-week leave with pay following the birth. During the nursing period, the mother must be given extra rest periods each day for nursing the baby. Equal wages must be paid for equal work, regardless of sex or nationality. Workers are entitled to a participation in the profits of an enterprise (i.e., profit sharing). Overtime work must carry double pay. Employers are responsible for and must pay appropriate compensation for injuries received by workers in the performance of their duties or for occupational diseases. In 1917, such provisions were viewed as astounding and revolutionary.

Unfulfilled Promises

Unfortunately, many of the goals of 1917 have yet to be achieved. A number of writers, frustrated by the slow pace of change, concluded long ago that the Mexican Revolution was dead. Leading thinkers and writers, such as the celebrated Carlos Fuentes, have bitterly criticized the failure of the Revolution to shape a more equitable society. Corruption, abuse of power, self-serving opportunism, and a general air of degeneration characterize Mexico today.

One of the failed goals of the Revolution, in the eyes of critics, was an agrarian reform program that fell short of achieving a wholesale change of land ownership or even of raising the standard of living in rural areas. Over the years, however, small scale agriculture has sown the seeds of its own destruction. Plots of land that are barely adequate for subsistence farming have been further divided by peasant farmers anxious to satisfy the inheritance rights of their sons.

More recently, government price controls on grain and corn have driven many marginal producers out of the market and off their lands.

Land Reform: One Story

Juan Rulfo, a major figure in the history of postrevolutionary literature, captured the frustration of peasants who have "benefited" from agrarian reform. "But sir," the peasant complained to the government official overseeing the land reform, "the earth is all washed away and hard. We don't think the plow will cut into the earth . . . that's like a rock quarry. You'd have to make with a pick-axe to plant the seed, and even then you can't be sure that anything will come up...." The official, cold and indifferent, responded: "You can state that in writing. And now you can go. You should be attacking the large-estate owners and not the government that is giving you the land."

More frequently, landowners have attacked peasants. During the past several years in Mexico, insistent peasant demands for a new allocation of lands have been the occasion of a number of human-rights abuses—some of a very serious character. Some impatient peasants who have occupied lands in defiance of the law have been killed or have "disappeared." In one notorious case in 1982, 26 peasants were murdered in a dispute over land in the state of Puebla. The peasants, who claimed legal title to the land, were killed by mounted gunmen, reportedly hired by local ranchers. Political parties reacted to the massacre in characteristic fashion—all attempted to manipulate the event to their own advantage rather than to address the problem of land reform. Yet years later, paramilitary bands and local police controlled by political bosses or landowners still routinely threatened and/or killed peasant activists. Indeed, access to the land was a major factor in the Maya uprising in the southern state of Chiapas that began in 1994 and, in 1999, remained unresolved.

The Promise of the Revolution

While critics of the 1910 Revolution are correct in identifying its failures, the Constitution of 1917 represents more than dashed hopes. The very radical nature of the document allows governments (should they desire) to pursue aggressive egalitarian policies and still be within the law. For example, when addressing citizens, Mexican public officials often invoke the Constitution—issues tend to become less controversial if they are placed within the broad context of 1917. When President Adolfo López Mateos declared in 1960 that his government would be "extremely leftist," he quickly added that his position would be "within the Constitution." In 1982, with the Mexican economy bordering on collapse, outgoing president José López Portillo nationalized the banks. The nationalization, allowable under the Constitution, was of little practical value, but it demonstrated to Mexicans that the government was serious about tackling economic problems and that the spirit of the Revolution of 1910 was still alive.

Women's Rights

Although the Constitution made reference to the equality of women in Mexican society, it was not until World War II that the women's-rights movement gathered strength. Women won the right to vote in 1955; by the 1970s, they had challenged laws and social customs that were prejudicial to women. Some women have served on presidential cabinets, and one woman became governor of the state of Colima. The most important victory for women occurred in 1974, however, when the Mexican Congress passed legislation that, in effect, asked men to grant women full equality in society—including jobs, salaries, and legal standing.

But attitudes are difficult to change with legislation, and much social behavior in Mexico still has a sexist orientation. Many Mexican men feel that there are male and female roles in society, regardless of law. Government, public corporations, private businesses, the Roman Catholic Church, and the armed forces represent important areas of male activity. The home, private religious rituals, and secondary service roles represent areas of female activity. One is clearly dominant, the other subordinate.

The Role of the Church

Under the Constitution of 1917, no religious organization is allowed to administer or teach in Mexico's primary, secondary, or normal (higher education) schools; nor may clergy

(United Nations photo/Heidi Larson)

Mexican women won the right to vote in 1955. These women, at a political rally in Oaxaca, demonstrate their political consciousness.

participate in the education of workers or peasants. Yet between 1940 and 1979, private schools expanded to the point where they enrolled 1.5 million of the country's 17 million pupils. Significantly, more than half of the private-school population attended Roman Catholic schools. Because they exist despite the fact that they are prohibited by law, the Catholic schools demonstrate the kinds of accommodation and flexibility that are possible in Mexico. It is in the best interests of the ruling party to satisfy as many interest groups as is possible, in order to achieve a certain societal balance.

From the perspective of politicians, the Roman Catholic Church has increasingly tilted the balance in the direction of social justice in recent years. Some Mexican bishops have been particularly outspoken on the issue; but when liberal or radical elements in the Church embrace social change, they may cross into the jurisdiction of the state. Under the Constitution, the state is responsible for improving the welfare of its people. Some committed clergy, however, believe that religion must play an active role in the transformation of society; it must not only have compassion for the poor but must also act to relieve poverty and eliminate injustice.

In 1991, Mexican bishops openly expressed their concern about the torture and mistreatment of prisoners, political persecution, corruption, discrimination against indigenous peoples, mistreatment of Central American refugees, and electoral fraud. In previous years, the government would have reacted sharply against such charges emanating from the Church. But, in this case, there was a significant rapprochement between the Roman Catholic Church and the state in Mexico. Begun by President Manuel de la Madrid and further elaborated by President Carlos Salinas de Gortari, the new relationship culminated in 1990 with the exchange of diplomatic representatives and Pope John Paul II's successful and popular visit to Mexico in May. Despite better relations at the highest level, in 1999 the Bishop of Chiapas vigorously criticized the government for backing away from a 1996 accord between the state and leaders of a guerrilla insurgency and returning to a policy of violent repression.

MEXICO'S STABILITY

The stability of the Mexican state, as has been suggested, depends on the ability of the ruling elite to maintain a state of relative equilibrium among the multiplicity of interests and demands in the nation. The whole political process is characterized by bargaining among elites with various views on politics, social injustice, economic policy, and the conduct of foreign relations.

It is the Institutional Revolutionary Party (PRI), in power since 1929, that sets policies and decides what is possible or desirable. All change is generated from above, from the president and presidential advisers. Although the Constitution provides for a federal system, power is effectively centralized. In the words of one authority, Mexico, with its one-party rule, is not a democracy but, rather, "qualified authoritarianism." Peruvian author Mario Vargas Llosa has referred to Mexico as a "perfect dictatorship." Indeed, the main role of the PRI in the political system is political domination, not power sharing. Paternalistic and all-powerful, the state controls the bureaucracies that direct the labor unions, peasant organizations, student groups, and virtually every other dimension of organized society.

Historically, politicians have tended to be more interested in building their careers than in responding to the demands of their constituents. According to political scientist Peter Smith, Mexican politicians are forever bargaining with one another, seeking favors from their superiors, and communicating in a language of "exaggerated deference." They have learned how to maximize power and success within the existing political structure. By following the "rules of the game," they move ahead. The net result is a consensus at the upper echelons of power.

In the past few decades, that consensus has been undermined. One of the great successes of the Revolution of 1910 was the rise to middle-class status of millions of people. But the recent economic crisis has alienated that upwardly mobile sector from the PRI. People have registered their dissatisfaction at the polls; in 1988, in fact, the official party finished second in Mexico City and other urban centers. In 1989, the PRI's unbroken winning streak of 60 years, facilitated by widespread electoral corruption, was broken in the state of Baja California del Norte, where the right-wing National Action Party (PAN) won the governorship. A decade of worrisome political losses prompted the PRI to consider long-overdue reforms. The party's poor showing in the presidential elections of 1988 gave President-Elect Carlos Salinas de Gortari all the justification he needed to reform the PRI and open an unaccustomed dialogue with the opposition. In 1993, the PRI announced a broad range of proposals to reform the Mexican political process in anticipation of the elections of 1994.

In other ways President Salinas behaved traditionally, essentially as a *patrón* to his people. This was apparent on a political trip that he took through northern Mexico in 1989. Mexicans felt that such trips were, in the words of *New York Times* reporter Larry Rohter, "essential to the functioning of the country's political system, which invests the President with an aura of omnipotence and consequently demands that he appear to have a hand in every decision made in his name." The primacy of the executive branch in the Mexican political system convinces people that only the president has both the authority and the credibility to correct injustices and to get things done. In the words of one of Salinas's cabinet ministers: "This is a presidential system par excellence. People want to see the President and to hear things from his own mouth." People crowded to get close to Salinas to deliver their very personal letters and petitions.

The most dramatic setback for the PRI occurred in the summer of 1997, when the left-of-center Party of the Demo-

(Agence Franc Presse/Corbis-Bettmann)

The Institutional Revolutionary Party (PRI) has been in power since 1929, but elections in the mid-1990s gave the National Action Party (PAN) substantial clout in Mexico. The presidency continues to be held by the PRI (here, Ernesto Zedillo Ponce de León is pictured in September 1997, presenting his third government report to members of Congress in Mexico City), but the PRI must reform itself so that it may take its place as one party among others, not *the* party.

cratic Revolution (PRD) scored stunning victories in legislative, gubernatorial, and municipal elections. For the first time, the PRI lost its stranglehold on the Chamber of Deputies, the lower house of Congress. Significantly, Cuauhtemoc Cardenas of the PRD was swept into power as mayor of Mexico City in the first direct vote for that position since 1928. In gubernatorial contests, the PAN won two elections and controlled an impressive seven of Mexico's 31 governorships.

Within the PRI, a new generation of leaders now sees the need for political and economic change. Old-fashioned party and union bosses, on the other hand, see any change as threatening to their entrenched positions. Elections, to their way of thinking, were never meant to allow anyone but PRI candidates to win. In the words of political scientist George Grayson, "the *carro completo* or clean sweep enables labor chieftains and peasant leaders to reward their loyalists." Reform, in such instances, is difficult, but not impossible. Electoral results, even if rigged, could be used to foster change. Historically, the PRI could register its dissatisfaction with one of its own politicians by reducing the candidate's winning margin. This was a sign that, if the politician did not shape up, then he or she was in danger of being ousted.

But President Ernesto Zedillo, worried about his party's prospects in the general elections of 2000, has, over the objections of old-line conservatives, pushed a series of reforms in the PRI. For the first time, the party will use state primaries and a national convention to choose the PRI's presidential candidate. This democratization of the party has its reflection in Zedillo's stated commitment to transform Mexican politics by giving the opposition a fair playing field. Voting is now more resistant to tampering and, as a consequence, the three major parties will have to campaign for the support of the voters.

In the southern state of Chiapas, however, the rhetoric of change failed to ease the reality of abuses perpetrated by local landowners against Maya Indians. Rebellion broke out in January 1994. The Maya insurgents were led by Subcommandant Marcos, an articulate and shrewd activist who quickly became a hero not only in Chiapas but also in much of the rest of Mexico, where he symbolized the widespread dissatisfaction with the Salinas government. The Maya were not intent on the destruction of the Mexican government, but they were insistent that their demands for justice be considered seriously. In an election year, a negotiated settlement seemed likely. Then, in March 1994, the PRI's presidential candidate, Luis Donaldo Colosio, was assassinated, further clouding Mexico's political future.

As mentioned earlier, the conflict in Chiapas remains unresolved. In February 1996, the government and the insurgents signed the Agreements of San Andres, which assured the Maya of independence in issues of local governance. But lack of implementation of the agreements, in combination with attacks by the military on the Maya, doomed the accord from the outset.

ORGANIZED LABOR

Organized labor provides an excellent example of the ways in which power is wielded in Mexico and how social change occurs. Mexican trade unions have the right to organize, negotiate, and strike. Most unions, however, are not independent of the government. The major portion of the labor movement is affiliated with the PRI through an umbrella organization known as the Confederation of Mexican Workers (CTM). The Confederation, with a membership of 3.5 million, is one of the PRI's most ardent supporters. Union bosses truck in large crowds for campaign rallies, help PRI candidates win impressive victory margins at election time, and secure from union members approval of government policies. Union bosses are well rewarded by the system they help to support. Most become moderately wealthy and acquire status and prestige. Fully one third of Mexico's senators and congressional representatives, as well

as an occasional governor, come from the ranks of union leadership.

Such a relationship must be reciprocal if it is to function properly. The CTM has used an impressive array of left-wing slogans for years to win gains for its members. It has projected an aura of radicalism when, in fact, it is not. The image is important to union members, however, for it gives them the feeling of independence from the government, and it gives a role to the true radicals in the movement.

Cracks have begun to appear in the foundation of union support for the government. The economic crisis has resulted in sharp cutbacks in government spending. Benefits and wage increases have fallen far behind the pace of inflation; layoffs and unemployment have led many union members to question the value of their special relationship with the government. Indeed, during the 1988 elections, the Mexican newspaper *El Norte* reported that Joaquín Hernández Galicia, the powerful leader of the Oil Workers' Union, was so upset with trends within the PRI that he directed his membership to vote for opposition candidates. Not surprisingly, President Salinas responded by naming a new leader to the Oil Workers' Union.

Independent unions outside the Confederation of Mexican Workers have capitalized on the crisis and increased their memberships. For the first time, these independent unions seem to possess sufficient power to challenge government policies. To negate the challenge from the independents, the CTM has invited them to join the larger organization. Incorporation of the dissidents into the system is seen as the only way in which the system's credibility can be maintained. It illustrates the state's power to neutralize opposing forces by absorbing them into its system. The demands of labor today are strong, and the government will have to make significant concessions. But if the system is preserved and dissidents are transformed into supporters of the state, the costs will be worthwhile.

ECONOMIC CRISIS

As has been suggested, the primary threat to the consensus politics of the PRI has come from the economic crisis that began to build in Mexico and other Latin American countries (notably Brazil, Venezuela, and Argentina) in the early 1980s. In the 1970s, Mexico undertook economic policies designed to foster rapid and sustained industrial growth. Credit was readily available from international lending agencies and banks at low rates of interest. Initially, the development plan seemed to work, and Mexico achieved impressive economic growth rates, in the range of 8 percent per year. The government, confident in its ability to pay back its debts from revenues generated by the vast deposits of petroleum beneath Mexico, recklessly expanded its economic infrastructure.

A glut on the petroleum market in late 1981 and 1982 led to falling prices for Mexican oil. Suddenly, there was not enough money available to pay the interest on loans that were

| Hernán Cortés lands at Vera Cruz 1519 | Destruction of the Aztec Empire 1521 | Mexico proclaims its independence from Spain 1810 | War with the United States; Mexico loses four fifths of its territory 1846–1848 | The French take over the Mexican throne and install Emperor Maximillian 1862–1867 | Era of dictator Porfirio Díaz: modernization 1876–1910 | The Mexican Revolution 1910–1917 |

coming due, and the government had to borrow more money—at very high interest rates—to cover the unexpected shortfall. By the end of 1982, between 35 and 45 percent of Mexico's export earnings were devoured in interest payments on a debt of $80 billion. Before additional loans could be secured, foreign banks and lending organizations, such as the International Monetary Fund, demanded that the Mexican government drastically reduce state spending. This demand translated into layoffs, inadequate funding for social-welfare programs, and a general austerity that devastated the poor and undermined the high standard of living of the middle class.

Although political reform was important to President Salinas, he clearly recognized that economic reform was of more compelling concern. Under Salinas, the foreign debt was renegotiated and substantially reduced.

The North American Free Trade Agreement among Mexico, the United States, and Canada is seen as essential if these advances are to continue and jobs are to be generated. Opposition politicians on the left have generally opposed any free-trade agreement, which they see as binding Mexico to the imperialist designs of the United States and giving the United States control over Mexican oil.

In the meantime, there has been a high social cost to economic reform: standards of living continue a downward spiral. The minimum wage for workers since 1982 has not been adequate to sustain a family above the poverty line. Indeed, since the devaluation of the peso in 1994, Mexican consumers have had to adjust to a drop of 39 percent in their purchasing power.

Many of those workers will continue to make their way to the U.S. border, which remains accessible despite the passage of immigration-reform legislation and the uncertain promise of free trade with the colossus of the north. Others will be absorbed by the so-called informal sector, or underground economy. When walking in the streets of Mexico City, one quickly becomes aware that there exists an economy that is not recognized, licensed, regulated, or "protected" by the government. Yet, in the 1980s, this informal sector of the economy produced 25 to 35 percent of Mexico's gross domestic product and served as a shield for millions of Mexicans who might otherwise have been reduced to destitution. According to George Grayson, "Extended families, which often have several members working and others hawking lottery tickets or shining shoes, establish a safety net for upward of one third of the workforce in a country where social security coverage is limited and unemployment compensation is nonexistent."

FOREIGN POLICY

The problems created by Mexico's economic policy have been balanced by a visibly successful foreign policy. Historically, Mexican foreign policy, which is noted for following an independent course of action, has been used by the government for domestic purposes. In the 1980s, President Miguel de la Madrid identified revolutionary nationalism as the historical synthesis, or melding, of the Mexican people. History, he argued, taught Mexicans to be nationalist in order to resist external aggression, and history made Mexico revolutionary in order to enable it to transform unequal social and economic structures. These beliefs, when tied to the formulation of foreign policy, have fashioned policies with a definite leftist bias.

The country has often been sympathetic to social change and has identified, at least in principle, with revolutionary causes all over the globe. The Mexican government opposed the economic and political isolation of Cuba that was so heartily endorsed by the United States. It supported the Marxist regime of Salvador Allende in Chile at a time when the United States was attempting to destabilize his government. Mexico was one of the first nations to break relations with President Anastasio Somoza of Nicaragua and to recognize the legitimacy of the struggle of the Sandinista guerrillas. In 1981, Mexico joined with France in recognizing the opposition front and guerrilla coalition in El Salvador. More recently, Mexico, together with several other Latin American countries, urged a negotiated solution to the armed conflict in Central America.

Mexico's leftist foreign policy balances conservative domestic policies. A foreign policy identified with change and social justice has the effect of softening the impact of leftist demands in Mexico for land reform or political change. Mexicans, if displeased with government domestic policies, are soothed by a vigorous foreign policy that places Mexico in a leadership role, often in opposition to the United States. As is the case in virtually every aspect of Mexican life, there is a sense of balance.

HARD TIMES

Mexico's future is fraught with uncertainty. In December 1994, the economy collapsed after the government could no longer sustain an overvalued peso. In just a few months, the peso fell in value by half, while the stock market, in terms of the peso, suffered a 38 percent drop. The crash was particularly acute because the Salinas government had not invested foreign aid in factories and job creation, but had instead put most of the money into Mexico's volatile stock market. It then proceeded to spend Mexico's reserves to prop up the peso

Land distribution
under President
Cárdenas
1934–1940
●

Nationalization of
foreign petroleum
companies
1938
●

Women win the
right to vote
1955
●

The Olympic
Games are held
in Mexico City;
riots and violence
1968
●

Severe economic
crisis; the peso is
devalued;
inflation soars;
the foreign-debt
crisis escalates

Maya insurgency
in the state of
Chiapas
1980s
●

1990s

NAFTA is
passed; Ernesto
Zedillo Ponce de
León is elected
president

The PRI loses
ground in
legislative,
gubernatorial,
and municipal
elections

Presidential
elections are
scheduled for
July 2000

when the decline gathered momentum. Salinas's successor, President Ernesto Zedillo, had to cut public spending, sell some state-owned industries, and place strict limits on wage and price increases.

To further confound the economic crisis, the Maya insurgency in Chiapas succeeded in generating much antigovernment support in the rest of Mexico. President Zedillo has claimed that the rebels, who call themselves the Zapatista Army of National Liberation (EZLN, named for Emiliano Zapata, one of the peasant leaders of the Mexican Revolution), are "neither popular, nor indigenous, nor from Chiapas." Nobel Laureate Octavio Paz condemned the uprising as an "interruption of Mexico's ongoing political and economic liberalization." The interests of the EZLN leadership, he said, are those of intellectuals rather than those of the peasantry. In other words, what happened in Chiapas is an old story of peasant Indians being used by urban intellectuals—in this instance, to challenge the PRI. Indeed, the real identity of "Subcomandante Marcos" was revealed as Rafael Sebastian Guillen Vicente, a 37-year-old former professor from a rich provincial family who had worked with Tzotzil and Tzeltal Maya Indians since 1984.

George Collier, however, argues that the rebellion is a response to changing governmental policies, agricultural modernization, and cultural and economic isolation. While the peasants of central Chiapas profited from PRI policies, those in the eastern part of the state were ignored. Thus, the rebellion, in essence, was a demand to be included in the largesse of the state. The demands of the EZLN were instructive: democratic reform by the state, limited autonomy for indigenous communities, an antidiscrimination law, teachers, clinics, doctors, electricity, better housing, child-care centers, and a radio station for indigenous peoples. Only vague statements were made about subdivision of large ranches.

In summary, the insurgency can be seen to have several roots and to serve many purposes. It is far more complex than a "simple" uprising of an oppressed people.

THE FUTURE

Journalist Igor Fuser, writing in the Brazilian newsweekly *Veja,* observed: "For pessimists, the implosion of the PRI is the final ingredient needed to set off an apocalyptic bomb composed of economic recession, guerrilla war, and the desperation of millions of Mexicans facing poverty. For optimists, the unrest is a necessary evil needed to unmask the most carefully camouflaged dictatorship on the planet."

Be that as it may, the key to Mexico's immediate future lies in the state of the nation's economy. Although the political and social systems are remarkably durable and resilient, rampant corruption, persistent inflation, high domestic interest rates, the devaluation of the peso and collapse of the stock market, foreign debt, austerity in state spending and associated reductions in social programs, and high unemployment and underemployment have significantly undermined the PRI's consensus politics. If the government complies with new election laws to reduce corruption, brings inflation under control, and can secure further loans abroad, and if the North American Free Trade Agreement lives up to expectations in terms of foreign-exchange earnings and job creation, then Mexico will survive this latest challenge to its stability.

DEVELOPMENT

President Zedillo's 1999 budget is among the leanest on record and is designed to combat inflation and encourage investment. In March 1999, top executives of foreign firms informed the Mexican government that they planned to invest $10 billion in factories and other projects—an amount equal to the total foreign investment in Mexico for all of 1998.

FREEDOM

Announced political reforms should help to eliminate much of the corruption and vote tampering that has traditionally accompanied national elections in Mexico. But political progress must be set against the continuing human-rights abuses perpetrated against the Maya by the military in the southern state of Chiapas.

HEALTH/WELFARE

Violence against women in Mexico first became an issue of public policy when legislation was introduced in 1990 to amend the penal code with respect to sexual crimes. Among the provisions were specialized medical and social assistance for rape victims and penalties for sexual harassment.

ACHIEVEMENTS

Mexican writers and artists have won world acclaim. The works of novelists such as Carlos Fuentes, Mariano Azuela, and Juan Rulfo have been translated into many languages. The graphic-art styles of Posada and the mural art of Diego Rivera, José Clemente Orozco, and David Siqueiros are distinctively Mexican.

Central America

Much of Central America shares important historical milestones. In 1821, the states of Guatemala, Honduras, El Salvador, Costa Rica, and Nicaragua declared themselves independent of Spain. In 1822, they joined the Empire of Mexico; in 1823, they formed the United Provinces of Central America. This union lasted until 1838, when each member state severed its relations with the federation and went its own way. Since 1838, there have been more than 25 attempts to restore the union—but to no avail.

Central America: Lands in Turmoil

LIFE IN THE MOUTH OF THE VOLCANO

Sons of the Shaking Earth, a well-known study of Middle America by anthropologist Eric Wolf, captures in its title the critical interplay between people and the land in Central America. It asserts that the land is violent and that the inhabitants of the region live in an environment that is often shaken by natural disaster.

The dominant geographical feature of Central America is the impressive and forbidding range of volcanic mountains that runs from Mexico to Panama. These mountains have always been obstacles to communication, to the cultivation of the land, and to the national integration of the countries in which they lie. The volcanoes rest atop major fault lines; some are dormant, others are active, and new ones have appeared periodically. Over the centuries, eruptions and earthquakes have destroyed thousands of villages. Some have recovered, but others remain buried beneath lava and ash. Nearly every Central American city has been destroyed at one time or another; and some, such as Managua, Nicaragua, have suffered repeated devastation.

An ancient Indian philosophy speaks of five great periods of time, each doomed to end in disaster. The fifth period, which is the time in which we now live, is said to terminate with a world-destroying earthquake. "Thus," writes Wolf, "the people of Middle [Central] America live in the mouth of the volcano. Middle America . . . is one of the proving grounds of humanity."

Earthquakes and eruptions are not the only natural disasters that plague the region. Rains fall heavily between May and October each year, and devastating floods are common. On the Caribbean coast, hurricanes often strike in the late summer and early autumn, threatening coastal cities and leveling crops.

The constant threat of natural disaster has had a deep impact on Central Americans' views of life and development. Death and tragedy have conditioned their attitudes toward the present and the future.

GEOGRAPHY

The region is not only violent but also diverse. In political terms, Central America consists of seven independent nations: Belize, Costa Rica, El Salvador, Guatemala, Honduras, Nicaragua, and Panama. With the exception of Costa Rica and Panama, where national borders coincide with geographical and human frontiers, political boundaries are artificial and were marked out in defiance of both the lay of the land and the cultural groupings of the region's peoples.

Geographically, Central America can be divided into four broad zones: Petén–Belize; the Caribbean coasts of Guatemala, Honduras, and Nicaragua; the Pacific volcanic region; and Costa Rica–Panama.

The northern Guatemalan territory of Petén and all of Belize are an extension of Mexico's Yucatán Peninsula. The region is heavily forested with stands of mahogany, cedar, and pine, whose products are a major source of revenue for Belize.

The Caribbean lowlands, steamy and disease-ridden, are sparsely settled. The inhabitants of the Caribbean coast in Nicaragua include Miskito Indians and the descendants of English-speaking blacks who first settled the area in the seventeenth century. The Hispanic population there was small until recently. Coastal Honduras, however, presents a different picture. Because of heavy investments by foreign companies in the region's banana industry, it is a pocket of relative prosperity in the midst of a very poor country whose economy is based on agricultural production and textiles.

The Pacific volcanic highlands are the cultural heartland of Central America. Here, in highland valleys noted for their springlike climate, live more than 80 percent of the population of Central America; here are the largest cities. In cultural terms, the highlands are home to the whites, mixed bloods, Hispanicized Indians known as Ladinos, and pure-blooded Indians who are descended from the Maya. These highland groups form a striking ethnic contrast to the Indians (such as the Miskito), mulattos, and blacks of the coastlands. The entire country of El Salvador falls within this geographical

The threat of earthquakes and other natural disasters affects all Central Americans. Above, residents of Guatemala City, Guatemala, begin the long clean-up process after an earthquake.

zone. Unlike its neighbors, there is a uniformity to the land and people of El Salvador.

The fourth region, divided between the nations of Costa Rica and Panama, constitutes a single geographical unit. Mountains form the spine of the isthmus. In Costa Rica, the Central Mesa has attracted 70 percent of the nation's population, because of its agreeable climate.

CLIMATE AND CULTURE

The geographic and biological diversity of Central America—with its cool highlands and steaming lowlands, its incredible variety of microclimates and environments, its seemingly infinite types of flora and fauna, and its mineral wealth—has been a major factor in setting the course of the cultural history of Central America. Before the Spanish conquest, the environmental diversity favored the cultural cohesion of peoples. The products of one environmental niche could easily be exchanged for the products of another. In a sense, valley people and those living higher up in the mountains depended on one another. Here was one of the bases for the establishment of the advanced culture of the Maya.

The cultural history of Central America has focused on the densely populated highlands and Pacific plains—those areas most favorable for human occupation. Spaniards settled in the same regions, and centers of national life are located there today. But, if geography has been a factor in bringing peoples together on a local level, it has also contributed to the formation of regional differences, loyalties, interests, and jealousies. Neither Maya rulers nor Spanish bureaucrats could triumph over the natural obstacles presented by the region's harsh geography. The mountains and rain forests have mocked numerous attempts to create a single Central American state.

CULTURES IN CONFLICT

Although geography has interacted with culture, the contact between Indians and Spaniards since the sixteenth century has profoundly shaped the cultural face of today's Central America. According to historian Ralph Woodward, the religious traditions of the Indians, with Christianity imperfectly superimposed over them, "together with the violence of the Conquest and the centuries of slavery or serfdom which followed, left clear impressions on the personality and mentality of the Central American Indian."

To outsiders, the Indians often appear docile and obedient to authority, but beneath this mask may lie intense emotions, including distrust and bitterness. The Indians' vision is usually local and oriented toward the village and family; they do not identify themselves as Guatemalan or Nicaraguan. When challenged, Indians have fought to defend their rights, and a long succession of rebellions from colonial days until the present attests to their sense of what is just and what is not. The Indians, firmly tied to their traditional beliefs and values, have tried to resist modernization, despite government pro-

(United Nations photo/Jerry Frank)

Central American Indians are firmly tied to their traditional beliefs and have strongly resisted the influence of European culture, as evidenced by this Cuna woman of Panama's Tubala Island.

grams and policies designed to counter what urbanized whites perceive as backwardness and superstition.

Population growth, rather than government programs and policies, has had a great impact on the region's Indian peoples and has already resulted in the recasting of cultural traditions. Peasant villages in much of Central America have traditionally organized their ritual life around the principle of *mayordomía,* or sponsorship. Waldemar Smith, an anthropologist who has explored the relationship between the *fiesta* (ceremony) system and economic change, has shown the impact of changing circumstances on traditional systems. In any Central American community in any given year, certain families are appointed *mayordomos,* or stewards, of the village saints; they are responsible for organizing and paying for the celebrations in their names. This responsibility ordinarily lasts for a year. One of the outstanding features of the fiesta system is the phenomenal costs that the designated family must bear. An individual might have to expend the equivalent of a year's earnings or more to act as a sponsor in a community fiesta. Psychological and social burdens must also be borne by the mayordomos, for they represent their community before its saints. Mayordomos, who in essence are priests for a year, are commonly expected to refrain from sexual activity for long periods as well as to devote much time to ritual forms.

The office, while highly prestigious, can also be dangerous. Maya Indians, for example, believe that the saints use the weather as a weapon to punish transgressions, and extreme weather is often traced to ritual error or sins on the part of the mayordomo, who might on such occasions actually be jailed.

Since the late 1960s, the socioeconomic structure of much of the area heavily populated by Indians has changed, forcing changes in traditional cultural forms, including the fiesta system. Expansion of markets and educational opportunity, the absorption of much of the workforce in seasonal plantation labor, more efficient transportation systems, and population growth have precipitated change. Traditional festivals in honor of a community's saints have significantly diminished in importance in a number of towns. Costs have been reduced or several families have been made responsible for fiesta sponsorship. This reflects not only modernization but also crisis. Some communities have become too poor to support themselves—and the expensive fiestas have, naturally, suffered.

This increasing poverty is driven in part by population growth, which has exerted tremendous pressure on people's access to land. Families that cannot be sustained on traditional lands must now seek seasonal wage labor on sugarcane, coffee, or cotton plantations. Others emigrate. The net result is a culture under siege. Thus, while the fiestas may not vanish, they are surely in the process of change.

The Ladino World

The word *Ladino* can be traced back to the Roman occupation of Spain. It referred to someone who had been "Latinized" and was therefore wise in the ways of the world. The word has several meanings in Central America. In Guatemala, it refers to a person of mixed blood, or *Mestizo*. In most of the rest of Central America, however, it refers to an Indian who has adopted white culture.

The Ladinos are caught between two cultures, both of which initially rejected them. The Ladinos attempted to compensate for their lack of cultural roots and cultural identity by aggressively carving out a place in Central American society.

Often acutely status-conscious, Ladinos typically contrast sharply with the Indians they physically resemble. Ladinos congregate in the larger towns and cities, speak Spanish, and seek a livelihood as shopkeepers or landowners. They compose the local elite in Guatemala, Nicaragua, Honduras, and El Salvador (the latter country was almost entirely Ladinoized by the end of the nineteenth century), and they usually control regional politics. They are often the most aggressive members of the community, driven by the desire for self-advancement. Their vision is frequently much broader than that of the Indian; they have a perspective that includes the capital city and the nation. The vast majority of the population speak

(United Nations photo)

Many Central Americans migrate from rural areas to the urban centers, but it is frequently beyond the capacity of urban areas to support them. The child pictured above has to get the family's water from a single, unsanitary community tap.

Spanish; few villages retain the use of their original, native tongues.

The Elite

For the elite, who are culturally "white," the city dominates their social and cultural horizons. For them, the world of the Indian is unimportant—save for the difficult questions of social integration and modernization. Businesspeople and bureaucrats, absentee landlords, and the professional class of doctors, lawyers, and engineers constitute an urban elite who are cosmopolitan and sophisticated. Wealth, status, and "good blood" are the keys to elite membership.

The Disadvantaged

The cities have also attracted disadvantaged people who have migrated from poverty-stricken rural regions in search of economic opportunity. Many are self-employed as peddlers, small-scale traders, or independent craftspeople. Others seek low-paying, unskilled positions in industry, construction work, and transportation. Most live on the edge of poverty and are the first to suffer in times of economic recession.

But there exist Hispanic institutions in this harsh world that help people of all classes to adjust. In each of the capital cities of Central America, lower-sector people seek help and sustenance from the more advantaged elements in society. They form economic and social alliances that are mutually beneficial. For example, a tradesman might approach a well-to-do merchant and seek advice or a small loan. In return, he can offer guaranteed service, a steady supply of crafts for the wholesaler, and a price that is right. It is a world built on mutual exchanges.

These networks, when they function, bind societies together and ease the alienation and isolation of the less advantaged inhabitants. Of course, networks that cut through class lines can effectively limit class action in pursuit of reforms; and, in many instances, the networks do not exist or are exploitive.

POPULATION MOVEMENT

For many years, Central Americans have been peoples in motion. Migrants who have moved from rural areas into the cities have often been driven from lands they once owned, either because of the expansion of landed estates at the expense of the smaller landholdings, population pressure, or division of the land into plots so small that subsistence farming is no longer possible. Others have moved to the cities in search of a better life.

Population pressure on the land is most intense in El Salvador. No other Latin American state utilizes the whole of its territory to the extent that El Salvador does. Most of the land is still privately owned and is devoted to cattle farming or to raising cotton and coffee for the export market. There is not enough land to provide crops for a population that has grown

(World Bank photo/Jaime Martin-Escobal)

The migration of poor rural people to Central American urban centers has caused large numbers of squatters to take up residence in slums. The crowded conditions in urban El Salvador, as shown in this photograph, are typical results of this phenomenon.

at one of the most rapid rates in the Western Hemisphere. There are no empty lands left to occupy. Agrarian reform, even if successful, will still leave hundreds of thousands of peasants without land.

Many Salvadorans have moved to the capital city of San Salvador in search of employment. Others have crossed into neighboring countries. In the 1960s, thousands moved to Honduras, where they settled on the land or were attracted to commerce and industry. By the end of that decade, more than 75 percent of all foreigners living in Honduras had crossed the border from El Salvador. Hondurans, increasingly concerned by the growing presence of Salvadorans, acted to stem the flow and passed restrictive and discriminatory legislation against the immigrants. The tension, an ill-defined border, and festering animosity ultimately brought about a brief war between Honduras and El Salvador in 1969.

Honduras, with a low population density (about 130 persons per square mile, as compared to El Salvador's 700), has attracted population not only from neighboring countries but also from the Caribbean. Black migrants from the "West Indian" Caribbean islands known as the Antilles have been particularly attracted to Honduras's north coast, where they have been able to find employment on banana plantations or in the light industry that has increasingly been established in the area. The presence of these Caribbean peoples in moderate numbers has more sharply focused regional differences in Honduras. The coast, in many respects, is Caribbean in its peoples' identity and outlook; while peoples of the highlands of the interior identify with the capital city of Tegucigalpa, which is Hispanic in culture.

THE REFUGEE PROBLEM

Recent turmoil in Central America created yet another group of people on the move—refugees from the fighting in their own countries or from the persecution by extremists of the political left and right. For example, thousands of Salvadorans crowded into Honduras's western province. In the south, Miskito Indians, fleeing from Nicaragua's Sandinista government, crossed the Río Coco in large numbers. Additional thousands of armed Nicaraguan counterrevolutionaries camped along the border. Only in 1990–1991 did significant numbers of Salvadorans move back to their homeland. With the declared truce between Sandinistas and Contras and the election victory of Violeta Chamorro, Nicaraguan refugees were gradually repatriated. Guatemalan Indians sought refuge in southern Mexico, and Central Americans of all nationalities resettled in Costa Rica and Belize.

El Salvadorans, who began to emigrate to the United States in the 1960s, did so in much greater numbers with the onset of the El Salvadoran Civil War, which killed approximately 70,000 people and displaced about 25 percent of the nation's population. The Urban Institute, a Washington, D.C.–based research group, estimated in 1986 that there were then about ¾ million El Salvadorans—of a total population of just over

5 million—living in the United States. Those emigrants became a major source of dollars for El Salvador; it is estimated that they now send home about $500 million a year.

While that money has undoubtedly helped to keep the nation's economy above water, it has also generated, paradoxically, a good deal of anti–U.S. sentiment in El Salvador. Lindsey Gruson, a reporter for *The New York Times*, studied the impact of expatriate dollars in Intipuca, a town 100 miles southwest of the capital, and concluded that they had a profound impact on Intipuqueño culture. The influx of money was an incentive not to work, and townspeople said that the "free" dollars "perverted cherished values" and were "breaking up many families."

THE ROOTS OF VIOLENCE

Central America still feels the effects of civil war and violence. Armies, guerrillas, and terrorists of the political left and right have exacted a high toll on human lives and property. The civil wars and guerrilla movements that spread violence to the region sprang from each of the societies in question.

A critical societal factor was (and remains) the emergence of a middle class in Central America. In some respects, people of the middle class resemble the Mestizos or Ladinos, in that their wealth and position have placed them above the masses. But, like the Mestizos and Ladinos, they have been denied access to the upper reaches of power, which is the special preserve of the elite. Since World War II, it has been members of the middle class who have called for reform and a more equitable distribution of the national wealth. They have also attempted to forge alliances of opportunity with workers and peasants.

Nationalistic, assertive, restless, ambitious, and, to an extent, ruthless, people of the middle class (professionals, intellectuals, junior officers in the armed forces, office workers, businesspeople, teachers, students, and skilled workers) demand a greater voice in the political world. They want governments that are responsive to their interests and needs; and, when governments have proven unresponsive or hostile, elements of the middle class have chosen confrontation.

In the civil war that removed the Somoza family from power in Nicaragua in 1979, for example, the middle class played a critical leadership role. Guerrilla leaders in El Salvador were middle class in terms of their social origins, and there was significant middle-class participation in the unrest in Guatemala.

Indeed, Central America's middle class is among the most revolutionary groups in the region. Although middle-class people are well represented in antigovernment forces, they also resist changes that would tend to elevate those below them on the social scale. They are also significantly represented among right-wing groups, whose reputation for conservative views is accompanied by systematic terror.

(United Nations photo/J. P. Laffont)

Rapid population growth has put severe strains on the resources of many Central American nations. In Guatemala, government policy has driven Indians from their ancestral villages to crowded urban "resettlement" areas, such as the one pictured above.

Other societal factors also figure prominently in the violence in Central America. The rapid growth of population since the 1960s has severely strained each nation's resources. Many rural areas have become overpopulated, poor agricultural practices have caused extensive erosion, the amount of land available to subsistence farmers is inadequate, and poverty and misery are pervasive. These problems have combined to compel rural peoples to migrate to the cities or to whatever frontier lands are still available. In Guatemala, government policy drove Indians from ancestral villages in the highlands to "resettlement" villages in the low-lying, forested Petén to the north. Indians displaced in this manner often—not surprisingly—joined guerrilla movements. They were not attracted to insurgency by the allure of socialist or communist ideology; they simply responded to violence and the loss of their lands with violence against the governments that pursued such policies.

The conflict in this region does not always pit landless, impoverished peasants against an unyielding elite. Some members of the elite see the need for change. Most peasants have not taken up arms, and the vast majority wish to be left in peace. Others who desire change may be found in the ranks of the military or within the hierarchy of the Roman Catholic Church. Reformers are drawn from all sectors of society. It is thus more appropriate to view the conflict in Central America as a civil war rather than a class struggle, as civil wars cut through the entire fabric of a nation.

ECONOMIC PROBLEMS

Central American economies, always fragile, have in recent years been plagued by a combination of vexing problems. Foreign debt, inflation, currency devaluations, recession, and, in some instances, outside interference have had deleterious effects on the standard of living in all the countries. Civil war, insurgency, corruption and mismanagement, and population growth have added fuel to the crisis—not only in the region's economies but also in their societies. Nature, too has played an important contributory role in the region's economic and social malaise. Hurricane Mitch, which struck Central American in 1998, killed thousands, destroyed crops and property, and disrupted the infrastructure of roads and bridges in Honduras, Nicaragua, Guatemala, and El Salvador.

Civil war in El Salvador brought unprecedented death and destruction and was largely responsible for economic deterioration and a decline of well over one third of per capita income from 1980 to 1992. Today, fully two thirds of the working-age population are either unemployed or underemployed. The struggle of the Sandinista government of Nicaragua against U.S.–sponsored rebels routinely consumed 60 percent of government spending; even with peace, much of the budget of the Chamorro regime was earmarked for economic recovery. In Guatemala, a savage civil war lasted more than a generation; took more than 140,000 lives; strained the economy; depressed wages; and left unaddressed pressing social problems in education, housing, and welfare. Although the violence has subsided, the lingering fears conditioned by that violence have not. U.S. efforts to force the ouster of Panamanian strongman Manuel Antonio Noriega through the application of economic sanctions probably harmed middle-class businesspeople in Panama more than Noriega.

Against this backdrop of economic malaise there have been some creative attempts to solve, or at least to confront, pressing problems. In 1987, the Costa Rican government proposed a series of debt-for-nature swaps to international conservation groups, such as the Nature Conservancy. The first of the transactions took place in 1988, when several organizations purchased more than $3 million of Costa Rica's foreign debt at 17 percent of face value. The plan called for the government to exchange with the organizations part of Costa Rica's external debt for government bonds; the conservation groups would then invest the earnings of the bonds in the management and protection of Costa Rican national parks. According to the National Wildlife Federation, while debt-for-nature swaps are not a cure-all for the Latin American debt crisis, at least the swaps can go some distance toward protecting natural resources and encouraging ecologically sound, long-term economic development.

INTERNAL AND EXTERNAL DIMENSIONS OF CONFLICT

The continuing violence in much of Central America suggests that internal dynamics are perhaps more important than the overweening roles formerly ascribed to Havana, Moscow, and Washington. The removal of foreign "actors" from the stage lays bare the real reasons for violence in the region: injustice, power, greed, revenge, and racial and ethnic discrimination. Havana, Moscow, and Washington, among others, merely used Central American violence in pursuit of larger policy goals. And Central American governments and guerrilla groups were equally adept at using foreign powers to advance their own interests, be they revolutionary or reactionary.

Panama offers an interesting scenario in this regard. It, like the rest of Central America, is a poor nation consisting of subsistence farmers, rural laborers, urban workers, and unemployed and underemployed people dwelling in the shantytowns ringing the larger cities. For years, the pressures for reform in Panama were skillfully rechanneled by the ruling elite toward the issue of the Panama Canal. Frustration and anger were deflected from the government, and an outdated social structure was attributed to the presence of a foreign power—the United States—in what Panamanians regarded as their territory.

Central America, in summary, is a region of diverse geography and is home to peoples of many cultures. It is a region of strong local loyalties; its problems are profound and perplexing. The violence of the land is matched by the violence of its peoples as they fight for something as noble as justice or human rights, or as ignoble as political power or self-promotion.

Belize

GEOGRAPHY

Area in Square Miles (Kilometers):
8,866 (22,963) (about the size of Massachusetts)

Capital (Population): Belmopan (5,300)

Environmental Concerns: deforestation; water pollution

Geographical Features: flat, swampy coastal plain; low mountains in south

Climate: tropical; very hot and humid

PEOPLE

Population

Total: 230,200

Annual Growth Rate: 2.42%

Rural/Urban Population Ratio: 54/46

Ethnic Makeup: 44% Mestizo; 30% Creole; 11% Maya; 7% Garifuna; 2% East Indian; 6% others

Major Languages: English; Spanish; Maya; Garifuna

Religions: 62% Roman Catholic; 30% Protestant; 6% others; 2% unaffiliated

Health

Life Expectancy at Birth: 67 years (male); 71 years (female)

Infant Mortality Rate (Ratio): 32.3/1,000

Average Caloric Intake: 111% of FAO minimum

Physicians Available (Ratio): 1/1,708

Education

Adult Literacy Rate: 70.3%

Compulsory (Ages): 5–14

COMMUNICATION

Televisions: 1 per 6 people

TRANSPORTATION

Highways in Miles (Kilometers): 1,396 (2,240)

Railroads in Miles (Kilometers): none

Usable Airfields: 44

GOVERNMENT

Type: parliamentary democracy

Independence Date: September 21, 1981 (from the United Kingdom)

Head of State/Government: Governor General Sir Colville Young (represents Queen Elizabeth II); Prime Minister Said Musa

Political Parties: People's United Party, United Democratic Party; National Alliance for Belizean Rights

Suffrage: universal at 18

MILITARY

Military Expenditures (% of GDP): 2%

Current Disputes: border dispute with Guatemala

ECONOMY

Currency ($ U.S. Equivalent): 2 Belize dollars = $1

Per Capita Income/GDP: $3,000/$680 million

GDP Growth Rate: 2.9%

Inflation Rate: 1%

Unemployment Rate: 13%

Labor Force: 71,000

Natural Resources: arable land; timber; fish

Agriculture: bananas; cocoa; citrus fruits; sugarcane; lumber; fish; cultured shrimp

Industry: garment production; food processing; tourism; construction

Exports: $166 million (primary partners United States, United Kingdom, European Union countries)

Imports: $262 million (primary partners United States, Mexico, United Kingdom)

http://lcweb2.loc.gov/frd/cs/ bztoc.html
http://www.belize.com

Belize

Capital — River
Major city --- Road
City/Town

| 0 | 75 | 150 Miles |
| 0 | 75 | 150 Kilometers |

Elevation in feet.

Belize is settled
by English
logwood cutters
1638

Belize is
declared an
independent
Crown colony
1884

Guatemala
threatens to
invade
1972

Independence
from Great Britain
1981

1990s

Guatemala
continues
territorial claims
to Belize

Belize becomes
an ecotourism
destination

Said Musa is
elected prime
minister

A LITTLE BIT OF ENGLAND

Belize was settled in the late 1630s by English woodcutters who also indulged in occasional piracy at the expense of the Spanish crown. The loggers were interested primarily in dye-woods, which, in the days before chemical dyes, were essential to British textile industries. The country's name is derived from Peter Wallace, a notorious buccaneer who, from his base there, haunted the coast in search of Spanish shipping. The natives shortened and mispronounced Wallace's name until he became known as "Belize."

As a British colony (called "British Honduras"), Belize enjoyed relative prosperity as an important entrepôt, or storage depot for merchandise, until the completion of the Panama Railway in 1855. With the opening of a rail route to the Pacific, commerce shifted south, away from Caribbean ports. Belize entered an economic tailspin (from which it has never entirely recovered). Colonial governments attempted to diversify the colony's agricultural base and to attract foreign immigration to develop the land. But, except for some Mexican settlers and a few former Confederate soldiers who came to the colony after the U.S. Civil War, the immigration policy failed. Economically depressed, its population exposed to the ravages of yellow fever, malaria, and dengue (a tropical fever), Belize was once described by British novelist Aldous Huxley in the following terms: "If the world had ends, Belize would be one of them."

Living conditions improved markedly by the 1950s, and the colony began to move toward independence from Great Britain. Although self-governing by 1964, Belize did not become fully independent until 1981, because of Guatemalan threats to invade what it even today considers a lost province, stolen by Britain. British policy calls for a termination of its military presence, even though Guatemalan intentions toward Belize are ambivalent.

Culturally, Belize is English with Caribbean overtones. English common law is practiced in the courts, and politics are patterned on the English parliamentary system. Thirty percent of the people are Protestants. The Belizeans are primarily working-class poor and middle-class shopkeepers and merchants. There is no great difference between the well-to-do and the poor in Belize, and few people fall below the absolute poverty line.

Thirty percent of the population are Creole (black and English mixture), 7 percent Garifuna (black and Indian mixture). The Garifuna originally inhabited the Caribbean island of St. Vincent. In the eighteenth century, they joined with native Indians in an uprising against the English authorities. As punishment, virtually all the Garifuna were deported to Belize.

Despite a pervasive myth of racial democracy in Belize, discrimination exists. Belize is not a harmonious, multiethnic island in a sea of violence. For example, sociologist Bruce Ergood notes that in Belize it "is not uncommon to hear a light Creole bad-mouth 'blacks,' even though both are considered Creole. This reflects a vestige of English colonial attitude summed up in the saying, 'Best to be white, less good to be mulatto, worst to be black....' "

A shift in population occurred in the 1980s because of the turmoil in neighboring Central American states. For years, well-educated, English-speaking Creoles had been leaving Belize in search of better economic opportunities in other countries; but this was more than made up for by the inflow of perhaps as many as 40,000 Latin American refugees fleeing the fighting in the region. Spanish is now the primary language of a significant percentage of the population, and some Belizeans are concerned about the "Hispanicization" of the country.

Women in Belize suffer discrimination that is deeply rooted in the cultural, social, and economic structures of the society, even though the government promotes their participation in the nation's politics and development process. Great emphasis is placed on education and health care. Tropical diseases, once the primary cause of death in Belize, were brought under control by a government program of spraying. Health and nutritional awareness are emphasized in campaigns to encourage breastfeeding and the selection and preparation of meals using local produce.

DEVELOPMENT

Belize has combined its tourism and environmental-protection offices into one ministry, which holds great promise for ecotourism. Large tracts of land have been set aside to protect jaguars and other endangered species. But there is also pressure on the land from rapid population growth.

FREEDOM

The House and Senate established a Joint Select Committee to "canvass the views of the Belizean people and to make recommendations for bringing about political reform in the country."

HEALTH/WELFARE

In a speech to the Christian Workers Union, PM Musa said: "Higher wages will not mean much if families cannot obtain quality and affordable health care services. What good are higher wages if there are not enough classrooms in which to place the children? What good are higher wages if we are forced to live in fear of the criminal elements in society? A workers' movement must . . . concern itself not only with wages but also with the overall quality of life of its members."

ACHIEVEMENTS

Recent digging by archaeologists has uncovered several Maya sites that have convinced scholars that the indigenous civilization in the region was more extensive and refined than experts had previously believed.

Costa Rica (Republic of Costa Rica)

GEOGRAPHY
Area in Square Miles (Kilometers):
19,700 (51,022) (smaller than West Virginia)
Capital (Population): San José (920,000)
Environmental Concerns: deforestation; soil erosion
Geographical Features: coastal plains separated by rugged mountains

PEOPLE

Population
Total: 3,605,000
Annual Growth Rate: 1.95%
Rural/Urban Population Ratio: 50/50
Major Language: Spanish
Ethnic Makeup: 96% white (including a few Mestizos); 2% black; 1% Indian; 1% Chinese
Religions: 95% Roman Catholic; 5% others

Health
Life Expectancy at Birth: 73 years (male); 78 years (female)
Infant Mortality Rate (Ratio): 13.1/1,000
Average Caloric Intake: 118% of FAO minimum
Physicians Available (Ratio): 1/870

Education
Adult Literacy Rate: 95%
Compulsory (Ages): 6–15; free

COMMUNICATION
Telephones: 1 per 6.1 people
Daily Newspaper Circulation: 99 per 1,000 people
Televisions: 1 per 7 people

TRANSPORTATION
Highways in Miles (Kilometers): 22,189 (35,560)
Railroads in Miles (Kilometers): 593 (950)
Usable Airfields: 158
Motor Vehicles in Use: 130,000

GOVERNMENT
Type: democratic republic
Independence Date: September 15, 1821 (from Spain)
Head of State/Government: President Miguel Angel Rodríguez is both head of state and head of government
Political Parties: Social Christian Unity Party; National Liberation Party; National Integration Party; People United Party; Democratic Party; National Independent Party; others

Suffrage: universal and compulsory at 18

MILITARY
Military Expenditures (% of Central Government Expenditures): 2%
Current Hostilities: none

ECONOMY
Currency ($ U.S. Equivalent): 296.85 colones = $1
Per Capita Income/GDP: $5,500/$19.6 billion
GDP Growth Rate: 3%
Inflation Rate: 11.2%
Unemployment Rate: 5.7%; much under employment
Labor Force: 868,300

Natural Resources: hydropower potential
Agriculture: coffee; bananas; sugar; corn; rice; beans; potatoes; beef; timber
Industry: food processing; textiles and clothing; construction materials; fertilizer; plastic products; tourism
Exports: $2.9 billion (primary partners United States, Germany, Guatemala)
Imports: $3.4 billion (primary partners United States, Japan, Mexico)

http://www.cia.gov/cia/publications/factbook/cs.html
http://www.infocstarica.com/interactive/sitemap.html

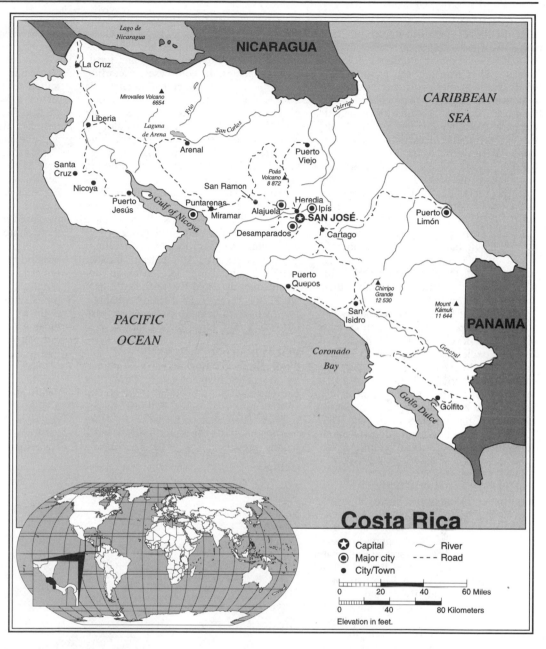

Costa Rica

- ⭐ Capital
- ◎ Major city
- ● City/Town
- ～ River
- - - - Road

0   20   40   60 Miles
0   40   80 Kilometers
Elevation in feet.

COSTA RICA:
A DIFFERENT TRADITION?

Costa Rica has often been singled out as politically and socially unique in Latin America. It is true that the nation's historical development has not been as directly influenced by Spain as its neighbors' have, but this must not obscure the essential Hispanic character of the Costa Rican people and their institutions. Historian Ralph Woodward has observed that historically, Costa Rica's "uniqueness was the product of her relative remoteness from the remainder of Central America, her slight economic importance to Spain, and her lack of a non-white subservient class and corresponding lack of a class of large landholders to exploit its labors." Indeed, in 1900, Costa Rica had a higher percentage of farmers with small- and medium-range operations than any other Latin American country.

The nature of Costa Rica's economy allowed a wider participation in politics and fostered the development of political institutions dedicated to the equality of all people, which existed only in theory in other Latin American countries. Costa Rican politicians, since the late nineteenth century, have endorsed programs that have been largely middle class in content. The government has consistently demonstrated a commitment to the social welfare of its citizens.

AN INTEGRATED SOCIETY

Despite the recent atmosphere of crisis and disintegration in Central America, Costa Rica's durable democracy has avoided the twin evils of oppressive authoritarianism and class warfare. But what might be construed as good luck is actually a reflection of Costa Rica's history. In social, racial, linguistic, and educational terms, Costa Rica is an integrated country without the fractures and cleavages that typify the rest of the region.

Despite its apparent uniqueness, Costa Rica is culturally an integral part of Latin America and embodies what is most positive about Hispanic political culture. The government has long played the role of benevolent patron to the majority of its citizens. Opposition and antagonism have historically been defused by a process of accommodation, mutual cooperation, and participation. In the early 1940s, for example, modernizers who wanted to create a dynamic capitalist economy took care to pacify the emerging labor movement with appropriate social legislation and benefits. Moreover, to assure that development did not sacrifice social welfare, the state assumed a traditional role with respect to the economy—that is, it took an active role in the production and distribution of income. After much discussion, in 1993, the Costa Rican Congress authorized the privatization of the state-owned cement and fertilizer companies. In both cases, according to *Latin American Regional Reports,* "a 30% stake [would] be reserved for employees, 20% [would] be offered to private investors, and the remainder [would] be shared out between trade unions . . . and cooperatives." Tight controls were retained on banking, insurance, oil refining, and public utilities.

Women, who were granted the right to vote in the 1940s, have participated freely in Costa Rica's elections. Women have served as a vice president, minister of foreign commerce, and president of the Legislative Assembly. Although in broader terms the role of women is primarily domestic, they are legally unrestricted. Equal work, in general, is rewarded by equal pay for men and women. But women also hold, as a rule, lower-paying jobs.

POLITICS OF CONSENSUS

Costa Rica's political stability is assured by the politics of consensus. Deals and compacts are the order of the day among various competing elites. Political competition is open, and participation by labor and peasants is expanding. Election campaigns provide a forum to air differing viewpoints, to educate the voting public, and to keep politicians in touch with the population at large.

Costa Rica frequently has had strong, charismatic leaders who have been committed to social democracy and have rejected a brand of politics grounded in class differences. The country's democracy has always reflected the paternalism and personalities of its presidents.

This tradition was again endorsed when José María Figueres Olsen won the presidential election on February 6, 1994. Figueres was the son of the founder of the modern Costa Rican democracy, and he promised to return to a reduced version of the welfare state. But, by 1996, in the face of a sluggish economy, the populist champion adopted policies that were markedly pro-business. As a result, opinion polls rapidly turned against him. In the 1998 presidential election, an unprecedented 13 political parties ran candidates, which indicated to the three leading parties that citizens no longer believed in them and that political reforms were in order.

Other oft-given reasons for Costa Rica's stability are the high levels of tolerance exhibited by its people and the absence of a military establishment. Costa Rica has had no military establishment since a brief civil war in 1948. Government officials have long boasted that they rule over a

(United Nations photo/Milton Grant)

Costa Rica has a widely varied landscape. Pictured above is the volcanic mountain Miravalles, which has the potential of generating geothermal energy that can be used to produce electricity.

| Spain establishes its first settlements in Costa Rica **1522** | Independence from Spain **1821** | Costa Rica is part of the United Provinces of Central America **1823** | Costa Rica becomes independent as a separate state **1838** | Civil war; reforms; abolition of the army **1948** | Costa Rica takes steps to protect its tropical rain forests and dry forests **1980s** |

1990s

| Border tensions increase with Nicaragua over Costa Rican access to the San Juan River | Ecotourism to Costa Rica increases | Miguel Angel Rodríguez is elected president |

country that has more teachers than soldiers. There is also a strong public tradition that favors demilitarization. Costa Rica's auxiliary forces, however, could form the nucleus of an army in a time of emergency.

The Costa Rican press is among the most unrestricted in Latin America, and differing opinions are openly expressed. Human-rights abuses are virtually nonexistent in the country, but there is a general suspicion of Communists in this overwhelmingly middle-class, white society. And some citizens are concerned about the antidemocratic ideas expressed by ultraconservatives.

The aftermath of Central America's civil wars is still being felt. Although thousands of refugees returned to Nicaragua with the advent of peace, many thousands more remained in Costa Rica. Economic malaise in Nicaragua combined with the devastation of Hurricane Mitch in 1998 sent thousands of economic migrants across the border into Costa Rica. "Ticos" are worried by the additional strain placed on government resources in a country where more than 80 percent of the population are covered by social-security programs, and approximately 60 percent are provided with pensions and medical benefits.

The economy has been under stress since 1994, and President Figueres was forced to reconsider many of his statist policies. While the export sector remained healthy, domestic industry languished and the internal debt ballooned. The Costa Rican–American Chamber of Commerce observed that "Costa Rica, with its tiny $8.6 billion GDP and 3.5 million people, can not afford a government that consistently overspends its budget by 5 percent or more and then sells short-term bonds, mostly to state institutions, to finance the

deficit." In 1997, there was a vigorous debate over the possible privatization of many state entities in an effort to reduce the debt quickly. But opponents of privatization noted that state institutions were important contributors to the high standard of living in the country. In 1999, the International Monetary Fund identified Costa Rica's main economic problems as inflation, the deficit, low levels of domestic savings, and the need for greater efficiency in the public sector. IMF guidelines also suggested a greater role for the private sector in the economy, even though this was opposed by many Costa Ricans.

THE ENVIRONMENT

At a time when tropical rain forests globally are under assault by developers, cattle barons, and land-hungry peasants, Costa Rica has taken concrete action to protect its environment. Minister of Natural Resources Álvaro Umana was one of those responsible for engineering an imaginative debt-for-nature swap. In his words: "We would like to see debt relief support conservation . . . a policy that everybody agrees is good." Since 1986, the Costa Rican government has authorized the conversion of $75 million in commercial debt into bonds. Interest generated by those bonds has supported a variety of projects, such as the enlargement and protection of La Amistad, a 1.7 million-acre reserve of tropical rain forest.

About 13 percent of Costa Rica's land is protected currently in a number of national parks. It is hoped that very soon about 25 percent of the country will be designated as national parkland in order to protect tropical rain forests as well as the even more endangered tropical dry forests.

Much of the assault on the forests typically has been dictated by economic necessity and/or greed. In one all-too-

common scenario, a small- or middle-size cacao grower discovers that his crop has been decimated by a blight. Confronted by disaster, he will usually farm the forest surrounding his property for timber and then torch the remainder. Ultimately, he will likely sell his land to a cattle rancher, who will transform what had once been rain forest or dry forest into pasture.

In an effort to break this devastating pattern, at least one Costa Rican environmental organization has devised a workable plan to save the forests. Farmers are introduced to a variety of cash crops so that they will not be totally dependent on a single crop. Also, in the case of cacao, for example, the farmer will be provided with a disease- or blight-resistant strain to lessen further the chances of crop losses and subsequent conversion of land to cattle pasture.

Scientists in Costa Rica are concerned that tropical forests are being destroyed before their usefulness to humankind can be fully appreciated. Such forests contain a treasure-trove of medicinal herbs. In Costa Rica, for example, there is at least one plant common to the rain forests that might be beneficial in the struggle against AIDS.

DEVELOPMENT

Despite government claims that deforestation has been brought under control, environmentalists charge that more trees were cut in the last logging season than in previous years, according to a report in *The Tico Times*. Recent laws with regard to logging have loopholes that allow loggers to destroy the few forests remaining outside Costa Rica's national-park system.

FREEDOM

Despite Costa Rica's generally enviable human-rights record, there is some de facto discrimination against blacks, Indians, and women (domestic violence against women is a serious problem). The press is free. A stringent libel law, however, makes the media cautious in reporting of personalities.

HEALTH/WELFARE

Costa Ricans enjoy the highest standard of living in Central America. But Costa Rica's indigenous peoples, in part because of their remote location, have inadequate schools, health care, and access to potable water. Moreover, because many lack citizenship papers, they cannot vote or hold office.

ACHIEVEMENTS

In a region torn by civil war and political chaos, Costa Rica's years of free and democratic elections stand as a remarkable achievement in political stability and civil rights. President Óscar Arias was awarded the Nobel Peace Prize in 1987; he remains an internationally recognized and respected world leader.

El Salvador (Republic of El Salvador)

GEOGRAPHY
Area in Square Miles (Kilometers):
8,292 (21,476) (about the
size of Massachusetts)
Capital (Population): San
Salvador (1,214,000)
Environmental Concerns:
deforestation; soil erosion;
water pollution
Geographical Features: a hot
coastal plain in south rises to
a cooler plateau and valley
region; mountainous in north,
including many volcanoes
Climate: tropical; distinct wet
and dry seasons

PEOPLE

Population
Total: 5,752,000
Annual Growth Rate: 1.57%
Rural/Urban Population Ratio:
55/45
Ethnic Makeup: 94% Mestizo;
5% Amerindian; 1% white
Major Language: Spanish
Religions: 75% Roman Catholic;
25% Protestant groups

Health
Life Expectancy at Birth: 66
years (male); 73 years (female)
Infant Mortality Rate (Ratio):
29/1,000
Average Caloric Intake: 94%
of FAO minimum
Physicians Available (Ratio):
1/1,219

Education
Adult Literacy Rate: 71.5%
Compulsory (Ages): 7–16

COMMUNICATION
Telephones: 1 per 19 people
Daily Newspaper Circulation:
50 per 1,000 people
Televisions: 1 per 12 people

TRANSPORTATION
Highways in Miles (Kilometers): 6,196
(9,977)
Railroads in Miles (Kilometers): 374 (602)
Usable Airfields: 88
Motor Vehicles in Use: 62,000

GOVERNMENT
Type: republic
Independence Date: September 15, 1821
(from Spain)
Head of State/Government: President
Francisco Flores is both head of state
and head of government
Political Parties: Farabundo Martí
National Liberation Front; National
Republican Alliance; National Concili-
ation Party; Christian Democratic Party;
Democratic Convergence; others
Suffrage: universal at 18

MILITARY
Military Expenditures (% of GDP): 0.9%
Current Disputes: none

ECONOMY
Currency ($ U.S. Equivalent): 8.78 colons
= $1
Per Capita Income/GDP: $3,000/$17.8
billion
GDP Growth Rate: 4%
Inflation Rate: 2%
Unemployment Rate: 7.7%
Labor Force: 2,260,000

Natural Resources: hydropower; geothermal
power; petroleum
Agriculture: coffee; sugarcane; corn; rice;
beans; oilseed; cotton; sorghum; beef;
dairy products; shrimp
Industry: food processing; beverages;
petroleum; chemicals; fertilizer; textiles;
furniture; light metals
Exports: $1.96 billion (primary partners
United States, Guatemala, Germany)
Imports: $3.5 billion (primary partners
United States, Guatemala, Mexico)

http://lcweb2.loc.gov/frd/cs/
svtoc.html
http://home.tampabay.rr.com/
latinoconnect/elsalvad.html

EL SALVADOR: A TROUBLED LAND

El Salvador, a small country, was engaged until 1992 in a civil war that cut through class lines, divided the military and the Roman Catholic Church, and severely damaged the social and economic fabric of the nation. It was the latest in a long series of violent sociopolitical eruptions that have plagued the country since its independence in 1821.

In the last quarter of the nineteenth century, large plantation owners—spurred by the sharp increase in the world demand for coffee and other products of tropical agriculture—expanded their lands and estates. Most of the new land was purchased or taken from Indians and Mestizos (those of mixed white and Indian blood), who, on five occasions between 1872 and 1898, took up arms in futile attempts to preserve their land. The once-independent Indians and Mestizos were reduced to becoming tenant farmers, sharecroppers, day laborers, or peons on the large estates. Indians, when deprived of their lands, also lost much of their cultural and ethnic distinctiveness. Today, El Salvador is an overwhelmingly Mestizo society.

The uprooted peasantry was controlled in a variety of ways. Some landowners played the role of *patrón* and assured workers the basic necessities of life in return for their labor. Laws against "vagabonds" (those who, when stopped by rural police, did not have a certain amount of money in their pockets) assured plantation owners a workforce and discouraged peasant mobility.

To enforce order further, a series of security organizations—the National Guard, the National Police, and the Treasury Police—were created by the central government. Many of these security personnel actually lived on the plantations and estates and followed the orders of the owner. Although protection of the economic system was their primary function, over time, elements of these organizations became private armies.

This phenomenon lay at the heart of much of the "unofficial" violence in El Salvador in recent years. In Salvadoran society, personal loyalties to relatives or local strongmen competed with and often superseded loyalty to government officials. Because of this, the government was unable to control some elements within its security forces.

In an analysis of the Salvadoran Civil War, it is tempting to place the rich, rightwing landowners and their military allies on one side; and the poor, the peasantry, and the guerrillas on the other. Such a division is artificial, however, and fails to reflect the complexities of the conflict. Granted, the military and landowners had

enjoyed a mutually beneficial partnership since 1945. But there were liberal and conservative factions within the armed forces, and, since the 1940s, there had been some movement toward needed social and economic reforms. It was a military regime in 1949 that put into effect the country's first social-security legislation. In 1950, a Constitution was established that provided for public-health programs, women's suffrage, and extended social-security coverage. The reformist impulse continued in the 1960s, when it became legal to organize opposition political parties.

A TIME FOR CHANGE

Food production increased in the 1970s by 44 percent, a growth that was second in Latin America only to Brazil's. Although much of the food grown was exported to world markets, some of the revenue generated was used for social programs in El Salvador. Life expectancy increased; the death rate fell; illiteracy declined; and the percentage of government expenditures on public health, housing, and education was among the highest in Latin America.

The programs and reforms, in classic Hispanic form, were generated by the upper classes. The elite believed that state-sponsored changes could be controlled in such a way that traditional balances in society would remain intact and elite domination of the government would be assured.

El Salvador's Civil War may be traced to 1972, when the Christian Democratic candidate for president, José Napoleón Duarte, is believed to have won the popular vote but was deprived of his victory when the army declared the results false and handed the victory to its own candidate. Impatient and frustrated, middle-class politicians and student leaders from the opposition began to consider more forceful ways to oust the ruling class.

By 1979, guerrilla groups had become well established in rural El Salvador, and some younger army officers grew concerned that a successful left-wing popular revolt was a distinct possibility. Rather than wait for revolution from below, which might result in the destruction of the military as an institution, the officers chose to seize power in a coup and manipulate change from above. Once in power, this *junta*, or ruling body, moved quickly to transform the structure of Salvadoran society. A land-reform program, originally developed by civilian reformers and Roman Catholic clergy, was adopted by the military. It would give the *campesinos* ("peasants") not only land but also status, dignity, and respect.

In its first year, 1980, the land-reform program had a tremendous impact on the

landowning elite—37 percent of the lands producing cotton and 34 percent of the coffee-growing lands were confiscated by the government and redistributed. The junta also nationalized the banks and assumed control of the sale of coffee and sugar. Within months, however, several peasant members of the new cooperatives and the government agricultural advisers sent to help them were gunned down. The violence spread. Some of the killings were attributed to government security men in the pay of dispossessed landowners, but most of the killings may have been committed by the army.

In the opinion of a land-reform program official, the army was corrupt and had returned to the cooperatives that it had helped to establish in order to demand money for protection and bribes. When the peasants refused, elements within the army initiated a reign of terror against them.

In 1989, further deterioration of the land-reform program was brought about by Supreme Court decisions and by policies adopted by the newly elected right-wing government of President Alfredo Cristiani. Former landowners who had had property taken for redistribution to peasants successfully argued that seizures under the land reform were illegal. Subsequently, five successive land-reform cases were decided by the Supreme Court in favor of former property owners.

Cristiani, whose right-wing National Republican Alliance Party (ARENA) fought hard against land reform, would not directly attack the land-reform program—only because such a move would further alienate rural peasants and drive them into the arms of left-wing guerrillas. Instead, Cristiani favored the reconstitution of collective farms as private plots. Such a move, according to the government, would improve productivity and put an end to what authorities perceived as a form of U.S.–imposed "socialism." Critics of the government's policy charged that the privatization plan would ultimately result in the demise of land reform altogether.

Yet another problem was that many of the collectives established under the reform were (and remain) badly in debt. A 1986 study by the U.S. Agency for International Development reported that 95 percent of the cooperatives could not pay interest on the debt they were forced to acquire to compensate the landlords. *New York Times* reporter Lindsey Gruson noted that the world surplus of agricultural products as well as mismanagement by peasants who suddenly found themselves in the unfamiliar role of owners were a large part of the reason for the failures. But the government did not help. Technical assistance was not provided, and the tremendous debt gave the cooperatives a poor credit rating, which made it difficult for them to secure needed fertilizer and pesticides.

Declining yields and, for many families, lives of increasing desperation have been the result. Some peasants must leave the land and sell their plots to the highest bidder. This will ultimately bring about a re-concentration of land in the hands of former landlords.

Other prime farmland lay untended because of the Civil War. Violence drove many peasants from the land to the slums of the larger cities. And free-fire zones established by the military (in an effort to destroy the guerrillas' popular base) and guerrilla attacks against cooperatives (in an effort to sabotage the economy and further destabilize the country) had a common victim: the peasantry.

Some cooperatives and individual families failed to bring the land to flower because of the poor quality of the soil they inherited. Reporter Gruson told the story of one family, which was, unfortunately, all too common:

José . . . received 1.7 acres on a rock-pocked slope an hour's walk from his small shack. José . . . used to sell some of his beans and rice to raise a little cash. But year after year his yields

have declined. Since he cannot afford fertilizers or insecticides, the corn that survives the torrential rainy season produces pest-infested ears the size of a baby's foot. Now, he has trouble feeding his wife and seven children.

"The land is no good," he said. "I've been working it for 12 years and my life has gotten worse every year. I don't have anywhere to go, but I'll have to leave soon."

After the coup, several governments came and went. The original reformers retired, went into exile, or went over to the guerrillas. The Civil War continued into 1992, when a United Nations–mediated cease-fire took effect. The extreme right and left regularly utilized assassination to eliminate or terrorize both each other and the voices of moderation who still dared to speak out. The death squads and guerrillas claimed their victims from all social classes. Some leaders, such as former president Duarte, described a culture of violence in El Salvador that had become part of the national character.

HUMAN-RIGHTS ISSUES
Through 1992, human-rights abuses still occurred on a wide scale in El Salvador. Public order was constantly disrupted by military operations, guerrilla raids, fac-

tional hatreds, acts of revenge, personal grudges, pervasive fear, and a sense of uncertainty about the future. State-of-siege decrees suspended all constitutional rights to freedom of speech and press. However, self-censorship, both in the media and by individuals, out of fear of violent reprisals, was the leading constraint on free expression in El Salvador.

Release of the report in 1993 by the UN's "Truth Commission," a special body entrusted with the investigation of human-rights violations in El Salvador, prompted the right wing–dominated Congress to approve an amnesty for those named. But progress has been made in other areas. The National Police have been separated from the Defense Ministry; and the National Guard, Civil Defense forces, and the notorious Treasury Police have been abolished. A new National Civilian Police, comprised of 20 percent of National Police, 20 percent former Farabundo Martí National Liberation Front (FMLN) guerrillas, and 60 percent with no involvement on either side in the Civil War, was instituted in 1994.

In El Salvador, as elsewhere in Latin America, the Roman Catholic Church was divided. The majority of Church officials backed government policy and supported the United States' contention that the violence in El Salvador was due to Cuban-

(Y. Nagata/PAS United Nations photo)

Civil strife disrupted much of the agrarian production, and lack of fishery planning necessitated importing from other parts of the world. With a new and efficient program to take advantage of fish in domestic waters, El Salvador has been able to develop an effective food industry from the sea.

| Present-day El Salvador is occupied by Spanish settlers from Mexico 1524 | Independence from Spain is declared 1821 | El Salvador is part of the United Provinces of Central America 1822 | El Salvador becomes independent as a separate state 1838 | A brief war between El Salvador and Honduras 1969 | Guerrilla warfare in El Salvador 1970 | Army officers seize power in a coup; Civil War 1979 | Right-wing President Alfredo Cristiani is elected 1989 | 1990s |

The cease-fire takes effect on February 1, 1992, officially ending the Civil War

Conservative candidate Francisco Flores claims victory in the 1999 presidential election

backed subversion. Other clergy strongly disagreed and argued convincingly that the violence was deeply rooted in historical social injustice.

GOVERNANCE

The election to the presidency of José Napoleón Duarte in 1984 was an important first step in establishing the legitimacy of government in El Salvador, as were municipal elections in 1985. The United States supported Duarte as a representative of the "democratic" middle ground between the guerrillas of the FMLN and the right-wing ARENA party. Ironically, U.S. policy in fact undermined Duarte's claims to legitimacy and created a widespread impression that he was little more than a tool for U.S. interests.

Yet, while the transfer of power to President Cristiani via the electoral process in 1989 reflected the will of those who voted, it did not augur well for the lessening of human-rights abuses. With respect to the guerrillas of the FMLN, Cristiani made it clear that the government would set the terms for any talks about ending the Civil War. For its part, the FMLN warned that it would make the country "ungovernable." In effect, then, the 1989 election results polarized the country's political life even more.

After several unsuccessful efforts to bring the government and the guerrillas to the negotiating table, the two sides reached a tentative agreement in April 1991 on constitutional reforms at a UN-sponsored meeting in Mexico City. The military, judicial system, and electoral process were all singled out for sweeping changes. By October, the FMLN had promised to lay down its arms; and near midnight on December 31, the final points of a peace accord were agreed upon. Final refinements of the agreement were drawn up in New York, and a formal signing ceremony was staged in Mexico City on January 16, 1992. The official cease-fire took effect February 1, thus ending the 12-year Civil War that had claimed more than 70,000 lives and given El Salvador the reputation of a bloody and abusive country.

Implementation of the agreement reached between the government and the FMLN has proven contentious. "But," according to *Boston Globe* correspondent Pamela Constable, "a combination of war-weariness and growing pragmatism among leaders of all persuasions suggests that once-bitter adversaries have begun to develop a modus vivendi."

President Cristiani reduced the strength of the army from 63,000 to 31,500 by February 1993, earlier than provided for by the agreement; and the class of officers known as the *tondona,* who had long dominated the military and were likely responsible for human-rights abuses, were forcibly retired by the president on June 30, 1993. Land, judicial, and electoral reforms followed. Despite perhaps inevitable setbacks because of the legacy of violence and bitterness, editor Juan Comas wrote that "most analysts are inclined to believe that El Salvador's hour of madness has passed and the country is now on the road to hope."

In 1998, President Armando Calderón Sol surprised both supporters and opponents when he launched a bold program of reforms. The first three years of his administration were characterized by indecision. Political scientist Tommie Sue Montgomery noted that his "reputation for espousing as policy the last viewpoint he has heard has produced in civil society both heartburn and black humor." But a combination of factors created new opportunities for Calderón. The former guerrillas of the FMLN were divided and failed to take advantage of ARENA's apparent weak leadership; a UN–sponsored program of reconstruction and reconciliation was short of funds and, by 1995, had lost momentum; and presidential elections were looming in 1999. A dozen years of civil war had left the economic infrastructure in disarray. The economy had, at best, remained static, and while the war raged, there had been no attempt to modernize. During his final year in office, Calderón developed reform policies of modernization, privatization, and free-market competition. Interestingly, his reforms generated opposition from former guerrillas, who are now represented in the Legislature by the FMLN, as well as from some members of the traditional conservative economic elite.

Perhaps one result of Calderón's reforms was the decisive victory of ARENA at the polls in 1999, where it won at least half of the votes cast. It remains to be seen if the new president, Francisco Flores, will embrace the reform package of his predecessor or strike out in his own direction.

DEVELOPMENT

Since 1991, the government has been able to attract substantial investment in a new industry of low-wage, duty-free assembly plants patterned after the *maquiladora* industries along Mexico's border with the United States. Advantageous tax laws and a free-market climate favorable to business are central to the government's development policy.

FREEDOM

The end of the Civil War brought an overall improvement in human rights in El Salvador. The number of extrajudicial killings fell significantly, and politically motivated killings seem to be on the wane. News from across the political spectrum, often critical of the government, is reported in El Salvador, although foreign journalists seem to be the target of an unusually high level of muggings, robberies, and burglaries.

HEALTH/WELFARE

Many Salvadorans suffer from parasites and malnutrition. El Salvador has one of the highest infant mortality rates in the Western Hemisphere, largely because of polluted water. Potable water is readily available to only 10% of the population. Violence against women is widespread. Judges often dismiss rape cases on the pretext that the victim provoked the crime.

ACHIEVEMENTS

Despite the violence of war, political power has been transferred via elections at both the municipal and national levels. Elections have helped to establish the legitimacy of civilian leaders in a region usually dominated by military regimes.

Guatemala (Republic of Guatemala)

GEOGRAPHY
Area in Square Miles (Kilometers):
42,000 (108,780) (about the size of Tennessee)
Capital (Population): Guatemala City (2,205,000)
Environmental Concerns: deforestation; soil erosion; water pollution
Geographical Features: mostly mountains, with narrow coastal plains and rolling limestone plateau (Peten)
Climate: temperate in highlands; semitropical on coasts

PEOPLE

Population
Total: 12,008,000
Annual Growth Rate: 2.7%
Rural/Urban Population Ratio: 61/39
Ethnic Makeup: 56% Ladino (Mestizo and Westernized Indian); 44% Amerindian
Major Languages: Spanish; Maya languages
Religions: predominantly Roman Catholic; also Protestant and traditional Maya

Health
Life Expectancy at Birth: 63 years (male); 68 years (female); 44 years (Indian population)
Infant Mortality Rate (Ratio): 47.6/1,000
Average Caloric Intake: 93% of FAO minimum
Physicians Available (Ratio): 1/2,356

Education
Adult Literacy Rate: 55.6%
Compulsory (Ages): 7–14; free

COMMUNICATION
Telephones: 1 per 37 people
Daily Newspaper Circulation: 23 per 1,000 people
Televisions: 1 per 19 people

TRANSPORTATION
Highways in Miles (Kilometers): 8,135 (13,100)
Railroads in Miles (Kilometers): 552 (884)
Usable Airfields: 479
Motor Vehicles in Use: 199,000

GOVERNMENT
Type: republic
Independence Date: September 15, 1821 (from Spain)
Head of State/Government: President Alvaro Arzu Irigoyen is both head of state and head of government

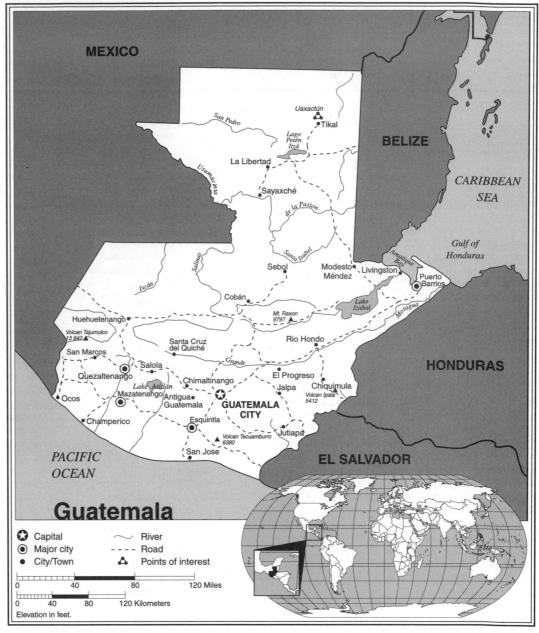

Guatemala

★ Capital
◉ Major city
● City/Town
∿ River
- - - Road
⌂ Points of interest

0   40   80   120 Miles
0   40   80   120 Kilometers
Elevation in feet.

Political Parties: National Centrist Union; Christian Democratic Party; National Advancement Party; National Liberation Movement; Social Democratic Party; Revolutionary Party; Guatemalan Republican Front; Democratic Union; New Guatemalan Democratic Front
Suffrage: universal at 18

MILITARY
Military Expenditures (% of GDP): 0.66%
Current Disputes: border dispute with Belize

ECONOMY
Currency ($ U.S. Equivalent): 7.68 quetzals = $1
Per Capita Income/GDP: $4,000/$45.8 billion
GDP Growth Rate: 4.1%
Inflation Rate: 9%

Unemployment Rate: 5.2%
Labor Force: 3,320,000
Natural Resources: petroleum; nickel; rare woods; fish; chicle
Agriculture: sugarcane; corn; bananas; coffee; beans; cardamom; livestock
Industry: sugar; textiles and clothing; furniture; chemicals; petroleum; metals; rubber; tourism
Exports: $2.9 billion (primary partners United States, El Salvador, Honduras)
Imports: $3.3 billion (primary partners United States, Mexico, Venezuela)

http://www.cia.gov/cia/publications/factbook/gt.html
http://www.guatemalaweb.com

GUATEMALA:
PEOPLES IN CONFLICT

Ethnic relations between the descendants of Maya Indians, who comprise 44 percent of Guatemala's population, and whites and Ladinos (Hispanicized Indians) have always been unfriendly and have contributed significantly to the nation's turbulent history. During the colonial period and since independence, Spaniards, Creoles (in Guatemala, whites born in the New World—as opposed to in Nicaragua, where Creoles are native-born blacks), and Ladinos have repeatedly sought to dominate the Guatemalan Indian population, largely contained in the highlands, by controlling the Indians' land and their labor.

The process of domination was accelerated between 1870 and 1920, as Guatemala's entry into world markets hungry for tropical produce such as coffee resulted in the purchase or extensive seizures of land from Indians. Denied sufficient lands of their own, Indians were forced onto the expanding plantations as debt peons. Others were forced to labor as seasonal workers on coastal plantations; many died there because of the sharp climatic differences.

THE INDIAN AND INTEGRATION

Assaulted by the Ladino world, highland Indians withdrew into their own culture and built social barriers between themselves and the changing world outside their villages. Those barriers have persisted until the present.

For the Guatemalan governments that have thought in terms of economic progress and national unity, the Indians have always presented a problem. (In 1964, the Guatemalan national census separated the population into two social categories: whites and Ladinos, and Indians.) Traditionally, the white world has perceived them as a burden. "Backward," "custom-bound," "superstitious," "uneducated," and "unassimilable" is how the Indians were described in the late nineteenth century. Those same descriptions are often used today.

According to anthropologist Leslie Dow, Jr., Guatemalan governments too easily explain the Indian's lack of material prosperity in terms of the "deficiencies" of Indian culture. Indian "backwardness" is better explained by elite policies calculated to keep Indians subordinate. Social, political, and economic deprivations have consistently and consciously been utilized by governments anxious to maintain the Indian in an inferior status.

Between 1945 and 1954, however, there was a period of remarkable social reform in Guatemala. Before the reforms were cut short by the resistance of landowners, fac-

tions within the military, and a U.S. Central Intelligence Agency–sponsored invasion, Guatemalan governments made a concerted effort to integrate the Indian into national life. Some Indians who lived in close proximity to large urban centers such as the capital, Guatemala City, learned that their vote had the power to effect changes to their benefit. They also realized that they were unequal not because of their illiteracy, "backwardness," poverty, or inability to converse in Spanish, but because of governments that refused to reform their political, social, and economic structures.

In theory, indigenous peoples in Guatemala enjoy equal legal rights under the Constitution. In fact, however, they remain largely outside the national culture, do not speak Spanish, and are not integrated into the national economy. Indian males are far more likely to be impressed into the army or guerrilla units. Indigenous peoples in Guatemala have suffered most of the combat-related casualties and repeated abuses of their basic human rights. There remains a pervasive discrimination against Indians in white society.

Indians have on occasion challenged state policies that they have considered inequitable and repressive. But, if they become too insistent on change, threaten violence or societal upheaval, or support and/or join guerrilla groups, government repression is usually swift and merciless.

GUERRILLA WARFARE

A civil war, which was to last for 36 years, developed in 1960. Guatemala was plagued by violence, attributed both to left-wing insurgencies in rural areas and to armed forces' counterinsurgency operations. Led by youthful middle-class rebels, guerrillas gained strength because of several factors: the radical beliefs of some Roman Catholic priests in rural areas; the ability of the guerrillas to mobilize Indians for the first time; and the "demonstration effect" of events elsewhere in Central America. Some of the success is explained by the guerrilla leaders' ability to converse in Indian languages. Radical clergy increased the recruitment of Indians into the guerrilla forces by suggesting that revolution was an acceptable path to social justice. The excesses of the armed forces in their search for subversives drove other Indians into the arms of the guerrillas. In some parts of the highlands, the loss of ancestral lands to speculators or army officers was sufficient to inspire the Indians to join the radical cause.

According to the *Latin American Regional Report* for Mexico and Central America, government massacres of guer-

rillas and their actual or suspected supporters were frequent and "characterized by clinical savagery." At times, the killing was selective, with community leaders and their families singled out. In other instances, entire villages were destroyed and all the inhabitants slaughtered. "Everything depends on the army's perception of the local level of support for the guerrillas," according to the report.

To counterbalance the violence, once guerrillas were cleared from an area, the government implemented an "Aid Program to Areas in Conflict." Credit was offered to small farmers to boost food production in order to meet local demand, and displaced and jobless people were enrolled in food-for-work units to build roads or other public projects.

By the mid-1980s, most of the guerrillas' military organizations had been destroyed. This was the result not only of successful counterinsurgency tactics by the Guatemalan military but also of serious errors of judgment by guerrilla leaders. Impatient and anxious for change, the guerrillas overestimated the willingness of the Guatemalan people to rebel. They also underestimated the power of the military establishment. Surviving guerrilla units maintained an essentially defensive posture for the remainder of the decade. In 1989, however, the guerrillas regrouped. The subsequent intensification of human-rights abuses and the climate of violence were indicative of the military's response.

There was some hope for improvement in 1993, in the wake of the ouster of President Jorge Serrano, whose attempt to emulate the "self-coup" of Peru's Alberto Fujimori failed. Guatemala's next president, Ramiro de León Carpio, was a human-rights activist who was sharply critical of security forces in their war against the guerrillas of the Guatemalan National Revolutionary Unity (URNG). Peace talks between the government and guerrillas had been pursued with the Roman Catholic Church as intermediary for several years, with sparks of promise but no real change. In July 1993, de León announced a new set of proposals to bring to an end the decades of bloodshed that had resulted in 140,000 deaths. Those proposals were the basis for the realization of a peace agreement worked out under the auspices of the United Nations in December 1996.

But the underlying causes of the violence still must be addressed. Colin Woodard, writing in *The Chronicle of Higher Education*, reported that the peace accords promised to "reshape Guatemala as a democratic, multicultural society." But an estimated 70 percent of the Maya Indians still live in poverty, and more than 80 percent are illiterate. Estuardo Zapeta, Guatemala's first Maya newspaper columnist, writes: "This is a multicultural, multilingual society.... As long as we leave the Maya illiterate, we're condemning them to being peasants. And if that happens, their need to acquire farmland will lead us to another civil war." This, however, is only one facet of a multifaceted set of issues. The very complexity of Guatemalan society, according to political scientist Rachel McCleary, "make[s] it extremely difficult to attain a consensus at the national level

on the nature of the problems confronting society." But the new ability of leaders from many sectors of society to work together to shape a meaningful peace is a hopeful sign.

Although the fighting has ended, the fear persists. Journalist Woodard wrote in July 1997: "In many neighborhoods [in Guatemala City] private property is protected by razor wire and patrolled by guards with pump-action shotguns." One professor at the University of San Carlos observed, "It is good that the war is over,

but I am pessimistic about the peace.... There is intellectual freedom now, but we are very unsure of the permanence of that freedom. It makes us very cautious."

URBAN VIOLENCE

Although most of the violence occurred in rural areas, urban Guatemala did not escape the horrors of the Civil War. The following characterization of Guatemalan politics, written by an English traveler in 1839, is still relevant today: "There is but one side to the politics in Guatemala. Both

(United Nations photo/152/271/Antoinette Jongen)

This elderly Indian woman of San Mateo looks back on a life of economic and social prejudice. In recent years, Indians in Guatemala have pursued their rights by exercising their voting power. On occasion, they have resorted to violence, which has been repressed swiftly and mercilessly by the government. But the power of the ballot box has finally begun to reap gains.

Guatemala is conquered by Spanish forces from Mexico
1523

Independence
1821

Guatemala is part of the United Provinces of Central America
1822–1838

Guatemala becomes independent as a separate state
1838

Revolution; many reforms
1944

A CIA–sponsored coup deposes the reformist government
1954

Miguel Ángel Asturias wins the Nobel Prize
1967

An earthquake leaves 22,000 dead
1976

Human-rights abuses lead to the termination of U.S. aid
1977

1990s

Alvaro Arzu Irigoyen is elected president; talks between the government and guerrillas end 36 years of violence

Two reports, one by the Catholic Church and the other by the UN, acknowledge human-rights abuses during the Civil War

Volcanic eruptions near Guatemala force evacuations

parties have a beautiful way of producing unanimity of opinion, by driving out of the country all who do not agree with them."

During the Civil War, right-wing killers murdered dozens of leaders of the moderate political left to prevent them from organizing viable political parties that might challenge the ruling elite. These killers also assassinated labor leaders if their unions were considered leftist or antigovernment. Leaders among university students and professors "disappeared" because the national university had a reputation as a center of leftist subversion. Media people were gunned down if they were critical of the government or the right wing. Left-wing extremists also assassinated political leaders associated with "repressive" policies, civil servants (whose only "crime" was government employment), military personnel and police, foreign diplomats, peasant informers, and businesspeople and industrialists associated with the government.

Common crime rose to epidemic proportions in Guatemala City (as well as in the capitals of other Central American republics). Many of the weapons that once armed the Nicaraguan militias and El Salvador's civil-defense patrols found their way onto the black market, where, according to the Managua newspaper *Pensamiento Propio,* they were purchased by the Guatemalan Army, the guerrillas of the URNG, and criminals.

The fear of official or unofficial violence has always inhibited freedom of the press in Guatemala. Early in the 1980s, the Conference on Hemispheric Affairs noted that restrictions on the print media and the indiscriminate brutality of the death squads "turned Guatemala into a virtual no-man's land for journalists." Lin

gering fears and memories of past violence tend to limit the exercise of press freedoms guaranteed by the Constitution. The U.S. State Department's *Country Reports* notes that "the media continues to exercise a degree of self-censorship on certain topics. . . . The lack of aggressive investigative reporting dealing with the military and human rights violations apparently is due to self-censorship."

HEALTH CARE AND NUTRITION

In rural Guatemala, half the population have a diet that is well below the minimum daily caloric intake established by the Food and Agricultural Organization. Growth in the staple food crops (corn, rice, beans, wheat) has failed to keep pace with population growth. Marginal malnutrition is endemic.

Health services vary, depending on location, but are uniformly poor in rural Guatemala. The government has begun pilot programs in three departments to provide basic primary health care on a wide scale. But some of these well-intentioned policies have failed because of a lack of sensitivity to cultural differences. Anthropologist Linda Greenberg has observed that the Ministry of Health, as part of its campaign to bring basic health-care services to the hinterlands, introduced midwives ignorant of Indian traditions. For Guatemalan Indians, pregnancy is considered an illness and demands specific care, calling for certain foods, herbs, body positions, and interpersonal relations between expectant mother and Indian midwife. In the Mayan culture, traditional medicine has spiritual, psychological, physical, social, and symbolic dimensions. Ministry of Health workers too often dismiss traditional practices as superstitious

and unscientific. This insensitivity and ignorance creates ineffectual health-care programs.

THE FUTURE

In February 1999, a UN-sponsored Commission for Historical Clarification, in a harsh nine-volume report, blamed the Guatemalan government for acts of genocide against the Maya during the long Civil War. The purpose of the report was not to set the stage for criminal prosecutions but to examine the root causes of the Civil War and explain how the conflict developed over time. Hopefully, the report signals the first steps toward national reconciliation and recognizes the need to address human-rights issues, long ignored by those in power. But the high command of the military and its civilian allies, accused of planning and executing a broad range of atrocities against the Maya, may see the report as a threat to their position and their future.

DEVELOPMENT

The Guatemalan economy has grown at a modest average 4% rate over the past few years, and inflation has stabilized at about 9%. Since 1985, the government has taken steps to open the economy in an effort to combat high unemployment and underemployment (estimated to be as high as 45%) and poverty. Good international prices for coffee, sugar, and cardamom have stimulated export earnings.

FREEDOM

Former president Ramiro de León Carpio warned those who would violate human rights, saying that the law would punish those guilty of abuses, "whether or not they are civilians or members of the armed forces." The moment has come, he continued, "to change things and improve the image of the army and of Guatemala."

HEALTH/WELFARE

While constitutional bars on child labor in the industrial sector are not difficult to enforce, in the informal and agricultural sectors, such labor is common. It is estimated that 5,000 Guatemalan children live on the streets and survive as best they can. They are often targeted for elimination by police and death squads.

ACHIEVEMENTS

Guatemalan novelist Miguel Ángel Asturias gained an international reputation for his works about political oppression. In 1967, he was awarded the Nobel Prize for Literature. Rigoberta Menchú Tum won the Nobel Peace Prize in 1992 for her passionate support of the Maya peoples of Guatemala.

Honduras (Republic of Honduras)

GEOGRAPHY

Area in Square Miles (Kilometers):
43,267 (112,090) (slightly
larger than Tennessee)
Capital (Population): Tegucigalpa
(995,000)
Environmental Concerns:
urbanization; deforestation;
land degradation and soil
erosion; mining pollution
Geographical Features: mostly
mountainous in interior;
narrow coastal plains
Climate: subtropical, but varies
with elevation (temperate
highlands)

PEOPLE

Population

Total: 5,862,000
Annual Growth Rate: 2.3%
Rural/Urban Population Ratio:
56/44
Ethnic Makeup: 90% Mestizo
(European and Indian mix);
7% Indian; 2% African; 1%
European, Arab, and Asian
Major Language: Spanish
Religions: 97% Roman Catholic;
a small Protestant minority

Health

Life Expectancy at Birth: 66
years (male); 71 years (female)
Infant Mortality Rate (Ratio):
42/1,000
Average Caloric Intake: 96%
of FAO minimum
Physicians Available (Ratio):
1/1,586

Education

Adult Literacy Rate: 72.7%
Compulsory (Ages): 7–13; free

COMMUNICATION

Telephones: 1 per 35 people
Daily Newspaper Circulation:
44 per 1,000 people
Televisions: 1 per 13 people

TRANSPORTATION

Highways in Miles (Kilometers): 9,563
(15,400)
Railroads in Miles (Kilometers): 369 (595)
Usable Airfields: 122
Motor Vehicles in Use: 115,000

GOVERNMENT

Type: republic
Independence Date: September 15, 1821
(from Spain)
Head of State/Government: President
Carlos Roberto Flores Facusse is both
head of state and head of government

Political Parties: Liberal Party; National
Party of Honduras; National Innovation
and Unity Party–Social Democratic
Party; Christian Democratic Party; others
Suffrage: universal and compulsory at 18

MILITARY

Military Expenditures (% of GDP): 1.5%
Current Disputes: boundary disputes with
El Salvador and Nicaragua

ECONOMY

Currency ($ U.S. Equivalent): 14.59
lempiras = $1
Per Capita Income/GDP: $2,200/$12.7 billion
GDP Growth Rate: 4.5%
Inflation Rate: 15%

Unemployment Rate: 6.3%; 30%
underemployment
Labor Force: 1,300,000
Natural Resources: timber; gold; silver;
copper; lead; zinc; iron ore; antimony;
coal; fish
Agriculture: bananas; coffee; citrus fruits;
beef; timber; shrimp
Industry: sugar; coffee; textiles and cloth-
ing; wood products
Exports: $1.3 billion (primary partners
United States, Germany, Belgium)
Imports: $1.8 billion (primary partners
United States, Guatemala, Japan)

 http://lcweb2.loc.gov/frd/cs/
hntoc.html

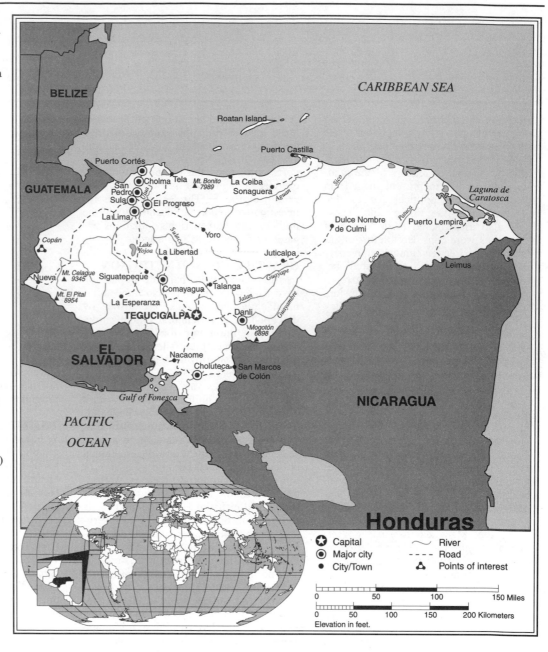

HONDURAS:
PEACEABLE KINGDOM?

In political terms, Honduras resembles much of the rest of Central America. Frequent changes of government, numerous constitutions, authoritarian presidents, widespread corruption, and an inability to solve basic problems are common to Honduras and to the region. A historian of Honduras once wrote that his country's history could be "written in a tear."

In terms of social policy, however, Honduras stands somewhat apart from its neighbors. It was slower to modernize, there were no great extremes of wealth between landowners and the rest of the population, and society appeared more paternalistic and less exploitive than was the case in other Central American states.

Honduras is a poor country. Its people have serious problems—widespread illiteracy, malnutrition, and inadequate health care. "Ironically," notes journalist Loren Jenkins, "the land's precarious existence as a poor and unstable backwater has proven almost as much a blessing as a curse." Honduras lacks the sharp social divisions that helped to plunge Nicaragua, El Salvador, and Guatemala into rebellion and civil war. And Honduran governments have seemed somewhat more responsive to demands for change.

A WILLINGNESS TO CHANGE

In 1962 and 1975, agrarian-reform laws were passed and put into effect with relative success. The Honduran government, with the aid of peasant organizations and organized labor, was able to resettle 30,000 families on their own land. Today, two thirds of the people who use the land either own it or have the legal right to its use. Labor legislation and social-security laws were enacted in the early 1960s. Even the Honduran military, usually corrupt, has at times brought about reform. An alliance of the military and organized labor in the early 1970s produced a series of reforms in response to pressure from the less advantaged sectors of the population; in 1974, the military government developed a five-year plan to integrate the rural poor into the national economy and to increase social services in the area. The state has often shown a paternalistic face rather than a brutal, repressive one. The capacity for reform led one candidate in the 1981 presidential campaign to comment: "We Hondurans are different. There is no room for violence here."

There are now many signs of change. Agrarian reform slowed after 1976, prompting a peasant-association leader to remark: "In order to maintain social peace in the countryside, the peasants' needs will have to be satisfied to avoid revolt." In 1984, the Honduran government initiated a land-titling program and issued about 1,000 titles per month to landless peasants. The government's agrarian-reform program, which is under the control of the National Agrarian Institute, has always been characterized by the carrot and the stick. While some *campesinos* ("peasants") have been granted titles to land, others have been jailed or killed.

Honduran campesinos, according to *Central America Report*, "have had a long and combative history of struggling for land rights." In 1987, hundreds of peasants were jailed as "terrorists" as a result of land invasions. Occupation of privately owned lands has become increasingly common in Honduras and reflects both population pressure on and land hunger of the peasantry. Land seizures by squatters are sometimes recognized by the National Agrarian Institute. In other cases, the government has promoted the relocation of people to sparsely populated regions of the country. Unfortunately, the chosen relocation sites are in tropical rain forests, which are already endangered throughout the region. The government wishes to transform the forests into rubber and citrus plantations or into farms to raise rice, corn, and other crops.

Peasants who fail to gain access to land usually migrate to urban centers in search of a better life. What they find in cities such as the capital, Tegucigalpa, are inadequate social services, a miserable standard of living, and a municipal government without the resources to help. In 1989, Tegucigalpa was deeply in debt, mortgaged to the limit, months behind in wage payments to city workers, and plagued by garbage piling up in the streets.

The nation's economy as a whole fared badly in the late 1980s. But by 1992, the economy, following painful adjustments occasioned by the reforms of the government of President Rafael Callejas, again showed signs of growth. Real gross domestic product reached 3.5 percent, and inflation was held in check. Unemployment remained a persistent problem; some agencies calculated that two thirds of the workforce lacked steady employment. A union leader warned: "Unemployment leads to desperation and becomes a time bomb that could explode at any moment."

In addition to internal problems, pressure has been put on Honduras by the International Monetary Fund. According to the *Caribbean & Central America Report,* the first phase of a reform program agreed to with the IMF succeeded in stabilizing the economy through devaluation of the lempira (the Honduran currency), public-

spending cuts, and increased taxes. But economic growth declined, and international agencies urged a reduction in the number of state employees as well as an accelerated campaign to privatize state-owned enterprises. The government admitted that there was much room for reform, but one official complained: "As far as they [the IMF] are concerned, the Honduran state should make gigantic strides, but our position is that this country cannot turn into General Motors overnight."

Opposition to the demands of international agencies was quick to materialize. One newspaper warned that cuts in social programs would result in violence. Trade-union and Church leaders condemned the social costs of the stabilization program despite the gains recorded in the credit-worthiness of Honduras.

HUMAN AND CIVIL RIGHTS

In theory, despite the continuing violence in the region, basic freedoms in Honduras are still intact. The press is privately owned and free of government censorship. There is, however, a quietly expressed concern about offending the government, and self-censorship is considered prudent. Moreover, it is an accepted practice in Honduras for government ministries and other agencies to have journalists on their payrolls.

Honduran labor unions are free to organize and have a tradition of providing their rank-and-file certain benefits. They are allowed to bargain, but labor laws guard against "excessive" activity. A complex procedure of negotiation and arbitration must be followed before a legal strike can be called. If a government proves unyielding, labor will likely pass into the ranks of the opposition.

In 1992, Honduras's three major workers' confederations convinced the private sector to raise the minimum wage by 13.7 percent, the third consecutive year of increases. Nevertheless, the minimum wage, which varies by occupation and location, is not adequate to provide a decent standard of living, especially in view of inflation. One labor leader pointed out that the minimum wage will "not even buy tortillas." To compound workers' problems, the labor minister admitted that about 30 percent of the enterprises under the supervision of his office paid wages *below* the minimum. To survive, families must pool the resources of all their working members. Predictably, health and safety laws are usually ignored. As is the case in the rural sector, the government has listened to the complaints of workers—but union leaders have also on occasion been jailed.

The government is also confronted with the problem of an increasing flow of rural

Honduras is
settled by
Spaniards from
Guatemala
1524

Independence
from Spain
1821

Honduras is part
of the United
Provinces of
Central America
1822–1838

Honduras
becomes
independent as a
separate country
1838

Brief border war
with El Salvador
1969

Tensions with
Nicaragua grow
1980s

1990s

Honduras joins
the Central
American Free
Trade Zone

Carlos Flores
Facusse is
elected president

Hurricane Mitch
spreads death
and destruction

poor into the cities. Employment opportunities in rural areas have declined as landowners convert cropland into pasture for beef cattle. Because livestock raising requires less labor than growing crops, the surplus rural workers seek to better their opportunities in the cities. But the new migrants have discovered that Honduras's commercial and industrial sectors are deep in recession and cannot provide adequate jobs.

Fortunately, many of the 300,000 refugees from Nicaragua and El Salvador have returned home. With the election of President Violeta Chamorro in Nicaragua, most of the 20,000 rebel Contras laid down their arms and went home, thus eliminating—from the perspective of the Honduran government—a source of much violence in its border regions.

To the credit of the Honduran government, which is under strong pressure from conservative politicians and businesspeople as well as elements within the armed forces for tough policies against dissent, allegations vis-à-vis human-rights abuses are taken seriously. (In one celebrated case, the Inter-American Court of Human Rights, established in 1979, found the government culpable in at least one person's "disappearance" and ordered the payment of an indemnification to the man's family. While not accepting any premise of guilt, the government agreed to pay. More important, according to the COHA *Washington Report*, the decision sharply criticized "prolonged isolation" and "incommunicado detention" of prisoners and equated such abuses with "cruel and inhuman punishment.") former president Carlos Roberto Reina was a strong advocate of human rights as part of his "moral revolution." In 1995, he took three steps in this direction: a special prosecutor was created to investigate human-rights violations, human-rights

inquiries were taken out of the hands of the military and given to a new civilian Department of Criminal Investigation, and promises were made to follow up on cases of disappearances during previous administrations. While Honduras may no longer be characterized as "the peaceable kingdom," the government has not lost touch with its people and still acts out a traditional role of patron.

From the mid-1980s to the mid-1990s, the most serious threat to civilian government came from the military. The United States' Central American policy boosted the prestige, status, and power of the Honduran military, which grew confident in its ability to forge the nation's destiny. With the end of the Contra–Sandinista armed struggle in Nicaragua, there was a dramatic decline in military assistance from the United States. This allowed President Reina to assert civilian control over the military establishment.

The sharp drop in U.S. economic assistance to Honduras—it fell from $229 million in 1985 to about $50 million in 1997—has revealed deep problems with the character of that aid. *Wall Street Journal* reporter Carla Anne Robbins writes that "Honduras's experience suggests that massive, politically motivated cash transfers . . . can buy social peace, at least temporarily, but can't guarantee lasting economic growth or social development." Rather, such unconditional aid "may have slowed development by making it possible for the government to put off economic reform." On the other hand, some of the aid that found its way to programs that were not politically motivated has also been lost. One program provided access to potable water and was credited with cutting the infant mortality rate by half. Other programs funded vaccinations and primary-education projects. In the words of newspaperman and development expert

Juan Ramón Martínez: "Just when you [the United States] started getting it right, you walked away."

President Reina's "moral revolution" also moved to confront the problem of endemic official corruption. In June 1995, Reina alluded to the enormity of the task when he said that if the government went after all of the guilty, "there would not be enough room for them in the prisons." One of those who agreed to appear in court was former president Callejas; but he insisted that he would not surrender his immunity as a member of the Central American Parliament because, as reported by *Caribbean & Central America Report,* he feared that "political persecution" by Reina's government would deny him justice.

In 1998, Reina handed over power to Carlos Roberto Flores Facusse of the Liberal Party, who won the presidential election of November 1997 with 53 percent of the vote.

ECONOMIC MALAISE
In 1998, just as the Honduran economy was beginning to recover from economic setbacks occasioned by turmoil in the influential Asian financial markets, Hurricane Mitch wreaked havoc on the nation's infrastructure. Roads, bridges, schools, clinics, and homes were destroyed, and thousands of lives were lost. Freshwater wells had to be reconstructed. Banana plantations were severely damaged. Recovery from this natural disaster will be prolonged and costly.

DEVELOPMENT

The Central American Free Trade Zone, of which Honduras is a member, will reduce tariffs by 5% to 20% on more than 5,000 products traded within the region. In the coming years, more products will be included and tariffs will be progressively lowered.

FREEDOM

President Reina reduced the power of the Honduran military. Constitutional reforms in 1994–1995 replaced obligatory military service and the press-gang recruitment system with voluntary service. As a result, the size of the army declined.

HEALTH/WELFARE

Honduras remains one of the region's poorest countries. Serious shortcomings are evident in education and health care, and economic growth is essentially erased by population growth. In 1997, 67% of the population lived in poverty.

ACHIEVEMENTS

The small size of Honduras, in terms of territory and population, has produced a distinctive literary style that is a combination of folklore and legend.

Nicaragua (Republic of Nicaragua)

GEOGRAPHY
Area in Square Miles (Kilometers):
49,985 (129,494) (about the
size of New York)
Capital (Population): Managua
(1,124,000)
Environmental Concerns:
deforestation; soil erosion;
water pollution
Geographical Features:
extensive Atlantic coastal
plains rising to central
interior mountains; narrow
Pacific coastal plain
interrupted by volcanoes
Climate: tropical, but varies with
elevation (temperate highlands)

PEOPLE

Population
Total: 4,584,000
Annual Growth Rate: 2.9%
Rural/Urban Population Ratio:
37/63
Ethnic Makeup: 69% Mestizo;
17% white; 9% black; 5%
Indian
Major Language: Spanish
Religions: 95% Roman Catholic;
5% Protestant

Health
Life Expectancy at Birth: 64
years (male); 69 years (female)
Infant Mortality Rate (Ratio):
42.2/1,000
Average Caloric Intake: 99% of
FAO minimum
Physicians Available (Ratio):
1/1,566

Education
Adult Literacy Rate: 65.7%
Compulsory (Ages): 7–13; free

COMMUNICATION
Telephones: 1 per 43 people
Daily Newspaper Circulation:
30 per 1,000 people
Televisions: 1 per 15 people

TRANSPORTATION
Highways in Miles (Kilometers): 11,178
(18,000)
Railroads in Miles (Kilometers): none
Usable Airfields: 185
Motor Vehicles in Use: 148,000

GOVERNMENT
Type: republic
Independence Date: September 15, 1821
(from Spain)
Head of State/Government: President
Arnoldo Alemán Lâcayo is both head
of state and head of government
Political Parties: Liberal Constitutionalist
Party; Neoliberal Party; Conservative

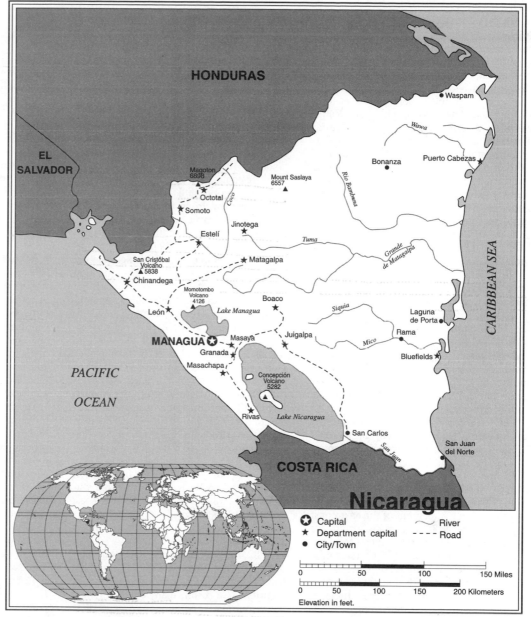

Action Party; National Action Party;
Sandinista National Liberation Front;
many others
Suffrage: universal at 16

MILITARY
Military Expenditures (% of GDP): 1.35%
Current Disputes: territorial or boundary
disputes with Colombia, Honduras, and
El Salvador

ECONOMY
Currency ($ U.S. Equivalent): 12.17
córdobas = $1
Per Capita Income/GDP: $2,100/$9.3 billion
GDP Growth Rate: 6%
Inflation Rate: 11.6%
Unemployment Rate: 16% (official rate);
substantial underemployment

Labor Force: 1,500,000
Natural Resources: gold; silver; copper;
tungsten; lead; zinc; timber; fish
Agriculture: coffee; bananas; sugarcane;
cotton; rice; corn; cassava (tapioca);
citrus fruits; beans; livestock
Industry: food processing; chemicals;
metals products; textiles and clothing;
petroleum; beverages; footwear
Exports: $635 million (primary partners
United States, Central America)
Imports: $1.1 billion (primary partners
Central America, United States,
Venezuela)

http://lcweb2.loc.gov/frd/cs/
nitoc.html
http://home.tampabay.rr.com/
latinoconncct/nicaragu.html

NICARAGUA:
A NATION IN RECOVERY

Nicaraguan society, culture, and history have been molded to a great extent by the country's geography. A land of volcanoes and earthquakes, the frequency of natural disasters in Nicaragua has profoundly influenced its peoples' perceptions of life, death, and fate. What historian Ralph Woodward has written about Central America is particularly apt for Nicaraguans: Fatalism may be said to be a "part of their national mentality, tempering their attitudes toward the future. Death and tragedy always seem close in Central America. The primitive states of communication, transportation, and production, and the insecurity of human life, have been the major determinants in the region's history. . . ."

Nicaragua is a divided land, with distinct geographic, cultural, racial, ethnic, and religious zones. The west-coast region, which contains about 90 percent of the total population, is overwhelmingly white or Mestizo (mixed blood), Catholic, and Hispanic. The east coast is a sharp contrast, with its scattered population and multiplicity of Indian, Creole (in Nicaragua, native-born blacks), and Hispanic ethnic groups.

The east coast's geography, economy, and isolation from Managua, the nation's capital city, have created a distinct identity among its people. Many east-coast citizens think of themselves as *costeños* ("coast dwellers") rather than Nicaraguans. Religion reinforces this common identity. About 70 percent of the east-coast population, regardless of ethnic group, are members of the Protestant Moravian Church. After more than 135 years of missionary work, the Moravian Church has become "native," with locally recruited clergy. Among the Miskito Indians, Moravian pastors commonly replace tribal elders as community leaders. The Creoles speak English and originally arrived either as shipwrecked or escaped slaves or as slave labor introduced by the British to work in the lumber camps and plantations in the seventeenth century. Many Creoles and Miskitos feel a greater sense of allegiance to the British than to Nicaraguans from the west coast, who are regarded as foreigners.

SANDINISTA POLICIES

Before the successful 1979 Revolution that drove the dictator Anastasio Somoza from power, Nicaraguan governments generally ignored the east coast. Revolutionary Sandinistas—who took their name from a guerrilla, Augusto César Sandino, who fought against occupying U.S. forces in the late 1920s and early 1930s—adopted a new policy toward the neglected region. The Sandinistas were concerned with the east coast's history of rebelliousness and separatism, and they were attracted by the economic potential of the region (palm oil and rubber). Accordingly, they hastily devised a bold campaign to unify the region with the rest of the nation. Roads, communications, health clinics, economic development, and a literacy campaign for local inhabitants were planned. The Sandinistas, in defiance of local customs, also tried to organize the local population into mass formations—that is, organizations for youth, peasants, women, wage earners, and the like. It was believed in Managua that such groups would unite the people behind the government and the Revolution and facilitate the economic, political, and social unification of the region.

In general, the attempt failed, and regional tensions within Nicaragua persist to this day. Historically, costeños were unimpressed with the exploits of the guerrilla Sandino, who raided U.S. companies along the east coast in the 1930s. When the companies left or cut back on operations, workers who lost their jobs blamed Sandino rather than the worldwide economic crisis of the 1930s. Consequently, there was a reluctance to accept Sandino as the national hero of the new Nicaragua. Race and class differences increased due to an influx of Sandinistas from the west. Many of the new arrivals exhibited old attitudes and looked down on the east-coast peoples as "uncivilized" or "second class."

The Miskito Question

In 1982, the government forced 10,000 Indians from their ancestral homes along the Río Coco because of concern with border security. As a result, many Indians joined the Contras, U.S.–supported guerrillas who fought against the Sandinista regime. In an attempt to win back the Miskito and associated Indian groups, the government decided on a plan of regional autonomy. In 1985, Interior Minister Tomás Borge finished a draft plan whose main proposals included the following features: a regional assembly for the east coast, with each of the six ethnic groups (Miskito, Sumo, Rama, Garifuna, Creole, Mestizo) having the same number of representatives; regional control over Sandinista federal officials working in the region; natural resources under the control of regional governments; and bilingual-education programs. Defense of the east-coast region remained in the hands of Managua, in coordination with the autonomous governments. The Sandinista government initiated a "repatriation" scheme in 1984, allowing 1,000 Miskitos to return to their homes.

The significance of the Sandinista policy was that the government finally appreciated how crucial regional differences are in Nicaragua. Cultural and ethnic differences must be respected if Managua expects to rule its peoples effectively. The lesson learned by the Sandinistas was taken to heart by the subsequent Chamorro government, which was the first in history to appoint a Nicaraguan of Indian background to a ministerial-level position. The limited self-government granted to the east-coast region by the Sandinistas in 1987 has been maintained; local leaders were elected to office in 1990.

A Mixed Record

The record of the Sandinista government was mixed. When the rebels seized power in 1979, they were confronted by an economy in shambles. Nineteen years of civil war had taken an estimated 50,000 lives and destroyed half a billion dollars' worth of factories, businesses, medical facilities, and dwellings. Living standards had tumbled to 1962 levels, and unemployment had reached an estimated 25 percent.

Despite such economic difficulties, the government made great strides in the areas of health and nutrition. A central goal of official policy was to provide equal access to health services. The plan had more success in urban areas than in rural ones. The government emphasized preventive, rather than curative, medicine. Preventive medicine included the provision of clean water, sanitation, immunization, nutrition, and maternal and child care. People were also taught basic preventive medical techniques. National campaigns to wipe out malaria, measles, and polio had reasonable success. But because of restricted budgets, the health system was overloaded, and there was a shortage of medical supplies. In the area of nutrition, basic foodstuffs such as grains, oil, eggs, and milk were paid for in part by the government in an effort to improve the general nutritional level of Nicaraguans.

By 1987, the Sandinista government was experiencing severe economic problems that badly affected all social programs. In 1989, the economy, for all intents and purposes, collapsed. Hyperinflation ran well over 100 percent a month; and in June 1989, following a series of mini-devaluations, the nation's currency was devalued by an incredible 100 percent. Commerce was virtually paralyzed.

The revolutionary Sandinista government, in an attempt to explain the economic debacle, with some justice argued that the Nicaragua that it had inherited in 1979 had been savaged and looted by former dictator Somoza. The long-term costs of economic reconstruction; the restructuring of the economy to redistribute wealth; the trade embargo erected by the United States and North American diplomatic pressure, designed to discourage lending or aid from international institutions such as the International Monetary Fund; and the high cost of fighting a war against the U.S.–supported Contra rebels formed the backdrop to the crisis. Opposition leaders added to this list various Sandinista economic policies that discouraged private business.

The impact of the economic crisis on average Nicaraguans was devastating. Overnight, prices of basic consumer goods such as meat, rice, beans, milk, sugar, and cooking oil were increased 40 to 80 percent. Gasoline prices doubled. Schoolteachers engaged in work stoppages in an effort to increase their monthly wages of about $15, equal to the pay of a domestic servant. (To put the teachers' plight into perspective, note that the cost of a liter of milk absorbed fully 36 percent of a day's pay.)

As a hedge against inflation, other Nicaraguans purchased U.S. dollars on the black market. *Regionews,* published in Managua, noted that conversion of córdobas into dollars was "seen as a better proposition than depositing them in savings accounts."

Economic travail inevitably produces dissatisfaction; opinion polls taken in July 1989 signaled political trouble for the Sandinistas. The surveys reflected an electorate with mixed feelings. While nearly 30 percent favored the Sandinistas, 57 percent indicated that they would not vote for President Daniel Ortega.

The results of the election of 1990 were not surprising, for the Sandinistas had lost control of the economy. They failed to survive a strong challenge from the opposition, led by the popular Violeta Chamorro.

Sandinista land reform, for the most part, consisted of the government's confiscation of the huge estates of the ousted Somoza family. These lands amounted to more than 2 million acres, including about 40 percent of the nation's best farmland. Some peasants were given land, but the government preferred to create cooperatives. This policy prompted the criticism that the state had simply become an old-style landowner. The Sandinistas replied that "the state is not the same state as before; it is a state of producers; we organized production and placed it at the disposal of the people." In 1990, there were several reports of violence between Sandinista security forces and peasants

and former Contras who petitioned for private ownership of state land.

The Role of the Church

The Revolution created a sharp division within the Roman Catholic Church in Nicaragua. Radical priests, who believed that Christianity and Marxism share similar goals and that the Church should play a leading role in social change and revolution, were at odds with traditional priests fearful of "godless communism." Since 1979, many radical Catholics had become involved in social and political projects; several held high posts in the Sandinista government.

One priest of the theology of liberation was interviewed by *Regionews*. The interviewer stated that an "atheist could say, 'These Catholics found a just revolution opposed by the Church hierarchy. They can't renounce their religion and are searching for a more convenient theology. But it's their sense of natural justice that motivates them.'" The priest replied: "I think that's evident and that Jesus was also an 'atheist,' an atheist of the religion as practiced in his time. He didn't believe in the God of the priests in the temples who were allied with Caesar. Jesus told of a new life. And the 'atheist' that exists in our people doesn't believe in the God that the hierarchy often offers us. He believes in life, in man, in development. God manifests Himself there. A person who believes in life and justice in favor of the poor is not an atheist." The movement, he noted, would continue "with or without approval from the hierarchy."

The Drift to the Left

As has historically been the case in revolutions, after a brief period of unity and excitement, the victors begin to disagree over policies and power. For a while in Nicaragua, there was a perceptible drift to the left, and the Revolution lost its image of moderation. While radicalization was a

(United Nations photo/Jerry Frank)

This lakeside section of Managua, Nicaragua, was destroyed by an earthquake in 1974. The region is often shaken by both large and small earthquakes.

Nicaragua is explored by Gil González
1522

Independence from Spain
1821

Nicaragua joins the United Provinces of Central America
1823

Nicaragua becomes independent as a separate state
1838

William Walker and filibusters (U.S. insurgents) invade Nicaragua
1855

Augusto César Sandino leads guerrillas against occupying U.S. forces
1928–1934

Domination of Nicaragua by the Somoza family
1934–1979

Sandinista guerrillas oust the Somoza family
1979

Sharp deterioration of relations with the United States
1980s

1990s

A cease-fire allows an opening for political dialogue

Former Managua mayor Arnoldo Alemán Lâcayo wins the presidency

Hurricane Mitch devastates the country

dynamic inherent in the Revolution, it was also pushed in a leftward direction by a hostile U.S. foreign policy that attempted to bring down the Sandinista regime through its support of the Contras. In 1987, however, following the peace initiatives of Latin American governments, the Sandinista government made significant efforts to project a more moderate image in the region. *La Prensa*, the main opposition newspaper, which the Sandinistas had shut down in 1986, was again allowed to publish. Radio Católica, another source of opposition to the government, was given permission to broadcast after its closure the year before. And antigovernment demonstrations were permitted in the streets of Managua.

Significantly, President Ortega proposed reforms in the country's election laws in April 1989, to take effect before the national elections in 1990. Although the Bush administration was not convinced that the changes would ensure free elections, a report prepared by the Hispanic Division of the Library of Congress was generally favorable. The new Nicaraguan legislation was based on Costa Rican and Venezuelan models and in some instances was even more forward-looking.

An important result of the laws was the enhancement of political pluralism, which allowed for the National Opposition Union (UNO) victory in 1990. Rules for organizing political parties, once stringent, were loosened; opposition parties were granted access to the media; foreign funding of political parties was allowed; the system of proportional representation permitted minority parties to maintain a presence; and the opposition was allowed to monitor the elections closely.

The Sandinistas realized that, to survive, they had to make compromises. In need of breathing space, the government embraced the Central American Peace Plan designed by Costa Rican president Óscar Arias and designed moderate policies to isolate the United States.

On the battlefield, the cease-fire unilaterally declared by the Sandinistas was eventually embraced by the Contras as well, and both sides moved toward a political solution of their differences. Armed conflict formally ended on June 27, 1990, although sporadic violence continued in rural areas.

A PEACEFUL TRANSITION

It was the critical state of the Nicaraguan economy that in large measure brought the Sandinistas down in the elections of 1990. Even though the government of Violeta Chamorro made great progress in the demilitarization of the country and national reconciliation, the economy remained a time bomb.

The continuing economic crisis and disagreements over policy directions destroyed the original base of Chamorro's political support. Battles between the legislative and executive branches of government virtually paralyzed the country. At the end of 1992, President Chamorro closed the Assembly building and called for new elections. But by July 1995, an accord had been reached between the two contending branches of government. Congress passed a "framework law" that created the language necessary to implement changes in the Sandinista Constitution of 1987. The Legislative Assembly, together with the executive branch, are pledged to the passage of laws on matters such as property rights, agrarian reform, consumer protection, and taxation. The July agreement also provided for the election of the five-member Consejo Supremo Electoral (Supreme Electoral Council), which oversaw the presidential elections in November 1996.

The election marked something of a watershed in Nicaraguan political history. Outgoing president Chamorro told reporters at the inauguration of Arnoldo Alemán Lâcayo: "For the first time in more than 100 years . . . one civilian, democratically elected president will hand over power to another." But the election did not mask the fact that Nicaragua was still deeply polarized and that the Sandinistas only grudgingly accepted their defeat.

President Alemán sought a dialogue with the Sandinistas, and both sides agreed to participate in discussions to study poverty, property disputes occasioned by the Sandinista policy of confiscation, and the need to attract foreign investment. While defeated Sandinista candidate Daniel Ortega agreed to talk, he also intimated that Nicaragua could return to violence if the new government followed policies detrimental to the poor.

The new administration faces a host of difficult problems. Only Haiti is poorer in the hemisphere. Perhaps 80 percent of the population are unemployed or underemployed, and more than 70 percent of the population live below the poverty line. However, the nation has begun to emerge from the economic chaos of the 1980s. In 1996, the economy grew at a healthy rate of 5.5 percent, and there were expectations of an even stronger economy in the late 1990s. Unfortunately, Hurricane Mitch, which devastated the countryside in 1998, profoundly set back development efforts, as all available resources had to be husbanded to reconstruct much of Nicaragua's infrastructure.

DEVELOPMENT

The possibility of the construction of a "dry canal" across Nicaragua has raised the hopes of thousands for a better future. A group of Asian investors is investigating the construction of a 234-mile-long rail link between the oceans to carry container cargo.

FREEDOM

Diverse points of view have been freely and openly discussed in the media. Radio, the most important medium for news distribution in Nicaragua, has conveyed a broad range of opinion.

HEALTH/WELFARE

Nicaragua's deep debt and the austerity demands of the IMF have had a strongly negative effect on citizens' health. As people have been driven from the health service by sharp cuts in government spending, the incidence of malnutrition in children has risen. Reported deaths from diarrhea and respiratory problems are also on the increase.

ACHIEVEMENTS

The Nicaraguan poet Rubén Dario was the most influential representative of the Modernist Movement, which swept Latin America in the late nineteenth century. Dario was strongly critical of injustice and oppression.

Panamá (Republic of Panama)

GEOGRAPHY

Area in Square Miles (Kilometers): 30,185 (78,200) (about the size of South Carolina)

Capital (Population): Panama City (967,000)

Environmental Concerns: water pollution; deforestation; land degradation

Geographical Features: interior mostly steep, rugged mountains and dissected upland plains; coastal areas largely plains and rolling hills

Climate: tropical

PEOPLE

Population

Total: 2,736,000

Annual Growth Rate: 1.56%

Rural/Urban Population Ratio: 44/56

Major Languages: Spanish; English

Ethnic Makeup: 70% Mestizo; 14% West Indian; 10% white; 6% Indian and others

Religions: 85% Roman Catholic; 15% Protestant and others

Health

Life Expectancy at Birth: 72 years (male); 77 years (female)

Infant Mortality Rate (Ratio): 24/1,000

Average Caloric Intake: 103% of FAO minimum

Physicians Available (Ratio): 1/808

Education

Adult Literacy Rate: 90.8%

Compulsory (Ages): for 6 years between 6–15; free

COMMUNICATION

Telephones: 1 per 8.8 people

Daily Newspaper Circulation: 62 per 1,000 people

Televisions: 1 per 5.9 people

TRANSPORTATION

Highways in Miles (Kilometers): 6,893 (11,100)

Railroads in Miles (Kilometers): 208 (355)

Usable Airfields: 109

Motor Vehicles in Use: 190,000

GOVERNMENT

Type: constitutional republic

Independence Date: November 3, 1903 (from Colombia)

Head of State/Government: President Mireya Moscoso is both head of state and head of government

Political Parties: Nationalist Republican Liberal Movement; Solidarity Party; Authentic Liberal Party; Arnulfista Party; Christian Democratic Party; Papa Egoro Movement; Democratic Revolutionary Party; Independent Democratic Union; National Liberal Party; Labor Party; others

Suffrage: universal and compulsory at 18

MILITARY

Military Expenditures (% of GDP): 1%

Current Disputes: none

ECONOMY

Currency ($ U.S. Equivalent): 1 balboa = $1

Per Capita Income/GDP: $6,700/$18 billion

GDP Growth Rate: 3.6%

Inflation Rate: 1.2%

Unemployment Rate: 13.1%

Labor Force: 1,044,000

Natural Resources: copper; mahogany forests; shrimp

Agriculture: bananas; rice; corn; coffee; sugarcane; vegetables; livestock; fishing

Industry: construction; petroleum, brewing; sugar milling; canal traffic/tourism

Exports: $592 million (primary partners United States, European Union, Central America and Caribbean)

Imports: $2.95 billion (primary partners United States, European Union, Central America and Caribbean)

 http://lcweb2.loc.gov/frd/cs/patoc.html
http://home.tampabay.rr.com/latinoconnect/panama.html

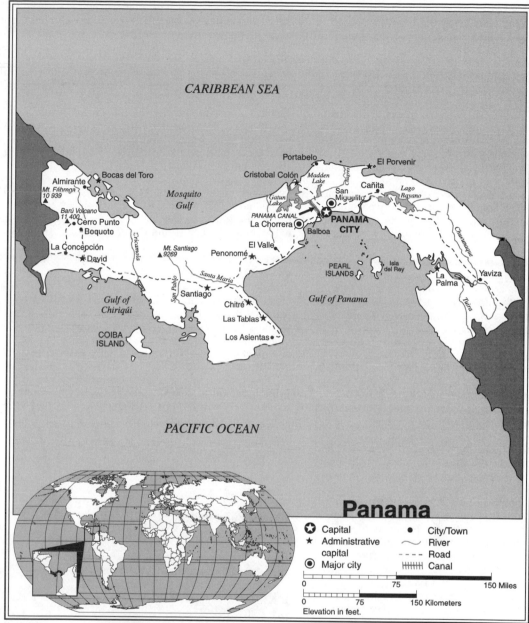

Panama

- ⊛ Capital
- ★ Administrative capital
- ◉ Major city
- • City/Town
- ～ River
- - - - Road
- ╫╫╫╫╫ Canal

0   75   150 Miles

0   75   150 Kilometers

Elevation in feet.

PANAMA:
A NATION AND A CANAL

The Panama Canal, opened to shipping in 1914, has had a sharp impact on Panamanian political life, foreign policy, economy, and society. Panama is a country of minorities and includes blacks, Mestizos (mixed Indian and white), Indians, and Chinese. Many of the blacks and Chinese are the children or grandchildren of the thousands of workers who were brought to Panama to build the canal. Unable to return home, they remained behind, an impoverished people, ignored for decades by a succession of Panamanian governments.

The government has usually been dominated by whites, although all of the country's minorities are politically active. In areas where Indians comprise a majority of the population, they play significant roles in provincial political life. Some, such as the San Blas islanders—famous for the art form known as Mola, which consists of different colored fabrics that are cut away to make designs—live in self-governing districts. Although Indians are not restricted to tribal areas, most remain by choice, reflecting a long tradition of resistance to assimilation and defense of their cultural integrity.

Panama's economy has both profited and suffered from the presence of the canal. Because governments traditionally placed too much reliance on the direct and indirect revenues generated by the canal tolls, they tended to ignore other types of national development. Much of Panama's economic success in the 1980s, however, was the result of a strong service sector associated with the presence of a large number of banks, the Panama Canal, and the Colón Free Zone. Agriculture and industry, on the other hand, usually experienced slow growth rates.

Because of U.S. control of the canal and the Canal Zone, this path between the seas continuously stoked the fires of Panamanian nationalism. The high standard of living and the privileges enjoyed by U.S. citizens residing in the zone contrasted sharply with the poverty of Panamanians. President Omar Torrijos became a national hero in 1977 when he signed the Panama Canal Treaties with U.S. president Jimmy Carter. The treaties provided for full Panamanian control over the canal and its revenues by 1999.

Panamanian officials spoke optimistically of their plans for the bases they would soon inherit, citing universities, modern container ports, luxury resorts, and retirement communities. But there was much concern over the loss of an estimated $500 million that tens of thousands of American troops, civilians, and their dependents have long pumped into the Panamanian economy. Moreover, while all agreed that the canal itself will be well run, because Panamanians have been phased into its operation, there was pessimism about the lack of planning for ancillary facilities.

In 1995, more than 300 poor, landless people a day were moving into the Zone and were clearing forest for crops. The rain forest in the Canal Basin supplies not only the water essential to the canal but also the drinking water for about 40 percent of Panama's population. Loss of the rain forest could prove catastrophic. One official noted: "If we lose the Canal Basin we do not lose only our water supply, it will also be the end of the Canal itself."

A RETURN TO CIVILIAN GOVERNMENT

President Torrijos, who died in a suspicious plane crash in 1981, left behind a legacy that included much more than the treaties. He elevated the National Guard to a position of supreme power in the state and ruled through a National Assembly of community representatives.

The 1984 elections appeared to bring to fruition the process of political liberalization initiated in 1978. But even though civilian rule was officially restored, the armed forces remained the real power behind the throne. Indeed, spectacular revelations in 1987 strongly suggested that Defense Forces chief general Manuel Antonio Noriega had rigged the 1984 elections. He was also accused of drug trafficking, gun running, and money laundering.

Indeed, in February 1988, Noriega was indicted by two U.S. grand juries and charged with using his position to turn Panama into a center for the money-laundering activities of the Medellín, Colombia, drug cartel and providing protection for cartel members living temporarily in Panama.

Attempts by Panamanian president Eric Arturo Delvalle to oust the military strongman failed, and Delvalle himself was forced into hiding. Concerted efforts by the United States to remove Noriega from power—including an economic boycott, plans to kidnap the general and have the CIA engineer a coup, and saber-rattling by the dispatch of thousands of U.S. troops to the Canal Zone—proved fruitless.

The fraud and violence that accompanied an election called by Noriega in 1989 to legitimize his government and the failure of a coup attempt in October ultimately resulted in the invasion of Panama by U.S. troops in December. Noriega was arrested, brought to the United States for

(Photo Library of Congress)

The Panama Canal has been of continuing importance to the country since it opened in 1914. Full control of the canal was turned over to Panama in 1999, marking the end of U.S. involvement and representing a source of Panamanian nationalism.

Panama City is
established
1518

Panama is a
department of
Colombia
1821–1903

Independence
from Colombia
1903

The signing of
the Panama
Canal Treaties
1977

The death of
President Omar
Torrijos creates a
political vacuum

American troops
invade Panama;
Noriega
surrenders to
face drug
charges in the
United States
1980s

1990s

Mireya Moscoso
is elected as
Panama's first
woman president

The last U.S.
troops leave
Panama

The Panama
Canal passes
to wholly local
control

trial, and eventually was convicted on drug-trafficking charges.

The U.S. economic sanctions succeeded in harming the wrong people. Noriega and his cronies were shielded from the economic crisis by their profits from money laundering. But many other Panamanians were devastated by the U.S. policy.

Nearly a decade after the invasion by U.S. troops to restore democracy and halt drug trafficking, the situation in Panama remains problematic. The country is characterized by extremes of wealth and poverty, and corruption is pervasive. The economy is still closely tied to drug-money laundering, which has reached levels higher than during the Noriega years.

Elections in 1994 reflected the depth of popular dissatisfaction. Three quarters of the voters supported political movements that had risen in opposition to the policies and politics imposed on Panama by the U.S. invasion. The new president, Ernesto Pérez Balladares, a 48-year-old economist and businessman and a former supporter of Noriega, promised "to close the Noriega chapter" in Panama's history. During his term, he pushed ahead with privatization, the development of the Panama Canal Zone, a restructuring of the foreign debt, and initiatives designed to enhance tourism.

Unfortunately, Pérez seemed to have inherited some of the personalist tendencies of his predecessors. In 1998, he pushed for a constitutional change that would have allowed him to run for reelection in 1999. When put to a referendum in August 1998, Panamanians resoundingly defeated the ambitions of the president.

The 1999 elections, without the participation of Pérez, produced a close campaign between Martín Torrijos, the son of

Omar, and Mireya Moscoso, the widow of the president who had been ousted by Omar Torrijos. Moscoso emerged as a winner, with 44 percent of the vote, and became Panama's first woman president.

Moscoso opposes many of Pérez's free-market policies and has been especially critical of any further plans to privatize state-owned industries. Moscoso has identified her administration with the inauguration of a "new era" for Panama's poor. Her social policies stand in direct contrast to the more economically pragmatic approach of her predecessors. Continued domination of the Legislature by the opposition will render social reform difficult, but the president feels that she must intercede on behalf of the poor, who constitute one third of the population. Diversification of the economy remains a need, as Panama is still overly dependent on canal revenues and traditional agricultural exports.

SOCIAL POLICIES
As is the case in most Latin American nations, Panama's Constitution authorizes the state to direct, regulate, replace, or create economic activities designed to increase the nation's wealth and to distribute the benefits of the economy to the greatest number of people. President Moscoso is aware that she has the constitutional authority to push for meaningful social changes. The harsh reality is that the income of one third of Panama's population frequently fails to provide for families' basic needs.

Women, who won the right to vote in the 1940s, are accorded equal political rights under the law and hold a number of important government positions, including the presidency. But as in all of Latin America, women do not enjoy the same opportunities for advancement as men. There are also profound domestic constraints to their freedom. Panamanian law, for example, does not recognize community property; divorced or deserted women have no protection and can be left destitute, if that is the will of their former spouses. Many female heads-of-household from poor areas are obliged to work for the government, often as street cleaners, in order to receive support funds from the authorities.

With respect to human rights, Panama's record is mixed. The press and electronic media, while theoretically free, have experienced some harassment. In 1983, the Supreme Court ruled that journalists need not be licensed by the government. Nevertheless, both reporters and editors still exercise a calculated self-censorship, and press conduct in general is regulated by an official "Morality and Ethics Commission," whose powers are broad and vague,

DEVELOPMENT

Although President Pérez's economic policies sought to accelerate private ownership of state enterprises and attract foreign investment to a broad range of economic activities, by the time he left office, foreign investment continued to be narrowly focused on the maritime trades and industries.

FREEDOM

Panama's indigenous population of 194,000 have the same political rights as other citizens. In 1992, Cuna Indians asked for the creation of an additional reserve to prohibit incursions by squatters into areas traditionally considered their own.

HEALTH/WELFARE

Deforestation and other environmental damage have reached such a point, according to *Latin American Regional Report*, that, unless a halt is called now, "Panama could be without drinking water within 20 years." Climatic changes accelerated by deforestation have already significantly reduced average rainfall.

ACHIEVEMENTS

The Panama Canal, which passed wholly to Panamanian control in 1999, is one of the greatest engineering achievements of the twentieth century. A maze of locks and gates, it cuts through 50 miles of the most difficult terrain on Earth.

South America

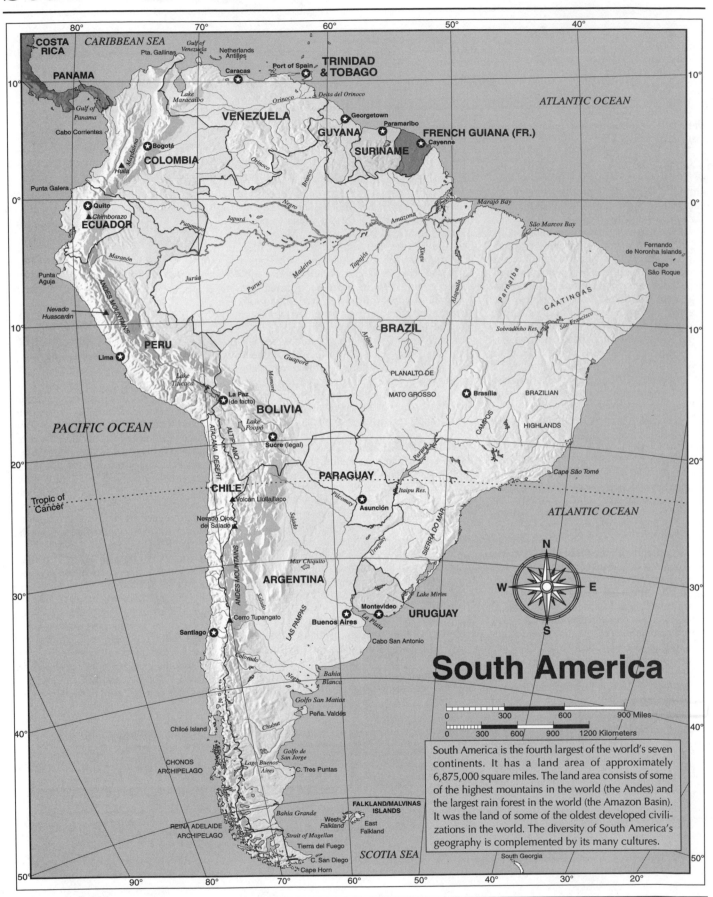

South America is the fourth largest of the world's seven continents. It has a land area of approximately 6,875,000 square miles. The land area consists of some of the highest mountains in the world (the Andes) and the largest rain forest in the world (the Amazon Basin). It was the land of some of the oldest developed civilizations in the world. The diversity of South America's geography is complemented by its many cultures.

South America: An Imperfect Prism

Any overview of South America must first address the incredible geographic and climatic diversity of the region. Equatorial rain forests are found in Brazil, Ecuador, Colombia, Venezuela, and other countries; and the coastal deserts in Peru and northern Chile are among the driest and most forbidding in the world (naturalist Charles Darwin described the area as "a complete and utter desert"). More hospitable are the undulating pampas and plains of Argentina, Uruguay, central Venezuela, eastern Colombia, and southeastern Brazil. The spine of the continent is formed by the Andes Mountains, majestic and snowcapped. Because of its topography and the many degrees of latitude in which it lies, South America has extremes of temperature, ranging from desert heat to the steaming humidity of the tropics to the cold gales of Tierra del Fuego, which lies close to the Antarctic Circle. To add further to the perils of generalization, wide-ranging differences often occur *within* a country. Geography has played a critical role in the evolution of each of the nations of South America; it has been one of several major influences in their histories and their cultures.

NATURE'S CHALLENGE

Nature has presented the inhabitants of South America with an unrelenting challenge. On the west coast, most of the major cities are located in geologically active zones. All too frequently, earthquakes, tidal waves, volcanic activity, and landslides have taken a staggering toll of human life. And throughout the region, floods and droughts make agriculture a risky business. In 1982–1983, for example, the worst

(Photo Lisa Clyde)

The Spanish colonial influence is apparent in South America, as seen in this sixteenth-century building in Andean Venezuela. It was originally a monastery. Later, it was used as a hunting lodge; most recently, it was turned into a hotel.

drought in living memory struck Peru and Bolivia. With food supplies dwindling, thousands of farming families were forced to migrate to the cities.

REGIONALISM

South America's diverse topography has also helped to foster a deep-seated regionalism that has spawned innumerable civil wars and made national integration an extremely difficult task. In Colombia, for instance, the Andes fan out into three distinct ranges, separated by deep valleys. Each of the nation's three major cities—Bogotá, Medellín, and Cali—dominates a valley and is effectively isolated from the others by the mountains. The broad plains to the east have remained largely undeveloped because of the difficulty of access from the centers of population. Troubling to Colombian governments is the fact that, in terms of topography, the eastern plains are tied to Venezuela and not to the Colombian cities to the west.

Similarly, mountains divide Ecuador, Peru, Bolivia, and Venezuela. In all of these nations, there is a permanent tension between the capital cities and the hinterlands. As is the case in those republics that have large Indian populations, the tension often is as much cultural as it is a matter of geography. But in the entire region, geography interacts with culture, society, politics, and economics. Regionalism has been a persistent theme in the history of Ecuador, where there has been an often bitter rivalry between the capital city of Quito, located high in the central mountains, and the port city of Guayaquil. Commonly, port cities, with their window on the world outside, tend to be more cosmopolitan, liberal, and dynamic than cities that are more isolated. Such is the case with freewheeling Guayaquil, which stands in marked contrast to conservative, traditional, deeply Catholic Quito.

Venezuela boasts six distinct geographical regions, which include mountains and valleys, plains and deserts, rivers and jungles, and a coastline. Historian John Lombardi has observed that each of these regions has had an important role in identifying and defining the character of Venezuela's past and present: "Over the centuries the geographical focus has shifted from one region to another in response to internal arrangements and external demands."

THE SOUTHERN CONE

The cultures of the countries of the so-called Southern Cone—Argentina, Uruguay, Paraguay, and Chile—have also been shaped by the geographical environment. Argentina, Uruguay, and Brazil's southern state of Rio Grande do Sul developed subcultures that reflected life on the vast, fertile plains, where cattle grazed by the millions. The *gaucho* ("cowboy") became symbolic of the "civilization of leather." Fierce, independent, a law unto himself, the gaucho was mythologized by the end of the nineteenth century. At a time when millions of European immigrants were flooding into the region, the gaucho emerged as a nationalist symbol of Argen-

(United Nations photo)

The cultures of the countries of the Southern Cone—Argentina, Uruguay, Paraguay, and Chile—have been profoundly influenced by the geography of their vast, fertile plains. These latter-day gauchos herd their animals to the auction pens.

BRAZIL

Historian Rollie Poppino has noted that the "major miracle of Brazil is its existence as a single nation." What he implies is that Brazil embraces regions that are so distinct that they could well be separate countries. "There are actually many Brazils within the broad expanse of the national territory, and the implication of uniformity conveyed by their common flag and language is often deceptive." In Brazil, there exists a tremendous range of geographical, racial, cultural, and economic contrasts. But part of the Brazilian "miracle" lies in the ability of its people to accept the diversity as normal. Many Brazilians were unaware of the great differences within their country for years, until the improvement of internal transportation and communications as well as the impact of the mass media informed them not only of their common heritage but also of their profound regional differences.

DIVERSE PEOPLES

In many respects, the peoples of South America are as diverse as its geography. While the populations of Argentina and Uruguay are essentially European, with virtually no Indian intermixture, Chilean society is descended from Spanish conquerors and the Indians they dominated. The Indian presence is strongest in the Andean republics of Bolivia, Peru, and Ecuador—the heart of the ancient Inca civilization. Bolivia is the most Indian, with well over half its population classified as such. Mestizos (mixed white and Indian) constitute about a quarter of the population, and whites make up only about one tenth.

Three ethnic groups are found among the populations of Colombia and Venezuela: Spanish and Indian predominate, and there are small black minorities. About 60 percent of the populations of both countries are of Mestizo or *pardo* (mixed blood) origin. One of Brazil's distinctive features is the rich racial mixture of its population. Peoples of Indian, European, African, and Japanese heritage live in an atmosphere largely free of racial enmity.

Taken as a whole, the predominant culture is Iberian (that is, Spanish or Portuguese), although many mountain areas are overwhelmingly Indian in terms of ethnic makeup. With the conquest and colonization of South America in the sixteenth century, Spain and Portugal attempted to fasten their cultures, languages, and institutions on the land and its peoples. Spanish cities in South America—laid out in the familiar grid pattern consisting of a large central plaza bordered by a Catholic church, government buildings, and the dwellings of the ruling elite—represented the conscious intention of the conquerors to impose their will, not only on the defeated Indian civilizations but also on nature itself.

By way of contrast, the Brazilian cities that were laid out by early Portuguese settlers tended to be less formally structured, suggesting that their planners and builders were more flexible and adaptable to the new world around them. Roman Catholicism, however, was imposed on all citizens by the central authority. Government, conforming to Hispanic po-

tina and Uruguay, standing firm in the face of whatever natives viewed as "foreign."

Landlocked Paraguay, surrounded by powerful neighbors, has for most of its history been an introspective nation, little known to the outside world. Because of its geography, most of Paraguay's population is concentrated near the capital city of Asunción. A third of the nation is tropical and swampy—not suitable for settlement. To the west, the desolate Chaco region, with its lack of adequate sources of drinkable water, is virtually uninhabitable.

Chile, with a coastline 2,600 miles long, is a country of topographic and climatic extremes. If superimposed on a map of North America, Chile would stretch from Baja California to the Yukon in Alaska. It is on Chile's border with Argentina that the Andes soar to their greatest heights. Several peaks, including Aconcagua, reach to nearly 23,000 feet in elevation. That mountain barrier has historically isolated Chile from eastern South America and from Europe. The central valley of Chile is the political, industrial, social, and cultural heart of the nation. With the capital city of Santiago and the large port of Valparaíso, the valley holds about 70 percent of Chile's population. The valley's Mediterranean climate and fertile soil have long acted as a magnet for Chileans from other, less hospitable, parts of the country.

(Photo Lisa Clyde)

The northern Andes Mountains meet the Caribbean Sea in Venezuela.

litical culture, was authoritarian in the colonial period and continues to be so today. The conquerors created a stratified society of essentially two sectors: a ruling white elite and a ruled majority. But Spain and Portugal also introduced institutions that knit society together. Paternalistic patron–client relationships that bound the weak to the strong were common; they continue to be so today.

INDIAN CULTURE

Among the isolated Indian groups of Ecuador, Peru, and Bolivia, Spanish cultural forms were strongly and, for the most part, successfully resisted. Suspicious and occasionally hostile, the Indians refused integration into the white world outside their highland villages. By avoiding integration, in the words of historian Frederick Pike, "they maintain the freedom to live almost exclusively in the domain of their own language, social habits, dress and eating styles, beliefs, prejudices, and myths."

Only the Catholic religion was able to make some inroads, and that was (and still is) imperfect. The Catholicism practiced by Quechua- and Aymara-speaking Indians is a blend of Catholic teachings and ancient folk religion. For example, in an isolated region in Peru where eight journalists were massacred by Indians, a writer who investigated the incident reported in *The New York Times* that while Catholicism was "deeply rooted" among the Indians, "it has not displaced old beliefs like the worship of the *Apus,* or god mountains." When threatened, the Indians are "zealous defenders of their cus-

toms and mores." The societies' two cultures have had a profound impact on the literature of Ecuador, Peru, and Bolivia. The plight of the Indian, social injustice, and economic exploitation are favorite themes of these nations' authors.

Other Indian groups more vulnerable to the steady encroachment of "progress" did not survive. In the late nineteenth century, pampas Indians were virtually destroyed by Argentine cavalry armed with repeating rifles. Across the Andes, in Chile, the Araucanian Indians met a similar fate in the 1880s. Unfortunately, relations between the "civilized" world and the "primitive" peoples clinging to existence in the rain forests of Brazil, Peru, Bolivia, and Venezuela have generally improved little. Events in Brazil, Ecuador, and Venezuela in the early 1990s, however, may signal a significant shift toward greater Indian rights. Indigenous peoples throughout the Amazon Basin, however, are still under almost daily assault from settlers hungry for land, road builders, developers, and speculators—most of whom care little about the cultures they are annihilating.

AFRICAN-AMERICAN CULTURE

In those South American countries where slavery was widespread, the presence of a large black population has contributed yet another dimension to Hispanic culture (or, in the case of Guyana and Suriname, English and Dutch culture). Slaves, brutally uprooted from their cultures in Africa, developed new cultural forms that were often a combination of Christian and pagan. To insulate themselves against the rigors of forced labor and to forge some kind of common identity, slaves embraced folk religions that were heavily oriented toward magic. Magic helped blacks to face an uncertain destiny, and folk religions built bridges between peoples facing a similar, horrible fate. Folk religions not only survived the emancipation of slaves but have remained a common point of focus for millions of Brazilian blacks.

This phenomenon had become so widespread that in the 1970s, the Roman Catholic Church made a concerted effort to win Afro-Brazilians to a religion that was more Christian and less pagan. This effort was partly negated by the development of close relations between Brazil and Africa, which occurred at the same time as the Church's campaign. Brazilian blacks became more acutely aware of their African origins and began a movement of "re-Africanization." So pervasive had the folk religions become that one authority stated that Umbada (one of the folk religions) was now the religion of Brazil. The festival of *Carnaval* ("Carnival") in Rio de Janeiro, Brazil, is perhaps the best-known example of the blending of Christianity with spiritism. Even the samba, a sensuous dance form that is central to the Carnaval celebration, had its origins in black folk religions.

IMMIGRATION AND CULTURE

Italians, Eastern and Northern Europeans, Chinese, and Japanese have also contributed to the cultural, social, and economic development of several South American nations. The great outpouring of Europe's peoples that brought millions of immigrants to the shores of the United States also brought millions to South America. From the mid-1800s to the outbreak of World War I in 1914, great numbers of Italians and Spaniards and much smaller numbers of Germans, Russians, Welsh, Scots, Irish, and English boarded ships that would carry them to South America.

Many were successful in the New World. Indeed, immigrants were largely responsible for the social restructuring of Argentina, Uruguay, and southern Brazil, as they created a large and dynamic middle class where none had existed before.

Italians

Many of the new arrivals came from urban areas, were literate, and possessed a broad range of skills. Argentina received the greatest proportion of immigrants. So great was the influx that an Argentine political scientist labeled the years 1890–1914 the "alluvial era" (flood). His analogy was apt, for by 1914, half the population of the capital city of Buenos Aires were foreign-born. Indeed, 30 percent of the total Argentine population were of foreign extraction. Hundreds of thousands of immigrants also flocked into Uruguay.

In both countries, they were able to move quickly into middle-class occupations in business and commerce. Others found work on the docks or on the railroads that carried the produce of the countryside to the ports for export to foreign markets. Some settled in the interior of Argentina, where they usually became sharecroppers or tenant farmers, although a sizable number were able to purchase land in the northern province of Santa Fe or became truck farmers in the immediate vicinity of Buenos Aires. Argentina's wine industry underwent a rapid transformation and expansion with the arrival of Italians in the western provinces of Mendoza and San Juan. In the major cities of Argentina, Uruguay, Chile, Peru, and Brazil, Italians built hospitals and established newspapers; they formed mutual aid societies and helped to found the first labor unions. Their presence is still strong today, and Italian words have entered into everyday discourse in Argentina and Uruguay.

Other Groups

Other immigrant groups also made their contributions to the formation of South America's societies and cultures. Germans colonized much of southern Chile and were instrumental in creating the nation's dairy industry. In the wilds of Patagonia, Welsh settlers established sheep ranches and planted apple, pear, and cherry trees in the Río Negro Valley.

In Buenos Aires, despite the 1982 conflict over the Falkland Islands, there remains a distinct British imprint. Harrod's is the largest department store in the city, and one can board a train on a railroad built with English capital and journey to suburbs with names such as Hurlingham, Temperley, and Thames. In both Brazil and Argentina, soccer was introduced by the English, and two Argentine teams still bear the names "Newell's Old Boys" and "River Plate." Collectively, the immigrants who flooded into South America in the late nineteenth and early twentieth centuries introduced a host of new ideas, methods, and skills. They were especially important in stimulating and shaping the modernization of Argentina, Uruguay, Chile, and southern Brazil.

In other countries that were bypassed earlier in the century, immigration has become a new phenomenon. Venezuela— torn by political warfare, its best lands long appropriated by the elite, and its economy developing only slowly—was far less attractive than the lands of opportunity to its north (the United States) and south (Argentina, Uruguay, and Brazil). In the early 1950s, however, Venezuela embarked on a broadscale development program that included an attempt to attract European immigrants. Thousands of Spaniards, Portuguese, and Italians responded to the economic opportunity. Most of the immigrants settled in the capital city of Caracas, where many eventually became important in the construction business, retail trade, and the transportation industry.

INTERNAL MIGRATION

Paralleling the movement of peoples from across the oceans to parts of South America has been the movement of populations from rural areas to urban centers. In every nation, cities have been gaining in population for years. What prompts people to leave their homes and strike out for the unknown? In the cases of Bolivia and Peru, the very real prospect of famine has driven people out of the highlands and into the larger cities. Frequently, families will plan the move carefully. Vacant lands around the larger cities will be scouted in advance, and suddenly, in the middle of the night, the new "settlers" will move in and erect a shantytown. With time, the seizure of the land is usually recognized by city officials and the new neighborhood is provided with urban services. Where the land seizure is resisted, however, violence and loss of life are common.

Factors other than famine also force people to leave their ancestral homes. Population pressure and division of the land into parcels too small to sustain families compel people to migrate. Others move to the cities in search of economic opportunities or chances for social advancement that do not exist in rural regions. Tens of thousands of Colombians illegally crossed into Venezuela in the 1970s and 1980s in search of employment. As is the case with Mexicans who enter the United States, Colombians experienced discrimination and remained on the margins of urban society, mired in low-paying, unskilled jobs. Those who succeeded in finding work in industry were a source of anger and frustration to labor-union members, who resented Colombians who accepted low rates of pay. Other migrants sought employment in the agricultural sector on coffee plantations or the hundreds of cattle

ranches that dot the *llanos,* or plains. In summary, a combination of push and pull factors are involved in a family's decision to begin a new life.

Since World War II, indigenous migration in South America has rapidly increased urban populations and has forced cities to reorganize. Rural people have been exposed to a broad range of push–pull pressures to move to the cities. Land hunger, extreme poverty, and rural violence might be included among the push factors; while the hope of a better job, upward social mobility, and a more satisfying life help to explain the attraction of a city. The phenomenon can be infinitely complex.

In Lima, Peru, there has been a twofold movement of people. While the unskilled and illiterate, the desperately poor and unemployed, the newly arrived migrant, and the delinquent have moved to or remained in inner-city slums, former slum dwellers have in turn moved to the city's perimeter. Although less centrally located, they have settled in more spacious and socially desirable shantytowns. In this way, some 16,000 families created a squatter settlement practically overnight in the south of Lima. Author Hernando DeSoto, in his groundbreaking and controversial book *The Other Path,* captures the essence of the shantytowns: "Modest homes

(United Nations photo/M. Grant)

Colombia, as is the case with many other Latin American nations, has experienced rapid urbanization. Large numbers of migrants from rural areas have spread into slums on the outskirts of cities, as exemplified by this picture of a section of Colombia's capital, Bogotá. Most of the migrants are poorly paid, and the struggle to meet basic needs precludes political activism.

cramped together on city perimeters, a myriad of workshops in their midst, armies of vendors hawking their wares on the street, and countless minibus lines crisscrossing them—all seem to have sprung from nowhere, pushing the city's boundaries ever outward."

Significantly, DeSoto notes, collective effort has increasingly been replaced by individual effort, upward mobility exists even for the inner-city slum dwellers, and urban culture and patterns of consumption have been transformed. Opera, theater, and *zarzuela* (comic opera) have gradually been replaced by movies, soccer, folk festivals, and television. Beer, rice, and table salt are now within the reach of much of the population; consumption of more expensive items, however, such as wine and meat, has declined.

On the outskirts of Buenos Aires there exists a *villa miseria* (slum) built on the bottom and sides of an old clay pit. Appropriately, the *barrio,* or neighborhood, is called La Cava (literally "The Digging"). The people of La Cava are very poor; most have moved there from rural Argentina or from Paraguay. Shacks seem to be thrown together from whatever is available—scraps of wood, packing crates, sheets of tin, and cardboard. There is no source of potable water, garbage litters the narrow alleyways, and there are no sewers. Because of the concave character of the barrio, the heat is unbearable in the summer. Rats and flies are legion. At times, the smells are repulsive. The visitor to La Cava experiences an assault on the senses; this is Latin America at its worst.

But there is another side to the slums of Buenos Aires, Lima, and Santiago. A closer look at La Cava, for example, reveals a community in transition. Some of the housing is more substantial, with adobe replacing the scraps of wood and tin; other homes double as places of business and sell general merchandise, food, and bottled drinks. One advertises itself as a food store, bar, and butcher shop. Another sells watches and repairs radios. Several promote their merchandise or services in a weekly newspaper that circulates in La Cava and two other *barrios de emergencia* ("emergency"— that is, temporary—neighborhoods). The newspaper addresses items of concern to the inhabitants. There are articles on hygiene and infant diarrhea; letters and editorials plead with people not to throw their garbage in the streets; births and deaths are recorded. The newspaper is a chronicle of progress as well as frustration: people are working together to create a viable neighborhood; drainage ditches are constructed with donated time and equipment; collections and raffles are held to provide materials to build sewers and, in some cases, to provide minimal street lighting; and men and women who have contributed their labor are singled out for special praise.

The newspaper also reproduces municipal decrees that affect the lives of the residents. The land on which the barrio sits was illegally occupied, the stores that service the neighborhood were opened without the necessary authorization, and the housing was built without regard to municipal codes, so city ordinances such as the following aimed at the barrios

de emergencia are usually restrictive: "The sale, renting or transfer of *casillas* [homes] within the boundaries of the barrio de emergencia is prohibited; casillas can not be inhabited by single men, women or children; the opening of businesses within the barrio is strictly prohibited, unless authorized by the Municipality; dances and festivals may not be held without the express authorization of the Municipality." But there are also signs of accommodation: "The Municipality is studying the problem of refuse removal." For migrants, authority and the legal system are not helpful; instead, they are hindrances.

Hernando DeSoto found this situation to be true also of Peru, where "the greatest hostility the migrants encountered was from the legal system." Until the end of World War II, the system had either absorbed or ignored the migrants "because the small groups who came were hardly likely to upset the status quo." But when the rural-to-urban flow became a flood, the system could no longer remain disinterested. Housing and education were barred to them, businesses would not hire them. The migrants discovered over time that they would have to fight for every right and every service from an unwilling establishment. Thus, to survive, they became part of the informal sector, otherwise known as the underground or parallel economy.

On occasion, however, municipal laws can work to the advantage of newly arrived migrants. In the sprawling new communities that sprang up between Lima and its port city of Callao, there are thousands of what appear to be unfinished

(United Nations photo/Bruno J. Zehnder)

South America's Indian cultures and modern development have never really mixed. The native cultures persist in many areas, as exemplified by this Indian woman at a market in Ecuador.

homes. In almost every instance, a second floor was begun but, curiously, construction ceased. The reason for the incomplete projects relates to taxes—they are not assessed until a building is finished.

These circumstances are true not only of the squatter settlements on the fringes of South America's great cities but also of the inner-city slums. Slum dwellers *have* been able to improve their market opportunities and *have* been able to acquire better housing and some urban services, because they have organized on their own, outside formal political channels. In the words of sociologist Susan Eckstein, "They refused to allow dominant class and state interests to determine and restrict their fate. Defiance and resistance won them concessions which quiescence would not."

DeSoto found this to be the case with Lima: Migrants, "if they were to live, trade, manufacture, or even consume . . . had to do so illegally. Such illegality was not antisocial in intent, like trafficking in drugs, theft, or abduction, but was designed to achieve such essentially legal objectives as building a house, providing a service, or developing a business."

This is also the story of Buenos Aires's La Cava. To open a shop in the barrio with municipal approval, an aspiring businessperson must be a paragon of patience. Various levels of bureaucracy, with their plethora of paperwork and fees, insensitive municipal officials, inefficiency, and interminable waiting, drive people outside the system where the laws do not seem to conform to social need.

AN ECCLESIASTICAL REVOLUTION

During the past 20 years, there have been important changes in the religious habits of many South Americans. Virtually everywhere, Roman Catholicism, long identified with the traditional order, has been challenged by newer movements such as Evangelical Protestantism and the Charismatics. Within the Catholic Church, the theology of liberation once gained ground. The creation of Christian communities in the barrios, people who bond together to discuss their beliefs and act as agents of change, has become a common phenomenon throughout the region. Base communities from the Catholic perspective instill Christian values in the lives of ordinary people. But it is an active form of religion that pushes for change and social justice. Hundreds of these communities exist in Peru, thousands in Brazil.

NATIONAL MYTHOLOGIES

In the midst of geographical and cultural diversity, the nations of South America have created national mythologies designed to unite people behind their rulers. Part of that mythology is rooted in the wars of independence that tore through much of the region between 1810 and 1830. Liberation from European colonialism imparted to South Americans a sense of their own national histories, replete with military heroes such as José de San Martín, Simón Bolívar, Bernardo O'Higgins, and Antonio José de Sucre, as well as a host of revolutionary myths. This coming to nationhood paralleled what the United States experienced when it won its independence from Britain. South Americans, at least those with a stake in the new society, began to think of themselves as Venezuelans, Chileans, Peruvians, or Brazilians. The architects of Chilean national mythology proclaimed the emergence of a new and superior being who was the result of the symbolic and physical union of Spaniards and the tough, heroic Araucanian Indians. The legacy of Simón Bolívar lives on in particular in Venezuela, his homeland; even today, the nation's foreign policymakers speak in Bolivarian terms about Venezuela's rightful role as a leader in Latin American affairs. In some instances, the mythology generated by the wars for independence became a shield against foreign ideas and customs and was used to force immigrants to become "Argentines" or "Chileans." It was an attempt to bring national unity out of diversity.

Argentines have never solved the question of their identity. Many consider themselves European and hold much of the rest of Latin America in contempt. Following Argentina's loss in the Falklands War with Britain, one scholar suggested that perhaps Argentines should no longer consider themselves as "a forlorn corner of Europe" but should wake up to the reality that they are Latin Americans. Much of Argentine literature reflects this uncertain identity and may help to explain author Jorge Luis Borges's affinity for English gardens and Icelandic sagas. It was also an Argentine military government that invoked Western Catholic civilization in its fight against a "foreign" and "godless" communism in the 1970s.

THE ARTIST AND SOCIETY

There is a strongly cultured and humane side of South America. Jeane Franco, an authority on Latin American cultural movements, has observed that to "declare oneself an artist in Latin America has frequently involved conflict with society." The art and literature of South America in particular and Latin America in general represent a distinct tradition within the panorama of Western civilization.

The art of South America has as its focus social questions and ideals. It expresses love for one's fellow human beings and "has kept alive the vision of a more just and humane form of society." It rises above purely personal relationships and addresses humanity.

Much change is also evident at the level of popular culture. Andean folk music, for example, is being replaced by the more urban and upbeat chicha music in Peru; and in Argentina, the traditional tango has lost much of its early appeal. Radio and television programs are more and more in the form of soap operas, adventure programs, or popular entertainment, once considered vulgar by cosmopolitan city dwellers.

South America is rather like a prism. It can be treated as a single object or region. Yet when exposed to a shaft of sunlight of understanding, it throws off a brilliant spectrum of colors that exposes the diversity of its lands and peoples.

Argentina (Argentine Republic)

GEOGRAPHY

Area in Square Miles (Kilometers):
1,100,000 (2,771,300) (about 4
times the size of Texas)

Capital (Population): Buenos
Aires (11,802,000)

Environmental Concerns: soil
erosion; soil degradation;
desertification; air and water
pollution

Geographical Features: rich plains
of the Pampas in northern
half; flat to rolling plateau of
Patagonia in south; rugged Andes along western border

Climate: varied; predominantly
temperate; subantarctic in
southwest

PEOPLE

Population
Total: 36,266,000
Annual Growth Rate: 1.3%
Rural/Urban Population Ratio:
12/88
Major Languages: Spanish; Italian
Ethnic Makeup: 85% white; 15%
Mestizo, Indian, and others
Religions: 90% Roman Catholic
(fewer than 20% practicing);
2% Protestant; 2% Jewish;
6% others

Health
Life Expectancy at Birth: 71
years (male); 78 years (female)
Infant Mortality Rate (Ratio):
19/1,000
Average Caloric Intake: 125%
of FAO minimum
Physicians Available (Ratio): 1/376

Education
Adult Literacy Rate: 96.2%
Compulsory (Ages): 6–14; free

COMMUNICATION
Telephones: 1 per 6.3 people
Daily Newspaper Circulation: 138 per
1,000 people
Televisions: 1 per 4.6 people

TRANSPORTATION
Highways in Miles (Kilometers): 135,549
(218,276)
Railroads in Miles (Kilometers): 23,542 (37,910)
Usable Airfields: 1,411
Motor Vehicles in Use: 5,900,000

GOVERNMENT
Type: republic
Independence Date: July 9, 1816 (from Spain)
Head of State/Government: President
Fernando de la Rua is both head of
state and head of government

Political Parties: Radical Civic Union;
Justicialist Party (Peronist); Union of
the Democratic Center; others
Suffrage: universal at 18

MILITARY
Military Expenditures (% of GDP): 1.5%
Current Disputes: indefinite boundary
with Chile; claims UK-administered
South Georgia and South Sandwich
Islands, and Falkland Islands (Islas
Malvinas); territorial claim in Antarctica

ECONOMY
Currency ($ U.S. Equivalent): 0.999 peso = $1
Per Capita Income/GDP: $9,700/$348.2 billion
GDP Growth Rate: 8.4%
Inflation Rate: 0.3%

Unemployment Rate: 13.7%; substantial
underemployment
Labor Force: 14,500,000
Natural Resources: fertile plains; lead;
zinc; tin; copper; iron ore; manganese;
petroleum; uranium
Agriculture: wheat; corn; sorghum;
soybeans; sugar beets; livestock
Industry: food processing; motor vehicles;
consumer durables; textiles; chemicals and
petrochemicals; printing; metallurgy; steel
Exports: $25.4 billion (primary partners
Brazil, United States, Chile)
Imports: $30.3 billion (primary partners
Brazil, United States, Italy)

http://www.cia.gov/cia/publications/
factbook/ar.html

ARGENTINA:
THE DIVIDED LAND
Writers as far back as the mid-1800s have perceived two Argentinas. Domingo F. Sarmiento, the president of Argentina in the 1860s, entitled his classic work about his country *Civilization and Barbarism.* More contemporary writers speak of Argentina as a divided land or as a city *and* a nation. All address the relationship of the capital city, Buenos Aires, to the rest of the country. Buenos Aires is cultured, cosmopolitan, modern, and dynamic. The rural interior is in striking contrast in terms of living standards, the pace of life, and, perhaps, expectations as well. For many years, Buenos Aires and other urban centers have drawn population away from the countryside: Today, Argentina is 88 percent urban.

There are other contrasts. The land is extremely rich and produces a large share of the world's grains and beef. Few Argentines are malnourished, and the annual per capita consumption of beef is comparable to that of the United States. Yet this land of promise, which seemed in the 1890s to have a limitless future, has slowly decayed. Its greatness is now more mythical than real. Since the Great Depression of the 1930s, the Argentine economy has, save for brief spurts, never been able to return to the sustained growth of the late nineteenth and early twentieth centuries.

Today, the Argentine economy is more stable than it has been for years. Inflation has dropped from 200 percent per year to less than 1 percent; inefficient and costly

state enterprises have been privatized, including petroleum, traditionally a strategic sector reserved to the state; the foreign debt is under control; and the pace of business activity, employment, and foreign investment has quickened. The nation's economy is vulnerable to events in other parts of the world, however. The collapse of the Mexican peso in the early 1990s and the economic crises in Russia and, especially, Asia in the late 1990s had profound negative effects in Argentina.

A healthy economy with sustained growth is problematical, however, for Argentine economic history has been typified by unrealized potential and unfulfilled promises. Much depends on the confidence of the Argentine people in the leadership and policies of their elected representatives.

AUTHORITARIAN GOVERNMENT
In political terms, Argentina has revealed a curious inability to bring about the kind of stable democratic institutions that seemed assured in the 1920s. Since 1930, the military has seized power at least half a dozen times. It must be noted, however, that it has been civilians who have encouraged the generals to play an active role in politics. Historian Robert Potash writes: "The notion that Argentine political parties or other important civilian groups have consistently opposed military takeovers bears little relation to reality."

Argentina has enjoyed civilian rule since 1983, but the military is still a presence. Indeed, one right-wing faction, the *carapintadas* ("painted faces"), responsi-

ble for mutinies against President Raúl Alfonsín in 1987 and 1988, have organized a nationwide party and have attracted enough votes to rank as an important political force. An authoritarian tradition is very much alive in Argentina, as is the bitter legacy of the so-called Dirty War.

THE DIRTY WAR
What made the most recent period of military rule different is the climate of political violence that gripped Argentina starting in the late 1960s. The most recent period of violence began with the murder of former president Pedro Aramburu by left-wing guerrillas (Montoneros) who claimed to be fighting on behalf of the exiled popular leader Juan Perón (president from 1946 to 1955 and from 1973 to 1974). The military responded to what it saw as an armed challenge from the left with tough antisubversion laws and official violence against suspects. Guerrillas increased their activities and intensified their campaign to win popular support.

Worried by the possibility of a major popular uprising and divided over policy, the military called for national elections in 1973, hoping that a civilian government would calm passions. The generals could then concentrate their efforts on destroying the armed left. The violence continued, however, and even the brief restoration of Juan Perón to power failed to bring peace.

In March 1976, with the nation on the verge of economic collapse and guerrilla warfare spreading, the military seized power once again and declared a state of internal war, popularly called the Dirty War. Between 1976 and 1982, approximately 6,000 Argentine citizens "disappeared." Torture, the denial of basic human rights, harsh press censorship, officially directed death squads, and widespread fear came to characterize Argentina.

The labor movement—the largest, most effective, and most politically active on the continent—was, in effect, crippled by the military. Identified as a source of leftist subversion, the union movement was destroyed as an independent entity. Collective-bargaining agreements were dismantled, pension plans were cut back, and social-security and public-health programs were eliminated. The military's intent was to destroy a labor movement capable of operating on a national level.

The press was one of the immediate victims of the 1976 coup. A law was decreed warning that anyone spreading information derived from organizations "dedicated to subversive activities or terrorism" would be subject to an indefinite sentence. To speak out against the military was punishable by a 10-year jail term. The state

(United Nations photo/P. Teuscher)

Few people are malnourished in Argentina. Well known for its abundant grains and beef, Argentina also has a large fishing industry. These fishing boats are in the bay of the Plata River in Buenos Aires.

also directed its terrorism tactics against the media, and approximately 100 journalists disappeared. Hundreds more received death threats, were tortured and jailed, or fled into exile. Numerous newspapers and magazines were shut down, and one, *La Opinión,* passed to government control.

The ruling junta justified these excesses by portraying the conflict as the opening battle of "World War III," in which Argentina was valiantly defending Western Christian values and cultures against hordes of Communist, "godless" subversives. It was a "holy war," with all of the unavoidable horrors of such strife.

By 1981, leftist guerrilla groups had been annihilated. Argentines slowly began to recover from the shock of internal war and talked of a return to civilian government. The military had completed its task; the nation needed to rebuild. Organized labor attempted to re-create its structure and threw the first tentative challenges at the regime's handling of the economy. The press carefully criticized both the economic policies of the government and the official silence over the fate of *los desaparecidos* ("the disappeared ones"). Human-rights groups pressured the generals with redoubled efforts.

OPPOSITION TO THE MILITARY

Against this backdrop of growing popular dissatisfaction with the regime's record, together with the approaching 150th anniversary of Great Britain's occupation of Las Islas Malvinas (the Falkland Islands), President Leopoldo Galtieri decided in 1982 to regain Argentine sovereignty and attack the Falklands. A successful assault, the military reasoned, would capture the popular imagination with its appeal to Argentine nationalism. The military's tarnished image would regain its luster. Forgiven would be the excesses of the Dirty War. But the attack ultimately failed.

In the wake of the fiasco, which cost thousands of Argentine and British lives, the military lost its grip on labor, the press, and the general population. Military and national humiliation, the continuing economic crisis made even worse by war costs, and the swelling chorus of discontent lessened the military's control over the flow of information and ideas. Previously forbidden subjects—such as the responsibility for the disappearances during the Dirty War—were raised in the newspapers.

The labor movement made a rapid and striking recovery and is now in the forefront of renewed political activity. Even though the movement is bitterly divided into moderate and militant wings, it is a force that cannot be ignored by political parties on the rebound.

The Falklands War may well prove to be a watershed in recent Argentine history. A respected Argentine observer, Torcuato DiTella, argues that the Falklands crisis was a "godsend," for it allowed Argentines to break with "foreign" economic models that had failed in Argentina. Disappointed with the United States and Europe over their support of Great Britain, he concludes: "We belong in Latin America and it is better to be a part of this strife-torn continent than a forlorn province of Europe."

Popularly elected in 1983, President Raúl Alfonsín's economic policies initially struck in bold new directions. He forced the International Monetary Fund to renegotiate Argentina's huge multi-billion-dollar debt in a context more favorable to Argentina, and he was determined to bring order out of chaos.

One of his most difficult problems centered on the trials for human-rights abuses against the nation's former military rulers. According to *Latin American Regional Reports,* Alfonsín chose to "distinguish degrees of responsibility" in taking court action against those who conducted the Dirty War. Impressively, Alfonsín put on trial the highest authorities, to be followed by action against those identified as responsible for major excesses.

Almost immediately, however, extreme right-wing nationalist officers in the armed forces opposed the trials and engineered a series of mutinies that undermined the stability of the administration. In 1987, during the Easter holiday, a rebellion of dissident soldiers made its point, and the Argentine Congress passed legislation that limited the prosecution of officers who killed civilians during the Dirty War to those only at the highest levels. Mini-mutinies in 1988 resulted in further concessions to the mutineers by the Alfonsín government, including reorganization of the army high command and higher wages.

Political scientist Gary Wynia aptly observed: "The army's leadership is divided between right-wing officers willing to challenge civilian authorities with force and more romantic officers who derive gratification from doing so. Many of the latter refuse to accept the contention that they are 'equal' to civilians, claiming that they have a special role that prevents their subordination to civilian authorities." To this day, the Argentine military has come to terms neither with itself nor with democratic government.

President Carlos Menem was supported by the military in the elections of May 1989, with perhaps 80 percent of the officer corps casting their votes for the Peronist Party. Menem adopted a policy of rapprochement with the military, which included the 1990 pardon of former junta members convicted of human-rights abuses. Historian Peter Calvert argues that Menem chose the path of amnesty because elements in the armed forces "would not be content until they got it." Rebellious middle-rank officers were well disposed toward Peronists, and Menem's pardon was "a positive gain in terms of the acceptance of the Peronists among the military themselves." In essence, then, Menem's military policy was consistent with other policies in terms of its pragmatic core.

On the other hand, significant progress has been made with regard to "disappeared" people. In 1992, President Menem agreed to create a commission to deal with the problem of children of the disappeared who were adopted by other families. Many have had their true identities established as a result of the patient work of "The Grandmothers of the Plaza de Mayo" and by the technique of cross-generational genetic analysis. (In 1998, former junta chief Admiral Emilio Massera was arrested on charges of kidnapping—that is, the distribution to families of babies born to victims of the regime.) In 1995, the names of an additional 1,000 people were added to the official list of the missing. Also, a retired military officer revealed his part in pushing drugged prisoners out of planes over the South Atlantic Ocean.

ECONOMIC TRAVAIL AND RECOVERY

President Alfonsín was fond of telling the following story of the frustrations of high office. George Bush, praying in the White House, asked God, "Will the hostages in the Middle East ever be released?" The reply came from above: "Yes, but not during your term in office." Similarly, Mikhail Gorbachev, alone in his library in the Kremlin, looked heavenward and asked: "Will perestroika succeed?" Once again the reply was heard: "Yes, but not during your time in office." And then, Alfonsín continued, "I myself looked up to God and asked, 'Will Argentina's economic, military and political crises ever be solved?'" Once more comes God's answer: "Yes, but not in *my* time in office." The humor is bitter and suggests the intractable character of crisis in Argentina. Indeed, Argentina's runaway inflation forced President Alfonsín to hand over power to Carlos Menem six months early.

Menem's government worked a bit of an economic miracle, despite an administration nagged by corruption and early policy indecision, which witnessed the ap-

1990s

Constitutional reform allows President Carlos Menem to serve a second consecutive term

Economic crises in Mexico, Russia, and Asia slow the Argentine economy

Fernando de la Rua is elected president in 1999

pointment of 21 ministers to nine cabinet positions during his first 18 months in office. In Menem's favor, he was not an ideologue but, rather, an adept politician whose acceptance by the average voter was equaled by his ability to do business with almost anyone. He quickly identified the source of much of Argentina's chronic inflation: the state-owned enterprises. From the time of Perón, these industries were regarded as wellsprings of employment and cronyism rather than as instruments for the production of goods or the delivery of services such as electric power and telephone service. "Ironically," says Luigi Manzetti, writing in *North-South FOCUS,* "it took a Peronist like Menem to dismantle Perón's legacy." While Menem's presidential campaign stressed "traditional Peronist themes like social justice and government investments" to revive the depressed economy, once he was in power, "having inherited a bankrupt state and under pressure from foreign banks and domestic business circles to enact a stiff adjustment program, Menem reversed his stand." He embraced the market-oriented policies of his political adversaries, "only in a much harsher fashion." State-owned enterprises were sold off in rapid-fire order. Argentina thus underwent a rapid transformation, from one of the world's most closed economies to one of the most open.

Economic growth began again in 1991, but the social costs were high. Thousands of public-sector workers lost their jobs; a third of Argentina's population lived below the poverty line, and the gap between the rich and poor tended to increase. But both inflation and the debt were eventually contained, foreign investment increased, and confidence began to return to Argentina.

In November 1993, former president Alfonsín supported a constitutional reform that allowed Menem to serve another term. Menem accepted some checks on executive power, including reshuffling the Supreme Court, placing members of the political opposition in charge of certain state offices, creating a post similar to that of prime minister, awarding a third senator to each province, and shortening the presidential term from six to four years. With these reforms in place, Menem easily won another term in 1995.

Convinced that his mandate should not end with the conclusion of his second term, Menem lobbied hard in 1998 for yet another constitutional reform to allow him to run again. This was not supported by either the Supreme Court or by 70 percent of the respondents in an opinion poll taken in March 1999. Presidential elections were held in late 1999 without Menem as the Justicialist Party's standard bearer.

FOREIGN POLICY

The Argentine government's foreign policy has usually been determined by realistic appraisals of the nation's best interests. Since 1946, the country has moved between the two poles of pro-West and nonaligned. President Menem has firmly supported the foreign-policy initiatives of the United States and the United Nations. Argentine participation in the Persian Gulf War and the presence of Argentine troops under United Nations command in Croatia, Somalia, and other trouble spots paid dividends: Washington agreed to supply Argentina with military supplies for the first time since the Falklands War in 1982. Such a policy obviously won points for Menem with the Argentine military.

ARGENTINA'S FUTURE

The Argentine economy, despite recent successes, still remains volatile. Although the growth rate since 1991 has averaged 6 percent a year, unemployment surged from 6 percent in 1991 to 17 percent in 1996, receding slightly, to less than 14 percent in 1998. Unemployment and underemployment trouble 30 percent of the workforce and have multiple causes—according to the *Buenos Aires Herald,* the increasing entry of women into the workforce; advances in technology and productivity; and, most important, the lack of training, not only for the post-40 generation but also for youths. Education and training are critical for the future health of the economy. Politically, however, Argentina's experiment with constitutional reform must be judged a success. And the military seems to have been contained; military spending has been halved, the army has been reduced from 100,000 to 20,000 soldiers, military enterprises have been divested, and mandatory service has been abandoned in favor of a professional force.

DEVELOPMENT

Argentina, in its rapid pursuit of privatization of state-owned industries, was the first Latin American country to sell its energy company. The remarkable economic progress made between 1991 and 1997, slowed to nearly zero in 1998 because of the shocks to the economy as a result of the Asian and other financial crises.

FREEDOM

In 1998, Argentines were again reminded of the horrors of the Dirty War with the arrest of former junta member Admiral Emilio Massera on kidnapping charges associated with the illegal adoption of babies born to victims of the regime. Kidnapping, in the eyes of the courts, was a crime not covered by earlier presidential pardons.

HEALTH/WELFARE

In recent years, inflation has had an adverse impact on the amount of state spending on social services. Moreover, the official minimum wage falls significantly lower than the $12,000 per year considered necessary to support a family of four.

ACHIEVEMENTS

Argentine citizens have won four Nobel Prizes—two for peace and one each for chemistry and medicine. The nation's authors— Jorge Luis Borges, Julio Cortazar, Manuel Puig, and Ricardo Guiraldes, to name only a few—are world-famous.

Bolivia (Republic of Bolivia)

GEOGRAPHY

Area in Square Miles (Kilometers): 424,162 (1,098,160) (about 3 times the size of Montana)

Capital (Population): La Paz (de facto) (1,250,000); Sucre (legal)

Environmental Concerns: deforestation; soil erosion; desertification; loss of biodiversity; water pollution

Geographical Features: rugged Andes Mountains with a highland plateau (Altiplano), hills, lowland plains of the Amazon Basin

Climate: varies from humid and tropical to semiarid and cold

PEOPLE

Population

Total: 7,827,000

Annual Growth Rate: 2%

Rural/Urban Population Ratio: 39/61

Major Languages: Spanish; Quechua; Aymara

Ethnic Makeup: 30% Quechua; 25% Aymara; 30% Mestizo; 15% white

Religions: 95% Roman Catholic; Protestant

Health

Life Expectancy at Birth: 58 years (male); 64 years (female)

Infant Mortality Rate (Ratio): 63.8/1,000

Average Caloric Intake: 91% of FAO minimum

Physicians Available (Ratio): 1/3,663

Education

Adult Literacy Rate: 83%

Compulsory (Ages): 6–14; free

COMMUNICATION

Telephones: 1 per 21 people

Daily Newspaper Circulation: 69 per 1,000 people

Televisions: 1 per 8.8 people

TRANSPORTATION

Highways in Miles (Kilometers): 32,426 (52,216)

Railroads in Miles (Kilometers): 2,292 (3,691)

Usable Airfields: 1,153

Motor Vehicles in Use: 547,000

GOVERNMENT

Type: republic

Independence Date: August 6, 1825 (from Spain)

Head of State/Government: President Hugo Banzer Suárez is both head of state and head of government

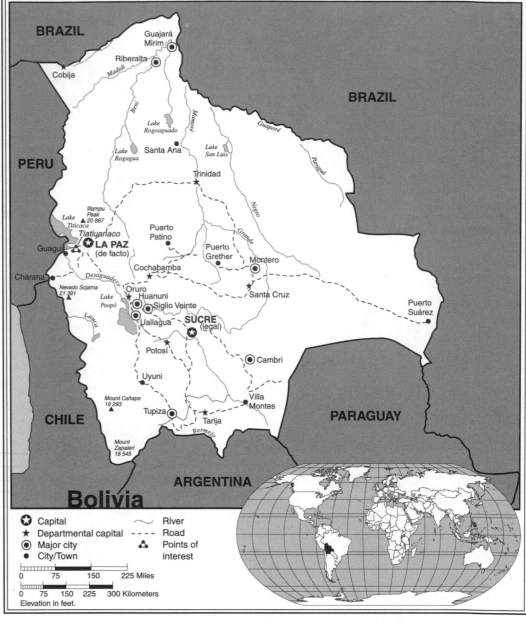

Bolivia

Legend	
✪ Capital	∿ River
★ Departmental capital	- - - Road
◉ Major city	△ Points of interest
● City/Town	

0   75   150   225 Miles
0   75   150   225   300 Kilometers
Elevation in feet.

Political Parties: Free Bolivia Movement; Revolutionary Front of the Left; Nationalist Revolutionary Movement; Christian Democratic Party; Nationalist Democratic Action; popular Patriotic Movement; Unity and Progress Movement; many others

Suffrage: universal and compulsory at 18 if married, 21 if single

MILITARY

Military Expenditures (% of GDP): 1.9%

Current Disputes: dispute with Chile over Rio Lauca water rights; seeks sovereign corridor to the South Pacific Ocean

ECONOMY

Currency ($ U.S. Equivalent): 5.95 bolivianos = $1

Per Capita Income/GDP: $3,000/$23.1 billion

GDP Growth Rate: 4.4%

Inflation Rate: 7%

Unemployment Rate: 10%

Labor Force: 2,500,000

Natural Resources: tin; natural gas; petroleum; zinc; tungsten; antimony; silver; iron; lead; gold; timber

Agriculture: coffee; coca; cotton; corn; sugarcane; rice; potatoes; timber

Industry: mining; smelting, petroleum; food and beverages; tobacco; handicrafts; clothing

Exports: $1.4 billion (primary partners United States, United Kingdom, Colombia)

Imports: $1.7 billion (primary partners United States, Japan, Brazil)

 http://lcweb2.loc.gov/frd/cs/botoc.html

BOLIVIA: AN INDIAN NATION

Until recently, the images of Bolivia captured by the world's press were uniformly negative. Human-rights abuses were rampant, a corrupt and brutal military government was deeply involved in cocaine trafficking, and the nation was approaching bankruptcy.

Other images might include Bolivia's complex society. So intermixed has this multiethnic culture become that one's race is defined by one's social status. So-called whites, who look very much like the Indians with whom their ancestors intermarried, form the upper classes only because of their economic, social, and cultural positions—that is, the degree to which they have embraced European culture.

Another enduring image fixed in the literature is Bolivia's political instability. The actual number of governments over the past 200 years is about 80, however, and not the 200 commonly noted. Indeed, elected governments have been in power for the past two decades. What outsiders perceive as typical Latin American political behavior clouds what is unusual and positive about Bolivia.

One nineteenth-century leader, Manuel Belzu, played an extremely complex role that combined the forces of populism, nationalism, and revolution. Belzu encouraged the organization of the first trade unions, abolished slavery, promoted land reform, and praised Bolivia's Indian past.

In 1952, a middle-class–led and popularly supported revolution swept the country. The ensuing social, economic, and political reforms, while not erasing an essentially dual society of "whites" and Indians, did significantly ease the level of exploitation. Most of the export industries, including those involved with natural resources, were nationalized. Bolivia's evolution—at times progressive, at times regressive—continues to reflect the impulse for change.

THE SOCIETY: POSITIVE AND NEGATIVE ASPECTS

Bolivia, despite the rapid and startling changes that have occurred in the recent past, remains an extremely poor society. In terms of poverty, life expectancy, death rates, and per capita income, the country ranks among the worst in the Western Hemisphere.

Rights for women have made slow progress, even in urban areas. In 1975, a woman was appointed to the Bolivian Supreme Court; and in 1979, the Bolivian Congress elected Lidia Gueiler Tejada, leader of the lower house, as president. Long a supporter of women's rights, Tejada had drafted and pushed through Congress a bill that created a ministry to provide social benefits for women and children. That remarkable advanced legislation has not guaranteed that women enjoy a social status equal to that of men, however. Furthermore, many women are likely unaware of their rights under the law.

Bolivia's press is reasonably free, although many journalists are reportedly paid by politicians, drug traffickers, and officials to increase their exposure or suppress negative stories. A few journalists who experienced repression under previous governments still practice self-censorship.

URBANIZATION

Santa Cruz has been transformed in the last 50 years from an isolated backwater into a modern city with links to the other parts of the country and to the rest of South America. From a population of 42,000 in 1950, the number of inhabitants quickly rose to half a million in the mid-1980s and is now growing at the rate of about 8 percent a year. Bolivia's second-largest city, its population is expected to surpass that of the de facto capital, La Paz, in this decade.

The city's political and economic strength has kept pace with the population growth. Politically, Santa Cruz represents the interests of lowland regionalism against the traditional hegemony of the highlands. Santa Cruz is also a growing commercial center; much of its wealth derives from the production and export of cocaine.

Most of the city's population growth has been the result of rural-to-urban migration, a phenomenon closely studied by geographer Gil Green. On paper, Santa Cruz is a planned city, but, since the 1950s, there has been a running battle between city planners and new settlers wanting land. "Due to the very high demand for cheap land and the large amount of flat, empty, nonvaluable land surrounding it, the city has tended to expand by a process of land invasion and squatting. Such invasions are generally overtly or covertly organized by political parties seeking electoral support of the low-income population." In the wake of a successful "invasion," the land is divided into plots that are allocated to the squatters, who then

(United Nations photo)

Bolivia has a complex society, tremendously affected by the continued interplay of multiethnic cultures. The influence of indigenous peoples on Bolivia remains strong.

Spanish settle
the altiplano
(high plain)
1538

Bolivian
declaration of
independence
of Spain
1825

The War of the
Pacific with Chile;
Bolivia loses
access to the sea
1879–1880

The Chaco War
with Paraguay
1932–1935

Reforms:
nationalization of
mines, land
reform, universal
suffrage, creation
of labor federation
1952–1964

1990s

Privatization of
the economy
accelerates; labor
unrest grips the
mining sector

Bolivia's
indigenous
people achieve
a new political
voice

Hugo Banzer
Suárez is elected
president

build houses from whatever materials are at hand. Then begins the lengthy process of settlement consolidation and regularization of land tenure. Once again the new land is subdivided and sold cheaply to the low-income population.

Mass migration to Santa Cruz has drawn people from different geographical regions in Bolivia who are also different from one another in terms of their ethnicity. Once they arrive in Santa Cruz, they are labeled either as *Cambas* or *Kollas*. Cambas, from the tropical lowlands, are of European stock and speak Spanish. They are the politically dominant ethnic group in Santa Cruz, and discriminate against the Kollas. Kollas are Aymara- or Quechua-speaking Indians from the Andean highlands.

The labels are used by the city dwellers to determine how one should behave in social interactions and reflect profound differences in language, dress, food, and music. Racial differences reinforce the tensions between the two groups. Kollas are particularly unwilling to adopt the lowland culture of the city, for the Indians' cultural heritage is an important part of their identity. The constant infusion of highland culture into Santa Cruz is resisted by Cambas, who use racial and cultural differences to retain their own "elite" status in the city. In Green's words: "What may in fact be happening, is that whilst some cultural divisions are becoming less marked, the ideology of difference is maintained in order that city residents born in certain areas of the country are excluded from local positions of power."

One's migrant status usually determines housing status in Santa Cruz. Kollas, who are long-distance migrants and the most recent arrivals in the city, lack information about Santa Cruz and have the fewest contacts to offer them help with accommodations. Thus, they are forced to rent.

Cambas, who are city natives or long-term residents, for the most part have well-developed support networks of interdependence with other Camba residents. They know the city and can best take advantage of land invasions and sales of cheap property. Kin and acquaintances are a critical part of the process.

FOREIGN POLICY AND DRUGS

Nonalignment has characterized Bolivian foreign policy since the 1952 Revolution. Relations with the United States have been strained occasionally because of official involvement in drug trafficking. Bolivian politicians have repeatedly promised to put an end to the trade and substitute other crops, a policy that most Bolivians view with suspicion.

Estimates in the early 1990s suggested that illegal exports of coca paste and cocaine contributed the equivalent of 13 to 15 percent of Bolivia's gross domestic product and that coca by-products accounted for about 40 percent of total exports, legal and illegal. Today, about 400,000 Bolivians are estimated to live off coca and cocaine production. U.S. wishes run afoul of the multifaceted heritage of coca, the sacred plant of the Incas. There is virtually no activity in domestic, social, or religious life in which coca does not play a role; thus, attempts to limit its cultivation would have profound repercussions among the peasantry.

CHALLENGES

Bolivia's problems are formidable. Although the economic horizon is less threatening and the country is blessed with substantial natural resources, Bolivia's people remain the poorest, most malnourished, and least educated in the Andean region; and extensive drug trafficking and the widespread corruption associated with

it may prove resistant to any action the Bolivian government may choose to take.

The 1997 presidential election was won by Hugo Banzer Suárez, with only 22.3 percent of the votes cast. His victory may in part be explained by a campaign strategy that negotiated agreements with other major parties as well as the new image he projected as a populist leader. In a previous political incarnation, Banzer seized power in 1971 in a coup d'etat and ruled with an iron fist until 1978. In a recent interview with the Argentine newspaper *La Nación,* he said that he wants "to humanize the neoliberal model" and that privatization was behind the increase in poverty and unemployment. Some critics claim that he has ties to narcotraffickers, but his vice president announced that the new administration would eradicate drug production by the end of Banzer's term in 2002.

DEVELOPMENT

President Banzer signed a bilateral agreement with the United States that, among other things, calls for the creation of free-trade zones between Andean Pact nations and Mercosur. Banzer also pressed on with reform of the market and promoted an open, free economy.

FREEDOM

A corrupt judicial system, overcrowded prisons, and violence and discrimination against women and indigenous peoples are perennial problems in Bolivia, despite protective legislation. A government campaign against narcotics traffickers has resulted not only in abuses by the police but also the further corruption of law enforcement.

HEALTH/WELFARE

Provisions against child labor in Bolivia are frequently ignored; many children may be found shining shoes, selling lottery tickets, and as street vendors. Although urban children generally attend school through the elementary level, more than half of rural children do not. Taken together, fewer than 30% of children are educated beyond elementary school.

ACHIEVEMENTS

The Bolivian author Armando Chirveches, in his political novel *La Candidatura de Rojas* (1909), produced one of the best examples of this genre in all of Latin America. The book captures the politics of the late nineteenth century extraordinarily well.

Brazil (Federative Republic of Brazil)

GEOGRAPHY

Area in Square Miles (Kilometers):
3,285,670 (8,512,100) (larger than the 48 contiguous U.S. states)

Capital (Population): Brasília (1,600,000)

Environmental Concerns: deforestation; water and air pollution; land degradation

Geographical Features: mostly flat to rolling lowlands in north; some plains, hills, mountains, and a narrow coastal belt

Climate: mostly tropical or semitropical; temperate zone in the south

PEOPLE

Population

Total: 169,807,000

Annual Growth Rate: 1.24%

Rural/Urban Population Ratio: 21/79

Ethnic Makeup: 55% white; 38% mixed; 6% black; 1% others

Major Languages: Portuguese; Spanish; English; French

Religions: 70% nominal Roman Catholic; 30% others

Health

Life Expectancy at Birth: 59 years (male); 70 years (female)

Infant Mortality Rate (Ratio): 40/1,000

Average Caloric Intake: 107% of FAO minimum

Physicians Available (Ratio): 1/681

Education

Adult Literacy Rate: 83.3%

Compulsory (Ages): 7–14; free

COMMUNICATION

Telephones: 1 per 13 people

Daily Newspaper Circulation: 45 per 1,000 people

Televisions: 1 per 4.8 people

TRANSPORTATION

Highways in Miles (Kilometers): 1,229,580 (1,980,000)

Railroads in Miles (Kilometers): 16,702 (26,895)

Usable Airfields: 3,291

Motor Vehicles in Use: 15,200,000

GOVERNMENT

Type: federal republic (from Portugal)

Independence Date: September 7, 1822

Head of State/Government: President Fernando Henrique Cardoso is both head of state and head of government

Political Parties: Brazilian Democratic Movement Party; Liberal Front Party; Workers' Party; Brazilian Workers' Party; Democratic Labor Party; Popular Socialist Party; Liberal Party; others

Suffrage: voluntary at 16; compulsory between 18 and 70; voluntary at 70

MILITARY

Military Expenditures (% of GDP): 1.9%

Current Disputes: small boundary disputes with Paraguay and Uruguay

ECONOMY

Currency ($ U.S. Equivalent): 1.85 reals = $1

Per Capita Income/GDP: $6,300/$1.04 trillion

GDP Growth Rate: 3%

Inflation Rate: 4.8%

Unemployment Rate: 7%

Labor Force: 57,000,000

Natural Resources: bauxite; gold; iron ore; manganese; nickel; phosphates; plantinum; tin; uranium; petroleum; hydropower; timber

Agriculture: coffee; rice; corn; sugarcane; soybeans; cotton; manioc; oranges

Industry: textiles; shoes; chemicals; cement; lumber; iron ore; tin; steel; aircraft; motor vehicles and parts; other machinery and equipment

Exports: $53 billion (primary partners European Union, Latin America, United States)

Imports: $61.4 billion (primary partners European Union, United States, Argentina)

 http://lcweb2.loc.gov/frd/cs/ brtoc.html
http://www.brazilinfo.net

BRAZIL:
A TROUBLED GIANT
In 1977, Brazilian president Ernesto Geisel stated that progress was based on "an integrated process of political, social, and economic development." Democracy, he argued, was the first necessity in the political arena. But democracy could only be achieved "if we also further social development..., if we raise the standard of living of Brazilians." The standard of living, he continued, "can only be raised through economic development."

It was clear from his remarks that the three broad objectives of democratization, social progress, and economic development were interconnected. He could not conceive of democracy in a poor country or in a country where there were "gaps, defects, and inadequacies in the social realm."

CONCEPTS OF PROGRESS
Geisel's comments offer a framework within which to consider not only the current situation in Brazil but also historical trends that reach back to the late nineteenth century—and, in some instances, to Portugal. Historically, most Brazilians have believed that progress would take place within the context of a strong, authoritarian state. In the nineteenth century, for example, a reform-minded elite adapted European theories of modernization that called for government-sponsored changes. The masses would receive benefits from the state; in this way, the elite reasoned, pressure for change from the poorer sectors of society would be eliminated. There would be progress with order. *Ordem e Progresso* ("Order and Progress") is the motto that graces the Brazilian flag; the motto is as appropriate today as it was in 1889, when the flag first flew over the new republic.

The tension among modernization, social equity, and order and liberty was first obvious in the early 1920s, when politically isolated middle-class groups united with junior military officers (*tenentes*) to challenge an entrenched ruling class of coffee-plantation owners. By the mid-1920s, the tenentes, bent on far-reaching reforms, conceived a new role for themselves. With a faith that bordered at times on the mystical and a philosophy that embraced change in the vaguest of terms, they felt that only the military could shake Brazil from its lethargy and force it to modernize. Their program demanded the ouster of conservative, tradition-minded politicians; an economic transformation of the nation; and, eventually, a return to strong, centralized constitutional rule. The tenentes also proposed labor reforms that included official recognition of trade unions, a minimum wage and maximum work week, restraints on child labor, land reform, nationalization of natural resources, and a radical expansion of educational facilities. Although the tenentes were frustrated in their attempts to mold policy, many of their reforms were taken up by Getulio Vargas, who seized power in 1930 and imposed a strong, authoritarian state on Brazil.

THE 1964 REVOLUTION
In some respects, the goals of the tenentes were echoed in 1964 when a broad coalition of civilians—frustrated by an economy that seemed to be disintegrating, concerned with the "leftist" slant of the government of João Goulart, and worried about a social revolution that might well challenge the status and prestige of the wealthy and the middle classes—called on the military to impose order on the country.

The military leaders did not see their intervention as just another coup but, rather, as a revolution. They foresaw change but believed that it would be dictated from above. Government was highly centralized, the traditional parties were virtually frozen out of the political process, and the military and police ruthlessly purged Brazil of elements considered "leftist" or "subversive." (The terms were used interchangeably.) Order and authority triumphed over liberty and freedom. The press was muzzled, and human-rights abuses were rampant.

Brazil's economic recovery eventually began to receive attention. The military gave economic growth and national security priority over social programs and political liberalization. Until the effects of

(United Nations photo/Jef Foxx)

Certain areas of Brazil attract enormous numbers of visitors from all over the world. This beach in Rio de Janeiro has one of the most famous skylines in South America.

the oil crisis generated by the Organization of Petroleum Exporting Countries (OPEC) in 1973 began to be felt, the recovery of the Brazilian economy was dubbed a "miracle," with growth rates averaging 10 percent a year.

The benefits of that growth went primarily to the upper and middle classes, who enjoyed the development of industries based largely on consumer goods. Moreover, Brazil's industrialization was flawed. It was heavily dependent on foreign investment, foreign technology, and foreign markets. It required large investments in machinery and equipment but needed little labor, and it damaged the environment through pollution of the rivers and air around industrial centers. Agriculture was neglected to the point that even basic foodstuffs had to be imported.

THE IMPACT OF RURAL–URBAN MIGRATION

The stress on industrialization tremendously increased rural-to-urban migration and complicated the government's ability to keep up with the expanded need for public health and social services. In 1970, nearly 56 percent of the population were concentrated in urban areas; by the late 1990s, 79 percent of the population were so classified. These figures also illustrate the inadequacies of an agrarian program based essentially on a "moving frontier." Peasants evicted from their plots have run out of new lands to exploit, unless they move to the inhospitable Amazon region. As a result, many have been attracted by the cities.

The pressure of the poor on the cities, severe shortages of staple foods, and growing tension in rural areas over access to the land forced the government to act. In 1985, the civilian government of José Sarney announced an agrarian-reform plan to distribute millions of acres of unused private land to peasants. Implementation of the reform was not easy, and confrontations between peasants and landowners occurred.

MILITARY RULE IS CHALLENGED

Nineteen seventy-four was a crucial year for the military government of Brazil. The virtual elimination of the urban-guerrilla threat challenged the argument that democratic institutions could not be restored because of national security concerns.

Pressure grew from other quarters as well. Many middle- and upper-class Brazilians were frightened by the huge state-controlled sector in the economy that had been carved out by the generals. The military's determination to promote the rapid development of the nation's resources, to

control all industries deemed vital to the nation's security, and to compete with multinational corporations concerned Brazilian businesspeople, who saw their role in the economy decreasing.

Challenges to the military regime also came from the Roman Catholic Church, which attacked the government for its brutal violations of human rights and constantly called for economic and social justice. One Brazilian bishop publicly called the government "sinful" and in "opposition to the plans of God" and noted that it was the Church's moral and religious obligation to fight it. After 1974, as Brazil's economic difficulties mounted, the chorus of complaints grew insistent.

THE RETURN OF DEMOCRACY

The relaxation of political repression was heralded by two laws passed in 1979. The Amnesty Bill allowed for the return of hundreds of political exiles; the Party Reform Bill in essence reconstructed Brazilian politics. Under the provisions of the Party Reform Bill, new political parties could be established—provided they were represented in nine states and in 20 percent of the counties of those states. The new parties were granted the freedom to formulate political platforms, as long as they were not ideological and did not favor any one economic class. The Communist Party was outlawed, and the creation of a workers' party was expressly forbidden. (Communist parties were legalized again in 1985.)

The law against the establishment of a workers' party reflected the regime's concern that labor, increasingly anxious about the state of the economy, might withdraw its traditional support for the state. Organized labor had willingly cooperated with the state since the populist regime of Getulio Vargas (1937–1945). For Brazilian workers in the 1930s, the state was their "patron," the source of benefits. This dependence on the government, deeply rooted in Portuguese political culture, replaced the formation of a more independent labor movement and minimized industrial conflict. The state played the role of mediator between workers and management. President Vargas led the workers to believe that the state was the best protector of their interests. (Polls have indicated that workers still cling to that belief.)

If workers expect benefits from the state, however, the state must then honor those expectations and allocate sufficient resources to assure labor's loyalty. A deep economic crisis, such as the one that occurred in the early 1960s and again in the early 1990s, endangers the state's control

of labor. In 1964, organized labor supported the coup, because workers felt that the civilian regime had failed to perform its protective function. This phenomenon also reveals the extremely shallow soil in which Brazilian democracy has taken root.

Organized labor tends not to measure Brazilian governments in political terms, but within the context of the state's ability to address labor's needs. For the rank-and-file worker, it is a question not of democracy or military authoritarianism, but of bread and butter. Former president Sarney, in an effort to keep labor loyal to the government, sought the support of union leaders for a proposal to create a national pact with businesspeople, workers, and his government. But pervasive corruption, inefficient government, and a continuing economic crisis eventually eroded the legitimacy of the elites and favored nontraditional parties in the 1989 election. The candidacy of Luís Inácio da Silva, popularly known as "Lula" and leader of the Workers' Party, "was stunning evidence of the Brazilian electorate's dissatisfaction with the conduct of the country's transition to democracy and with the political class in general." He lost the election by a very narrow margin.

Yet workers continue to regard the state as the source of benefits, as do other Brazilians. Many social reformers, upset with the generals for their neglect of social welfare, believe that social reform should be dispensed from above by a strong and paternalistic state. Change is possible, even welcome—but it must be the result of compromise and conciliation, not confrontation or non-negotiable demands.

THE NEW CONSTITUTION

The *abertura* (political liberalization) of Brazil climaxed in January 1985 with the election of President Sarney, a civilian, following 21 years of military rule. Importantly, the Brazilian military promised to respect the Constitution and promised a policy of nonintervention in the political process. In 1987, however, with the draft of a new constitution under discussion, the military strongly protested language that removed its responsibility for internal law and order and restricted the military's role to that of defense of the nation against external threats. According to *Latin American Regional Reports: Brazil*, the military characterized the draft constitution as "confused, inappropriate, at best a parody of a constitution, just as Frankenstein was a gross and deformed imitation of a human being."

Military posturing aside, the new Constitution went into effect in October 1988. It reflects the input of a wide range of interests: The Constituent Assembly—which also served as Brazil's Congress—heard testimony and suggestions from Amazonian Indians, peasants, and urban poor as well as from rich landowners and the military. The 1988 Constitution is a document that captures the byzantine character of Brazilian politics and influence peddling and reveals compromises made by conservative and liberal vested interests.

The military's fears about its role in internal security were removed when the Constituent Assembly voted constitutional provisions to grant the right of the military independently to ensure law and order, a responsibility it historically has claimed. But Congress also arrogated to itself the responsibility for appropriating federal monies. This is important, because it gives Congress a powerful check on both the military and the executive office.

Nationalists won several key victories. The Constituent Assembly created the concept of "a Brazilian company of national capital" that can prevent foreigners from engaging in mining, oil-exploration risk contracts, and biotechnology. Brazilian-controlled companies were also given preference in the supply of goods and services to local, state, and national governments. Legislation reaffirmed and strengthened the principle of government intervention in the economy should national security or the collective interest be at issue.

Conservative congressional representatives were able to prevail in matters of land reform. They defeated a proposal that would have allowed the compulsory appropriation of property for land reform. Although a clause that addressed the "social function" of land was included in the Constitution, it was clear that powerful landowners and agricultural interests had triumphed over Brazil's landless peasantry.

In other areas, however, the Constitution is remarkably progressive on social and economic issues. The workweek was reduced to a maximum of 44 hours, profit sharing was established for all employees, time-and-a-half was promised for overtime work, and paid vacations were to include a bonus of 30 percent of one's monthly salary. Day-care facilities were to be established for all children under age six, maternity leave of four months and paternity leave of five days were envisaged, and workers were protected against "arbitrary dismissal." The Constitution also introduced a series of innovations that would increase significantly the ability of Brazilians to claim their guaranteed rights before the nation's courts and ensure the protection of human rights, particularly the rights of Indians and peasants involved in land disputes.

Despite the ratification of the 1988 Constitution, a functioning Congress, and an independent judiciary, the focus of power in Brazil is still the president. A legislative majority in the hands of the opposition in no way erodes the executive's ability to govern as he or she chooses. Any measure introduced by the president automatically becomes law after 40 days, even without congressional action. Foreign observers perceive "weaknesses" in the new parties, which in actuality are but further examples of well-established political practices. The parties are based on personalities rather than issues, platforms are vague, goals are so broad that they are almost illusions, and party organization conforms to traditional alliances and the "rules" of patronage. Democratic *forms* are in place in Brazil; the *substance* remains to be realized.

(United Nations photo)

By the late 1980s, agrarian reforms that were designed to establish peasants in plots of workable land had caused the depletion of Brazilian jungle and, as space and opportunities diminished, a large movement of these people to the cities. The profound urban crowding in Brazil is illustrated by this photo of a section of Rio de Janeiro.

The election of President Fernando Collor de Mello, who assumed office in March 1990, proves the point. As political scientist Margaret Keck explains, Collor fit well into a "traditional conception of elite politics, characterized by fluid party identifications, the predominance of personal relations, a distrust of political institutions, and reliance on charismatic and populist appeals to *o povo*, the people." Unfortunately, such a system is open to abuse; revelations of widespread corruption that reached all the way to the presidency brought down Collor's government in 1992 and gave Brazilian democracy its most difficult challenge to date. The scandal brought to light a range of strengths and weaknesses that presents insights into the Brazilian political system.

THE PRESS AND THE PRESIDENCY

Brazil's press was severely censored and harassed from the time of the military coup of 1964 until 1982. Not until passage of the Constitution of 1988 was the right of free speech and a free press guaranteed. It was the press, and in particular the news magazine *Veja*, that opened the door to President Collor's impeachment. In the words of *World Press Review*, "Despite government pressure to ease off, the magazine continued to uncover the president's malfeasance, tugging hard at the threads of Collor's unraveling administration. As others in the media followed suit, Congress was forced to begin an investigation and, in the end, indict Collor." The importance of the event to Brazil's press, according to *Veja* editor Mario Sergio Conti, is that "It will emerge with fewer illusions about power and be more rigorous. Reporting has been elevated to a higher plane. . . ."

While the failure of Brazil's first directly elected president in 29 years was tragic, it should not be interpreted as the demise of Brazilian democracy. Importantly, according to Brazilian journalist Carlos Eduardo Lins da Silva, writing in *Current History*, many "Brazilians and outside observers saw the workings of the impeachment process as a sign of the renewed strength of democratic values in Brazilian society. They were also seen as a healthy indicator of growing intolerance to corruption in public officials."

The military, despite persistent rumors of a possible coup, has to date allowed the constitutional process to dictate events. For the first time, most civilians do not see the generals as part of the solution to political shortcomings. And Congress, to its credit, chose to act responsibly and not be "bought off" by the executive office.

THE RIGHTS OF WOMEN AND CHILDREN

Major changes in Brazilian households have occurred over the last decade as the number of women in the workforce has dramatically increased. In 1990, just over 35 percent of women were in the workforce, and the number was expected to grow. As a result, many women are limiting the size of their families. More than 20 percent use birth-control pills, and Brazil is second only to China in the percentage of women who have been sterilized. The traditional family of 5.0 or more children has shrunk to an average of 3.4. With two wage earners, the standard of living has risen slightly for some families. Many homes now have electricity and running water. Television sales increased by more than 1,000 percent in the last decade.

In relatively affluent, economically and politically dynamic urban areas, women are more obvious in the professions, education, industry, the arts, media, and political life. In rural areas, however, especially in the northeast, traditional cultural attitudes, which call upon women to be submissive, are still well entrenched.

Women are routinely subjected to physical abuse in Brazil. Americas Watch, an international human-rights group, reports that more than 70 percent of assault, rape, and murder cases take place in the home and that many incidents are unreported. Even though Brazil's Supreme Court struck down the outmoded concept of a man's "defense of honor," local courts routinely acquit men who kill unfaithful wives. Brazil, for all intents and purposes, is still a patriarchy.

Children are also in many cases denied basic rights. According to official statistics, almost 18 percent of children between the ages of 10 and 14 are in the labor force, and they often work in unhealthy or dangerous environments. Violence against urban street children has reached frightening proportions. Between January and June 1992, 167 minors were killed in Rio de Janeiro; 306 were murdered in São Paulo over the first 7 months of the year. In July 1993, the massacre in a single night of seven street children in Rio de Janeiro resulted, for a time, in cries for an investigation of the matter. In February 1997, however, five children were murdered on the streets of Rio.

THE STATUS OF BLACKS

Scholars continue to debate the actual status of blacks in Brazil. Not long ago, an elected black member of Brazil's federal Congress blasted Brazilians for their racism. However, argues historian Bradford Burns, Brazil probably has less racial tension and prejudice than other multiracial societies.

A more formidable barrier, Burns says, may well be class. "Class membership depends on a wide variety of factors and their combination: income, family history and/or connections, education, social behavior, tastes in housing, food and dress, as well as appearance, personality and talent." But, he notes, "The upper class traditionally has been and still remains mainly white, the lower class principally colored." Upward mobility exists and barriers can be breached. But if such advancement depends upon a symbolic "whitening out," does not racism still exist?

This point is underscored by the 1988 celebration of the centennial of the abolition of slavery in Brazil. In sharp contrast to the government and Church emphasis on racial harmony and equality were the public protests by militant black groups claiming that Brazil's much-heralded "racial democracy" was a myth. In 1990, blacks earned 40 percent less than whites in the same professions.

THE INDIAN QUESTION

Brazil's estimated 200,000 Indians have suffered greatly in recent decades from the gradual encroachment of migrants from the heavily populated coastal regions and from government efforts to open the Amazon region to economic development. Highways have penetrated Indian lands, diseases for which the Indians have little or no immunity have killed thousands, and additional thousands have experienced a profound culture shock. Government efforts to protect the Indians have been largely ineffectual.

The two poles in the debate over the Indians are captured in the following excerpts from *Latin American Regional Reports: Brazil*. A Brazilian Army officer observed that the "United States solved the problem with its army. They killed a lot of Indians. Today everything is quiet there, and the country is respected throughout the world." And in the words of a Kaingang Indian woman: "Today my people see their lands invaded, their forests destroyed, their animals exterminated and their hearts lacerated by this brutal weapon that is civilization."

Sadly, the assault against Brazil's Indian peoples has accelerated, and disputes over land have become more violent. One case speaks for itself. In the aftermath of a shooting incident in which several Yanomamö Indians were killed by prospectors, the Brazilian federal government declared that all outsiders would be removed from Yanomamö lands, ostensibly to protect the Indians. Those expelled by the government included anthropologists, missionaries, doctors, and nurses. A large number of prospectors remained behind. By the end of 1988, while medical personnel had not been allowed back in, the number of prospectors had swelled to 50,000 in an area peopled by 9,000 Yanomamö. The Indians have been devastated by diseases, particularly malaria, and by mercury poisoning as a result of prospecting activities upriver from Yanomamö settlements. In 1991, cholera began to spread among indigenous Amazon peoples, due to medical waste dumped into rivers in cholera-ridden Peru and Ecuador.

The new Constitution devotes an entire chapter to the rights of Indians. For the first time in the country's history, Indians have the authority to bring suits in court to defend their rights and interests. In all such cases, they will be assisted by a public prosecutor. Even though the government established a large protected zone for Brazil's Yanomamö Indians in 1991, reports of confrontations between Indians and prospectors have persisted. There are also Brazilian nationalists who insist that a 150-mile-wide strip along the border with Venezuela be excluded from the reserve as a matter of national security. The Yanomamö cultural area extends well into

Venezuela; such a security zone would bisect Yanomamö lands.

THE BURNING OF BRAZIL

Closely related to the destruction of Brazil's Indians is the destruction of the tropical rain forests. The burning of the forests by peasants clearing land in the traditional slash-and-burn method, or by developers and landowners constructing dams or converting forest to pasture, has become a source of worldwide concern and controversy.

Ecologists are horrified by the mass extinction of species of plants, animals, and insects, most of which have not even been catalogued. The massive annual burning (equivalent in one recent year to the size of Kansas) also fuels the debate on the greenhouse effect and global warming. The problem of the burning of Brazil is indeed global, because we are all linked to the tropics by climate and the migratory patterns of birds and animals.

World condemnation of the destruction of the Amazon basin has produced a strong xenophobic reaction in Brazil. Foreign Ministry Secretary-General Paulo Tarso Flecha de Lima informed a 24-nation conference on the protection of the environment that the "international community cannot try to strangle the development of Brazil in the name of false ecological theories." He further noted that foreign criticism of his government in this regard was "arrogant, presumptuous and aggressive." The Brazilian military, according to *Latin American Regional Reports: Brazil,* has adopted a high-profile posture on the issue. The military sees the Amazon as "a kind of strategic reserve vital to national security interests." Any talk of transforming the rain forests into an international nature reserve is rejected out of hand.

Over the next decade, however, Brazilian and foreign investors will create a 2.5 million-acre "green belt" in an already devastated area of the Amazon rain forest. Fifty million seedlings have been planted in a combination of natural and commercial zones. It is hoped that responsible forestry will generate jobs to maintain and study the native forest and to log the commercial zones. Steady employment would help to stem the flow of migrants to cities and to untouched portions of the rain forest.

FOREIGN POLICY

If Brazil's Indian and environmental policies leave much to be desired, its foreign policy has won it respect throughout much of Latin America and the developing world. Cuba, Central America, Angola, and Mozambique seemed far less threat-

(United Nations photo/Shelley Rotner)

The status of blacks in Brazil is considered better than in most other multiracial societies. The class structure is determined by a number of factors: income, family history, education, social behavior, cultural tastes, and talent. Still, the upper class remains mainly white, and the lower class principally of color.

Pedro Alvares Cabral discovers and claims Brazil for Portugal **1500**	Declaration of Brazil's independence **1822**	The Golden Law abolishes slavery **1888**	The republic is proclaimed **1889**	The Brazilian Expeditionary Force participates in the Italian campaign **1944**	The military seizes power **1964**	Economic, social, and ecological crises **1980s**

1990s

President Fernando Collor de Mello is convicted on impeachment charges

The Asian financial crisis plunges Brazil into deep recession; the currency is devalued

President Fernando Henrique Cardoso is elected to a second term

ening during the cold war to the Brazilian government than they did to Washington. Brazil is more concerned about its energy needs, capital requirements, and trade opportunities. Its foreign policy, in short, is one of pragmatism.

ECONOMIC POLICY

In mid-1993, Finance Minister Fernando Henrique Cardoso announced a plan to restore life to an economy in shambles. The so-called Real Plan, which pegged the new Brazilian currency (the real) to the dollar, brought an end to hyperinflation and won Cardoso enough popularity to carry him to the presidency. Inflation, which had raged at a rate of 45 percent per month in July 1994, was only 2 percent per month in February 1995. His two-to-one victory in elections in October 1994 was the most one-sided win since 1945.

President Cardoso transformed the economy through carefully conceived and brilliantly executed constitutional reforms. A renovated tax system, an overhauled social-security program, and extensive privatization of state-owned enterprises were supported by a new generation of legislators pledged to support broad-based reform.

But, as was the case in much of Latin America in 1995, Mexico's financial crisis spread quickly to affect Brazil's economy, in large measure because foreign investors were unable to distinguish between Mexico and other Latin American nations. A similar problem occurred in 1998 with the collapse of Asian financial markets. Again, foreign investors shied away from Brazil's economy, and President Cardoso was forced to back away from a promise not to devalue the real. With devaluation in 1999 and signs of recovery in Asian markets, Brazil's economic prospects

brightened considerably. Exports rose, and Brazil was able to finance its foreign debt through bond issues. Life for average Brazilians remains difficult, however, and Cardoso's popularity has begun to wane. But his government has some breathing room, as the next presidential elections are not scheduled until 2002.

A fundamental problem remains the state of Brazilian industry. According to reports in *World Press Review,* in the 1980s the nation's industries "went into hibernation" and stopped investing in themselves. As a result, there was no increase in productive capacity. The steel industry is characterized as "lazy and rusty," and the automotive industry is described as the "least productive in the world and among the worst for quality." Electricity generation is stagnant. However, the scope of Brazilian industry is impressive; it "produces virtually everything."

Cardoso's laudable economic reforms have not as yet transformed the quality of Brazilian democracy. The lament of Brazilian journalist Lins da Silva is still accurate: "Brazilian elites have once again shown how capable they are of solving political crises in a creative and peaceful manner but also how unwilling to promote change in inequitable social structures." The wealth of the nation still remains in the hands of a few, and the educational system has failed to absorb and train as many citizens as it should. Police continue routinely to abuse their power.

On a positive note, though, Brazilians in record numbers have joined voluntary associations devoted to helping the less fortunate. This reflects a level of confidence in the government and an ability to transform society that augers well for the future. At a broader level, Brazil hopes to prosper from its membership in Mercosur, a regional trade organization that consists

of Argentina, Brazil, Paraguay, and Uruguay. The success of Mercosur has expanded relations with other countries, especially Chile, which became an "associate" member of sorts in 1997. Tariffs will be ended on 95 percent of goods traded among member nations. Brazilian manufacturers are pleased by the prospect of a 50 percent expansion of the duty-free area open to their products.

The military—which to its credit has remained aloof from recent political agonies—has spoken out about the dangers posed by poverty, unemployment, and inflation. In 1993, it identified the "struggle against misery" as a priority. Cardoso's economic successes together with a new style of politics that eschews self-interest for meaningful change should keep the military in the barracks.

DEVELOPMENT

Brazil's economy has refocused outward to the rest of South America and the world. The success of Mercosur has been instrumental in Brazil's "discovery" of its neighbors. Inflation has been cut back dramatically and has put more money into the hands of consumers. But Brazil, according to the World Bank, still has the world's worst distribution of income.

FREEDOM

Violence against street children, indigenous peoples, homosexuals, and common criminals at the hands of the police, landowners, vigilante groups, gangs, and hired thugs is commonplace. Homicide committed by police is the third-leading cause of death among children and adolescents. Investigation of such crimes is lax and prosecution of the perpetrators sporadic. Indians continue to clash with miners and landowners.

HEALTH/WELFARE

The quality of education in Brazil varies greatly from state to state, in part because there is no system of national priorities. The uneven character of education has been a major factor in the maintenance of a society that is profoundly unequal. The provision of basic health needs remains poor, and land reform is a perennial issue, although some advances were made in land redistribution in the northeast in 1999.

ACHIEVEMENTS

Brazil's cultural contributions to the world are many. Authors such as Joaquim Maria Machado de Assis, Jorge Amado, and Graciliano Ramos are evidence of Brazil's high rank in terms of important literary works. Brazilian music has won millions of devotees throughout the world, and Brazil's *Cinema Novo* (New Cinema) has won many awards.

Chile (Republic of Chile)

GEOGRAPHY

Area in Square Miles (Kilometers):
292,280 (756,945) (about
twice the size of Montana)
Capital (Population): Santiago
(4,891,000)
Environmental Concerns: air
and water pollution; deforestation; loss of biodiversity; soil
erosion; desertification
Geographical Features: low
coastal mountains; fertile
central valley; rugged Andes
Mountains in east
Climate: temperate; desert in
north; Mediterranean in center; cool and damp in south

PEOPLE

Population
Total: 14,788,000
Annual Growth Rate: 1.27%
Rural/Urban Population Ratio:
16/84
Major Language: Spanish
Ethnic Makeup: 95% European
and Mestizo; 3% Indian; 2%
others
Religions: 89% Roman
Catholic; 11% Protestant;
small Jewish population

Health
Life Expectancy at Birth: 72
years (male); 78 years (female)
Infant Mortality Rate (Ratio):
10.4/1,000
Average Caloric Intake: 114%
of FAO minimum
Physicians Available (Ratio): 1/875

Education
Adult Literacy Rate: 95.2%

COMMUNICATION
Telephones: 1 per 7.6
Daily Newspaper Circulation:
100 per 1,000 people
Televisions: 1 per 4.7 people

TRANSPORTATION
Highways in Miles (Kilometers): 49,556
(79,800)
Railroads in Miles (Kilometers): 4,212
(6,782)
Usable Airfields: 380
Motor Vehicles in Use: 1,358,000

GOVERNMENT
Type: republic
Independence Date: September 18, 1810
(from Spain)
Head of State/Government: President Ricardo Lagos is both head of state and
head of government

Political Parties: Christian Democratic
Party; Party for Democracy; Socialist
Party; National Renewal; Independent
Democratic Union; others
Suffrage: universal and compulsory at 18

MILITARY
Military Expenditures (% of GDP): 3.5%
Current Disputes: boundary or territorial
disputes with Argentina, Chile, and Bolivia; territorial claim in Antarctica

ECONOMY
Currency ($ U.S. Equivalent): 516.00 pesos = $1
Per Capita Income/GDP: $11,600/$168.5 billion
GDP Growth Rate: 7.1%
Inflation Rate: 6%
Unemployment Rate: 6.1%
Labor Force: 5,700,000

Natural Resources: copper; timber; iron
ore; nitrates; precious metals;
molybdenum; fish
Agriculture: wheat; corn; grapes; beans;
sugar beets; potatoes; fruit; beef;
poultry; wool; timber; fish
Industry: copper and other minerals; foodstuffs; fish processing; iron and steel;
wood and wood products; transport
equipment; cement; textiles
Exports: $16.9 billion (primary partners
Asia, European Union, Latin America)
Imports: $18.2 billion (primary partners Latin
America, United States, European Union)

http://www.lcweb2.loc.gov/frd/
cs/cltoc.html
http://www.chip.cl

CHILE: A NATION ON THE REBOUND

In September 1973, the Chilean military, with the secret support of the U.S. Central Intelligence Agency (CIA), seized power from the constitutionally elected government of President Salvador Allende. Chile, with its long-standing traditions of free and honest elections, respect for human rights, and freedom of the press, was quickly transformed into a brutal dictatorship that arrested, tortured, and killed thousands of its own citizens. In the larger sweep of Chilean history, however, the coup seemed to be the most recent and severe manifestation of a lengthy conflict between social justice, on the one hand, and the requirements of order dictated by the nation's ruling elite, on the other. This was true in the colonial period, when there was conflict over Indian rights between the Roman Catholic Church and landowners. It was also apparent in later confrontations among Marxists, reformers, and conservatives.

FORM, NOT SUBSTANCE

Form, as opposed to substance, had characterized the rule of the Christian Democrats in the 1960s, when they created many separate rural unions, supposedly to address the needs of *campesinos* ("peasants"). A divided union movement in effect became a form of government control that prevented the emergence of a single powerful rural organization.

In the early 1970s, President Allende—despite his talk of socialism and his genuine attempt to destroy the institutions and values of an old social order—used a centralized bureaucracy that would have been recognized by sixteenth-century viceroys and nineteenth-century presidents as his weapon of transformation. Allende's attempts to institute far-reaching social change led to a strong reaction from powerful sectors of Chilean society who felt threatened.

THE 1973 COUP D'ETAT

When the military ousted Allende, it had the support of many Chileans, including the majority of the middle class, who had been hurt by the government's economic policies, troubled by continuous political turmoil, and infuriated by official mismanagement. The military, led by General Augusto Pinochet, began a new experiment with another form of centrist rule: military authoritarianism. The generals made it clear that they had not restored order merely to return it to the "discredited" constitutional practices of the past. They spoke of regeneration, of a new Chile, and of an end to the immorality,

(Reuters/Bettmann)

On October 5, 1988, the voters of Chile denied the brutal dictator General Augusto Pinochet an additional eight-year term as president. To his credit, his military regime accepted defeat peacefully.

corruption, and incompetence of all civilian politics. The military announced in 1974 that, "guided by the inspiration of [Diego] Portales"—one of nineteenth-century Chile's greatest civilian leaders—"the government of Chile will energetically apply the principle of authority and drastically punish any outburst of disorder and anarchy."

The political, economic, and social reforms proposed by the military aimed at restructuring Chile to such an extent that there would no longer be a need for traditional political parties. Economic policy favored free and open competition as the main regulator of economic and social life. The Chilean state rid itself of hundreds of state-owned corporations, struck down tariffs designed to protect Chilean industry from foreign competition, and opened the economy to widespread foreign investment. The changes struck deeply at the structure of the Chilean economy and produced a temporary but sharp recession, high unemployment, and hundreds of bankruptcies. A steep decline in the standard of living for most Chileans was the result of the government's anti-inflation policy.

Social-welfare programs were reduced to a minimum. The private sector was encouraged to assume many functions and services once provided by the state. Pensions were moved entirely to the private sector as all state programs were phased out. In this instance, the state calculated that workers tied through pensions and other benefits to the success of private enterprise would be less likely to be attracted to "non-Chilean" ideologies such as Marxism, socialism, and even Christian democracy. State-sponsored health programs were also cut to the bone, and many of the poor now paid for services once provided by the government.

THE DEFEAT OF A DICTATOR

To attain a measure of legitimacy, Chileans expected the military government to produce economic achievement. By 1987, and continuing into 1989, the regime's economic policies seemed successful; the economic growth rate for 1988 was an impressive 7.4 percent. However, it masked critical weaknesses in the Chilean economy. For example, much of the growth was overdependent on exports of raw materials—notably, copper, pulp, timber, and fishmeal.

Modest economic success and an inflation rate of less than 20 percent convinced General Pinochet that he could take his political scenario for Chile's future to the voters for their ratification. But in the

October 5, 1988, plebiscite, Chile's voters upset the general's plans and decisively denied him an additional eight-year term. (He did, however, continue in office until the next presidential election determined his successor.) Importantly, the military regime (albeit reluctantly) accepted defeat at the polls, which signifies the reemergence of a deep-rooted civic culture and long democratic tradition.

Where had Pinochet miscalculated? Public-opinion surveys on the eve of the election showed a sharply divided electorate. Some political scientists even spoke of the existence of "two Chiles." In the words of government professor Arturo Valenzuela and *Boston Globe* correspondent Pamela Constable, one Chile "embraced those who had benefited from the competitive economic policies and welfare subsidies instituted by the regime and who had been persuaded that power was best entrusted to the armed forces." The second Chile "consisted of those who had been victimized by the regime, who did not identify with Pinochet's anti-Communist cause, and who had quietly nurtured a belief in democracy." Polling data from the respected Center for Public Policy Studies showed that 72 percent of those who voted against the regime were motivated by economic factors. These were people who had lost skilled jobs or who had suffered a decrease in real wages. While Pinochet's economic reforms had helped some, it had also created a disgruntled mass of downwardly mobile wage earners.

Valenzuela and Constable explain how a dictator allowed himself to be voted out of power. "To a large extent Pinochet had been trapped by his own mythology. He was convinced that he would be able to win and was anxious to prove that his regime was not a pariah but a legitimate government. He and other officials came to believe their own propaganda about the dynamic new Chile they had created." The closed character of the regime, with all lines of authority flowing to the hands of one man, made it "impossible for them to accept the possibility that they could lose." And when the impossible occurred and the dictator lost an election played by his own rules, neither civilians on the right nor the military were willing to override the constitutional contract they had forged with the Chilean people.

In March 1990, Chile returned to civilian rule for the first time in almost 17 years, with the assumption of the presidency by Patricio Aylwin. His years in power revealed that tensions still existed between civilian politicians and the military. In 1993, for example, General Pinochet mobilized elements of the army in Santiago—a move that, in the words of the independent newspaper *La Época,* "marked the crystallization of long-standing hostility" between the Aylwin government and the army. The military had reacted both to investigations into human-rights abuses during the Pinochet dictatorship and proposed legislation that would have subordinated the military to

civilian control. On the other hand, the commanders of the navy and air force as well as the two right-wing political parties refused to sanction the actions of the army.

President Aylwin regained the initiative when he publicly chastised General Pinochet. Congress, in a separate action, affirmed its supremacy over the judiciary in 1993, when it successfully impeached a Supreme Court justice for "notable dereliction of duty." The court system had been notorious for transferring human-rights cases from civil to military courts, where they were quickly dismissed. The impeachment augured well for further reform of the judicial branch.

Further resistance to the legacy of General Pinochet was expressed by the people when, on December 11, 1993, the center-left coalition candidate Eduardo Frei Ruiz-Tagle won the Chilean presidential election, with 58 percent of the vote. As part of his platform, Frei had promised to bring the military under civilian rule. The parliamentary vote, however, did not give him the two-thirds majority needed to push through such a reform. The trend toward civilian government, though, seemed to be continuing.

Perhaps the final chapter in Pinochet's career began in November 1998, while the former dictator was in London for medical treatment. At that time, the British government received formal extradition requests from the governments of Spain, Switzerland, and France. The charges against Pinochet included attempted mur-

(United Nations photo)

The rural areas of Chile have presented challenges for community development. Here, volunteers work on a road that will link the village of Tincnamar to a main road.

The founding of
Santiago de Chile
1541
●

Independence
of Spain is
proclaimed
1818
●

Revolution in
Liberty
dramatically
alters Chilean
society
1964–1970
●

A military coup
ousts President
Salvador Allende;
General Augusto
Pinochet
becomes
president
1973
●

1990s

Eduardo Frei
Ruiz-Tagle is
elected president

Asian financial
woes cut into
Chilean
economic growth

Ricardo Lagos, a
moderate
Socialist, wins
the presidency in
December
1999–January
2000 elections

der, conspiracy to murder, torture, conspiracy to torture, hostage taking, conspiracy to take hostages, and genocide, based on Pinochet's alleged actions while in power. The British courts ruled that the charges were valid, and Pinochet was placed under house arrest. In Chile, following some sharp protests from Pinochet's supporters, news of the general's plight was generally relegated to the inside pages of newspapers. Politicians from a broad range of parties admitted that the absence of Pinochet from Chile during the 1999–2000 presidential campaign was probably best for all concerned. In January 2000, the British courts ruled that Pinochet was too ill to stand trial. The return of Pinochet to Chile could prove tricky for the new government of Ricardo Lagos.

Until 1998, the Chilean economy had experienced 13 consecutive years of strong growth. But in 1998, the Asian financial crisis hit Chile hard, in part because 33 percent of the nation's exports in 1997 went to Asian markets. Copper prices tumbled; and because the largest copper mine is government-owned, state revenues contracted sharply. Even though there were signs of recovery in the first quarter of 1999, the Chilean budget, for the first time in years, was characterized as "austere." The social costs could be significant.

Planning Minister Roberto Pizarro, as reported in *El Mercurio* and *La Nación,* noted that poverty in Chile declined by 4 percent between 1994 and 1996. However, a quarter of the population—some 3 million people—still live in poverty. Pizarro credited the country's social programs and an economic policy that promoted growth while simultaneously reducing unemployment and inflation. Despite these positive signs, Chilean income distribution remains badly skewed. Between 1994 and 1996,

the lowest-income groups experienced an increase in their incomes of a meager 0.1 percent. The average per capita income of the poor was about $120 a month, while the top 10 percent averaged a monthly income of more than $4,000. Pizarro identified educational reform as critical to the future of the nation and said that the government must create more jobs, raise wages, support small- and medium-size companies, and promote labor reforms designed to give workers more bargaining power. The economic slowdown did little to alter these figures in 1998 and 1999.

Peruvian novelist and politician Mario Vargas Llosa observes that while Chile "is not paradise," it does have a "stability and economic dynamism unparalled in Latin America." Indeed, "Chile is moving closer to Spain and Australia and farther from Peru or Haiti." He suggests that there has been a shift in Chile's political culture. "The ideas of economic liberty, a free market open to the world, and private initiative as the motor of progress have become embedded in the people of Chile."

SIGNS OF CHANGE

Although the Chilean Constitution was essentially imposed on the nation by the military in 1980, there are signs of change. The term for president was reduced from eight to six years in 1993; and in 1997, the Chamber of Deputies, the lower house of the Legislature, approved legislation to further reduce the term of a president to four years, with a prohibition on reelection. Military courts, which have broader peacetime jurisdiction than most other countries in the Western Hemisphere, have also come under scrutiny by politicians. According to the *Revista Hoy,* as summarized by *CHIP News,* military justice reaches far beyond the ranks. If, for example, several people are involved in the

commission of a crime and one of the perpetrators happens to be a member of the military, all are tried in a military court. Another abuse noted by politicians is that the military routinely uses the charge of sedition against civilians who criticize it. Although the Frei government had no intention to pursue reform of the military, a group of Christian Democrats wants to limit the jurisdiction of the military to military crimes committed by military personnel; eliminate the participation of the army prosecutor in the Supreme Court, where he sits on the bench in cases related to the military; grant civilian courts the authority to investigate military premises; and accord civilian courts jurisdiction over military personnel accused of civilian-related crimes. The military disagrees. One prosecutor noted: "The country needs the Armed Forces and needs them to function well."

Another healthy sign of change is a concerted effort by the Chilean and Argentine governments to discuss issues that have been a historical source of friction between the two nations. Arms escalation, mining exploration and exploitation in border areas, and trade and investment concerns were on the agenda. The Chilean foreign relations minister and the defense minister sat down with their Argentine counterparts in the first meeting of its kind in the history of Argentine–Chilean relations.

DEVELOPMENT

Chile, with an average gross domestic product growth of 6% over the last decade, has become a model for other Latin American nations. Bilateral trade agreements have continued with Mexico, Venezuela, and Bolivia. Chile eventually hopes to join NAFTA but, in the meantime, has become an associate member of Mercosur.

FREEDOM

Chile's human-rights record has improved significantly in recent years. There is still the need to address hundreds of abuses committed during the years of military rule, however. The military pursues obstructionist tactics in this regard, but the Frei government, with its careful and methodical rule, made progress in this area. It remains to be seen how the government of President Ricardo Lagos will deal with this issue.

HEALTH/WELFARE

Since 1981, all new members of Chile's labor force have been required to contribute 10% of their monthly gross earnings to private pension-fund accounts, which they own. By 1995, more than 93% of the labor force were enrolled in 20 separate and competing private pension funds. The reforms increased the domestic savings rate to 26% of GDP.

ACHIEVEMENTS

Chile's great literary figures, such as Gabriela Mistral and Pablo Neruda, have a great sympathy for the poor and oppressed. This places Chilean authors in the mainstream of Latin American literature. Other major Chilean writers, such as Isabel Allende, have won worldwide acclaim.

Colombia (Republic of Colombia)

GEOGRAPHY
Area in Square Miles (Kilometers):
440,000 (1,139,600) (about 3
times the size of Montana)
Capital (Population): Bogotá
(6,079,000)
Environmental Concerns:
deforestation; soil damage;
air pollution
Geographical Features: flat
coastal lowlands; central highlands; high Andes Mountains;
eastern lowland plains
Climate: tropical on coast and
eastern plains; cooler in
highlands

PEOPLE

Population
Total: 38,581,000
Annual Growth Rate: 1.9%
Rural/Urban Population Ratio: 27/73
Major Language: Spanish
Ethnic Makeup: 58% Mestizo;
20% white; 14% mulatto; 4%
African; 3% African-Indian;
1% Indian
Religions: 95% Roman
Catholic; 5% others

Health
Life Expectancy at Birth: 66
years (male); 74 years (female)
Infant Mortality Rate (Ratio):
25.4/1,000; Indians 233/1,000
Average Caloric Intake: 108%
of FAO minimum
Physicians Available (Ratio):
1/1,078

Education
Adult Literacy Rate: 91.3%
Compulsory (Ages): for 5 years
between 6 and 12; free

COMMUNICATION
Telephones: 1 per 10 people
Daily Newspaper Circulation:
64 per 1,000 people
Televisions: 1 per 8.5 people

TRANSPORTATION
Highways in Miles (Kilometers): 66,447
(107,000)
Railroads in Miles (Kilometers): 2,103 (3,386)
Usable Airfields: 1,136
Motor Vehicles in Use: 1,700,000

GOVERNMENT
Type: republic
Independence Date: July 10, 1810 (from Spain)
Head of State/Government: President
Andrés Pastrana is both head of state
and head of government
Political Parties: Liberal Party; Conservative
Party; New Democratic Force; Demo-
cratic Alliance M-19; Patriotic Union

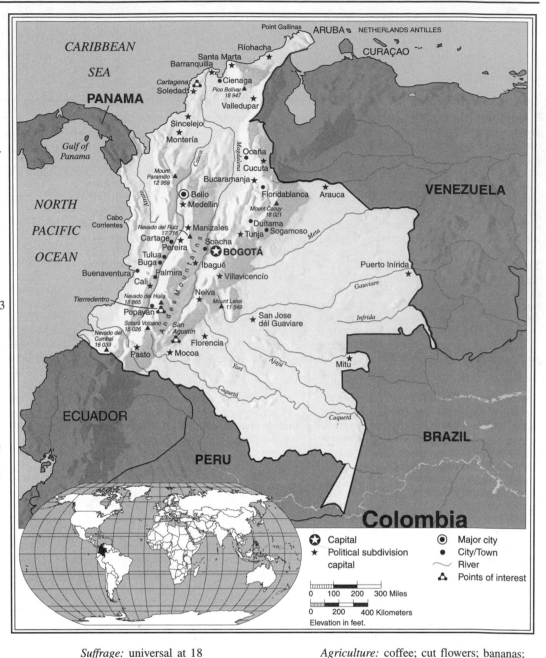

Colombia

Capital · Major city
★ Political subdivision ⊙ City/Town
capital ∼ River
▲ Points of interest

0 100 200 300 Miles
0 200 400 Kilometers
Elevation in feet.

Suffrage: universal at 18

MILITARY
Military Expenditures (% of GDP): 2.8%
Current Disputes: civil war; maritime
boundary dispute with Venezuela;
territorial disputes with Nicaragua

ECONOMY
Currency ($ U.S. Equivalent): 1,908.8
pesos = $1
Per Capita Income/GDP: $6,200/$231.1 billion
GDP Growth Rate: 3.1%
Inflation Rate: 17.7%
Unemployment Rate: 12.2%
Labor Force: 16,800,000
Natural Resources: petroleum; natural gas;
coal; iron ore; nickel; gold; copper;
emeralds

Agriculture: coffee; cut flowers; bananas;
rice; tobacco; corn; sugarcane; cocoa
beans; oilseed; vegetables; forest
products; shrimp farming
Industry: textiles; food processing; petroleum; clothing and footwear; beverages;
chemicals; cement; gold; coal; emeralds
Exports: $11.4 billion (primary partners
United States, European Union, Venezuela)
Imports: $13.5 billion (primary partners
United States, European Union, Japan)

http://lcweb2.loc.gov/frd/cs/
cotoc.html
http://home.tampabay.rr.com/
latinoconnect/colombi.html

74

COLOMBIA:
THE VIOLENT LAND

Colombia has long been noted for its violent political history. The division of political beliefs in the mid-nineteenth century into conservative and liberal factions produced not only debate but also civil war. To the winner went the presidency and the spoils of office. That competition for office came to a head during the savage War of the Thousand Days (1899–1902). Nearly half a century later, Colombia was again plagued by political violence, which took perhaps 200,000 lives. Although on the surface it is distinct from the nineteenth-century civil wars, *La Violencia* ("The Violence," 1946–1958) offers striking parallels to the violence of the last century. Competing factions were again led by conservatives and liberals, and the presidency was the prize. Explanations for this phenomenon have tended to be at once simple and powerful. Colombian writers blame a Spanish heritage and its legacy of lust for political power.

Gabriel García Márquez, in his classic novel *One Hundred Years of Solitude*, spoofed the differences between liberals and conservatives. "The Liberals," said Aureliano Buendía's father-in-law, "were Freemasons, bad people, wanting to hang priests, to institute civil marriage and divorce, to recognize the rights of illegitimate children as equal to those of legitimate ones, and to cut the country up into a federal system that would take power away from the supreme authority." On the other hand, "the Conservatives, who had received their power directly from God, proposed the establishment of public order and family morality. They were the defenders of the faith of Christ, of the principle of authority, and were not prepared to permit the country to be broken down into autonomous entities." Aureliano, when later asked if he was a Liberal or a Conservative, quickly replied: "If I have to be something I'll be a Liberal, because the Conservatives are tricky."

THE ROOTS OF VIOLENCE

The roots of the violence are far more complex than a simple quest for spoils caused by a flaw in national character. Historian Charles Bergquist has shown that "divisions within the upper class and the systematic philosophical and programmatic positions that define them are not merely political manifestations of cultural traits; they reflect diverging economic interests within the upper class." These opposing interests developed in both the nineteenth and twentieth centuries. Moreover, to see Colombian politics solely as a violent quest for office ignores long periods of relative peace (1902–1935). But, whatever the underlying causes of the violence, it has profoundly influenced contemporary Colombians.

La Violencia was the largest armed conflict in the Western Hemisphere since the Mexican Revolution (1910–1917). It was a civil war of ferocious intensity that cut through class lines and mobilized people from all levels of society behind the banner of either liberalism or conservatism. That elite-led parties were able to win popular support was evidence of their strong organization rather than their opponents' political weakness.

These multiclass parties still dominate Colombian political life, although the fierce interparty rivalry that characterized the civil wars of the nineteenth century as well as La Violencia has been stilled. In 1957, Colombia's social elite decided to bury partisan differences and devised a plan to end the widespread strife. Under this National Front agreement, the two parties agreed to divide legislative and bureaucratic positions equally and to alternate the presidency every four years from 1958 to 1974. This form of coalition government proved a highly successful means of elite compromise.

THE IMPACT OF LA VIOLENCIA

The violence has left its imprint on the people of Colombia in other ways. Some scholars have suggested that peasants now shun political action because of fear of renewed violence. Refugees from La Violencia generally experienced confusion and a loss of values. Usually, rising literacy rates, improved transportation and communications, and integration into the nation's life produce an upsurge of activism as people clamor for more rapid change. This has not been the case in rural Colombia. Despite guerrilla activity in the countryside—some of which is a spin-off from La Violencia, some of which until recently had a Marxist orientation, and some of which is banditry—the guerrillas have not been able to win significant rural support.

La Violencia also led to the professionalization and enlargement of the Colombian armed forces in the late 1950s and early 1960s. Never a serious participant in the nation's civil wars, the military acquired a new prestige and status unusual for Colombia. It must be considered an important factor in any discussion of Colombian politics today.

A standoff between guerrillas and the military prompted the government of Virgilio Barco to engage reluctantly in a dialogue with the insurgents, with the ultimate goal of peace. In 1988, he announced a three-phase peace plan to end the violence, to talk about needed reforms, and ultimately to reincorporate guerrillas into society. This effort came to fruition in 1991, when the guerrilla movement M-19 laid down its arms after 16 years of fighting and engaged in political dialogue. Other guerrilla groups, notably the long-lived (since 1961) Colombian Revolutionary Armed Forces (FARC) and the National Liberation Army (ELN), led by a Spanish priest, chose to remain in the field.

Numbering perhaps 10,000, the guerrillas claim that their armed insurgency is about social change; but, as *The Economist* has observed, lines between revolution and crime are increasingly blurred. Guerrillas ambush army units, attack oil pipelines, engage in blackmail, and kidnap rich ranchers and foreign oil executives for ransom. Some guerrillas are also apparently in the pay of the drug traffickers and collect a bounty for each helicopter they shoot down in the government's campaign to eradicate coca-leaf and poppy fields.

DRUGS AND DEATH

The guerrillas have a different perspective. One FARC leader asserted in an interview with the Colombian news weekly *Semana* that the guerrillas had both political and social objectives. Peace would come only if the government demilitarized large portions of the country and took action against the paramilitary organizations, some of them private and some of them supported by elements within the government. President Andrés Pastrana, who feared losing control of the country as well the credibility of his government, began to press for peace talks in January 1999 and, as a precondition to peace, agreed to demilitarize—that is, to withdraw government soldiers from a number of municipalities in southern Colombia. The United States objected that any policy of demilitarization would result in looser counternarcotics efforts and urged a broader program to eradicate coca crops through aerial spraying. Critics of the policy claim that crop eradication plays into the hands of the guerrillas, who come to the support of the peasants who grow the coca. There is substance in the criticism, for by late 1999 FARC guerrillas controlled about 40 percent of the countryside.

FARC leaders, contrary to reports of foreign news media, claim not to be involved in drug trafficking and have offered their own plan to counter the drug problem. It would begin with a government development plan for the peasants. In the words of a FARC leader: "Thousands of peasants need to produce and

GLOBAL STUDIES: LATIN AMERICA

grow drugs to live, because they are not protected by the state." Eradication can succeed only if alternative crops can take the place of coca. Rice, corn, cacao, or cotton might be substituted. " Shooting the people, dropping bombs on them, dusting their sown land, killing birds and leaving their land sterile" is not the solution.

The peace talks scheduled between the government and the guerrillas in 1999 stalled and then failed, in large measure because of distrust on the part of FARC. Although a large portion of southern Colombia was demilitarized, the activities of paramilitary organizations were not curbed, and the United States sought to intensify its eradication policy. In the meantime, the Colombian Civil War entered its 35th year.

In addition to the deaths attributed to guerrilla warfare, literally hundreds of politicians, judges, and police officers have been murdered in Colombia. It has been estimated that 10 percent of the nation's homicides are politically motivated. Murder is the major cause of death for men between ages 15 and 45. While paramilitary violence accounts for many deaths, drug trafficking and the unraveling of Colombia's fabric of law are responsible for most. As political scientist John D. Martz writes: "Whatever the responsibility of the military or the rhetoric of government, the penetration of Colombia's social and economic life by the drug industry [is] proving progressively destructive of law, security and the integrity of the political system."

Drug traffickers, according to *Latin American Update*, "represent a new economic class in Colombia; since 1981 'narcodollars' have been invested in real estate and large cattle ranches." The newsmagazine *Semana* noted that drug cartels had purchased 2.5 million acres of land since 1984 and now own one twelfth of the nation's productive farmland in the Magdalena River Basin. More than 100,000 acres of forest have been cut down to grow marijuana, coca, and opium poppies. Of particular concern to environmentalists is the fact that opium poppies are usually planted in the forests of the Andes at elevations above 6,000 feet. "These forests," according to *Semana,* "do not have great commercial value, but their tree cover is vital to the conservation of the sources of the water supply." The cartels have also bought up factories, newspapers, radio stations, shopping centers, soccer teams, and bullfighters. The emergence of Medellín as a modern city of gleaming skyscrapers and expensive cars also reflects the enormous profits of the drug business.

Political scientist Francisco Leal Buitrago argues that, while trafficking in narcotics in the 1970s was economically motivated, it had evolved into a social phenomenon by the 1980s. "The traffickers represent a new social force that wants to participate like other groups—new urban groups, guerrillas and peasant movements. Like the guerrillas, they have not been able to participate politically. . . ."

Domestic drug consumption has also emerged as a serious problem in Colombia's cities. *Latin American Regional Reports* noted that the increase in consumption of the Colombian form of crack, known as *bazuko,* "has prompted the growth of gangs of youths in slum areas running the bazuko business for small distributors." In Bogotá, police reported that more than 1,500 gangs operated from the city's slums.

URBANIZATION

As is the case in other Andean nations, urbanization has been rapid in Colombia. But the constantly spreading slums on the outskirts of the larger cities have not produced significant urban unrest or activism. Most of the migrants to the cities are first generation and are less frustrated and demanding than the general urban population. The new migrants perceive an improvement in their status and opportunities simply because they have moved into a more hopeful urban environment. Also, since most of the migrants are poorly paid, their focus tends to be on daily survival, not political activism.

Migrants make a significant contribution to the parallel Colombian economy. As is the case in Peru and other South American countries, the informal sector amounts to approximately 30 percent of gross domestic product.

The Roman Catholic Church in Colombia has also tended to take advantage of rapid urbanization. Depending on the individual beliefs of local bishops, the Church has to a greater or lesser extent embraced the migrants, brought them into the Church, and created or instilled a sense of community where none existed before. The Church has generally identified with the expansion and change taking place and has played an active social role.

Marginalized city dwellers are often the targets of violence. Hired killers, called *sicarios*, have murdered hundreds of petty thieves, beggars, prostitutes, indigents, and street children. Such "clean-up" campaigns are reminiscent of the activities of the Brazilian death squads since the 1960s. An overloaded judicial system and interminable delays have contributed to Colombia's high homicide rate. According to government reports, lawbreakers have

not been brought to justice in 97 to 99 percent of *reported* crimes. (Perhaps three quarters of all crimes remain unreported to the authorities.) Increasingly, violence and murder have replaced the law as a way to settle disputes; private justice is now commonly resorted to for a variety of disputes. Debts, for example, are more easily and quickly resolved through murder than by lengthy court proceedings.

SOCIAL CHANGE

Government has responded to calls for social change and reform. President Virgilio Barco sincerely believed that the eradication of poverty would help to eliminate guerrilla warfare and reduce the scale of violence in the countryside. Unfortunately, his policies lacked substance, and he was widely criticized for his indecisiveness.

President César Gaviria felt that political reform must precede social and economic change and was confident that Colombia's new Constitution would set the process of national reconciliation in motion. The constitutional debate generated some optimism about the future of liberal democracy in Colombia. As Christopher Abel writes, it afforded a forum for groups ordinarily denied a voice in policy formulation—"to civic and community movements in the 40 and more intermediate cities angry at the poor quality of basic public services; to indigenous movements. . . ; and to cooperatives, blacks, women, pensioners, small businesses, consumer and sports groups."

Unfortunately, the debates have not been transformed into a viable social policy. The distribution of income in Colombia has been deteriorating since 1983, and the significant improvement in the incomes of the poor in the 1970s has not been sustained. Successful social policy springs from committed politicians. But Colombia's political parties are in disarray, which in turn weakens the confidence of people in the ability of the state to govern.

ECONOMIC POLICIES

Colombia has a mixed economy. While state enterprises control domestic participation in the coal and oil industries and play a commanding role in the provision of electricity and communications, most of the economy is dominated by private business. At this point, Colombia is a moderate oil producer. (Recent attacks on pipelines and storage facilities by guerrillas have cut into export earnings from this growing sector.) A third of the nation's legal exports comes from the coffee industry, while exports of coal, cut flowers, seafood, and other nontraditional exports

The first Spanish settlement at Santa Marta 1525	Independence from Spain 1810	The creation of Gran Colombia (including Venezuela, Panama, and Ecuador) 1822	Independence as a separate country 1830	War of the Thousand Days 1899–1902	La Violencia; nearly 200,000 lose their lives 1946–1958	Women's suffrage 1957	The drug trade becomes big business 1980s

1990s

Government offensive against guerrillas, narcotraffickers, and organized crime	Violence hampers political, social, and economic progress in Colombia	An earthquake kills or injures thousands in central Colombia

have experienced significant growth. In that Colombia is not saddled with an onerous foreign debt, its economy is relatively prosperous.

Contributing to economic success is the large informal sector. Also of tremendous importance are the profits from the illegal-drug industry. *The Economist* estimated that Colombia grossed perhaps $1.5 billion in drug sales in 1987, as compared to official export earnings of $5.5 billion. Indeed, over the past 15 years, profits from drug trafficking have grown to emcompass between 25 and 35 percent of Colombia's legal exports. Perhaps half the profits are repatriated—that is, converted from dollars into local currency. An unfortunate side effect of the inflow of cash is an increase in the inflation rate.

FOREIGN POLICY

In the foreign-policy arena, President Barco's policies were attacked as low-profile, shallow, and too closely aligned to the policies of the United States. Presidents Gaviria, Samper, and Pastrana all adopted a more independent line, especially in terms of the drug trade.

With an uneasy peace reigning in Central America, Colombia's focus has turned increasingly toward its neighbors and a festering territorial dispute with Venezuela over waters adjacent to the Guajira Peninsula. Colombia has proposed a multilateral solution to the problem, perhaps under the auspices of the International Court of Justice. Venezuela continues to reject a multilateral approach and seeks to limit any talks to the two countries concerned. It is likely that a sustained deterioration of internal conditions in either Venezuela or Colombia will keep the territorial dispute in the forefront. A further detriment to better relations with Venezuela is the justified Venezuelan fears that Colombian violence as a result of guerrilla activity, military sweeps, and drugs will cross the border. As it is, thousands of Colombians have fled to Venezuela to escape their violent homeland.

More positively, the government's support of free-trade initiatives has bilateral trade with Venezuela. But in July 1999, Venezuela, in response to attacks in Colombia on Venezuelan truckers, closed its borders, with likely serious economic consequences for both countries. Mexico and Chile have also been targeted by the Colombian government for similar bilateral agreements to liberalize import policies, stimulate exports, and attract foreign capital.

THE CLOUDED FUTURE

Francisco Leal Buitrago, a respected Colombian academic, argues forcefully that his nation's crisis is, above all, "political": "It is the lack of public confidence in the political regime. It is not a crisis of the state itself. . . , but in the way in which the state sets the norms—the rules for participation—for the representation of public opinion. . . ."

Constitutional reforms have taken place in Colombia, but changes in theory must reflect the country's tumultuous realities. Many of those in opposition have looked for a political opening but in the meantime continue to wage an armed insurgency against the government. Other problems, besides drugs, that dog the government include corruption, violence, slow growth, high unemployment, a weak currency, inflation, and the need for major reforms in banking. To get the economy on track, the International Monetary Fund has recommended that Colombia broaden its tax base, enhance municipal tax collections, get tough on tax evasion, and reduce spending.

Endemic violence and lawlessness, the continued operation of guerrilla groups, the emergence of mini-cartels in the wake of the eclipse of drug kingpins, and the attitude of the military toward conditions in Colombia all threaten any kind of progress. The hard-line antidrug trafficking policy of the United States adds another complicated, and possibly counterproductive, dimension to the difficult task of governing Colombia.

DEVELOPMENT

In 1996, the government continued its economic liberalization program and the privatization of selected public industries. Exports of crude petroleum have increased to the point that they almost equaled coffee exports. Two new oil fields will likely increase the importance of petroleum to the Colombian economy.

FREEDOM

Colombia continues to have the highest rate of violent deaths in Latin America. Guerrillas, the armed forces, right-wing vigilante groups and drug traffickers are responsible for many deaths. On the positive side, a 1993 law that accorded equal rights to black Colombians resulted in the 1995 election of Piedad de Castro, the first black woman to hold the position, to the Senate.

HEALTH/WELFARE

Rape and other acts of violence against women are pervasive but seldom prosecuted. Spousal abuse was not considered a crime until 1996. Law 294 on family violence identifies as crimes violent acts committed within families, including spousal rape. Although the Constitution of 1991 prohibits it, discrimination against women persists in terms of access to employment and equal pay for equal work.

ACHIEVEMENTS

Colombia has a long tradition in the arts and humanities and has produced international figures such as the Nobel Prize–winning author Gabriel García Márquez; the painters and sculptors Alejandro Obregón, Fernando Botero, and Edgar Negret; the poet León de Greiff, and many others well known in music, art, and literature.

Ecuador (Republic of Ecuador)

GEOGRAPHY

Area in Square Miles (Kilometers):
109,454 (283,560) (about the size of Nevada)

Capital (Population): Quito (1,298,000)

Environmental Concerns: deforestation; soil erosion; desertification; water pollution

Geographical Features: coastal plain; inter-Andean central highlands; flat to rolling eastern jungle

Climate: varied; tropical on coast and inland jungle; cooler inland

PEOPLE

Population
Total: 12,337,000
Annual Growth Rate: 1.9%
Rural/Urban Population Ratio: 40/60
Major Languages: Spanish; Quechua and other Amerindian languages
Ethnic Makeup: 55% Mestizo; 25% Indian; 10% Spanish; 10% black
Religions: 95% Roman Catholic; 5% indigenous and others

Health
Life Expectancy at Birth: 69 years (male); 75 years (female)
Infant Mortality Rate (Ratio): 32/1,000
Average Caloric Intake: 97% of FAO minimum
Physicians Available (Ratio): 1/904

Education
Adult Literacy Rate: 90%
Compulsory (Ages): 6–14; free

COMMUNICATION
Telephones: 1 per 15 people
Daily Newspaper Circulation: 72 per 1,000 people
Televisions: 1 per 11 people

TRANSPORTATION
Highways in Miles (Kilometers): 26,858 (43,249)
Railroads in Miles (Kilometers): 599 (965)
Usable Airfields: 183
Motor Vehicles in Use: 480,000

GOVERNMENT
Type: republic
Independence Date: May 24, 1822 (from Spain)
Head of State/Government: President Jamil Mahuad is both head of state and head of government
Political Parties: Democratic Left; Social Christian Party; Popular Democracy; Popular Democratic Movement; others

Suffrage: universal and compulsory for literate people ages 18–65

MILITARY
Military Expenditures (% of GDP): 2.1%
Current Disputes: boundary disputes with Peru

ECONOMY
Currency ($ U.S. Equivalent): 17,700 sucres = $1
Per Capita Income/GDP: $4,400/$53.4 billion
GDP Growth Rate: 3.4%
Inflation Rate: 31%
Unemployment Rate: 6.9%; widespread underemployment
Labor Force: 4,200,000
Natural Resources: petroleum; fish; timber

Agriculture: bananas; coffee; cocoa; rice; potatoes; manioc; plantains; sugarcane; livestock; balsa wood; fish; shrimp

Industry: petroleum; food processing; textiles; metalwork; paper products; wood products; chemicals; plastics; fishing; lumber

Exports: $3.4 billion (primary partners United States, Latin America, European Union)

Imports: $2.9 billion (primary partners Latin America, United States, European Union)

http://www.lcweb2.loc/gov/frd/cs/ectoc.html
http://www.ecuador.org

Ecuador

✪ Capital	● City/Town	
★ Provincial capital	∿ River	
◉ Major city	---- Road	

Elevation in feet.

ECUADOR: A LAND OF CONTRASTS

Several of Ecuador's great novelists have had as the focus of their works the exploitation of the Indians. Jorge Icaza's classic *Huasipungo* (1934) describes the actions of a brutal landowner who first forces Indians to work on a road so that the region might be "developed" and then forces them, violently, from their plots of land so that a foreign company's operations will not be impeded by a troublesome Indian population.

That scenario, while possible in some isolated regions, is for the most part unlikely in today's Ecuador. In recent years, Ecuador has apparently made great strides forward in health care, literacy, human rights, press freedom, and representative government. Conaie, an organization of Ecuadoran Indians, has become increasingly assertive in national politics since 1990 and reflects developments in other Latin American countries with significant indigenous populations. Nobel Peace Prize–winner Rigoberta Menchú, a Quiché–Maya from Guatemala, has used her position to intervene in favor of indigenous peoples in countries like Ecuador. Conaie, which has from time to time aligned itself with urban unions, pressed for an agrarian-reform law from the center-right government of President Sixto Durán-Ballén.

Although Ecuador is still a conservative, traditional society, it has recently shown an increasing concern for the plight of its rural inhabitants, including the various endangered Indian groups inhabiting the Amazonian region. The new attention showered on rural Ecuador—traditionally neglected by policymakers in Quito, the capital city—reflects in part the government's concern with patterns of internal migration. Even though rural regions have won more attention from the state, social programs continue to be implemented only sporadically.

Two types of migration are currently taking place: the move from the highlands to the coastal lowlands and the move from the countryside to the cities. In the early 1960s, most of Ecuador's population was concentrated in the mountainous central highlands. Today, the population is about equally divided between that area and the coast, with more than half the nation's people crowded into the cities. So striking and rapid has the population shift been that the director of the National Institute of Statistics commented that it had assumed "alarming proportions" and that the government had to develop appropriate policies if spreading urban slums were not to develop into "potential focal points for insurgency."

Despite the large-scale movement of people in Ecuador, it still remains a nation of regions. Political rivalry has always characterized relations between Quito, in the sierras, and cosmopolitan Guayaquíl, on the coast. The presidential elections of 1988 illustrated the distinctive styles of the country. Rodrigo Borja's victory was regionally based, in that he won wide support in Ecuador's interior provinces. Usually conservative in its politics, the interior voted for the candidate of the Democratic Left, in part because of the extreme populist campaign waged by a former mayor of Guayaquíl, Abdalá Bucaram. Bucaram claimed to be a man of the people who was persecuted by the oligarchy. He spoke of his lower-class followers as the "humble ones," or, borrowing a phrase from former Argentine president Juan Perón, *los descamisados* ("the shirtless ones"). Bucaram, in the words of political scientist Catherine M. Conaghan, "honed a political style in the classic tradition of coastal populism. He combined promises of concrete benefits to the urban poor with a colorful anti-oligarchic style." Bucaram's style triumphed in 1996, when he won the presidential election.

EDUCATION AND HEALTH

Central to the government's policy of development is education. Twenty-nine percent of the national budget was set aside for education in the early 1980s, with in-creases proposed for the following years. Adult literacy improved from 74 percent in 1974 to 87 percent by 1995. In the central highlands, however, illiteracy rates of more than 35 percent are still common, largely because Quechua is still the preferred language among the Indian peasants.

The government has approached this problem with an unusual sensitivity to indigenous culture. Local Quechua speakers have been enlisted to teach reading and writing both in Quechua and Spanish. This approach has won the support of Indian leaders who are closely involved in planning local literacy programs built around indigenous values.

Health care has also shown steady improvement, but the total statistics hide sharp regional variations. Infant mortality and malnutrition are still severe problems in rural areas. In this sense, Ecuador suffers from a duality found in other Latin American nations with large Indian populations: Social and racial differences persist between the elite-dominated capitals and the Indian hinterlands. Income, services, and resources tend to be concentrated in the capital cities. Ecuador, at least, is attempting to correct the imbalance.

The profound differences between Ecuador's highland Indian and its European cultures is illustrated by the story of an Indian peasant who, when brought to a clinic, claimed that he was dying as the result of a spell. He told the doctor, trained in Western medicine, that, while traveling

(United Nations photo)

The migration of the poor to the urban areas of Ecuador has been very rapid and of great concern to the government. The increase in inner-city population can easily lead to political unrest. The graffito in this photo says, "We don't want a dictatorship."

First Spanish contact **1528**	Ecuador is part of Gran Colombia (with Panama, Venezuela, and Colombia); independence as a separate state **1822**		Women's suffrage **1929**	A border war with Peru **1941**	**1990s**

Modernization laws aim to speed the privatization of the economy

Jamil Mahuad is elected president

Popular dissatisfaction with the government's handling of the economy rises

a path from his highland village down to a valley, he passed by a sacred place, where a witch cast a spell on him. The man began to deteriorate, convinced that this had happened. The doctor, upon examination of the patient, could find no physical reason for the man's condition. Medicine produced no improvements. The doctor finally managed to save his patient, but only after a good deal of compromise with Indian culture. "Yes," he told the peasant, "a witch has apparently cast a spell on you and you are indeed dying." And then the doctor announced: "Here is a potion that will remove the spell." The patient's recovery was rapid and complete. Thus, though modern medicine can work miracles, health-care workers must also be sensitive to cultural differences.

THE ECONOMY

In 1998 and 1999, the Ecuadoran economy was hit hard by two crises. Falling petroleum prices in combination with the ravages of the El Niño weather phenomenon transformed a $598 million surplus in 1997 into a troubling $830 million deficit in 1998. Petroleum revenues fell to third place, behind exports of bananas and shrimp, which themselves were devastated by bad weather (in the case of shrimp, due to the dramatic warming of waters in the eastern Pacific as a result of El Niño).

Newly elected president Jamil Mahuad was confronted from the outset of his administration with some daunting policy decisions. A projected growth rate for 1998 of only 1 percent and an inflation rate that soared to 40 percent resulted in budget austerity and an emergency request to Congress to cut spending and prepare legislation for the privatization of Ecuador's telecommunications and electrical industries. The privatization plans raised the ire of nationalists. Since their celebra-

tion of the *nationalization* of the Trans-Ecuadoran Pipeline in 1989 and the Texaco-managed oil fields in 1990, the pace of the free-market reforms and privatizations had accelerated. In the mid-1990s, the government privatized more than 160 state-owned enterprises and, in an effort to modernize and streamline the economy, cut the number of public employees from 400,000 to 260,000.

Despite protests that were accentuated by the economic downturn of 1998 and 1999, debt negotiation with foreign lenders, the need to attract aid to rebuild an infrastructure heavily damaged by El Niño, and the reform of banking and financial institutions all required assistance from the International Monetary Fund. Muhuad's government was also aware of critical investments that had to be made in health and education. Not surprisingly, such drastic measures resulted in growing social and political unrest. The recovery of petroleum prices in 1999 only partly eased the nation's growing problems.

BITTER NEIGHBORS

A long legacy of boundary disputes that reached back to the wars for independence created a strained relationship between Ecuador and Peru which erupted in violence in July 1941. Ecuador initiated an undeclared war against Peru in an attempt to win territory along its southeastern border, in the Marañón River region, and, in the southwest, around the town of Zaramilla. In the 1942 Pact of Peace, Amity, and Limits, which followed a stunning Peruvian victory, Ecuador lost about 120,000 square miles of territory. The peace accord was guaranteed by Argentina, Brazil, Chile, and the United States. In January 1995, the usual tensions that grew each year as the anniversary of the conflict approached were given founda-

tion when fighting again broke out between Peru and Ecuador; Peruvian soldiers patrolling the region had stumbled upon well-prepared and waiting Ecuadoran soldiers. Three weeks later, with the intervention of the guarantors of the original pact, the conflict ended. The Peruvian armed forces were shaken from their smug sense of superiority over the Ecuadorans, and the Ecuadoran defense minister used the fight to support his political pretensions. The border war sent waves of alarm through the rest of Latin America, in that it reminded more than a dozen nations of boundary problems with their neighbors. Of particular concern were revelations made in 1998 and 1999 that individuals within the Argentine government and the military had sold arms to the Ecuadoran military during the conflict. Argentina was embarrassed because it was one of the original guarantors of the 1942 Pact of Peace.

On October 16, 1998, the Legislatures of Ecuador and Peru supported an agreement worked out by other governments in the region to end the border dispute. Under the terms of the agreement, Peru's sovereignty of the vast majority of the contested territory was affirmed. Ecuador won a major concession when it was granted navigation rights on the Amazon River and its tributaries within Peru and the right to establish trading centers on the river. In that both parties benefited from the negotiation, it is hoped that a lasting peace will have been effected.

DEVELOPMENT

Ecuador's development problems have been exacerbated by problems with debt negotiations with and interest payments to foreign creditors. Further complicating the picture is the uncertain future of petroleum revenues, which have fallen below expectations.

FREEDOM

Ecuador's media, with the exception of two government-owned radio stations, are in private hands and represent a broad range of opinion. They are often critical of government policies, but they practice a degree of self-censorship in coverage involving corruption among high-level military personnel.

HEALTH/WELFARE

Educational and economic opportunities in Ecuador are often not made available to women, blacks, and indigenous peoples. Most of the nation's peasantry, overwhelmingly Indian or Mestizo, are poor. Infant mortality, malnutrition, and epidemic disease are common among these people.

ACHIEVEMENTS

Ecuadoran poets have often made their poetry an expression of social criticism. The so-called Tzántzicos group has combined avant-garde techniques with social commitment and has won a measure of attention from literary circles.

Guyana (Co-operative Republic of Guyana)

GEOGRAPHY

Area in Square Miles (Kilometers):
82,990 (215,000) (about the size of Idaho)
Capital (Population):
Georgetown (248,500)
Environmental Concerns: water pollution; deforestation
Geographical Features: mostly rolling highlands; low coastal plain; savannah in south
Climate: tropical

PEOPLE

Population

Total: 708,000
Annual Growth Rate: 0.17%
Rural/Urban Population Ratio: 74/36
Major Languages: English; indigenous dialects
Ethnic Makeup: 51% East Indian; 43% African and mixed African; 4% Amerindian; 2% European and Chinese
Religions: 57% Christian; 33% Hindu; 9% Muslim; 1% others

Health

Life Expectancy at Birth: 60 years (male); 65 (female)
Infant Mortality Rate (Ratio): 48.7/1,000
Average Caloric Intake: 110% of FAO minimum
Physicians Available (Ratio): 1/3,000

Education

Adult Literacy Rate: 98%
Compulsory (Ages): 6–14; free

COMMUNICATION

Telephones: 1 per 19 people
Daily Newspaper Circulation: 97 per 1,000 people
Televisions: 1 per 26 people

TRANSPORTATION

Highways in Miles (Kilometers): 4,949 (7,970)
Railroads in Miles (Kilometers): 55 (88)
Usable Airfields: 50
Motor Vehicles in Use: 33,000

GOVERNMENT

Type: republic
Independence Date: May 26, 1966 (from the United Kingdom)
Head of State/Government: President Bharrat Jagdeo; Prime Minister Samuel Hinds
Political Parties: People's National Congress; Alliance for Guyana People's Progressive Party; United Force; Democratic Labour Movement; People's Democratic Movement; National Democratic Front; others
Suffrage: universal at 18

MILITARY

Military Expenditures (% of GDP): 1.7%
Current Disputes: territorial disputes with Venezuela and Suriname

ECONOMY

Currency ($ U.S. Equivalent): 180.50 Guyanese dollars = $1
Per Capita Income/GDP: $2,500/$1.8 billion
GDP Growth Rate: 5%
Inflation Rate: 4.5%
Unemployment Rate: 12%
Natural Resources: bauxite; gold; diamonds; hardwood timber; shrimp; fish
Agriculture: sugar; rice; wheat; vegetable oils; livestock; potential for fishing and forestry
Industry: bauxite; sugar; rice milling; timber; fishing; textiles; gold mining
Exports: $546 million (primary partners Canada, United States, United Kingdom)
Imports: $589 million (primary partners United States, Trinidad and Tobago, Netherland Antilles)

 http://www.lcweb2.loc.gov/frd/cs/gytoc.html
http://www.stabroeknews.com

Map labels:

ATLANTIC OCEAN
VENEZUELA
BRAZIL
SURINAME

Pert Katuma
Barima
Barama
Waini
Charty
Suddie
Cuyuni
disputed by Venezuela
Arimu Mine
GEORGETOWN
Mahaicony Village
New Amsterdam
Rose Hall
Bartica
Mazaruni
Peters Mine
Linden
Corriverton
Tiger Hill 350
Essequibo
Demerara
Ituni
Issano
Mount Roraima 9219
Potaro
Mount Ebini 2339
Berbice
Kwakwani
Kurupukari
Mount Makari 1679
Karasabai
Apoteri
Mount Makarapun 3063
Lethan
Rupununi
Essequibo
New
area disputed by Suriname

Guyana

⭐ Capital
◉ Major city
● City/Town
〜 River
- - - Road

0   100   200 Miles
0   100   200   300 Kilometers
Elevation in feet.

The first
permanent Dutch
settlements on
Essequibo River
1616

The Netherlands
cedes the
territory to Britain
1815

Independence
1966

President Forbes
Burnham dies
1985

1990s

Territorial
disputes with
Suriname and
Venezuela persist

The government
promises to end
racial and ethnic
discrimination

Janet Jagan is
elected president
in 1997; she later
steps down

GUYANA: RACIAL AND ETHNIC TENSIONS

Christopher Columbus, who cruised along what are now Guyana's shores in 1498, named the region *Guiana*. The first European settlers were the Dutch, who settled in Guyana late in the sixteenth century, after they had been ousted from Brazil by a resurgent Portuguese Crown. Dutch control ended in 1796, when the British gained control of the area. In 1815, as part of the treaty arrangements that brought the Napoleonic Wars to a close, the Dutch colonies of Essequibo, Demerera, and Berbice were officially ceded to the British. In 1831, the former Dutch colonies were consolidated as the Crown Colony of British Guiana.

Guyana is a society deeply divided along racial and ethnic lines. East Indians make up the majority of the population. They predominate in rural areas, constituting the bulk of the labor force on the sugar plantations, and they comprise nearly all of the rice-growing peasantry. They also dominate local businesses and are prominent in the professions. Blacks are concentrated in urban areas, where they are employed in clerical and secretarial positions in the public bureaucracy, in teaching, and in semiprofessional jobs. A black elite dominates the state bureaucratic structure.

Before Guyana's independence in 1966, plantation owners, large merchants, and British colonial administrators consciously favored some ethnic groups over others, providing them with a variety of economic and political advantages. The regime of President Forbes Burnham revived old patterns of discrimination for political gain.

Burnham, after ousting the old elite when he nationalized the sugar plantations and the bauxite mines, built a new regime that simultaneously catered to lower-class blacks and discriminated against East Indians. In an attempt to address the blacks' basic human needs, the Burnham government greatly expanded the number of blacks holding positions in public administration. To demonstrate his largely contrived black-power ideology, Burnham spoke out strongly in support of African liberation movements. The government played to the fear of communal strife in order to justify its increasingly authoritarian rule.

In the mid-1970s, a faltering economy and political mismanagement generated an increasing opposition to Burnham that cut across ethnic lines. The government increased the size of the military, packed Parliament through rigged elections, and amended the Constitution so that the president held virtually imperial power.

There has been some improvement since Burnham's death in 1985. The appearance of newspapers other than the government-controlled *Guyana Chronicle* and the public's dramatically increased access to television have served to curtail official control of the media. In politics, the election of Indo-Guyanese leader Cheddi Jagan to the presidency reflected deep-seated disfavor with the behavior and economic policies of the previous government of Desmond Hoyte. President Jagan identified the nation's foreign debt of $2 billion as a "colossally big problem, because the debt overhang impedes human development."

While president, Hoyte once pledged to continue the socialist policies of the late Forbes Burnham; but in the same breath, he talked about the need for privatization of the crucial sugar and bauxite industries. Jagan's economic policies, according to *Latin American Regional Reports,* outlined an uncertain course. During his campaign, Jagan stated that government should not be involved in sectors of the economy where private or cooperative ownership would be more efficient. In 1993, however, he backed away from the sale of the Guyana Electric Company and had some doubts about selling off the sugar industry. In Jagan's words: "Privatisation and divestment must be approached with due care. I was not elected president to preside over the liquidation of Guyana. I was mandated by the Guyanese people to rebuild the national economy and to restore a decent standard of living." Jagan's policies stimulated rapid socioeconomic progress as Guyana embarked on the road to economic recovery.

Following Jagan's death, new elections were held in December 1997, and Janet Jagan, the ex-president's 77-year-old widow, was named president. In August 1999, she stepped down due to health reasons. She named Finance Minister Bharrat Jagdeo to succeed her.

DEVELOPMENT

By the late 1990s, gold exports earned 32% more in value than more traditional exports of sugar, rice, and bauxite. An unfortunate effect of the intensified exploitation of the gold fields has been serious environmental degradation. The journal *Nature* notes a jungle "blasted, pulverized, and run through with cyanide solutions."

FREEDOM

One of the priorities of the Jagan governments was the elimination of all forms of ethnic and racial discrimination, a difficult task in a country where political parties are organized along racial lines. It was hoped that Guyana's indigenous peoples would be offered accelerated development programs to enhance their health and welfare.

HEALTH/WELFARE

The government has initiated policies designed to lower the cost of living for Guyanese. Prices for essentials have been cut. Money has been allocated for school lunch programs and for a "food-for-work" plan. Pensions have been raised for the first time in years. The minimum wage, however, will not sustain an average family.

ACHIEVEMENTS

The American Historical Association selected Walter Rodney for the 1982 Beveridge Award for his study of the Guyanese working people. The award is for the best book in English on the history of the United States, Canada, or Latin America. Rodney, the leader of the Working People's Alliance, was assassinated in 1980.

Paraguay

GEOGRAPHY

Area in Square Miles (Kilometers):
157,048 (406,752) (about the
size of California)

Capital (Population): Asunción
(1,081,000)

Environmental Concerns:
deforestation; water pollution;
problems with waste disposal

Geographical Features: grassy
plains and wooded hills east
of Rio Paraguay; Gran Chaco
region west of the river;
mostly marshy plain near the
river, dry forest and thorny
scrub elsewhere

Climate: temperate east of the
Paraguay River; semiarid to
the west

PEOPLE

Population

Total: 5,434,100
Annual Growth Rate: 2.6%
Rural/Urban Population Ratio: 47/53
Major Languages: Spanish;
Guaraní; Portuguese
Ethnic Makeup: 95% Mestizo;
5% white and Indian
Religions: 90% Roman Catholic;
10% Mennonite and other
Prostestant denominations

Health

Life Expectancy at Birth: 70
years (male); 74 years (female)
Infant Mortality Rate (Ratio):
36.5/1,000
Average Caloric Intake: 126%
of FAO minimum
Physicians Available (Ratio):
1/1,406

Education

Adult Literacy Rate: 92%
Compulsory (Ages): 7–20

COMMUNICATION

Telephones: 1 per 30 people
Daily Newspaper Circulation: 42 per
1,000 people
Televisions: 1 per 12 people

TRANSPORTATION

Highways in Miles (Kilometers): 18,320
(29,500)
Railroads in Miles (Kilometers): 602 (970)
Usable Airfields: 941
Motor Vehicles in Use: 125,000

GOVERNMENT

Type: republic
Independence Date: May 14, 1811 (from
Spain)
Head of State/Government: President Luis
Gonzalez Macchi is both head of state
and head of government

Political Parties: Colorado Party; Authentic Radical Liberal Party; Christian
Democratic Party; Febrerist Revolutionary Party; National Encounter
Suffrage: universal and compulsory from
18 to 60

MILITARY

Military Expenditures (% of GDP): 1.4%
Current Disputes: none

ECONOMY

Currency ($ U.S. Equivalent): 3,318
guaranis = $1
Per Capita Income/GDP: $3,700/$19.8 billion
GDP Growth Rate: –0.5%
Inflation Rate: 14.6%
Unemployment Rate: 8.2%
Labor Force: 1,800,000

Natural Resources: hydropower; timber;
iron ore; manganese; limestone
Agriculture: cotton; sugarcane; soybeans;
corn; wheat; tobacco; cassava (tapioca);
fruits; vegetables; livestock; timber
Industry: meat packing; oilseed crushing,
milling; brewing; textiles; other light
consumer goods; cement; construction
Exports: $1.1 billion (primary partners
Brazil, Netherlands, Argentina)
Imports: $2.5 billion (primary partners
Brazil, United States, Argentina)

http://www.lcweb2.loc.gov/frd/cs/
pytoc.html
http://home.tampabay.rr.com/
latinoconnect/paraguay.html

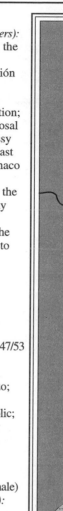

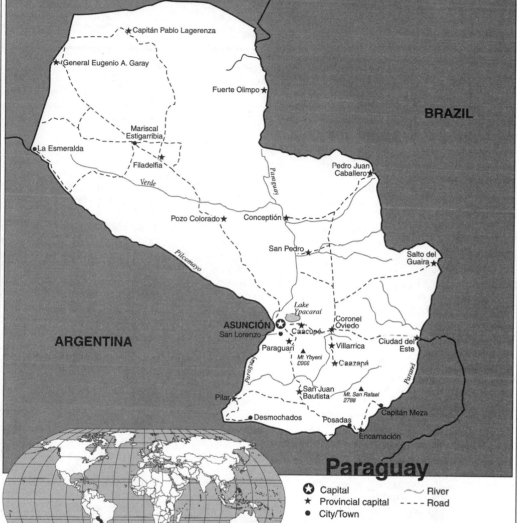

BOLIVIA

★ Capitán Pablo Lagerenza

★ General Eugenio A. Garay

Fuerte Olimpo ★

BRAZIL

Mariscal
Estigarribia

La Esmeralda ●

Filadelfia

Verde

Paraguay

Pedro Juan
Caballero ★

Pozo Colorado ★   Conceptión ★

San Pedro ●

Salto del
Guaira ★

Pilcomayo

ARGENTINA

Lake
Ypacaraí

ASUNCIÓN ✪
San Lorenzo ●

Caacupé ●

Coronel
Oviedo ●

Paraguarí ●   Villarrica ●   Ciudad del
Este ●

*Mt. Ybyeni
£006*   Caazapá ●

San Juan ★
Bautista   *Mt. San Rafael
2788* ▲

Pilar ●

Desmochados ●   Posadas ●

Capitán Meza ●

Encarnación

Paraguay

✪ Capital   〜 River
★ Provincial capital - - - - Road
● City/Town

0	100	200 Miles
0	100 200	300 Kilometers

Elevation in feet.

The Spanish
found Asunción
1537

Independence is
declared
1811

War against the
"Triple Alliance":
Argentina, Brazil,
and Uruguay
1865–1870

General Alfredo
Stroessner
begins his rule
1954

Women win the
right to vote
1961

Stroessner is
ousted in a coup
1989

1990s

A new
Constitution is
promulgated in
1993

President Raúl
Cubas is forced
to resign; the
Colorado Party is
in disarray

Luis Gonzalez
Macchi assumes
the presidency

A COUNTRY OF PARADOX

Paraguay is a country of paradox. Although there is little threat of foreign invasion and guerrilla activity is insignificant, a state of siege was in effect for 35 years, ending only in 1989 with the ouster of President (General) Alfredo Stroessner, who had held the reins of power since 1954. Government expenditures on health care in Paraguay are among the lowest in the Western Hemisphere, yet life expectancy is impressive, and infant mortality reportedly has fallen to levels comparable to more advanced developing countries. On the other hand, nearly a third of all reported deaths are of children under 5 years of age. Educational achievement, especially in rural areas, is low.

Paraguayan politics, economic development, society, and even its statistical base are comprehensible only within the context of its geography and Indo–Hispanic culture. Its geographic isolation in the midst of powerful neighbors has encouraged Paraguay's tradition of militarism and self-reliance—of being led by strongmen who tolerate little opposition. There is no tradition of constitutional government or liberal democratic procedures upon which to draw. Social values influence politics to the extent that politics is an all-or-nothing struggle for power and its accompanying prestige and access to wealth. These political values, in combination with a population that is poor and politically ignorant, contribute to the type of paternalistic, personal rule characteristic of a dictator such as Stroessner.

The paradoxical behavior of the Acuerdo Nacional, a block of opposition parties under Stroessner, was understandable within the context of a quest for power or at least a share of power. Stroessner, always eager to divide and conquer, identified the Acuerdo Nacional as a fruit-ful field for new alliances. Leaping at the chance for patronage positions but anxious to demonstrate to Stroessner that they were a credible political force worthy of becoming allies, Acuerdo members tried to win the support of unions and the peasantry. At the same time, the party purged its youth wing of leftist influences.

Just when it seemed that Stroessner would rule until his death, Paraguayans were surprised in February 1989 when General Andrés Rodríguez—second-in-command of the armed forces, a member of the Traditionalist faction of the Colorado Party, which was in disfavor with the president, and a relative of Stroessner—seized power. Rodríguez's postcoup statements promised the democratization of Paraguay, respect for human rights, repudiation of drug trafficking, and the scheduling of presidential elections. Not surprisingly, General Rodríguez emerged as President Rodríguez. When asked about voting irregularities, Rodríguez indicated that "real" democracy would begin with elections in 1993 and that his rule was a necessary "transition."

"Real" democracy, following the 1993 victory of President Juan Carlos Wasmosy, had a distinct Paraguayan flavor. Wasmosy won the election with 40 percent of the vote; and the Colorado Party, which won most of the seats in Congress, was badly divided. When an opposition victory seemed possible, the military persuaded the outgoing government to push through legislation to reorganize the armed forces. In effect, they were made autonomous.

Later attempts to reform the military precipitated an attempted coup in 1996 by General Lino Oviedo. The resultant furor further divided an already schismatic Colorado Party. Oviedo was arrested, but his friend Raúl Cubas Grau, who was elected president in 1998, immediately sought to release the general. There then followed in rapid succession a decision by the nation's Supreme Court to deny Oviedo's release; the assassination in March 1999 of Vice President Luis Maria Argana, who opposed both Cubas and Oviedo; the forced resignation of the president; and the elevation of the former president of the Senate, Luis Gonzalez Macchi, to the presidency. The new president presides over the first coalition government in Paraguay's history.

THE ECONOMY

It is difficult to acquire accurate statistics about the Paraguayan economy, in part because of the large informal sector and in part because of large-scale smuggling and drug trafficking. It is clear that neighboring Brazil's economic travails have hurt the Paraguayan economy. Officially, the country experienced negative growth in 1998. The new government's privatization plans, needed to raise revenue, must confront the military, which controls the most important state-owned enterprises. There is also concern about the "Brazilianization" of the eastern part of Paraguay, which has developed to the point at which Portuguese is heard as frequently as Spanish or Guaraní, the most common Indian language.

DEVELOPMENT

The devaluation of the Brazilian real in 1999 sent some shock waves through the Paraguayan economy. Also problematic for development was the decision of the U.S. Congress in March 1999 to refuse Paraguay "certification" in the war against drug trafficking as well as the nation's incredibly contentious and unpredictable political scene.

FREEDOM

Monolingual Guaraní speakers suffer from a marked disadvantage in the labor market. Where Guaraní speakers are employed, their wages are much lower than monolingual Spanish speakers. This differential is accounted for by the educational deficiencies of the Guaraní speakers as opposed to those who speak Spanish.

HEALTH/WELFARE

The Paraguayan government spends very little on human services and welfare. As a result, its population is plagued by health problems—including poor levels of nutrition, lack of drinkable water, absence of sanitation, and a prevalence of fatal childhood diseases.

ACHIEVEMENTS

Paraguay has produced several notable authors, including Gabriel Casaccia and Augusto Roa Bastos. Roa Bastos makes extensive use of religious symbolism in his novels as a means of establishing true humanity and justice.

Peru (Peruvian Republic)

GEOGRAPHY

Area in Square Miles (Kilometers):
496,087 (1,285,200) (about the size of Alaska)

Capital (Population): Lima (6,743,000)

Environmental Concerns: deforestation; overgrazing; soil erosion; desertification; air and water pollution

Geographical Features: western coastal plain; high and rugged Andes Mountains in center; eastern lowland jungle of Amazon Basin

Climate: coastal area, arid and mild; Andes, temperate to frigid, eastern lowlands, tropically warm and humid

PEOPLE

Population
Total: 26,625,000
Annual Growth Rate: 1.93%
Rural/Urban Population Ratio: 29/71
Major Languages: Spanish; Quechua; Aymara
Ethnic Makeup: 45% Indian; 37% Mestizo; 15% white; 3% black, Asian, and others
Religions: more than 90% Roman Catholic; others

Health
Life Expectancy at Birth: 68 years (male); 73 years (female)
Infant Mortality Rate (Ratio): 39/1,000
Average Caloric Intake: 98% of FAO minimum
Physicians Available (Ratio): 1/1,116

Education
Adult Literacy Rate: 88.7%
Compulsory (Ages): 6–16; free

COMMUNICATION
Telephones: 1 per 21 people
Daily Newspaper Circulation: 86 per 1,000 people
Televisions: 1 per 10 people

TRANSPORTATION
Highways in Miles (Kilometers): 44,803 (72,146)
Railroads in Miles (Kilometers): 1,267 (2,041)
Usable Airfields: 244
Motor Vehicles in Use: 736,000

GOVERNMENT
Type: republic
Independence Date: July 28, 1821 (from Spain)
Head of State/Government: President Alberto Fujimori is both head of state and head of government

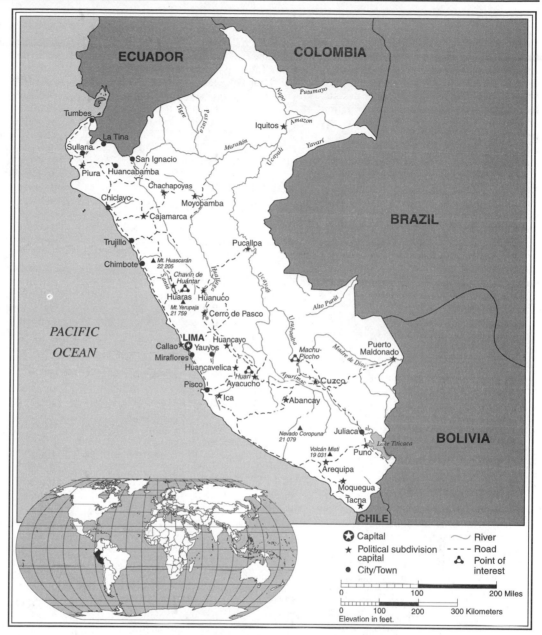

Political Parties: Change 90–New Majority; Union for Peru; Popular Action Party; Popular Christian Party; United Left; Civic Works Movement; Renovation Party; others
Suffrage: universal at 18

MILITARY
Military Expenditures (% of GDP): 1.4%
Current Disputes: boundary dispute with Ecuador being resolved

ECONOMY
Currency ($ U.S. Equivalent): 3.46 nuevo sols = $1
Per Capita Income/GDP: $4,300/$111.8 billion
GDP Growth Rate: 1.8%
Inflation Rate: 6.7%

Unemployment Rate: 8.2% (official rate); extensive underemployment
Labor Force: 7,600,000
Natural Resources: copper; silver; gold; petroleum; timber; fish; iron ore; coal; phosphate; potash
Agriculture: coffee; sugarcane; rice; wheat; potatoes, plantains; coca; livestock; wool; fish
Industry: mining; petroleum; fishing; textiles and clothing; food processing; cement; auto assembly; steel; shipbuilding; metal fabrication
Exports: $6.8 billion (primary partners United States, United Kingdom, Japan, China)
Imports: $10.3 billion (primary partners United States, Colombia, Chile, Venezuela)

PERU: HEIR TO THE INCAS

The culture of Peru, from pre-Hispanic days to the present, has in many ways reflected the nation's variegated geography and climate. While 55 percent of the nation is covered with jungle, coastal Peru boasts one of the world's driest deserts. Despite its forbidding character, irrigation of the desert is made possible by run-offs from the Andes. This allows for the growing of a variety of crops in fertile oases that comprise about 5.5 percent of the land area.

Similarly, in the highlands, or *sierra,* there is little land available for cultivation. Because of the difficulty of the terrain, only about 7 percent of the land can produce crops. Indeed, Peru contains the lowest per capita amount of arable land in South America. The lack of good land has had—and continues to have—profound social and political repercussions, especially in the southern highlands near the city of Ayacucho.

THE SUPREMACY OF LIMA

Historically, coastal Peru and its capital city of Lima have attempted to dominate the sierra—politically, economically, and, at times, culturally. Long a bureaucratic and political center, in the twentieth century Lima presided over the economic expansion of the coast. Economic opportunity in combination with severe population pressure in the sierra caused Lima and its port of Callao to grow tremendously in population, if not in services.

Ironically, the capital city has one of the worst climates for dense human settlement. Thermal inversions are common; between May and September, they produce a cloud ceiling and a pervasive cool fog.

Middle- and upper-class city dwellers have always been ignorant of the people of the highlands. Very few know either Quechua or Aymara, the Indian languages spoken daily by millions of Peruvians. Yet this ignorance of the languages—and, by extension, of the cultures—has not prevented government planners or well-meaning intellectuals from trying to impose a variety of developmental models on the inhabitants of the sierra. In the late nineteenth century, for example, modernizers known collectively in Latin America as Positivists sought in vain to transform indigenous cultures by Europeanizing them. Other reformers sought to identify with the indigenous peoples. In the 1920s, a young intellectual named Victor Raúl Haya de la Torre fashioned a political ideology called APRISMO, which embraced the idea of an alliance of Indoamerica to recover the American states for their original inhabitants. While his broader vision proved to be too idealistic, the specific re-

forms he recommended for Peru were put into effect by reform-minded governments in the 1960s and 1970s. Sadly, reform continued to be developed and imposed from Lima, without an understanding of the rationale behind existing agrarian systems or an appreciation of a peasant logic that was based not on production of a surplus but on attaining a satisfying level of well-being. Much of the turmoil in rural Peru today stems from the agrarian reform of 1968–1979.

AGRARIAN REFORM

From the mid-1950s, rural laborers in the central and southern highlands and on the coastal plantations demonstrated an increasingly insistent desire for agrarian reform. Peasant communities in the sierra staged a series of land invasions and challenged the domination of the large estate, or *hacienda,* from outside. Simultaneously, tenants living on the estates pressured the hacienda system from within. In both cases, peasants wanted land.

The Peruvian government responded with both the carrot and the stick. A military regime, on the one hand, tried to crush peasant insurgency in 1962 and, on the other, passed agrarian reform legislation. The laws had no practical effect, but they did give legal recognition to the problem of land reform. In the face of continued peasant unrest in the south, the military enacted more substantial land laws in 1963, confiscating some property and redistributing it to peasants. The trend toward reform continued with the election of Francisco Belaunde Terry as president of a civilian government. AP

In the face of continued peasant militancy, Belaunde promised far-ranging reforms, but a hostile Congress refused to provide sufficient funds to implement the proposed reforms. Peasant unrest increased, and the government feared the development of widespread rural guerrilla warfare.

Against this backdrop of rural violence, the Peruvian military again seized power in 1968. To the astonishment of most observers, the military chose not to crush popular unrest but, rather, to embrace reforms. Clearly, the military had become sensitive to the political, social, and economic inequalities in Peru that had bred unrest. The military was intent on revolutionizing Peru from the top down rather than waiting for revolution from below.

In addition to land reform, the military placed new emphasis on Peru's Indian heritage. Tupac Amaru, an Incan who had rebelled against Spanish rule in 1780–1781, became a national symbol. In 1975, Quechua, the ancient language of the Inca,

became Peru's second official language (along with Spanish). School curricula were revised and approached Peru's Indian heritage in a new and positive light.

NATIONALIZATION
AND INTEGRATION

Behind the reforms, which were extended to industry and commerce and included the nationalization of foreign enterprises, lay the military's desire to provide for Peru a stable social and political order. The military leaders felt that they could provide better leadership in the quest for national integration and economic development than could "inefficient" civilians. Their ultimate goal was to construct a new society based on citizen participation at all levels.

As is so often the case, however, the reform model was not based on the realities of the society. It was naively assumed by planners that the Indians of the sierra were primitive socialists and wanted collectivized ownership of the land. In reality, each family's interests tended to make it competitive, rather than cooperative, with every other peasant family. Collectivization in the highlands failed because peasant communities outside the old hacienda structure clamored for the return of traditional lands that had been taken from them over the years. The Peruvian government found itself, awkwardly, attempting to defend the integrity of the newly reformed units from peasants who wanted their own land.

THE PATRON

Further difficulties were caused by the disruption of the patron–client relationship in the more traditional parts of the sierra. Hacienda owners, although members of the ruling elite, often enjoyed a tight bond with their tenants. Rather than a boss–worker relationship, the patron–client tie came close to kinship. Hacienda owners, for example, were often godparents to the children of their workers. A certain reciprocity was expected and given. But, with the departure of the hacienda owners, a host of government bureaucrats arrived on the scene, most of whom had been trained on the coast and were ignorant of the customs and languages of the sierra. The peasants who benefited from the agrarian reform looked upon the administrators with a good deal of suspicion. The agrarian laws and decrees, which were all written in Spanish, proved impossible for the peasants to understand. Not surprisingly, fewer than half of the sierra peasants chose to join the collectives; and, in a few places, peasants actually asked for the return of the hacienda owner, someone to

(United Nations photo)

Machu Picchu, a famous Inca ruin, stands atop a 6,750-foot mountain in the Peruvian Andes.

whom they could relate. On the coast, the cooperatives did not benefit all agricultural workers equally, since permanent workers won the largest share of the benefits. In sum, the reforms had little impact on existing trends in agricultural production, failed to reverse income inequalities within the peasant population, and did not ease poverty.

The shortcomings of the reforms—in combination with drought, subsequent crop failures, rising food prices, and population pressure—created very difficult and tense situations in the sierra. The infant mortality rate rose 35 percent between 1978 and 1980, and caloric intake dropped well below the recommended minimum. More than half of the children under age 6 suffered from some form of malnutrition. Rural unrest continued.

RETURN TO CIVILIAN RULE
Unable to solve Peru's problems and torn by divisions within its ranks, the military stepped aside in 1980, and Belaunde was again elected as Peru's constitutional president. Despite the transition to civilian government, unrest continued in the highlands, and the appearance of a left-wing guerrilla organization known as Sendero Luminoso (Shining Path) led the government to declare repeated states of emergency and to lift civil guarantees.

In an attempt to control the situation, the Ministry of Agriculture won the power to restructure and, in some cases, to liquidate the cooperatives and collectives established by the agrarian reform. Land was divided into small individual plots and given to the peasants. Because the plots can be bought, sold, and mortgaged, some critics argue that the undoing of the reform may hasten the return of most of the land into the hands of a new landed elite.

Civilian rule, however, has not necessarily meant democratic rule for Peru's citizens. This helps to explain the spread of Sendero Luminoso despite its radical strategy and tactics of violence. By 1992, according to Diego García-Sayán, the executive director of the Andean Commission of Jurists, the Sendero Luminoso controlled "many parts of Peruvian territory. Through its sabotage, political assassinations, and terrorist actions, Sendero Luminoso has helped to make political violence, which used to be rather infrequent, one of the main characteristics of Peruvian society."

Violence was not confined to the guerrillas of Sendero Luminoso or of the Tupac Amaru Revolutionary Movement (MRTA). Economist Javier Iguíñiz, of the Catholic University of Lima, argued that a solution to the violence required an understanding that it flowed from disparate, autonomous, and competing sources, including guerrillas, right-wing paramilitary groups, the Peruvian military and police forces, and cocaine traffickers, "particularly the well-armed Colombians active in the Huallaga Valley." Sendero Luminoso, until recently, was also active in the Huallaga Valley and profited from taxing drug

traffickers. Raúl González, of Lima's Center for Development Studies, observed that, as both the drug traffickers and the guerrillas "operate[d] outside the law, there has evolved a relationship of mutual convenience in certain parts of Huallaga to combat their common enemy, the state."

President Alan García vacillated on a policy toward the Sendero Luminoso insurgency. But ultimately, he authorized the launching of a major military offensive against Sendero Luminoso bases thought to be linked to drug trafficking. Later, determined to confront an insurgency that claimed 29,000 victims, President Alberto Fujimori armed rural farmers, known as *rondas campesinas,* to fight off guerrilla incursions. (The arming of peasants is not new to Peru; it is a practice that dates to the colonial period.) Critics correctly feared that the accelerated war against insurgents and drug traffickers would only strengthen the Peruvian military's political power.

A BUREAUCRATIC REVOLUTION?
Peruvian author Hernando DeSoto's best-selling and controversial book *The Other Path* (as opposed to Sendero Luminoso, or Shining Path), argues convincingly that both left- and right-wing governments in Latin America in general and in Peru in particular are neo-mercantile—that is, both intervene in the economy and promote the expansion of state activities. "Both strengthened the role of the government's bureaucracy until they made it the main obstacle, rather than the main incentive, to progress, and together they produced, without consulting the electorate, almost 99 percent of the laws governing us." There are differences between left- and right-wing approaches: The left governs with an eye to redistributing wealth and well-being to the neediest groups, and the right tends to govern to serve foreign investors or national business interests. "Both, however, will do so with bad laws which explicitly benefit some and harm others. Although their aims may seem to differ, the result is that in Peru one wins or loses by political decisions. Of course, there is a big difference between a fox and a wolf but, for the rabbit, it is the similarity that counts."

DeSoto attacked the bureaucracy head-on when his private research center, the Institute for Liberty and Democracy, drafted legislation to abolish a collection of requirements built on the assumption that citizens are liars until proven otherwise. The law, which took effect in April 1989, reflected a growing rebellion against bureaucracy in Peru. Another law, which took effect in October 1989, radi-

The Inca Empire is at its height 1500	The Spanish found Lima 1535	Independence is proclaimed 1821	Women gain the right to vote 1955	A military coup: far-reaching reforms are pursued 1968	Debureaucratization campaign begins 1989

1990s

El Niño spreads economic havoc and human misery

Privatization; the economy slows

Fujimori plans a third term, despite constitutional prohibition; public protests mount

cally simplified the process of gaining title to land. (DeSoto discovered that, to purchase a parcel of state-owned land in Peru, one had to invest 56 months of effort and 207 visits to 48 different offices). The legislation will have an important impact on the slum dwellers of Lima, for it will take much less time to regularize land titles as the result of invasions and seizures. Slum dwellers with land titles, according to DeSoto, invest in home improvements at a rate 9 times greater than that of slum dwellers without titles. Slum dwellers who own property will be less inclined to turn to violent solutions to their problems.

The debureaucratization campaign has been paralleled by grassroots social movements that grew in response to a state that no longer could or would respond to the needs of its citizenry. Cataline Romero, director of the Bartolome de Las Cases Institute of Lima, said that "grass-roots social movements have blossomed into political participants that allow historically marginalized people to feel a sense of their own dignity and rights as citizens." Poor people have developed different strategies for survival as the government has failed to meet even their most basic needs. Most have entered the informal sector and have learned to work together through the formation of unions, mothers' clubs, and cooperatives. Concluded Romero: "As crisis tears institutions down, these communities are preparing the ground for building new institutions that are more responsive to the needs of the majority." DeSoto concurs and adds: "No one has ever considered that most poor Peruvians are a step ahead of the revolutionaries and are already changing the country's structures, and what politicians should be doing is guiding the change and giving it an appropriate institutional framework so that it can be properly used and governed."

DEMOCRACY AND THE "SELF-COUP"

In April 1992, President Fujimori, increasingly isolated and unable to effect economic and political reforms, suspended the Constitution, arrested a number of opposition leaders, shut down Congress, and openly challenged the power of the judiciary. The military, Fujimori's staunch ally, openly supported the *autogolpe*, or "self-coup," as did business leaders and about 80 percent of the Peruvian people. In the words of political scientist Cynthia McClintock, writing in *Current History*, "Fujimori emerged a new caudillo, destroying the conventional wisdom that institutions, whether civilian or military, had become more important than individual leaders in Peru and elsewhere in Latin America." In 1993, a constitutional amendment allowed Fujimori to run for a second consecutive term.

In April 1995, Fujimori won a comfortable victory, with 64 percent of the vote. This was attributable to his successful economic policies, which saw the Peruvian economy grow by 12 percent—the highest in the world for 1994—and the campaign against Sendero Luminoso.

To everyone's surprise, however, the guerrillas of MRTA openly challenged the government with their seizure of the Japanese Embassy in Lima in December 1996. The siege continued for months and was a source of embarrassment for the Fujimori administration. None of the guerrillas survived the assault on the embassy by the Peruvian military, although all but one of the hostages was rescued. Despite the apparent success of the operation, serious damage had been done to the prestige of the government. Public-opinion polls in July 1997 revealed that Fujimori's approval rate had fallen to only 19 percent, the lowest in his 7 years of rule. More than three quarters of the respondents felt that Fujimori's government was "dictatorial," and about half of Peruvians surveyed asserted that the government was essentially in the hands of the military. Others felt that the government lacked direction.

The combination of a financial crisis in Asia and the devastation wrought by El Niño storms put Peru to a severe test in 1998 and 1999. Heavy rains and flooding destroyed much of the country's economic infrastructure in coastal areas. Roads, bridges, schools, clinics, and houses were demolished, and marine life and seabirds were decimated. Growth slowed, inflation again became a problem, and political tensions were heightened as the market reforms of the last eight years adversely affected the poorest Peruvians.

Cognizant of presidential elections scheduled for the year 2000, President Fujimori scaled back his privatization program in 1999 to concentrate on a populist campaign designed to win him reelection. Despite constitutional constraints against a third term, Fujimori argues that the Constitution does not apply in his case, because his first term antedated the constitutional reforms that fixed two terms as the limit. To win, he will have to manage a rapid economic recovery, although his opposition is badly divided and there is some question as to whether it could mount a serious challenge.

DEVELOPMENT

Peru, despite some sharp shocks, was one of only three Latin American economies expected to grow in 1999. The manufacturing sector remained weak, and foreign funding was required to meet debt obligations. Weather-related factors reduced exports of fish, fish meal, and agricultural goods.

FREEDOM

Fujimori decided to pave the way for an unconstitutional third term regardless of the wishes of his opponents or, apparently, of the law. He claims that the current Constitution does not apply in his case and has openly harassed and intimidated journalists who have dared to criticize his administration. He seems intent on removing all obstacles to his continuance in office.

HEALTH/WELFARE

The newsweekly *Caretas* of Lima said that one of the keys to Fujimori's success has been a vast public-works program. In rural areas, jobs, health care, and a higher standard of living are issues of great concern. The president convinced rural dwellers that he could deliver on his promises.

ACHIEVEMENTS

Peru has produced a number of literary giants, including José Maria Mariategui, who believed that the "socialism" of the Indians should be a model for the rest of Peru; and Mario Vargas Llosa, always concerned with the complexity of human relationships.

Suriname (Republic of Suriname)

GEOGRAPHY

Area in Square Miles (Kilometers):
63,037 (163,265) (about the size of Georgia)

Capital (Population):
Paramaribo (201,000)

Environmental Concerns:
deforestation; water pollution; threatened wildlife populations

Geographical Features: mostly rolling hills; narrow coastal plain with swamps; mostly tropical rainforest

Climate: tropical

PEOPLE

Population

Total: 431,200

Annual Growth Rate: 0.71%

Rural/Urban Population Ratio: 50/50

Major Languages: Dutch; Sranantonga; English; Hindustani

Ethnic Makeup: 37% Hindustani (locally called East Indian); 31% Creole; 15% Javanese; 10% Bush Negro; 3% Amerindian; 3% Chinese

Religions: 27% Hindu; 25% Prostestants; 23% Roman Catholic; 20% Muslim; 5% others

Health

Life Expectancy at Birth: 68 years (male); 74 years (female)

Infant Mortality Rate (Ratio): 26.5/1,000

Average Caloric Intake: 108% of FAO minimum

Physicians Available (Ratio): 1/1,348

Education

Adult Literacy Rate: 93%

Compulsory (Ages): 6–16

COMMUNICATION

Telephones: 1 per 7.7 people

Daily Newspaper Circulation: 103 per 1,000 people

Televisions: 1 per 7.1 people

TRANSPORTATION

Highways in Miles (Kilometers): 2,813 (4,530)

Railroads in Miles (Kilometers): 103 (166)

Usable Airfields: 46

Motor Vehicles in Use: 66,000

GOVERNMENT

Type: republic

Independence Date: November 25, 1975 (from the Netherlands)

Head of State/Government: President Jules Wijdenbosch is both head of state and head of government

Political Parties: New Front; Progressive Reform Party; National Democratic Party; National Party; others

Suffrage: universal at 18

MILITARY

Military Expenditures (% of GDP): 1.6%

Current Disputes: territorial disputes with Guyana and French Guiana

ECONOMY

Currency ($ U.S. Equivalent): 691.53 Surinamese guilders = $1

Per Capita Income/GDP: $3,500/$1.48 billion

GDP Growth Rate: 2%

Inflation Rate: 20%

Unemployment Rate: 20%

Natural Resources: timber; hydropower; fish; kaolin; shrimp; bauxite; gold; nickel; copper; platinum; iron ore

Agriculture: paddy rice; bananas; palm kernels; coconuts; plantains; peanuts; livestock; forest products; shrimp

Industry: bauxite and gold mining; alumina and aluminum production; lumbering; fish processing; fishing

Exports: $548.8 million (primary partners Norway, Netherlands, United States)

Imports: $551.8 million (primary partners United States, Netherlands, United Kingdom)

 http://www.cia.gov/cia/publications/factbook/ns.html

Map

GUYANA

ATLANTIC OCEAN

Nieuw Nickerie

PARAMARIBO
New Amsterdam
Meerzorg
Wageningen
Totness
Groningen
Overwacht
Albina
Apoera
Nickerie
Bitagron
Brokopondo
Courantyne
Bakhuis
W.J. van Blommestein Lake
Poeloegoedoe Falls
FRENCH GUIANA
Tiger Falls
Hendrick Top ▲3198
Pokigron
Goddo
Kabalebo
Coppename
Saramacca
Suriname
Tapanahony
Maripa Falls
Juliana Top 4034 ▲
Lucie
Grandafoetoe Rapids
Oelemari
Lawa
Commewijne
Moroni
Bofroe Rapids
Courantyne
Polesemu
Litani
Sipaliwini

BRAZIL

Suriname

⊛ Capital
★ District capital
◎ Major city
● City/Town
~ River
---- Road

0 — 60 — 120 Miles
0 — 60 — 120 Kilometers
Elevation in feet.

89

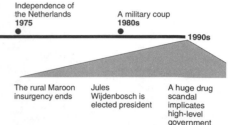

British colonization efforts **1651**

The Dutch receive Suriname from the British in exchange for New Amsterdam **1667**

Independence of the Netherlands **1975**

A military coup **1980s**

1990s

The rural Maroon insurgency ends

Jules Wijdenbosch is elected president

A huge drug scandal implicates high-level government officials

SURINAME:
A SMALL-TOWN STATE

Settled by the British in 1651, Suriname, a small colony on the coast of Guiana, prospered with a plantation economy based on cocoa, sugar, coffee, and cotton. The colony came under Dutch control in 1667; in exchange, the British were given New Amsterdam (Manhattan, New York). The colony was often in turmoil because of Indian and slave uprisings, which took advantage of a weak Dutch power. When slavery was finally abolished, in 1863, plantation owners brought contract workers from China, India, and Java.

Suriname, on the eve of independence of the Netherlands in 1975, was a complex multiracial society. Although existing ethnic tensions were heightened as communal groups jockeyed for power in the new state, other factors cut across racial lines. Even though Creoles (native-born whites) were dominant in the bureaucracy as well as in the mining and industrial sectors, there was sufficient economic opportunity for all ethnic groups, so acute socioeconomic conflict was avoided.

THE POLITICAL FABRIC

Until 1980, Suriname enjoyed a parliamentary democracy that, because of the size of the nation, more closely resembled a small town or extended family in terms of its organization and operation. The various ethnic, political, and economic groups that comprised Surinamese society were united in what sociologist Rob Kroes describes as an "oligarchic web of patron-client relations" that found its expression in government. Through the interplay of the various groups, integration in the political process and accommodation of their needs were achieved. Despite the fact that most interests had access to the center of power, and despite the spirit of accommo-

dation and cooperation, the military seized power early in 1980.

THE ROOTS OF MILITARY RULE

In Kroes's opinion, the coup originated in the army among noncommissioned officers, because they were essentially outside the established social and political system—they were denied their "rightful" place in the patronage network. The officers had a high opinion of themselves and resented what they perceived as discrimination by a wasteful and corrupt government. Their demands for reforms, including recognition of an officers' union, were ignored. In January 1980, one government official talked of disbanding the army altogether.

The coup, masterminded and led by Sergeant Desire Bouterse, had a vague, undefined ideology. It claimed to be nationalist; and it revealed itself to be puritanical, in that it lashed out at corruption and demanded that citizens embrace civic duty and a work ethic. Ideological purity was maintained by government control or censorship of a once-free media. Wavering between left-wing radicalism and middle-of-the-road moderation, the rapid shifts in Bouterse's ideological declarations suggest that this was a policy designed to keep the opposition off guard and to appease factions within the military.

The military rule of Bouterse seemed to come to an end early in 1988, when President Ramsewak Shankar was inaugurated. However, in December 1990, Bouterse masterminded another military coup. The military and Bouterse remained above the rule of law, and the judiciary was not able to investigate or prosecute serious cases involving military personnel.

With regard to Suriname's economic policy, most politicians see integration into Latin American and Caribbean mar-

kets as critical. The Dutch, who suspended economic aid after the 1990 coup, restored their assistance with the election of President Ronald Venetiaan in 1991. But civilian authorities were well aware of the roots of military rule and pragmatically allowed officers a role in government befitting their self-perceived status.

In 1993, Venetiaan confronted the military when it refused to accept his choice of officers to command the army. Army reform was still high on the agenda in 1995 and was identified by President Venetiaan as one of his government's three great tasks. The others were economic reform necessary to ensure Dutch aid and establish the country's eligibility for international credit; and the need to reestablish ties with the interior to consolidate an Organization of American States–brokered peace, after almost a decade of insurgency.

Bouterse made headlines again in 1999 when he was charged by the Dutch government of exporting $1\frac{1}{2}$ metric tons of cocaine to Europe. Particularly troubling was the fact that Bouterse was an adviser to President Jules Wijdenbosch.

DEVELOPMENT

Although Suriname is one of the world's largest bauxite producers, its economy has been in decline for a decade and a half. To compensate, logging rights in tropical rain forests have been signed over to Asian investors, raising merited fears of deforestation.

FREEDOM

The Venetiaan government successfully brought to an end the Maroon insurgency of 8 years' duration. Under the auspices of the Organization of American States, the rebels turned in their weapons, and an amnesty for both sides in the conflict was declared.

HEALTH/WELFARE

Amerindians and Maroons (the descendants of escaped African slaves) who live in the interior have suffered from the lack of educational and social services, partly from their isolation and partly from insurgency. With peace, however, it is hoped that the health, education, and general welfare of these peoples will improve.

ACHIEVEMENTS

Suriname, unlike most other developing countries, has a small foreign debt and a relatively strong repayment capacity. This is substantially due to its export industry.

Uruguay (Oriental Republic of Uruguay)

GEOGRAPHY

Area in Square Miles (Kilometers):
68,037 (176,215) (about the size of Washington State)
Capital (Population):
Montevideo (1,325,000)
Environmental Concerns:
transboundary pollution from Brazilian power plant; water pollution; waste disposal
Geographical Features: mostly rolling plains and low hills; fertile coastal lowland
Climate: warm temperate

PEOPLE

Population
Total: 3,309,000
Annual Growth Rate: 0.73%
Rural/Urban Population Ratio: 9/91
Major Languages: Spanish; Portunol: Brazilero
Ethnic Makeup: 88% white; 8% Mestizo; 4% black
Religions: 66% Roman Catholic; 2% Prostestant; 2% Jewish; 30% nonprofessing or others

Health
Life Expectancy at Birth: 73 years (male); 79 years (female)
Infant Mortality Rate (Ratio): 13.5/1,000
Average Caloric Intake: 110% of FAO minimum
Physicians Available (Ratio): 1/282

Education
Adult Literacy Rate: 97.3%
Compulsory (Ages): 6 years between 6 and 14; free

COMMUNICATION
Telephones: 1 per 5.1 people
Daily Newspaper Circulation: 237 per 1,000 people
Televisions: 1 per 4.3 people

TRANSPORTATION
Highways in Miles (Kilometers): 5,229 (8,420)
Railroads in Miles (Kilometers): 1,859 (2,994)
Usable Airfields. 65
Motor Vehicles in Use: 491,000

GOVERNMENT
Type: republic
Independence Date: August 25, 1828 (from Brazil)
Head of State/Government: President Jorge Battle is both head of state and head of government

Political Parties: National (Blanco) Party factions; Colorado Party factions; Broad Front Coalition; others
Suffrage: universal and compulsory at 18

MILITARY
Military Expenditures (% of GDP): 0.9%
Current Disputes: boundary disputes with Brazil

ECONOMY
Currency ($ U.S. Equivalent): 11.40 pesos = $1
Per Capita Income/GDP: $8,600/$28.4 billion
GDP Growth Rate: 3%
Inflation Rate: 8.6%
Unemployment Rate: 10.5%

Labor Force: 1,380,000
Natural Resources: fertile soil; hydropower; minor minerals; fisheries
Agriculture: wheat; rice; corn; sorghum; livestock; fish
Industry: meat processing; wool and hides; sugar; textiles; footwear; leather apparel; tires; cement; petroleum refining; wine
Exports: $2.7 billion (primary partners Brazil, Argentina, United States)
Imports: $3.7 billion (primary partners Brazil, Argentina, United States)

http://www.lcweb2.loc.gov/frd/cs/uytoc.html
http://www.embassy.org/uruguay/

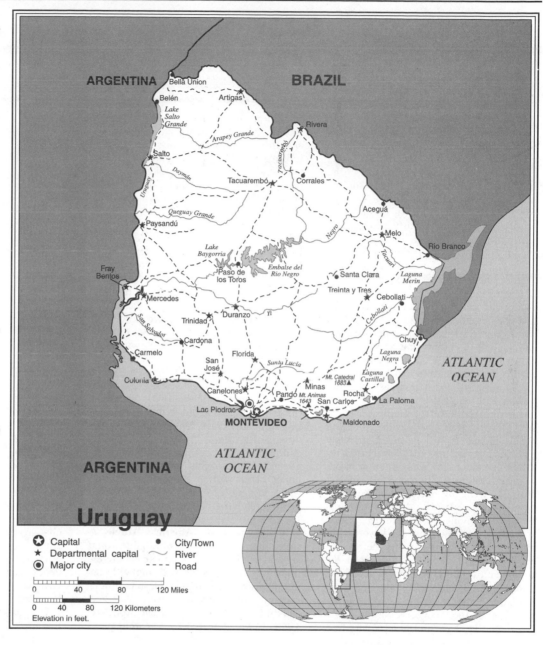

Uruguay

⬤ Capital   ● City/Town
★ Departmental capital   〜 River
◎ Major city   --- Road

0 40 80 120 Miles
0 40 80 120 Kilometers
Elevation in feet.

Jesuits and Franciscans establish missions in the region
1624

Uruguay is established as a buffer state between Argentina and Brazil
1828

The era of President José Batlle y Ordoñez; social reform
1903–1929

Women win the right to vote
1932

Tupamaro guerrillas wage war against the government
1963–1973

1990s

President Julio Maria Sanguinetti returns the Colorado Party to power

The government endorses sweeping economic and social reforms

Jorge Battle is elected president in 1999

URUGUAY: ONCE A PARADISE

The modern history of Uruguay begins with the administration of President José Batlle y Ordoñez. Between 1903 and 1929, Batlle's Uruguay became one of the world's foremost testing grounds for social change, and it eventually became known as the "Switzerland of Latin America." Batlle's Colorado Party supported a progressive role for organized labor and formed coalitions with the workers to challenge the traditional elite and win benefits. Other reforms included the formal separation of church and state, nationalization of key sectors of the economy, and the emergence of mass-based political parties. Batlle's masterful leadership was facilitated by a nation that was compact in size; had a small, educated, and homogeneous population; and had rich soil and a geography that facilitated easy communication and national integration.

Although the spirit of Batllismo eventually faded after his death in 1929, Batlle's legacy is still reflected in many ways. Reports on income distribution reveal an evenness that is uncommon in developing countries. Extreme poverty is unusual in Uruguay, and most of the population enjoy an adequate diet and minimal standards of living. Health care is within the reach of all citizens. And women in Uruguay are granted equality before the law, are present in large numbers at the national university, and have access to professional careers.

But this model state fell on bad times beginning in the 1960s. Runaway inflation, declining agricultural production, a swollen bureaucracy, official corruption, and bleak prospects for the future led to the appearance of youthful middle-class urban guerrillas. Known as Tupamaros, they first attempted to jar the nation to its senses with a Robin Hood–style approach

to reform. When that failed, they turned increasingly to violence and terrorism in an effort to destroy a state that resisted reform. The Uruguayan government was unable to quell the rising violence. It eventually called on the military, which crushed the Tupamaros and then drove the civilians from power in 1973.

RETURN TO CIVILIAN RULE

In 1980, the military held a referendum to try to gain approval for a new constitution. Despite extensive propaganda, 60 percent of Uruguay's population rejected the military's proposals and forced the armed forces to move toward a return to civilian government. Elections in 1984 returned the Colorado Party to power, with Julio Maria Sanguinetti as president.

By 1989, Uruguay was again a country of laws, and its citizens were anxious to heal the wounds of the 1970s. A test of the nation's democratic will involved the highly controversial 1986 Law of Expiration, which effectively exempted military and police personnel from prosecution for alleged human-rights abuses committed under orders during the military regime. Many Uruguayans objected and created a pro-referendum commission. They invoked a provision in the Constitution that is unique to Latin America: Article 79 states that, if 25 percent of eligible voters sign a petition, it will initiate a referendum, which, if passed, will implicitly annul the Law of Expiration. Despite official pressure, the signatures were gathered. The referendum was held on April 16, 1989. It was defeated by a margin of 57 to 43 percent.

The winds of free-market enterprise and privatization are starting to blow through the country. When Sanguinetti regained the presidency in 1994, he was expected, as the leader of the Colorado Party—the

party of Batlle—to maintain the economic status quo. But in 1995, he said that his first priority would be to reform the social-security system, which cannot pay for itself, in large part because people are allowed to retire years earlier than in other countries. Reform was also begun in other sectors of the economy. Government employees were laid off, tariffs were reduced, and a program to privatize state industries was inaugurated. The new policies, according to officials, would produce "a change of mentality and culture" in public administration. How Jorge Battle, Sanguinetti's successor, elected to the presidency late in 1999, will approach Uruguay's economic problems remains to be seen.

Uruguay's affiliation with Mercosur has had a profound effect on the country. According to *LatinFinance,* the regional free-trade association opened borders "so dramatically [that] the national has had to discard traditional secrecy, uncloak its historic insulation, unite with its big neighbors, and embrace competition."

DEVELOPMENT

Former president Sanguinetti inaugurated a reform program with a series of measures designed to reduce the size of Uruguay's public administration. The key provision aimed at reducing personnel in ministries and government agencies by 40%. The object of the downsizing was to reduce the fiscal deficit. President Battle's plan of attack remains to be seen.

FREEDOM

Uruguay's military is constitutionally prohibited from involvement in issues of domestic security unless ordered to do so by civilian authorities. The press is free and unrestricted, as is speech. The political process is open, and academic freedom is the norm in the national university.

HEALTH/WELFARE

Uruguay compares favorably with all of Latin America in terms of health and welfare. Medical care is outstanding, and the quality of public sanitation equals or exceeds that of other developing countries. Women, however, still experience discrimination in the workplace.

ACHIEVEMENTS

Of all the small countries in Latin America, Uruguay has been the most successful in creating a distinct culture. High levels of literacy and a large middle class have allowed Uruguay an intellectual climate that is superior to many much-larger nations.

Venezuela (Bolivarian Republic of Venezuela)

GEOGRAPHY

Area in Square Miles (Kilometers):
352,143 (912,050) (about twice the size of California)

Capital (Population): Caracas (3,007,000)

Environmental Concerns: sewage pollution; oil and urban pollution; deforestation; soil degradation; water and air pollution

Geographical Features: flat coastal plain and Orinoco Delta are bordered by Andes Mountains and hills; plains (llanos) extend between mountains and Orinoco; Guyana Highlands and plains are south of Orinoco

Climate: varies from tropical to temperate

PEOPLE

Population

Total: 23,204,000
Annual Growth Rate: 1.71%
Rural/Urban Population Ratio: 14/86
Major Languages: Spanish; indigenous dialects
Ethnic Makeup: 67% Mestizo; 21% white; 10% black; 2% Indian
Religions: 96% Roman Catholic; 4% Protestant and others

Health

Life Expectancy at Birth: 70 years (male); 76 years (female)
Infant Mortality Rate (Ratio): 27/1,000
Average Caloric Intake: 107% of FAO minimum
Physicians Available (Ratio): 1/576

Education

Adult Literacy Rate: 91%
Compulsory (Ages): 5–15; free

COMMUNICATION

Telephones: 1 per 9 people
Daily Newspaper Circulation: 215 per 1,000 people
Televisions: 1 per 6.1 people

TRANSPORTATION

Highways in Miles (Kilometers): 53,350 (84,300)
Railroads in Miles (Kilometers): 363 (584)
Usable Airfields: 371
Motor Vehicles in Use: 2,012,000

GOVERNMENT

Type: republic
Independence Date: July 5, 1811 (from Spain)
Head of State/Government: President Hugo Chavez Frias is both head of state and head of government

Political Parties: National Convergence; Social Christian Party; Democratic Action; Movement Toward Socialism; Radical Cause; Homeland for All
Suffrage: universal at 18

MILITARY

Military Expenditures (% of GDP): 1%
Current Disputes: territorial disputes with Guyana and Colombia

ECONOMY

Currency ($ U.S. Equivalent): = 643.90 bolívars = $1
Per Capita Income/GDP: $8,500/$194.5 billion
GDP Growth Rate: –0.9%
Inflation Rate: 30%
Unemployment Rate: 11.5%
Labor Force: 9,200,000
Natural Resources: petroleum; natural gas; iron ore; gold; bauxite; other minerals; hydropower; diamonds
Agriculture: corn; sorghum; sugarcane; rice; bananas; vegetables; coffee; livestock; fish
Industry: petroleum; mining; construction materials; food processing; textiles; steel; aluminum; motor-vehicle assembly
Exports: $16.9 billion (primary partners United States, Colombia, Brazil)
Imports: $12.4 billion (primary partners United States, Japan, Colombia)

http://www.lcweb2.loc.gov/frd/cs/vetoc.html
http://venezuela.mit.edu

Map

CARIBBEAN SEA

ATLANTIC OCEAN

GRENADA

TOBAGO

TRINIDAD

Gulf of Venezuela
Punto Fijo
Catia la Mar
San Juan de los Morros
Guacara
Petare
MARGARITA ISLAND
La Asunción
Cumana
Carúpano
Coro
San Felípe
CARACAS
Guanta
General Rafael
Cabimas
Maracay
Barcelona
Mount Turimiquire 8515
Lake Maracaibo
Barquisimeto
Valencia
Lake Valencia
Mount Platillán 6327
Maturín
Acarigua
San Carlos
Tucupita
Trujillo
Guanare
Curiapo
Valera
Barinas
Orinoco
Ciudad Guyana
Pico Bolívar 16 427
Mérida
Mapire
Ciudad Bolívar
Guri Reservoir
San Cristóbal
Apure
Cerro Bolívar 2000
Tumereme
San Fernando de Apure
Orinoco
La Escalera
GUYANA
COLOMBIA
Caura
Caroni
Puerto Ayacucho
Santa Elena
Orinoco
Mount Duida 7952
BRAZIL
Casiquiare
Orinoco

Venezuela

⊗ Capital
★ Political subdivision capital
◉ Major city
• City/Town
∿ River
- - - - Road

0   150   300 Miles
0   150   300   450 Kilometers
Elevation in feet.

93

VENEZUELA: CHANGING TIMES

Venezuela is a country in transition. After decades of rule by a succession of *caudillos* (strong, authoritarian rulers), national leaders can now point to four decades of unbroken civilian rule and peaceful transfers of presidential power. Economic growth—stimulated by mining, industry, and petroleum—has, until recently, been steady and, at times, stunning. With the availability of better transportation; access to radio, television, newspapers, and material goods; and the presence of the national government in once-isolated towns, regional diversity is less striking now than a decade ago. Fresh lifestyles and perspectives, dress and music, and literacy and health care are changing the face of rural Venezuela.

THE PROBLEMS OF CHANGE

Such changes have not been without problems—significant ones. Venezuela, despite its petroleum-generated wealth, remains a nation plagued by imbalances, inequalities, contradictions, and often bitter debate over the meaning and direction of national development. Some critics note the danger of the massive rural-to-urban population shift and the influx of illegal immigrants (from Colombia and other countries), both the result of Venezuela's rapid economic development. Others warn of the excessive dependence on petroleum as the means of development and are concerned about the agricultural output at levels insufficient to satisfy domestic requirements. Venezuela, once a food exporter, periodically has had to import large amounts of basic commodities—such as milk, eggs, and meat—to feed the expanding urban populations. Years of easy, abundant money also promoted undisciplined borrowing abroad to promote industrial expansion and has saddled the nation with a serious foreign-debt problem. Government corruption is rampant and, in fact, led to the impeachment of President Carlos Andrés Pérez in 1993.

THE CHARACTER OF MODERNIZATION

The rapid changes in Venezuelan society have produced a host of generalizations as to the nature of modernization in this Andean republic. Commentators who speak of a revolutionary break with the past—of a "new" Venezuela completely severed from its historic roots reaching back to the sixteenth century—ignore what is enduring about Venezuela's Hispanic culture.

Even before it began producing petroleum, Venezuela was not a sleepy backwater. Its Andean region had always been the most prosperous area in the South American continent and was a refuge from the civil wars that swept other parts of the country. There were both opportunity and wealth in the coffee-growing trade. With the oil boom and the collapse of coffee prices in 1929, the Andean region experienced depopulation as migrants left the farms for other regions or for the growing Andean cities. In short, Venezuela's rural economy should not be seen as a static point from which change began but as a part of a dynamic process of continuing change, which now has the production of petroleum as its focus.

CULTURAL IDENTITY

Historian John Lombardi has identified language, culture, and an urban network centered on the capital city of Caracas as primary forces in the consolidation of the nation. "Across the discontinuities of civil war and political transformation, agricultural and industrial economies, rural life styles and urban agglomerations, Venezuela has functioned through the stable network of towns and cities whose interconnections defined the patterns of control, the directions of resource distribution, and the country's identity."

One example of the country's cultural continuity can be seen by looking into one dimension of Venezuelan politics. Political parties are not organized along class lines but tend to cut across class divisions. This is not to deny the existence of class consciousness—which is certainly ubiquitous in Venezuela—but it is not a major *political* force. Surprisingly, popular support for elections and strong party affiliations are

(United Nations photo/H. Null)

When oil was discovered in Venezuela, rapid economic growth caused many problems in national development. By depending on petroleum as the major source of wealth, Venezuela was at the mercy of the fickle world energy market.

more characteristic of rural areas than of cities. The phenomenon cannot be explained as a by-product of modernization. Party membership and electoral participation are closely linked to party organization, personal ties and loyalties, and charismatic leadership. The party, in a sense, becomes a surrogate *patrón* that has power and is able to deliver benefits to the party faithful.

IMPACTS OF URBANIZATION

Another insight into Hispanic political culture can be found in the rural-to-urban shift in population that has often resulted in large-scale seizures of land in urban areas by peasants. Despite the illegality of the seizures, such actions are frequently encouraged by officials because, they argue, it provides the poor with enough land to maintain political stability and to prevent peasants from encroaching on richer neighborhoods. Pressure by the new urban dwellers at election time usually results in their receiving essential services from government officials. In other words, municipal governments channel resources in return for expected electoral support from the migrants. Here is a classic Hispanic response to challenge from below—to bend, to cooperate.

Cultural values also underlie both the phenomenon of internal migration and the difficulty of providing adequate skilled labor for Venezuela's increasingly technological economy. While the attraction of the city and its many opportunities is one reason for the movement of population out of rural areas, so too is the Venezuelan culture, which belittles the peasant and rural life in general. Similarly, the shortage of skilled labor is the result not only of inadequate training but also of social values that neither reward nor dignify skilled labor.

THE SOCIETY

The rapid pace of change has contributed to a reexamination of the roles and rights of women in Venezuela. In recent years, women have occupied positions in the cabinet and in the Chamber of Deputies; several women deputies have held important posts in political parties.

Yet while educated women are becoming more prominent in the professions, there is a reluctance to employ women in traditional "men's" jobs, and blatant inequality still blemishes the workplace. Women, for example, are paid less than men for similar work. And although modern feminist goals have become somewhat of a social and economic force, at least in urban centers, the traditional roles of wife and mother continue to hold the most prestige, and physical beauty is still often viewed as a woman's most precious asset. In addition, many men seek deference from women rather than embracing social equality. Nevertheless, the younger generations of Venezuelans are experiencing the social and cultural changes that have tended to follow women's liberation in Western industrialized nations: higher levels of education and career skills; broadened intellectualism; increasing freedom and equality for both men and women; relaxed social mores; and the accompanying personal turmoil, such as rising divorce and single-parenthood rates.

Venezuelans generally enjoy a high degree of individual liberty. Civil, personal, and political rights are protected by a strong and independent judiciary. Citizens generally enjoy a free press. There exists the potential for governmental abuse of press freedom, however. Several laws leave journalists vulnerable to criminal charges, especially in the area of libel. Journalists must be certified to work, and certification may be withdrawn by the government if journalists stray from the "truth," misquote sources, or refuse to correct "errors." But, as a rule, radio, televi-

(Photo Lioa Clydo)

Caracas, Venezuela, an ultra-modern city of 3 million exemplifying the extremes of poverty and wealth that exist in Latin America, sprawls for miles over mountains and valleys.

sion, and newspapers are free and are often highly critical of the government.

The civil and human rights enjoyed by most Venezuelans have not necessarily extended to the nation's Indian population in the Orinoco Basin. For years, extraregional forces—in the form of rubber gatherers, missionaries, and developers—have, to varying degrees, undermined the economic self-sufficiency, demographic viability, and tribal integrity of indigenous peoples. A government policy that stresses the existence of only one Venezuelan culture poses additional problems for Indians.

In 1991, however, President Pérez signed a decree granting a permanent homeland, encompassing some 32,000 square miles in the Venezuelan Amazon forest, to the country's 14,000 Yanomamö Indians. Venezuela will permit no mining or farming in the territory and will impose controls on existing religious missions. President Pérez stated that "the primary use will be to preserve and to learn the traditional ways of the Indians." As James Brooke reported in *The New York Times*, "Venezuela's move has left anthropologists euphoric."

Race relations are outwardly tranquil in Venezuela, but there exists an underlying racism in nearly all arenas. People are commonly categorized by the color of their skin, with white being the most prized. Indeed, race, not economic level, is still the major social-level determinant. This unfortunate reality imparts a sense of frustration and a measure of hopelessness to many of Venezuela's people, in that even those who acquire a good education and career training may be discriminated against in the workplace because they are "of color." Considering that only one fifth of the population are of white extraction, with 67 percent Mestizos and 10 percent blacks, this is indeed a widespread and debilitating problem.

A VIGOROUS FOREIGN POLICY

Venezuela has always pursued a vigorous foreign policy. In the words of former president Luis Herrera Campins: "Effective action by Venezuela in the area of international affairs must take certain key facts into account: economics—we are a producer-exporter of oil; politics—we have a stable, consolidated democracy; and geopolitics—we are at one and the same time a Caribbean, Andean, Atlantic, and Amazonian country." Venezuela has long assumed that it should be the guardian of Simón Bolívar's ideal of creating an independent and united Latin America. The nation's memory of its continental leadership, which developed during the Wars for Independence (1810–1826), has been rekindled in Venezuela's desire to

promote the political and economic integration of both the continent and the Caribbean. Venezuela's foreign policy remains true to the Bolivarian ideal of an independent Latin America. It also suggests a prominent role for Venezuela in Central America. In the Caribbean, Venezuela has emerged as a source of revenue for the many microstates in the region; the United States is not without competitors for its Caribbean Basin Initiative.

PROMISING PROSPECTS TURN TO DISILLUSIONMENT

The 1980s brought severe turmoil to Venezuela's economy. The boom times of the 1970s turned to hard times as world oil prices dropped. Venezuela became unable to service its massive foreign debt (currently $40.1 billion) and to subsidize the "common good," in the form of low gas and transportation prices and other amenities. In 1983, the currency, the bolívar, which had remained stable and strong for many years at 4.3 to the U.S. dollar, was devalued, to an official rate of 14.5 bolívars to the dollar. This was a boon to foreign visitors to the country, which became known as one of the world's greatest travel bargains, but a catastrophe for Venezuelans. (In early 2000, the exchange rate was about 650.0 bolívars to the dollar on the free market.)

President Jaime Lusinchi of the Democratic Action Party, who took office early in 1984, had the unenviable job of trying to cope with the results of the preceding years of free spending, high expectations, dependence on oil, and spiraling foreign debt. Although the country's gross national product grew during his tenure (agriculture growth contributed significantly, rising from 0.4 percent of GNP in 1983 to 6.8 percent in 1986), austerity measures were in order. The Lusinchi government was not up to the challenge. Indeed, his major legacy was a corruption scandal at the government agency Recadi, which was responsible for allocating foreign currency to importers at the official rate of 14.5 bolívars to the dollar. It was alleged that billions of dollars were skimmed, with a number of high-level government officials, including three finance ministers, implicated. Meanwhile, the distraught and economically pinched Venezuelans watched inflation and the devalued bolívar eat up their savings; the once-blooming middle class started getting squeezed out.

In the December 1988 national elections, another Democratic Action president, Carlos Andrés Pérez, was elected. Pérez, who had served as president from 1974 to 1979 (presidents may not serve consecutive terms), was widely rumored

to have stolen liberally from Venezuela's coffers during that tenure. Venezuelans joked at first that "Carlos Andrés is coming back to get what he left behind," but as the campaign wore on, some political observers were dismayed to hear the preponderance of the naive sentiment that "now he has enough and will really work for Venezuela this time."

One of Pérez's first acts upon re-entering office was to raise the prices of government-subsidized gasoline and public transportation. Although he had warned that tough austerity measures would be implemented, the much-beleaguered and disgruntled urban populace took to the streets in February 1989 in the most serious rioting to have occurred in Venezuela since it became a democracy. Army tanks rolled down the major thoroughfares of Caracas, the capital; skirmishes between the residents and police and military forces were common; looting was widespread. The government announced that 287 people had been killed. Unofficial hospital sources charge that the death toll was closer to 2,000. A stunned Venezuela quickly settled down in the face of the violence, mortified that such a debacle, widely reported in the international press, should take place in this advanced and peaceable country. But tourism, a newly vigorous and promising industry as a result of favorable currency-exchange rates, subsided immediately; it has yet to recover fully.

On February 4, 1992, another ominous event highlighted Venezuela's continuing political and economic weaknesses. Rebel military paratroopers, led by Hugo Chavez, attacked the presidential palace in Caracas and government sites in several other major cities. The coup attempt, the first in Venezuela since 1962, was rapidly put down by forces loyal to President Pérez, who escaped what he described as an assassination attempt. Reaction within Venezuela was mixed, reflecting widespread discontent with Pérez's tough economic policies, government corruption, and declining living standards. A second unsuccessful coup attempt, on November 27, 1992, followed months of public demonstrations against Pérez's government.

Perhaps the low point was reached in May 1993, when Pérez was suspended from office and impeachment proceedings initiated. Allegedly the president had embezzled more than $17 million and had facilitated other irregularities. Against a backdrop of military unrest, Ramón José Velásquez was named interim president.

In December 1993, Venezuelans elected Rafael Caldera, who had been president in a more prosperous and promising era (1969–1974). Caldera's presidency too

Timeline:

The first Spanish settlement at Cumaná
1520

Venezuela is part of Gran Colombia
1822–1829

Venezuela achieves independence as a separate country
1829

The first productive oil well
1922

Women win the right to vote
1947

Foreign oil companies are nationalized
1976

Booming public investment fuels inflation; Venezuela seeks renegotiation of foreign debt
1980s

1990s

Social and economic crisis grips the nation; failure of President Caldera's "Agenda Venezuela" program

Hugo Chavez wins the presidential elections of 1998 and sets about to redraft the Constitution

Chavez's government is challenged by massive flooding that leaves more than 30,000 people dead and many more homeless

was fraught with problems. In his first year, he had to confront widespread corruption in official circles, the devaluation of the bolívar, drug trafficking, a banking structure in disarray, and a high rate of violent crime in Caracas. Indeed, in 1997, a relative of President Caldera was mugged and a Spanish diplomat who had traveled to Caracas to negotiate a trade agreement with Venezuela was robbed in broad daylight.

In an attempt to restore order from chaos, President Caldera inaugurated his "Agenda Venezuela" program to address the difficult problems created by deep recession, financial instability, deregulation, privatization, and market reforms. The plan was showing signs of progress when it was undercut by the collapse of petroleum prices.

The stage was thus set for the emergence of a "hero" who would promise to solve all of Venezuela's ills. In the presidential election of 1998, the old parties were swept from power and a populist— the same Hugo Chavez who had attempted a coup in 1992—won with 55 percent of the popular vote. Those who expected change were not disappointed, although some of Chavez's actions have raised concerns about the future of democracy in Venezuela. A populist and a pragmatist, it is difficult to ascertain where Chavez's often contradictory policies will lead. Since taking power in February 1999, he has placed the army in control of the operation of medical clinics and has put soldiers to work on road and sewer repairs and in school and hospital construction. He has talked about the need to cut costs and uproot what he perceives as a deeply corrupt public sector—but he has refused

to downsize the bureaucracy. Chavez supports privatization of the nation's pension fund and electric utilities, but he wants to maintain state control over health care and the petroleum industry. He wants more free-trade initiatives with foreign nations but at the same time threatens to prohibit some agricultural imports.

Perhaps of greater concern is Chavez's successful bid to redraft Venezuela's Constitution, to provide "a better version." He claimed that the document had eroded democracy by allowing a political elite to rule without restraint for decades. Chavez's "democratic" vision demands special powers to revamp the economy without congressional approval. Through clever manipulation of the people by means of his own radio and television shows, and newspaper, Chavez intimidated Congress into granting him almost all the power he wanted to enact financial and economic legislation by decree. A referendum in April 1999 gave him a huge majority supporting the creation of an assembly to redraft the Constitution. A draft was completed in November. The political opposition was convinced that the new document would allow Chavez to seek a second consecutive term in office, which had been prohibited in Venezuela, and that he was doing nothing less than creating a dictatorship under the cover of democracy and the law. Their fears have been realized, as the new Constitution allows for consecutive six-year terms.

Equally radical and unpredictable is Chavez's policy toward neighboring Colombia. For years Venezuelan governments gave the military the task to monitor the border with Colombia. In 1995, the army moved through border ar-

eas and rounded up more than 1,000 illegal Colombian aliens, burned some of their homes and crops, and expelled them. Chavez, in response to violence directed at Venezuelan truckers in Colombia by guerrillas or bandits, took the extraordinary move in July 1999 of closing the border between the two countries. While this might demonstrate seriousness of purpose, the border closure had immediate and detrimental effects on the economics of both nations, given the large volume of cross border trade.

Venezuela's future is wholly unpredictable in large measure because its current government is unpredictable. It is not a formula that seems likely to assure long-term success.

DEVELOPMENT

The policies of President Chavez have led to a good deal of uncertainty in foreign and domestic economic, financial, and commercial circles. The fiscally responsible policies he announced just after taking office—including, bringing about a sharp reduction in the budget deficit by raising new taxes, cutting spending, restructuring debt, and imposing austerity, are in limbo.

FREEDOM

Venezuela has a free and vigorous daily press, numerous weekly news magazines, 3 nationwide television networks, and nearly 200 radio stations. Censorship or interference with the media on political grounds is rare. Venezuela has traditionally been a haven for refugees and displaced persons. "Justice" in the justice system remains elusive for the poor.

HEALTH/WELFARE

A 1997 survey of children working in the informal sector revealed that 25% were between ages 5 and 12; that they worked more than 7 hours a day and earned about $2; and that their "jobs" included garbage collection, lotteries and gambling, and selling drugs. Fewer than half attended school.

ACHIEVEMENTS

Venezuela's great novelists, such as Rómulo Gallegos and Artúro Uslar Pietri, have been attracted by the barbarism of the backlands and the lawlessness native to rural regions. Gallegos's classic *Doña Barbara*, the story of a female regional chieftain, has become world-famous.

The Caribbean

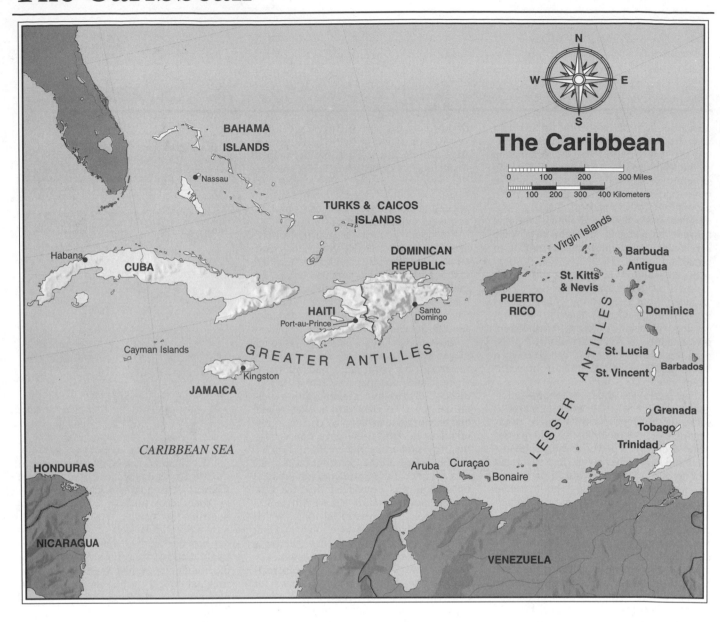

The Caribbean region consists of hundreds of islands stretching from northern South America to the southern part of Florida. Many of the islands cover just a few square miles and are dominated by a central range of mountains; only Cuba has any extensive lowlands. Almost every island has a ring of coral, making approaches very dangerous for ships. The land that can be used for agriculture is extremely fertile; but many islands grow only a single crop, making them vulnerable to fluctuations in the world market in that particular commodity.

The Caribbean: Sea of Diversity

To construct a coherent overview of the Caribbean is an extremely difficult task because of the region's profound geographical and cultural diversity. "The history of the Caribbean is the examination of fragments, which, like looking at a broken vase, still provides clues to the form, beauty, and value of the past." So writes historian Franklin W. Knight in his study of the Caribbean. Other authors have drawn different analogies: geographer David Lowenthal and anthropologist Lambros Comitas note that the West Indies "is a set of mirrors in which the lives of black, brown, and white, of American Indian and East Indian, and a score of other minorities continually interact."

For the geographer, the pieces fall into a different pattern, consisting of four distinct geographical regions. The first contains the Bahamas as well as the Turks and Caicos Islands. The Greater Antilles—consisting of Cuba, Hispaniola (Haiti and the Dominican Republic), Jamaica, the Cayman Islands, Puerto Rico, and the Virgin Islands—make up the second region. Comprising the third region are the Lesser Antilles—Antigua and Barbuda, Dominica, St. Lucia, St. Vincent and the Grenadines, Grenada, and St. Kitts and Nevis as well as various French departments and British and Dutch territories. The fourth group consists of islands that are part of the South American continental shelf: Trinidad and Tobago, Barbados, and the Dutch islands of Aruba, Curaçao, and Bonaire. Within these broad geographical regions, each nation is different. On each island there often is a firmly rooted parochialism—a devotion to a parish or a village, a mountain valley or a coastal lowland.

CULTURAL DIVERSITY

To break down the Caribbean region into culture groups presents its own set of problems. The term "West Indian" inadequately describes the culturally Hispanic nations of Cuba and the Dominican Republic. On the other hand, "West Indian" does capture the essence of the cultures of Belize, the Caribbean coast of Central America, and Guyana, Suriname, and Cayenne (French Guiana). In Lowenthal's view: "Alike in not being Iberian [Hispanic], the West Indies are not North American either, nor indeed do they fit any ordinary regional pattern. Not so much undeveloped as overdeveloped, exotic without being traditional, they are part of the Third World yet ardent emulators of the West."

EFFORTS AT INTEGRATION

To complicate matters further, few West Indians would identify themselves as such. They are Jamaicans, or Bajans (people from Barbados), or Grenadans. Their economic, political, and social worlds are usually confined to the islands on which they live and work. In the eyes of its inhabitants, each island, no matter how small, is—or should be—sovereign.

Communications by air, sea, and telephone with the rest of the world are ordinarily better than communications within the Caribbean region itself. Trade, even between neighboring islands, has always been minimal. Economic ties with the United States or Europe, and in some cases with Venezuela, are more important.

A British attempt to create a "West Indies Federation" in 1958 was reduced to a shambles by 1962. Member states had the same historical background; spoke the same languages; had similar economies; and were interested in the same kinds of food, music, and sports. But their spirit of independence triumphed over any kind of regional federation that "threatened" their individuality. In the words of a former Bajan prime minister, "We live together very well, but we don't like to live together *together.*" A Trinidadian explanation for the failure of the federation is found in a popular calypso verse from the early 1960s:

Plans was moving fine
When Jamaica stab we from behind
Federation bust wide open
But they want Trinidad to bear the burden.

Recently, however, the Windward Islands (Dominica, Grenada, St. Lucia, and St. Vincent and the Grenadines) have discussed political union. While each jealously guards its sovereignty, leaders are nevertheless aware that some integration is necessary if they are to survive in a changing world. The division of the world into giant economic blocs points to political union and the creation of a Caribbean state with a combined population of nearly half a million. Antigua and Barbuda resist because they believe that, in the words of former prime minister Vere Bird, "political union would be a new form of colonialism and undermine sovereignty."

While political union remains problematic, the 15 members of the Caribbean Community and Common Market (CARICOM, a regional body created in 1973) began long-term negotiations with Cuba in 1995 with regard to a free-trade agreement. CARICOM leaders informed Cuba that "it needs to open up its economy more." The free-market economies of CARICOM are profoundly different from Cuba's rigid state controls. "We need to assure that trade and investment will be mutually beneficial." Caribbean leaders have pursued trade with Cuba in the face of strong opposition from the United States. In general, CARICOM countries are convinced that "constructive engagement" rather than a policy of isolation is the best way to transform Cuba.

Political problems also plague the Dutch Caribbean. Caribbean specialist Aaron Segal notes that the six-island Netherlands Antilles Federation has encountered severe internal difficulties. Aruba never had a good relationship with the larger island of Curaçao and, in 1986, became a self-governing entity, with its own flag, Parliament, and currency, but still *within* the Netherlands. "The other Netherlands Antillean states have few complaints about their largely autonomous relations with the Netherlands but find it hard to get along with one another."

Interestingly, islands that are still colonial possessions generally have a better relationship with their "mother" countries than with one another. Over the past few decades, smaller islands—populations of about 50,000 or less—have learned that there are advantages to a continued colonial connection. The extensive subsidies paid by Great Britain, France, or the Netherlands have turned dependency into an asset. Tax-free offshore sites for banks and companies as well as tourism and hotel investments have led to modest economic growth.

CULTURAL IDENTIFICATION

Yet, despite the local focus of the islanders, there do exist some broad cultural similarities. To the horror of nationalists, who are in search of a Caribbean identity that is distinct from Western civilization, most West Indians identify themselves as English or French in terms of culture. Bajans, for example, take a special pride in identifying their country as the "Little England of the Caribbean." English or French dialects are the languages spoken in common.

Nationalists argue that the islands will not be wholly free until they shatter the European connection. In the nationalists' eyes, that connection is a bitter reminder of slavery. After World War II, several Caribbean intellectuals attacked the strong European orientation of the islands and urged the

islanders to be proud of their black African heritage. The shift in focus was most noticeable in the French Caribbean, although this new ethnic consciousness was echoed in the English-speaking islands as well in the form of a black-power movement during the 1960s and 1970s. It was during those years, when the islands were in transition from colonies to associated states to independent nations, that the Caribbean's black majorities seized political power by utilizing the power of their votes.

It is interesting to note that at the height of the black-power and black-awareness movements, sugar production was actually halted on the islands of St. Vincent, Antigua, and Barbuda—not because world market prices were low, but because sugar cultivation was associated with the slavery of the past.

African Influences

The peoples of the West Indies are predominantly black, with lesser numbers of "mixed bloods" and small numbers of whites. Culturally, the blacks fall into a number of groups. In Haiti, blacks, throughout the nineteenth century, strove to realize an African-Caribbean identity. African influences have remained strong on the island, although they have been blended with European Christianity and French civilization.

(United Nations photo/King)

These Jamaican agricultural workers, who reflect the strong African heritage of the Caribbean, contribute to the ethnic and cultural diversity of the region.

Mulattos, traditionally the elite in Haiti, have strongly identified with French culture in an obvious attempt to distance themselves from the black majority, who comprise about 95 percent of the population. African-Creoles, as blacks of the English-speaking islands prefer to be called, are manifestly less "African" than the mass of Haitians. An exception to this generalization is the Rastafarians, common in Jamaica and found in lesser numbers on some of the other islands. Convinced that they are Ethiopians, the Rastafarians hope to return to Africa.

Racial Tension

The Caribbean has for years presented an image of racial harmony to the outside world. Yet, in actuality, racial tensions are not only present but also have become sharper during the past few decades. Racial unrest broke to the surface in Jamaica in 1960 with riots in the capital city of Kingston. Tensions heightened again in 1980–1981 and in 1984, to the point that the nation's tourist industry drastically declined. A recent slogan of the Jamaican tourist industry, "Make It Jamaica Again," was a conscious attempt to downplay racial antagonism. The black-power movement in the 1960s on most of the islands also put to the test notions of racial harmony.

Most people of the Caribbean, however, believe in the myth of racial harmony. It is essential to the development of nationalism, which must embrace all citizens. Much racial tension is officially explained as class difference rather than racial prejudice. There is some merit to the class argument. A black politician on Barbuda, for example, enjoys much more status and prestige than a poor white "Redleg" from the island's interior. Yet if a black and a Redleg competed for the job of plantation manager, the white would likely win out over the black. In sum, race does make a difference, but so too does one's economic or political status.

East Indians

The race issue is more complex in Trinidad and Tobago, where there is a large East Indian (i.e., originally from India) minority. The East Indians, for the most part, are agricultural workers. They were originally introduced by the British between 1845 and 1916 to replace slave labor on the plantations. While numbers of East Indians have moved to the cities, they still feel that they have little in common with urban blacks. Because of their large numbers, East Indians are able to preserve a distinctive, healthy culture and community and to compete with other groups for political office and status.

East Indian culture has also adapted, but not yielded, to the West Indian world. In the words of Trinidadian-East Indian author V. S. Naipaul: "We were steadily adopting the food styles of others: The Portuguese stew of tomato and onions ... the Negro way with yams, plantains, breadfruit, and bananas," but "everything we adopted became our own; the outside was still to be dreaded...." The East Indians in

(Photo Lisa Clyde)

The weekly open-air market in St. Lucia provides a variety of local produce.

Jamaica, who make up about 3 percent of the population, have made even more accommodations to the cultures around them. Most Jamaican-East Indians have become Protestant (the East Indians of Trinidad have maintained their Hindu or Islamic faith).

East Indian conformity and internalization, and their strong cultural identification, have often made them the targets of the black majority. Black stereotypes of the East Indians describe them in the following terms: "secretive," "greedy," and "stingy." And East Indian stereotypes describing blacks as "childish," "vain," "pompous," and "promiscuous" certainly do not help to ease ethnic tensions.

REVOLUTIONARY CUBA

In terms of culture, the Commonwealth Caribbean (former British possessions) has little in common with Cuba or the Dominican Republic. But Cuba has made its presence felt in other ways. The Cuban Revolution, with the social progress that it entailed for many of its people and the strong sense of nationalism that it stimulated, impressed many West Indians. For new nation-states still in search of an identity, Cuba offered some clues as to how to proceed. For a time, Jamaica experimented with Cuban models of mass mobilization and programs designed to bring social services

Certain crops in Caribbean countries generate a disproportionate amount of the nations' foreign incomes—so much so that their entire economies are vulnerable to changes in world demand. This harvest of bananas in Dominica is ready for shipment to a fickle world market.

to the majority of the population. Between 1979 and 1983, Grenada saw merit in the Cuban approach to problems. The message that Cuba seemed to represent was that a small Caribbean state could shape its own destiny and make life better for its people.

The Cuba of Fidel Castro, while revolutionary, is also traditional. Hispanic culture is largely intact. The politics are authoritarian and personality-driven, and Castro himself easily fits into the mold of the Latin American leader, or *caudillo,* whose charisma and benevolent paternalism win him the widespread support of his people. Castro's relationship with the Roman Catholic Church is also traditional and corresponds to notions of a dualistic culture that has its roots in the Middle Ages. In Castro's words: "The same respect that the Revolution ought to have for religious beliefs, ought also to be had by those who talk in the name of religion for the political beliefs of others. And, above all, to have present that which Christ said: 'My kingdom is not of this world.' What are those who are said to be the interpreters of Christian thought doing meddling in the problems of this world?" Castro's comments should not be interpreted as a Communist assault on religion. Rather, they express a time-honored Hispanic belief that religious life and everyday life exist in two separate spheres.

The social reforms that have been implemented in Cuba are well within the powers of all Latin American governments to enact. Those governments, in theory, are duty-bound to provide for the welfare of their peoples. Constitutionally, the state is infallible and all-powerful. Castro has chosen to identify with the needs of the majority of Cubans, to be a "father" to his people. Again, his actions are not so much Communistic as Hispanic.

Where Castro has run against the grain is in his assault on Cuba's middle class. In a sense, he has reversed a trend that is evident in much of the rest of Latin America—the slow, steady progress of a middle class that is intent on acquiring a share of the power and prestige traditionally accorded to elites. Cuba's middle class was effectively shattered—people were deprived of much of their property; their livelihood; and, for those who fled into exile, their citizenship. Many expatriate Cubans remain bitter toward what they perceive as Castro's betrayal of the Revolution and the middle class.

EMIGRATION AND MIGRATION
Throughout the Caribbean, emigration and migration are a fact of life for hundreds of thousands of people. These are not new phenomena; their roots extend to the earliest days of European settlement. The flow of people looking for work is

deeply rooted in history, in contemporary political economy, and even in Caribbean island culture. The Garifuna (black–Indian mixture) who settled in Belize and coastal parts of Mexico, Guatemala, Honduras, and Nicaragua originally came from St. Vincent. There, as escaped slaves, they intermixed with remnants of Indian tribes who had once peopled the islands, and they adopted many of their cultural traits. Most of the Garifuna (or Black Caribs, as they are also known) were deported from St. Vincent to the Caribbean coast of Central America at the end of the eighteenth century.

From the 1880s onward, patois-speaking (French dialect) Dominicans and St. Lucians migrated to Cayenne (French Guiana) to work in the gold fields. The strong identification with Europe has drawn thousands more to what many consider their cultural homes.

High birth rates and lack of economic opportunity have forced others to seek their fortunes elsewhere. Many citizens of the Dominican Republic have moved to New York, and Haitian refugees have thrown themselves on the coast of Florida by the thousands. Other Haitians seek seasonal employment in the Dominican Republic or the Bahamas. There are sizable Jamaican communities in the Dominican Republic, Haiti, the Bahamas, and Belize.

On the smaller islands, stable populations are the exception rather than the rule. The people are constantly migrating to larger places in search of higher pay and a better life. Such emigrants moved to Panama when the canal was being cut in the early 1900s or sought work on the Dutch islands of Curaçao and Aruba when oil refineries were built there in the 1920s. They provided much of the labor for the banana plantations in Central America.

The greatest number of people by far have left the Caribbean region altogether and emigrated to the United States, Canada, and Europe. Added to those who have left because of economic or population pressures are political refugees. The majority of these are Cubans, most of whom have resettled in Florida.

Some have argued that the prime mover of migration from the Caribbean lies in the *ideology* of migration—that is, the expectation that all nonelite males will migrate abroad. Sugarcane slave plantations left a legacy that included little possibility of island subsistence; and so there grew the need to migrate to survive, a fact that was absorbed into the culture of lower-class blacks. But, for these blacks, there has also existed the expectation to return. (In contrast, middle- and upper-class migrants have historically departed permanently.) Historian Bonham Richardson writes: "By traveling away and returning the people have been able to cope more successfully with the vagaries of man and nature than they would have by staying at home. The small islands of the region are the most vulnerable to environmental and economic uncertainty. Time and again in the Lesser Antilles, droughts, hurricanes, and economic depressions have diminished wages, desiccated provision grounds, and destroyed livestock, and there has been no local recourse to disease or starvation." Hence men and women of the small West Indian islands have been obliged to migrate. "And like migrants everywhere, they have usually considered their travels tem-

(United Nations photo/J. Viesti)

Economic hardship in the Caribbean region is exemplified by this settlement in Port-au-Prince, Haiti. Such grinding poverty causes large numbers of people to migrate in search of a better life.

porary, partly because they have never been greeted cordially in host communities."

On the smaller islands, such as St. Kitts and Nevis, family and community ceremonies traditionally reinforce and sustain the importance of immigration and return. Funerals reunite families separated by vast distances; Christmas parties and carnival celebrations are also occasions to welcome returning family and friends.

Monetary remittances from relatives in the United States, or Canada, or the larger islands are a constant reminder of the importance of migration. According to Richardson: "Old men who have earned local prestige by migrating and returning exhort younger men to follow in their footsteps. . . . Learned cultural responses thereby maintain a migration ethos . . . that is not only valuable in coping with contemporary problems, but also provides continuity with the past."

The Haitian diaspora (dispersion) offers some significant differences. While Haitian migration is also a part of the nation's history, a return flow is noticeably absent. One of every six Haitians now lives abroad—primarily in Cuba, the Dominican Republic, Venezuela, Colombia, Mexico, and the Bahamas. In French Guiana, Haitians comprise more than 25 percent of the population. They are also found in large numbers in urban areas of the United States, Canada, and France. The typical Haitian emigrant is poor, has little education, and has few skills or job qualifications.

Scholar Christian A. Girault remarks that although "ordinary Haitian migrants are clearly less educated than the Cubans, Dominicans, Puerto Ricans and even Jamaicans, they are not Haiti's most miserable; the latter could never hope to buy an air ticket or boat passage, or to pay an agent." Those who establish new roots in host countries tend to remain, even though they experience severe discrimination and are stereotyped as "undesirable" because they are perceived as bringing with them "misery, magic and disease," particularly AIDS.

There is also some seasonal movement of population on the island itself. Agricultural workers by the tens of thousands are found in neighboring Dominican Republic. *Madames sara,* or peddlers, buy and sell consumer goods abroad and provide "an essential provisioning function for the national market."

AN ENVIRONMENT IN DANGER

When one speaks of soil erosion and deforestation in a Caribbean context, Haiti is the example that usually springs to mind. While that image is accurate, it is also too limiting, for much of the Caribbean is threatened with ecological disaster. Part of the problem is historical, for deforestation began with the development of sugarcane cultivation in the seventeenth century. But now, soil erosion and depletion as well as the exploitation of marginal lands by growing populations perpetuate a vicious cycle between inhabitants and the land on which they live. Cultivation of sloping hillsides creates a situation in which erosion is constant.

A 1959 report on soil conditions in Jamaica noted that, in one district of the Blue Mountains, on the eastern end of that island, the topsoil had vanished, a victim of rapid erosion. The problem is not unique to the large islands, however. Bonham Richardson observes that ecological degradation on the smallest islands is acute. Thorn scrub and grasses have replaced native forest. "A regional drought in 1977, leading to starvation in Haiti and producing crop and livestock loss south to Trinidad, was severe only partly because of the lack of rain. Grasses and shrubs afford little protection against the sun and thus cannot help the soil to retain moisture in the face of periodic drought. Neither do they inhibit soil loss."

Migration of the islands' inhabitants has at times exacerbated the situation. In times of peak migration, a depleted labor force on some of the islands has resulted in landowners resorting to the raising of livestock, which is not labor-intensive. But livestock contribute to further ecological destruction. "Emigration itself has thus indirectly fed the ongoing devastation of island environments, and some of the changes seem irreversible. Parts of the smaller islands already resemble moonscapes. They seem simply unable to sustain their local resident populations, not to mention future generations or those working abroad who may someday be forced to return for good."

MUSIC, DANCE, FOLKLORE, AND FOOD

Travel accounts of the Caribbean tend to focus on local music, dances, and foods. Calypso, the limbo, steel bands, reggae, and African–Cuban rhythms are well known. Much of the music derives from Amerindian and African roots.

Calypso music apparently originated in Trinidad and spread to the other islands. Calypso singers improvise on any theme; they are particularly adept at poking fun at politicians and their shortcomings. Indeed, governments are as attentive to the lyrics of a politically inspired calypso tune as they are to the opposition press. On a broader scale, calypso is a mirror of Caribbean society.

Some traditional folkways, such as storytelling and other forms of oral history, are in danger of being replaced by electronic media, particularly radio, tape recorders, and jukeboxes. The new entertainment is both popular and readily available.

Scholar Laura Tanna has gathered much of Kingston, Jamaica's, oral history. Her quest for storyteller Adina Henry took her to one of the city's worst slums, the Dungle, and was reprinted in *Caribbean Review:* "We walked down the tracks to a Jewish cemetery, with gravestones dating back to the 1600s. It, too, was covered in litter, decaying amid the rubble of broken stones. Four of the tombs bear the emblem of the skull and crossbones. Popular belief has it that Spanish gold is buried in the tombs, and several of them have been desecrated by treasure seekers. We passed the East Indian shacks, and completed our tour of Majesty Pen amidst greetings of 'Love' and 'Peace' and with the fragrance of ganja [mari-

(Photo Lisa Clyde)

These lush mountain peaks in St. Lucia are volcanic in origin.

juana] wafting across the way. Everywhere, people were warm and friendly, shaking hands, chatting, drinking beer, or playing dominos. One of the shacks had a small bar and jukebox inside. There, in the midst of pigs grunting at one's feet in the mud and slime, in the dirt and dust, people had their own jukeboxes, tape recorders, and radios, all blaring out reggae, the voice of the ghetto." Tanna found Miss Adina, whose stories revealed the significant African contribution to West Indian folk culture.

In recent years, Caribbean foods have become more accepted, and even celebrated, within the region as well as internationally. Part of the search for an identity involves a new attention to traditional recipes. French, Spanish, and English recipes have been adapted to local foods—iguana, frogs, seafood, fruits, and vegetables. Cassava, guava, and mangos figure prominently in the islanders' diets.

The diversity of the Caribbean is awesome, with its potpourri of peoples and cultures. Its roots lie in Spain, Portugal, England, France, the Netherlands, Africa, India, China, and Japan. There has emerged no distinct West Indian culture, and the Caribbean peoples' identities are determined by the island—no matter how small—on which they live. For the Commonwealth Caribbean, nationalist stirrings are still weak and lacking in focus; while people in Cuba and the Dominican Republic have a much surer grasp on who they are. Nationalism is a strong integrating force in both of these nations. The Caribbean is a fascinating and diverse corner of the world that is far more complex than the travel posters imply.

Antigua and Barbuda

GEOGRAPHY
Area in Square Miles (Kilometers): 171 (442) (about 2½ times the size of Washington, D.C.)
Capital (Population): Saint John's (35,600)
Environmental Concerns: water management; clearing of trees
Geographical Features: mostly low-lying limestone and coral islands, with some higher volcanic areas
Climate: tropical marine

PEOPLE

Population
Total: 64,250
Annual Growth Rate: 0.36%
Rural/Urban Population Ratio: 64/36
Major Languages: English; Creole
Ethnic Makeup: almost entirely black African origin; some of British, Portuguese, Lebanese, or Syrian origin
Religions: predominantly Anglican; other Protestant sects; some Roman Catholic

Health
Life Expectancy at Birth: 69 years (male); 74 years (female)
Infant Mortality Rate (Ratio): 20.7/1,000
Average Caloric Intake: 90% of FAO minimum
Physicians Available (Ratio): 1/1,083

Education
Adult Literacy Rate: 89%
Compulsory (Ages): 5–16

COMMUNICATION
Televisions: 1 per 2.7 people

TRANSPORTATION
Highways in Miles (Kilometers): 150 (240)
Railroads in Miles (Kilometers): 48 (77)
Usable Airfields: 3

GOVERNMENT
Type: parliamentary democracy
Independence Date: November 1, 1981 (from the United Kingdom)
Head of State/Government: Queen Elizabeth II; Prime Minister Lester Bryant Bird
Political Parties: Antigua Labour Party; United Progressive Party; a coalition of opposing parties

Suffrage: universal at 18

MILITARY
Current Disputes: tensions between Antiguans and Barbudans

ECONOMY
Currency ($ U.S. Equivalent): 2.7 East Caribbean dollars = $1
Per Capita Income/GDP: $7,900/$503 million
GDP Growth Rate: 6%
Inflation Rate: −1.1%
Unemployment Rate: 9%
Labor Force: 30,000

Natural Resources: negligible
Agriculture: cotton; fruits; vegetables; sugarcane; livestock
Industry: tourism; construction; light manufacturing
Exports: $37.8 million (primary partners Caribbean, Guyana, United States)
Imports: $325.5 million (primary partners United States, United Kingdom, Canada)

http://www.cia.gov/cia/publications/factbook/ac.html
http://www.antiguanice.com

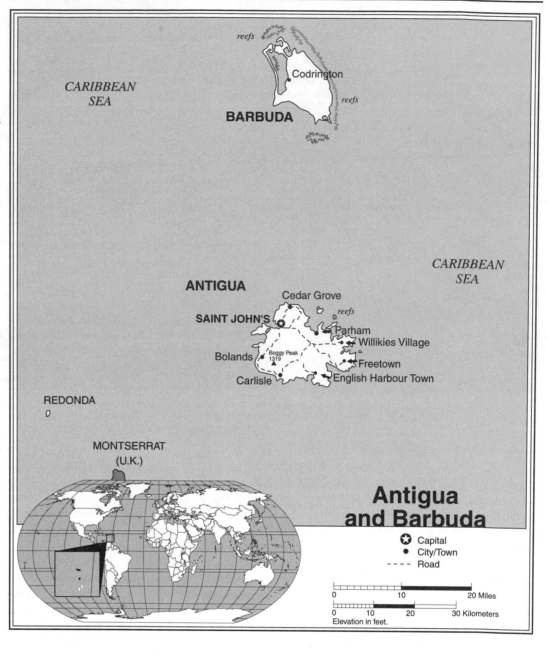

Antigua and Barbuda

★ Capital
● City/Town
- - - - Road

Elevation in feet.

The English
settle Antigua
1632
●

Antigua
abolishes slavery
1834
●

Antigua becomes
part of the West
Indies Federation
1958–1962
●

Independence
from Great Britain
1981
●

1990s

Barbuda talks of
secession

Hurricane Luís
devastates the
islands

Bird wins
reelection in
the 1999
presidential
contest

ANTIGUA AND BARBUDA: A STRAINED RELATIONSHIP

The nation of Antigua and Barbuda gained its independence from Great Britain on November 1, 1981. Both islands, tenuously linked since 1967, illustrate perfectly the degree of localism characteristic of the West Indies. Barbudans—who number approximately 1,200—culturally and politically believe that they are not Antiguans; indeed, since independence of Britain, they have been intent on secession. Barbudans view Antiguans as little more than colonial masters.

MEMORIES OF SLAVERY

Antigua was a sugar island for most of its history. This image changed radically in the 1960s, when the black-power movement then sweeping the Caribbean convinced Antiguans that work on the sugar plantations was "submissive" and carried the psychological and social stigma of historic slave labor. In response to the clamor, the government gradually phased out sugar production, which ended entirely in 1972. The decline of agriculture resulted in a strong rural-to-urban flow of people. To replace lost revenue from the earnings of sugar, the government promoted tourism.

Tourism produced the unexpected result of greater freedom for women, in that they gained access to previously unavailable employment opportunities. Anthropologist W. Penn Handwerker has shown that a combination of jobs and education for women has resulted in a marked decline in fertility. Between 1965 and the 1980s, real wages doubled, infant mortality fell dramatically, and the proportion of women ages 20 to 24 who completed secondary school rose from 3 percent to about 50 percent. "Women were freed from dependency on their children" as well as their men and created "conditions for a revolution in gender relations." Men outmigrated as the economy shifted, and women took the new jobs in tourism. Many of the jobs demanded higher skills, which in turn resulted in more education for women, followed by even better jobs. And notes Handwerker: "Women empowered by education and good jobs are less likely to suffer abuse from partners."

CULTURAL PATTERNS

Antiguans and Barbudans are culturally similar. Many islanders still have a strong affinity for England and English culture, while others identify more with what they hold to be their African–Creole roots. On Antigua, for example, Creole, which is spoken by virtually the entire population, is believed to reflect what is genuine and "natural" about the island and its culture. Standard English, even though it is the official language, carries an aura of falseness in the popular mind.

FOREIGN RELATIONS

Despite the small size of the country, Antigua and Barbuda are actively courted by regional powers. The United States maintains a satellite-tracking station on Antigua, and Brazil has provided loans and other assistance. A small oil refinery, jointly supported by Venezuela and Mexico, began operations in 1982.

FAMILY POLITICS

Since 1951, with only one interruption, Antiguan politics has been dominated by the family of Vere Bird and his Antigua Labour Party (ALP). Charges of nepotism, corruption, drug smuggling, and money laundering dogged the Vere Bird administration for years. Still, in 1994, Lester Bird managed to succeed his 84-year-old father, and the ALP won 11 of 17 seats in elections. Lester admitted that his father had been guilty of some "misjudgments" and quickly pledged that the ALP would improve education, better the status of women, and increase the presence of young people in government.

The younger Bird, in his State of the Nation address early in 1995, challenged Antiguans to transform their country on their own terms, rather than those dictated by the International Monetary Fund. His government would take "tough and unpopular" measures to avoid the humiliation of going "cap in hand" to foreign financial institutions. Those tough measures have included increases in contributions for medical benefits, property and personal taxes, and business and motor-vehicle licenses. Because Bird and the ALP control patronage and access to government jobs, it is unlikely that the opposition will be able to take advantage of such policies.

DEVELOPMENT

Land-use patterns in the islands show that 37% of the land is devoted to grazing, 34% to woodlands, 11% to settlements, 3% to tourist areas, and 3% to airports. Agricultural use accounts for only 8% of the land. Tourism, the leading generator of employment, has replaced agriculture as the prime generator of revenue. Perhaps 80% of foreign exchange derives from tourism.

FREEDOM

Pervasive government control of the electronic media has resulted in virtually no access for opposition parties or persons representing opinions divergent from or critical of those held by the government. Various governments have used the media in deliberate campaigns of disinformation.

HEALTH/WELFARE

The government has initiated programs to enhance educational opportunities for men and women and to assist in family planning. The new Directorate of Women's Affairs helps women to advance in government and in the professions. It has also sponsored educational programs for women in health, crafts, and business skills.

ACHIEVEMENTS

Antigua has preserved its rich historical heritage, from the dockyard named for Admiral Lord Nelson to the Ebenezer Methodist Church. Built in 1839, the latter was the "mother church" for Methodism in the Caribbean.

The Bahamas (Commonwealth of the Bahamas)

GEOGRAPHY
Area in Square Miles (Kilometers): 5,380 (13,934) (about the size of Connecticut)
Capital (Population): Nassau (172,000)
Environmental Concerns: coral-reef decay; waste disposal
Geographical Features: long, flat coral formations with some low, rounded hills
Climate: tropical marine

PEOPLE

Population
Total: 283,700
Annual Growth Rate: 1.36%
Rural/Urban Population Ratio: 13/87
Ethnic Makeup: 85% black; 15% white
Major Language: English
Religions: 32% Baptist; 22% Protestant; 20% Anglican; 19% Roman Catholic; 7% unaffiliated or unknown

Health
Life Expectancy at Birth: 71 years (male); 78 years (female)
Infant Mortality Rate (Ratio): 18.3/1,000
Average Caloric Intake: 98% of FAO minimum
Physicians Available (Ratio): 1/709

Education
Adult Literacy Rate: 98.2%
Compulsory (Ages): 5–16

COMMUNICATION
Telephones: 1 per 3.5 people
Daily Newspaper Circulation: 129 per 1,000 people
Televisions: 1 per 4.4 people

TRANSPORTATION
Highways in Miles (Kilometers): 1,672 (2,693)
Railroads in Miles (Kilometers): none
Usable Airfields: 62
Motor Vehicles in Use: 58,000

GOVERNMENT
Type: commonwealth
Independence Date: July 10, 1973 (from the United Kingdom)
Head of State/Government: Queen Elizabeth II; Prime Minister Hubert A. Ingraham
Political Parties: Free National Movement; Progressive Liberal Party
Suffrage: universal at 18

MILITARY
Current Disputes: none

ECONOMY
Currency ($ U.S. Equivalent): 1 Bahamian dollar = $1 (fixed rate)
Per Capita Income/GDP: $20,100/$5.63 billion
GDP Growth Rate: 4%
Inflation Rate: 0.4%
Unemployment Rate: 9%
Labor Force: 148,000
Natural Resources: salt; aragonite; timber
Agriculture: citrus fruits; vegetables; poultry
Industry: tourism; banking; cement; oil refining and transshipment; salt production; rum; aragonite; pharmaceuticals; steel pipe
Exports: $300 million (primary partners United States, European Union, United Kingdom)
Imports: $1.37 billion (primary partners United States, European Union, Japan)

http://www.cia.gov/cia/publications/factbook/bf.html
http://www.bahamas-on-line.com

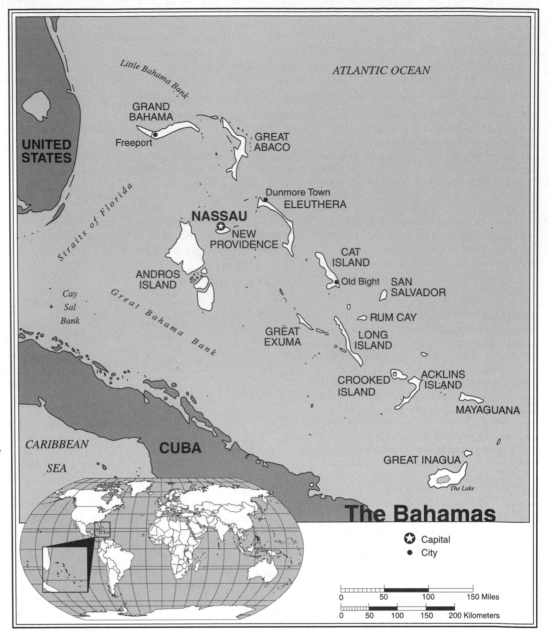

The Bahamas

⊙ Capital
● City

Christopher
Columbus first
sights the New
World at San
Salvador Island
1492
●

The first English
settlement in the
Bahamas
1647
●

Black-power
controversy
1967
●

Independence
from Great Britain
1973
●

Violent crime,
drug trafficking,
and narcotics
addiction
become serious
social problems
1980s
●

1990s

Hubert Ingraham,
leader of the Free
National
Movement, wins
a second term as
prime minister

New investments
create jobs
and cut the
unemployment
rate

Elections are
scheduled for
2002

BAHAMAS:
A NATION OF ISLANDS

Christopher Columbus made his first landfall in the Bahamas in 1492, when he touched ashore on the island of San Salvador. Permanent settlements on the islands were not established by the British until 1647, when the Eleutheran Adventurers, a group of English and Bermudan religious dissidents, landed. The island was privately governed until 1717, when it became a British Crown colony. During the U.S. Civil War, Confederate blockade runners used the Bahamas as a base. The tradition continued in the years after World War I, when Prohibition rum runners used the islands as a base. Today drug traffickers utilize the isolation of the out-islands for their illicit operations.

Although the Bahamas are made up of almost 700 islands, only 10 have populations of any significant size. Of these, New Providence and Grand Bahama contain more than 75 percent of the Bahamian population. Because most economic and cultural activities take place on the larger islands, other islands—particularly those in the southern region—have suffered depopulation over the years as young men and women have moved to the two major centers of activity.

Migrants from Haiti and Jamaica have also caused problems for the Bahamian government. There are an estimated 50,000 illegal Haitians now resident in the Bahamas—equivalent to more than one fifth of the total Bahamian population of 283,700. The Bahamian response was tolerance until late 1994, when the government established tough new policies that reflected a fear that the country would be "overwhelmed" by Haitian immigrants. In the words of one official, the large numbers of Haitians would "result in a very fundamental economic and

social transformation that even the very naïve would understand to be undesirable." Imprisonment, marginalization, no legal right to work, and even the denial of access to schools and hospitals are now endured by the immigrants, who have begun to abandon the Bahamas in large numbers.

Bahamian problems with Jamaicans are rooted differently. The jealous isolation of each of the new nations is reflected in the peoples' fears and suspicions of the activities of their neighbors. As a result, interisland freedom of movement is subject to strict scrutiny.

The Bahamas were granted their independence from Great Britain in 1973 and established a constitutional parliamentary democracy governed by a freely elected prime minister and Parliament. Upon independence, there was a transfer of political power from a small white elite to the black majority, who comprise 85 percent of the population. Whites continue to play a role in the political process, however, and several hold high-level civil-service and political posts.

The country has enjoyed a marked improvement in health conditions over the past few decades. Life expectancy has risen, and infant mortality has declined. Virtually all people living in urban areas have access to good drinking water, although the age and dilapidated condition of the capital's (Nassau) water system could present problems in the near future.

The government has begun a program to restructure education on the islands. The authorities have placed a new emphasis on technical and vocational training so that skilled jobs in the economy now held by foreigners will be performed by Bahamians. While the literacy rate has remained high, there remains a shortage of teachers, equipment, and supplies.

The government of Prime Minister Hubert A. Ingraham and his Free National Movement won a clear mandate in 1997 over the opposition Progressive Liberal Party to continue the policies and programs it initiated in 1992. *The Miami Herald* reported that the election "marked a watershed in Bahamian politics, with many new faces on the ballot and both parties facing leadership succession struggles before the next vote is due in 2002." Ideologically, the two contending political parties were similar; thus, voters made their decisions on the basis of who they felt would provide jobs and bring crime under control. Honest government and a history of working effectively with the private sector to improve the national economy have dramatically increased foreign investment in the Bahamas and strengthened Ingraham's position.

Despite new investments, unemployment is still a problem, and many young Bahamians out-migrate. The thousands of illegal Haitian immigrants have added pressure to the job market and worry some Bahamians that their own sense of identity may be threatened. But in general, there is a new sense of optimism in the islands.

DEVELOPMENT

Because the Bahamian economy is service-oriented, especially in tourism and offshore banking, there are no significant industrial and occupational health hazards. Tourism accounts for nearly half the gross national product.

FREEDOM

Women participate actively in all levels of government and business. The Constitution does, however, make some distinctions between males and females with regard to citizenship and permanent-resident status.

HEALTH/WELFARE

Cases of child abuse and neglect in the Bahamas rose in the 1990s. The Government and Women's Crisis Centre focused on the need to fight child abuse through a public-awareness program that had as its theme: "It shouldn't hurt to be a child."

ACHIEVEMENTS

The natural beauty of the islands has had a lasting effect on those who have visited them. As a result of his experiences in the waters off Bimini, Ernest Hemingway wrote his classic *The Old Man and the Sea*.

Barbados

GEOGRAPHY

Area in Square Miles (Kilometers): 166 (431) (about 2 ½ times the size of Washington, DC.)

Capital (Population): Bridgetown (97,500)

Environmental Concerns: pollution of coastal waters from waste disposal by ships; soil erosion; illegal solid-waste disposal

Geographical Features: relatively flat; rises gently to central highland region

Climate: tropical marine

PEOPLE

Population

Total: 259,200

Annual Growth Rate: 0.04%

Rural/Urban Population Ratio: 52/48

Major Language: English

Ethnic Makeup: 80% Black 16% mixed; 4% white

Religions: 67% Protestant (Anglican, Pentecostal, Methodist, others); 4% Roman Catholic; 17% unaffiliated; 12% others or unknown

Health

Life Expectancy at Birth: 72 years (male); 78 years (female)

Infant Mortality Rate (Ratio): 16.7/1,000

Average Caloric Intake: 129% of the FAO minimum

Physicians Available (Ratio): 1/842

Education

Adult Literacy Rate: 97.4%

Compulsory (Ages): 5–16

COMMUNICATION

Telephones: 1 per 2.9 people

Daily Newspaper Circulation: 159 per 1,000 people

Televisions: 1 per 3.6 people

TRANSPORTATION

Highways in Miles (Kilometers): 1,025 (1,650)

Railroads in Miles (Kilometers): none

Usable Airfields: 1

Motor Vehicles in Use: 53,100

GOVERNMENT

Type: parliamentary democracy; independent sovereign state within Commonwealth

Independence Date: November 30, 1966 (from the United Kingdom)

Head of State/Government: Queen Elizabeth II; Prime Minister Owen Seymour Arthur

Political Parties: Democratic Labour Party; Barbados Labour Party; National Democratic Party

Suffrage: universal at 18

MILITARY

Current Disputes: none

ECONOMY

Currency ($ U.S. Equivalent): 2 Bajan dollars = $1 (fixed rate)

Per Capita Income/GDP: $11,200/$2.9 billion

GDP Growth Rate: 3%

Inflation Rate: 3.6%

Unemployment Rate: 12%

Labor Force: 136,000

Natural Resources: petroleum; fish; natural gas

Agriculture: sugarcane; vegetables; cotton

Industry: tourism; sugar; light manufacturing; component assembly

Exports: $280 million (primary partners CARICOM, United States, United Kingdom)

Imports: $982 million (primary partners United States, CARICOM, United Kingdom)

 http://www.cia.gov/cia/publications/ factbook/bb.html

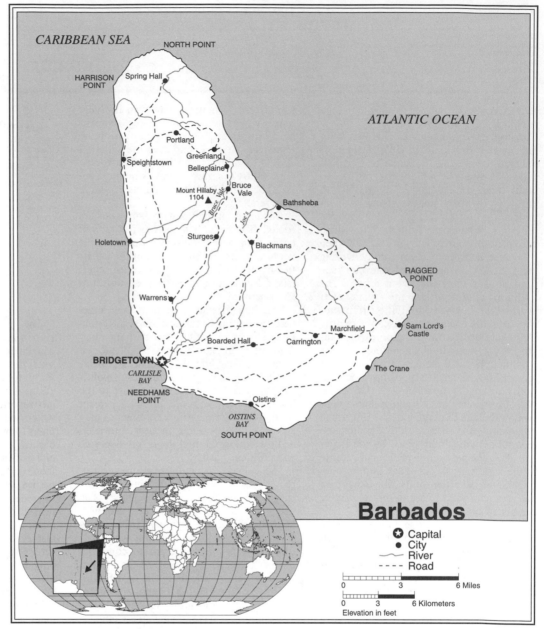

CARIBBEAN SEA
ATLANTIC OCEAN

NORTH POINT
HARRISON POINT
Spring Hall
Portland
Speightstown
Greenland
Belleplaine
Mount Hillaby 1104
Bruce Vale
Bathsheba
Holetown
Sturges
Blackmans
RAGGED POINT
Warrens
Marchfield
Sam Lord's Castle
Boarded Hall
Carrington
BRIDGETOWN
The Crane
CARLISLE BAY
NEEDHAMS POINT
Oistins
OISTINS BAY
SOUTH POINT

Barbados
⊛ Capital
● City
— River
--- Road
0 3 6 Miles
0 3 6 Kilometers
Elevation in feet

| Barbados is occupied by the English **1625** | The first sugar from Barbados is sent to England **1647** | Full citizenship is granted to nonwhites **1832** | Universal suffrage **1951** | Independence from Great Britain **1966** | **1990s** |

The Labour Party's Owen Arthur becomes prime minister

Barbados develops an offshore banking industry

The government pursues a policy of economic diversification

THE LITTLE ENGLAND OF THE CARIBBEAN

A parliamentary democracy that won its independence from Britain in 1966, Barbados boasts a House of Assembly that is the third oldest in the Western Hemisphere, after Bermuda's and Virginia's. A statement of the rights and privileges of Bajans (as Barbadians are called), known as the Charter of Barbados, was proclaimed in 1652 and has been upheld by those governing the island. The press is free, labor is strong and well organized, and human rights are respected.

While the majority of the populations of the English-speaking West Indies still admire the British, this admiration is carried to extremes in Barbados. In 1969, for example, Bajan soccer teams chose English names and colors—Arsenal, Tottenham Hotspurs, Liverpool, and Coventry City. Among the primary religions are Anglican and Methodist Protestantism.

Unlike most of the other islands of the Caribbean, European sailors initially found Barbados uninhabited. It has since been determined that the island's original inhabitants, the Arawak Indians, were destroyed by Carib Indians who overran the region and then abandoned the islands. Settled by the English, Barbados was always under British control until its independence.

A DIVERSIFYING ECONOMY

In terms of wealth, as compared to other West Indian nations, Barbados is well off. One important factor is that Barbados has been able to diversify its economy; thus, the country is no longer dependent solely on sugar and its by-products rum and molasses. Manufacturing, and high-technology industries now contribute to economic growth, and tourism has overtaken agriculture as a generator of foreign exhange.

The Constitution of 1966 authorized the government to promote the general welfare of the citizens of the island through equitable distribution of wealth. While governments have made a sincere effort to wipe out pockets of poverty, a great disparity in wealth still exists.

RACE AND CLASS

Barbados is a class- and race-conscious society. One authority noted that there are three classes (elite, middle class, and masses) and two colors (white/light and black). Land is highly concentrated; 10 percent of the population own 95 percent of the land. Most of the nation's landed estates and businesses are owned by whites, even though they comprise a very small percentage of the population (4 percent).

While discrimination based on color is legally prohibited, color distinctions continue to correlate with class differences and dominate most personal associations. Although whites have been displaced politically, they still comprise more than half of the group considered "influential" in the country.

Even though Barbados's class structure is more rigid than that of other West Indian states, there is upward social mobility for all people, and the middle class has been growing steadily in size. Poor whites, known as "Redlegs," have frequently moved into managerial positions on the estates. The middle class also includes a fairly large percentage of blacks and mulattos. Bajans have long enjoyed access to public and private educational systems, which have been the object of a good deal of national pride. Adequate medical care is available to all residents through local clinics and hospitals under a government health program. All Bajans are covered under government health insurance programs.

SEEKING A LEADERSHIP ROLE

Given the nation's relative wealth and its dynamism, Bajans have been inclined to seek a strong role in the region. In terms of Caribbean politics, economic development, and defense, Bajans feel they have a right and a duty to lead.

Some of that optimism was tempered in the early 1990s by economic recession. Recovery in 1993 saw a growth of 1 to 2 percent, a result of an International Monetary Fund–induced austerity program.

The Labour Party has continued to push privatization policies. In 1993, an important step was taken toward the greater diversification of the nation's economic base with the creation of offshore financial services. By 1995, the new industry had created many new jobs for Bajans and had significantly reduced the high unemployment rate.

DEVELOPMENT

Between 1971 and 1999, there was an approximate 30% decrease in land used for agriculture. Formerly agricultural land has been transformed into golf courses, residential areas, commercial developments, tourist facilities, or abandoned.

FREEDOM

Barbados has maintained an excellent human-rights record. The government officially advocates strengthening the human-rights machinery of the United Nations and the Organization of American States. Women are active participants in the country's economic, political, and social life.

HEALTH/WELFARE

The acting minister of Health and Welfare noted that the treatment of nutrition-related diseases cost taxpayers nearly $50 million in 1996–1997. He felt that the country depended too heavily on imported foods, which Bajans consider superior to locally grown foods.

ACHIEVEMENTS

Bajan novelist George Lamming has won attention from the world's literary community for his novels, each of which explores a stage in or an aspect of the colonial experience. Through his works, he explains what it is to be simultaneously a citizen of one's island and a West Indian.

Cuba (Republic of Cuba)

GEOGRAPHY

Area in Square Miles (Kilometers): 44,200 (114,471) (about the size of Pennsylvania)

Capital (Population): Havana (2,221,000)

Environmental Concerns: pollution of Havana Bay; threatened wildlife populations; deforestation

Geographical Features: mostly flat to rolling plains; rugged hills and mountains in southeast

Climate: tropical

PEOPLE

Population

Total: 11,096,400

Annual Growth Rate: 0.4%

Rural/Urban Population Ratio: 24/76

Ethnic Makeup: 51% mulatto; 37% white; 11% black; 1% Chinese

Major Language: Spanish

Religion: 85% Roman Catholic before Castro assumed power

Health

Life Expectancy at Birth: 73 years (male); 78 years (female)

Infant Mortality Rate (Ratio): 7.8/1,000

Average Caloric Intake: 121% of FAO minimum

Physicians Available (Ratio): 1/231

Education

Adult Literacy Rate: 95.7%

Compulsory (Ages): 6–11; free

COMMUNICATION

Telephones: 1 per 31 people

Daily Newspaper Circulation: 120 per 1,000 people

Televisions: 1 per 5.8 people

TRANSPORTATION

Highways—Miles (Kilometers): 37,793 (60,858)

Railroads—Miles (Kilometers): 2,985 (4,807)

Usable Airfields: 170

Motor Vehicles in Use: 449,000

GOVERNMENT

Type: Communist state

Independence Date: May 20, 1902 (from Spain)

Head of State/Government: President Fidel Castro Ruz is both head of state and head of government

Political Parties: Cuban Communist Party

Suffrage: universal at 16

MILITARY

Military Expenditures (% of GDP): 4% (est.)

Current Disputes: U.S. Naval Base at Guantanamo Bay is leased to the United States

ECONOMY

Currency ($ U.S. Equivalent): 1 Cuban peso = $1 (official rate)

Per Capita Income/GDP: $1,560/$17.3 billion

GDP Growth Rate: 1.2%

Unemployment Rate: 6.8%

Labor Force: 4,500,000

Natural Resources: cobalt; nickel; iron ore; copper; manganese; salt; timber; silica; petroleum

Agriculture: sugarcane; tobacco; citrus fruits; coffee; rice; potatoes; beans; livestock

Industry: sugar; petroleum; food; textiles; tobacco; chemicals; paper and wood products; metals; cement; fertilizers; consumer goods; agricultural machinery

Exports: $1.4 billion (primary partners Russia, Canada, Spain)

Imports: $3.6 billion (primary partners Spain, France, Canada)

http://www.odci.gov/cia/publications/factbook/cu.html

REFLECTIONS ON A REVOLUTION

Cuba, which contains about half the land area of the West Indies, has held the attention of the world since 1959. In that year, Fidel Castro led his victorious rebels into the capital city of Havana and began a revolution that has profoundly affected Cuban society. The Cuban Revolution had its roots in the struggle for independence of Spain in the late nineteenth century, in the aborted Nationalist Revolution of 1933, and in the Constitution of 1940. It grew from Cuba's history and must be understood as a Cuban phenomenon.

The Revolution in some respects represents the fulfillment of the goals of the Cuban Constitution of 1940, a radically nationalist document that was never fully implemented. It banned *latifundia* (the ownership of vast landed estates) and discouraged foreign ownership of the land. It permitted the confiscation of property in the public or social interest. The state was authorized to provide full employment for its people and to direct the course of the national economy. Finally, the Constitution of 1940 gave the Cuban state control of the sugar industry, which at the time was controlled by U.S. companies.

The current Constitution, written in 1976, incorporates 36 percent of the articles of the 1940 Constitution. In other words, many of Castro's policies and programs are founded in Cuban history and the aspirations of the Cuban people. Revolutionary Cuba—at least in its earlier years—has been very successful in solving the nation's most pressing problems of poverty. But those successes must be balanced against the loss of basic freedoms imposed by a strong authoritarian state.

ACHIEVEMENTS OF THE REVOLUTION

Education

One of the Revolution's most impressive successes has been in the area of education. In 1960, the Castro regime decided to place emphasis on raising the minimum level of education for the whole population. To accomplish this, some 200,000 Cubans were mobilized in 1961 under the slogan "Let those who know more teach those who know less." In a single year, the literacy rate rose from 76 to 96 percent. Free education was made available to all Cubans. The literacy campaign involved many Cubans in an attempt to recognize and attack the problems of rural impoverishment. It was the first taste of active public life for many women who were students or teachers and because of

their involvement, they began to redefine sex roles and attitudes.

While the literacy campaign was a resounding triumph, long-term educational policy was less satisfactory. Officials blamed the high dropout rate in elementary and junior high schools on poor school facilities and inadequate teacher training. Students also apparently lacked enthusiasm, and Castro himself acknowledged that students needed systematic, constant, daily work and discipline.

"Scholarship students and students in general," in Castro's words, "are willing to do anything, except to study hard."

Health Care

The Cuban Revolution took great strides forward in improving the health of the Cuban population, especially in rural regions. Success in this area is all the more impressive when one considers that between one third and one half of all doctors left the country between 1959 and 1962. Health care initially declined sharply, and the infant mortality rate rose rapidly. But, with the training of new health-care professionals, the gaps were filled. The infant mortality rate in Cuba is now at a level comparable to that of developed countries.

From the outset, the government decided to concentrate on rural areas, where the need was the greatest. Medical treatment was free, and newly graduated doctors had to serve for at least two years in the countryside. The Cuban health service was founded on the principle that good health for all, without discrimination, is a birthright of Cubans. All Cubans were included under a national health plan.

The first national health standards were developed between 1961 and 1965, and eight priority areas were identified: infant and maternal care, adult health care, care for the elderly, environmental health, nutrition, dentistry, school health programs, and occupational health. A program of spraying and immunization eradicated malaria and poliomyelitis. Cuban life expectancy became one of the highest in the world, and Cuba's leading causes of death became the same as in the United States—heart disease, cancer, and stroke.

Before the Revolution of 1959, there was very little health and safety regulation for workers. Afterward, however, important advances were made in the training of specialized inspectors and occupational physicians. In 1978, a Work Safety and Health Law was enacted, which defined the rights and responsibilities of government agencies, workplace administrators, unions, and workers.

Cuba also exported its health-care expertise; one health authority called Cuba

a "health power." It has had medical teams in countries from Nicaragua to Yemen and more doctors overseas than the World Health Organization.

Redistribution of Wealth

The third great area of change presided over by the Revolution was income redistribution. The Revolution changed the lives of rural poor and agricultural workers. They gained the most in comparison to other groups in Cuban society—especially urban groups. From 1962 to 1973, for example, agricultural workers saw their wages rise from less than 60 percent to 93 percent of the national average.

Still, Cuba's minimum wage was inadequate for most families. Many families needed two wage earners to make ends meet. All wages were enhanced by the so-called social wage, which consisted of free medical care and education, subsidized housing, and low food prices. Yet persistent shortages and tight rationing of food undermined a good portion of the social wage. Newly married couples found it necessary to live with relatives, sometimes for years, before they could obtain their own housing, which was in short supply. Food supplies, especially those provided by the informal sector, were adversely affected by a 1986 decision to eliminate independent producers because an informal private sector was deemed antithetical to "socialist morality" and promoted materialism.

Women in Cuba

From the outset of the Revolution, Fidel Castro appealed to women as active participants in the movement and redefined their political roles. Women's interests were protected by the Federation of Cuban Women, an integral part of the ruling party. The Family Code of 1975 equalized pay scales, reversed sexual discrimination against promotions, provided generous maternity leave, and gave employed women preferential access to goods and services. Although women comprised approximately 30 percent of the Cuban workforce, most were still employed in traditional female occupations; the Third Congress of the Cuban Communist Party admitted in 1988 that both racial minorities and women were underrepresented in responsible government and party positions at all levels. This continues to be a problem.

SHORTCOMINGS

Even at its best, the new Cuba had significant shortcomings. Wayne Smith, a former chief of the U.S. Interest Section in Havana who was sympathetic to the Revolution, wrote: "There is little freedom of expression and no freedom of the press at all. It is a command society, which still holds political prisoners, some of them under deplorable conditions. Further, while the Revolution has provided the basic needs of all, it has not fulfilled its promise of a higher standard of living for the society as a whole. Cuba was, after all, an urban middle-class society with a relatively high standard of living even before the Revolution. . . . The majority of Cubans are less well off materially."

Castro, to win support for his programs, did not hesitate to take his revolutionary message to the people. Indeed, the key reason why Castro enjoyed such widespread support in Cuba was because the people had the sense of being involved in a great historical process.

Alienation

Not all Cubans identified with the Revolution, and many felt a deep sense of betrayal and alienation. The elite and most of the middle class strongly resisted the changes that robbed them of influence, prestige, and property. Some were particularly bitter, for at its outset, the Revolution had been largely a middle-class movement. For them, Castro was a traitor to his class. Thousands fled Cuba, and some formed the core of an anti-Castro guerrilla movement based in South Florida.

There are many signs that Castro's government, while still popular among many people, has lost the widespread acceptance it enjoyed in the 1960s and 1970s. While Castro still has the support of the older generation and those in rural areas who benefited from the social transformation of the island, limited economic growth has led to dissatisfaction among urban workers and youth, who are less interested in Castro as a revolutionary hero and more interested in economic gains.

More serious disaffection may exist in the army. Journalist Georgie Anne Geyer, writing in *World Monitor,* suggests that the 1989 execution of General Arnaldo Ochoa, ostensibly for drug trafficking, was actually motivated by Castro's fears of an emerging competitor for power. "The 1930s-style show trial effectively revealed the presence of an 'Angola generation' in the Cuban military. . . . That generation, which fought in Angola between 1974 and 1989, is the competitor generation to Castro's own Sierra Maestra generation." The condemned officers argued that their dealings with drug traffickers were not for personal enrichment but were designed to earn desperately needed hard currency for the state. Some analysts are convinced that Castro knew about drug trafficking and condoned it; others claim that it took place

without his knowledge. But the bottom line is that the regime had been shaken at the highest levels, and the purge was the most far-reaching since the 1959 Revolution.

The Economy

The state of the Cuban economy and the future of the Cuban Revolution are inextricably linked. Writing in *World Today,* James J. Guy predicted that, given the economic collapse of the former Soviet Union and its satellites, "Cuba is destined to face serious structural unemployment: its agrarian economy cannot generate the white-collar, technical jobs demanded by a swelling army of graduates. . . . The entire system is deteriorating—the simplest services take months to deliver, water and electricity are constantly interrupted. . . ," and there is widespread corruption and black-marketeering.

Oil is particularly nettlesome. Just as Soviet oil imports fell off and Cuba was forced to make petroleum purchases on the world market, Kuwait was invaded by Iraq. Oil prices skyrocketed. Active development of the tourism industry offers some hope, but Western banks and governments since the mid-1980s have been reluctant to invest in Cuba.

Although Castro prides Cuba on being one of the last bulwarks of untainted Marxism-Leninism, in April 1991 he said: "We are not dogmatic . . . we are realistic. . . . Under the special conditions of this extraordinary period we are also aware that different forms of international cooperation may be useful." He noted that Cuba had contacted foreign capitalists

about the possibility of establishing joint enterprises and remarked that more than 49 percent foreign participation in state businesses was a possibility.

In 1993, Castro called for economic realism. Using the rhetoric of the Revolution, he urged the Legislative Assembly to think seriously about the poor condition of the Cuban economy: "It is painful, but we must be sensible. . . . It is not only with decisiveness, courage and heroism that one saves the Revolution, but also with intelligence. And we have the right to invent ways to survive in these conditions without ever ceasing to be revolutionaries."

A government decree in September 1993 allowed Cubans to establish private businesses; today, Cubans in some 140 professions can work on their own for a profit. At about the same time, the use of dollars was decriminalized, the Cuban currency became convertible, and, in the agricultural sector, the government began to transform state farms into cooperatives. Farmers are now allowed to sell some of their produce in private markets and, increasingly, market forces set the prices of many consumer goods. Managers in state-owned enterprises have been given unprecedented autonomy; and foreign investment, in contrast with past practice, is now encouraged.

Still, the Cuban economy has continued its decline. Mirta Ojito, writing in *The New York Times,* sees older revolutionaries "coming to terms with the failure of their dreams." Cuba now resembles most other underdeveloped countries, with "many needy, unhappy, sad people." The Revolu-

(United Nations photo)

Fidel Castro has been the prime minister of Cuba since he seized power in 1959. Pictured above is Castro at the United Nations, as he looked in 1960.

The island is discovered by Christopher Columbus 1492	The founding of Havana 1511	The Ten Years' War in Cuba 1868–1878	The Cuban War of Independence 1895–1898	The Republic of Cuba is established 1902	Cuba writes a new, progressive Constitution 1940	Fidel Castro seizes power 1959	An abortive U.S.–sponsored invasion at the Bay of Pigs 1961	The OAS votes to allow member states to normalize relations with Cuba 1975	Mass exodus from Cuba; trial and execution of top military officials for alleged dealing in drugs 1980s

1990s

Castro pursues economic liberalization	The economy rapidly deteriorates	The state cracks down on opposition; tensions flare between Cuba and the United States over the disposition of a young Cuban refugee, Elian González

tion was supposed to make Cuba prosperous, "not merely survive," and end the country's dependence on the U.S. dollar. By 1999, dollars in circulation in Cuba had created a parallel speculative economy. *The Economist* noted in January 1999 Cuba's "ruined economy, disintegrating public services, and uncertain future." With wages effectively frozen while prices have continued to rise, it is not surprising that prostitution, moonlighting, black-marketeering, and begging have rapidly increased. Castro has talked with CARICOM states about the possibilities of free trade, but the stifling bureaucracy makes it much easier to export from rather than export to Cuba.

Freedom Issues

Soon after the Revolution, the government assumed total control of the media. No independent news organization is allowed, and all printed publications are censored by the government or the Communist Party. The arts are subject to strict censorship, and even sports must serve the purposes of the Revolution. As Castro noted: "Within the Revolution everything is possible. Outside it, nothing."

In many respects, there is less freedom now in Cuba than there was before the Revolution. Cuba's human-rights record is not good. There are thousands of political prisoners, and rough treatment and torture—physical and psychological—occur. The Constitution of 1976 allows the repression of all freedoms for all those who oppose the Revolution. U.S. political scientist William LeGrande, who was sympathetic to the Revolution, nevertheless noted that "Cuba is a closed society. The Cuban Communist Party does not allow dissenting views on fundamental policy. It does not allow people to challenge the basic leadership of the regime." But here,

too, there are signs of change. In 1995, municipal elections were held under a new system that provides for run-offs if none of the candidates gains a clear majority. In an indication of a new competitiveness in Cuban politics, 326 out of 14,229 positions were subject to the run-off rule.

THE FUTURE

It will be difficult for Castro to maintain the support of the Cuban population for long. There must be continued positive accomplishments in the economy. Health and education programs are successful and will continue to be so. "Cubans get free health care, free education and free admission to sports and cultural events [and] 80% of all Cubans live in rent-free apartments, and those who do pay rent pay only between 6 and 10% of their salaries," according to James J. Guy.

But there must be a recovery of basic political and human freedoms. Criticism must not be the occasion for jail terms or exile. The Revolution must be more inclusive and less exclusive.

Although Castro has never been effectively challenged, there are signs of unrest on the island. The military, as noted, is a case in point. Castro has also lost a good deal of luster internationally, as most countries have moved away from statism and toward free-market economies and more open forms of government.

Even though a similar trend is apparent on the island, in 1994 and 1995, many Cubans grew increasingly frustrated with their lives and took to the sea in an attempt to reach the United States. Thousands were intercepted by the U.S. Coast Guard and housed in U.S. military facilities at Guantanamo Bay and Fort Howard in the Panama Canal Zone.

The question is increasingly asked, What will happen once Fidel, through

death or retirement, is gone from power? Castro's assumption is that the new Constitution, which institutionalizes the Revolution, will provide a mechanism for succession. Over the past few years, he has made some effort to depersonalize the Revolution; his public appearances are fewer and he does less traveling around the countryside. But there is no transition plan, and Castro continues to behave as if he is the embodiment of the Revolution. Despite an announcement that 1998 would be his last year in office, at this writing he still clings to power.

Change must come to Cuba. More than half of all Cubans alive today were born after the Revolution. They are not particularly attuned to the rhetoric of revolution and seem more interested in the attainment of basic freedoms and consumer goods. In January 1999, *The Economist* asked: "What will follow Fidel?" The magazine suggested that Cubans could be faced with violence and political turmoil, for there were "no plausible political heirs in sight, no credible opposition, and an exile community eager not only for return but also revenge."

DEVELOPMENT

The visit by the foreign minister of Belarus in 1997 signaled another step in the reestablishment of ties that existed between the former Soviet Republic and Cuba before 1991. Relations with the Dominican Republic, broken in 1959, were resumed in 1997.

FREEDOM

The Committee to Protect Journalists noted that those who try to work outside the confines of the state media face tremendous obstacles. "The problems of a lack of basic supplies . . . are dwarfed by Fidel Castro's campaign of harassment and intimidation against the fledgling free press."

HEALTH/WELFARE

In August 1997, the Cuban government reported 1,649 HIV cases, 595 cases of full-blown AIDS, and 429 deaths, a significant increase over figures for 1996. Cuban medical personnel are working on an AIDS vaccine. AIDS has been spread in part because of an economic climate that has driven more women to prostitution.

ACHIEVEMENTS

A unique cultural contribution of Cuba to the world was the Afro-Cuban movement, with its celebration of black song and dance rhythms. The work of contemporary prize-winning Cuban authors such as Alejo Carpentier and Edmundo Desnoes has been translated into many languages.

Dominica (Commonwealth of Dominica)

GEOGRAPHY

Area in Square Miles (Kilometers): 289 (752) (about 4 times the size of Washington, D.C.)

Capital (Population): Roseau (15,900)

Geographical Features: rugged mountains of volcanic origin

Climate: tropical

PEOPLE

Population

Total: 64,880

Annual Growth Rate: −1.41%

Rural/Urban Population Ratio: 30/70

Major Languages: English; French Creole

Ethnic Makeup: mostly black; some Carib Indians

Religions: 77% Roman Catholic; 15% Protestant; 8% others or unaffiliated

Health

Life Expectancy at Birth: 75 years (male); 81 years (female)

Infant Mortality Rate (Ratio): 8.7/1,000

Average Caloric Intake: 90% of FAO minimum

Physicians Available (Ratio): 1/2,112

Education

Adult Literacy Rate: 94%

Compulsory (Ages): 5–15; free

COMMUNICATION

Telephones: 4 per 4 people

Televisions: 1 per 13 people

TRANSPORTATION

Highways in Miles (Kilometers): 484 (780)

Railroads in Miles (Kilometers): none

Usable Airfields: 2

GOVERNMENT

Type: parliamentary democracy

Independence Date: November 3, 1978 (from the United Kingdom)

Head of State/Government: President Vernon Lorden Shaw; Prime Minister Edison C. James

Political Parties: United Workers Party; Dominica Freedom Party; Dominica Labour Party

Suffrage: universal at 18

MILITARY

Current Disputes: territorial dispute with Venezuela

ECONOMY

Currency ($ U.S. Equivalent): 2.7 East Caribbean dollars = $1

Per Capita Income/GDP: $3,300/$216 million

GDP Growth Rate: 1.8%

Inflation Rate: 2.2%

Unemployment Rate: 15%

Labor Force: 25,000

Natural Resources: timber

Agriculture: bananas; citrus fruits; mangoes; root crops; coconuts; forestry and fishing potential

Industry: soap; coconut oil; tourism; copra; furniture; cement blocks; shoes

Exports: $50.4 million (primary partners CARICOM, United Kingdom, United States)

Imports: $104.2 million (primary partners United States, CARICOM, United Kingdom)

http://www.cia.gov/cia/publications/factbook/do.html
http://www.dominica.dm

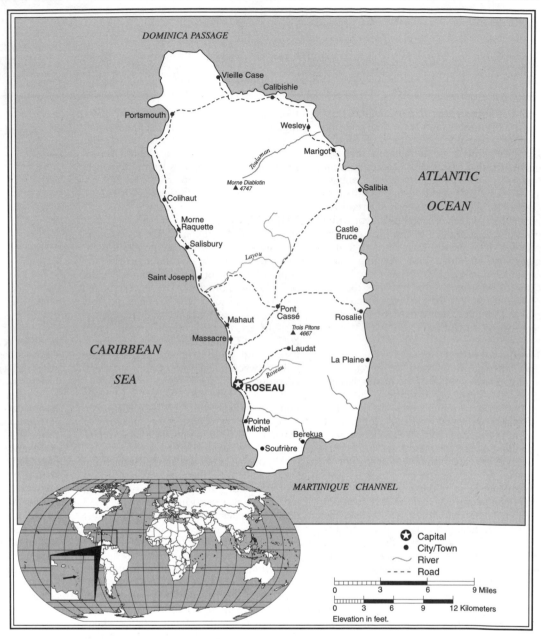

Dominica is sighted on Christopher Columbus's second voyage
1493

Dominica is deeded to the British by France
1783

Independence of Great Britain
1978

Hurricanes devastate Dominica's economy
1979–1980

Hurricane Hugo devastates the island
1980s

Mary Eugenia Charles becomes the Caribbean's first woman head of government

1990s

Dominica seeks stronger tourism revenues, especially in ecotourism

Territorial dispute with Venezuela over Bird Island

The banana industry is in crisis

A FRAGMENTED NATION

Dominica is a small and poor country that gained its independence of Great Britain in 1978. Culturally, the island reflects a number of patterns. Ninety percent of the population speak French patois (dialect), and most are Roman Catholic, while only a small minority speak English and are Protestant. Yet English is the official language. There are also small groups of Indians who may have descended from the original Carib inhabitants; they are alternately revered and criticized. Many Dominicans perceive the Carib Indians as drunken, lazy, and dishonest. Others see them as symbolically important because they represent an ancient culture and fit into the larger Caribbean search for cultural and national identity. There is also a small number of Rastafarians, who identify with their black African roots.

Christopher Columbus discovered the island of Dominica on his second voyage to the New World in 1493. Because of the presence of Carib Indians, who were known for their ferocity, Spanish efforts to settle the island were rebuffed. It was not until 1635 that France took advantage of Spanish weakness and claimed Dominica as its own. French missionaries became the island's first European settlers. Because of continued Carib resistance, the French and English agreed in 1660 that both Dominica and St. Vincent should be declared neutral and left to the Indians. Definitive English settlement did not occur until the eighteenth century, and the island again became a bone of contention between the French and English. It became Britain's by treaty in 1783.

Today, Dominica's population is broken up into sharply differentiated regions. The early collapse of the plantation economy left pockets of settlements, which are still isolated from one another. A difficult topography and poor communications exaggerate the differences between these small communities. This contrasts with nations such as Jamaica and Trinidad and Tobago, which have a greater sense of national awareness because there are good communications and mass media that reach most citizens and foster the development of a national perception.

EMIGRATION

Although Dominica has a high birth rate and its people's life expectancy has measurably increased over the past few years, the growth rate has been dropping due to significant out-migration. Out-migration is not a new phenomenon. From the 1880s until well into the 1900s, many Dominicans sought economic opportunity in the gold fields of French Guiana. Today, most move to the neighboring French departments of Guadeloupe and Martinique.

THE ECONOMY

Dominica's chief export, bananas, has suffered for some years from natural disasters and falling prices. Hurricanes blew down the banana trees in 1979, 1980, 1989, and 1995, and banana exports fell dramatically between 1993 and 1994. Attempts by the United States in 1995 to force the European Union to end special treatment for former colonies cast a further pall over the banana industry in Dominica. A drop in banana prices in 1997 prompted the opposition Dominica Freedom Party to demand that Dominica become part of a single market in order to take advantage of set prices enjoyed by the producers of Martinique and Guadeloupe. Prime Minister Edison James informed citizens that belt-tightening is necessary to confront the nation's difficult financial situation. Together with other banana-producing small states in the Caribbean, Dominica has increasingly turned to nontraditional crops, including root crops, cucumbers, flowers, hot peppers, tomatoes, and nonbanana tropical fruits.

POLITICAL FREEDOM

Despite economic difficulties and several attempted coups, Dominica still enjoys a parliamentary democracy patterned along British lines. The press is free and has not been subject to control—save for a brief state of emergency in 1981, which corresponded to a coup attempt by former prime minister Patrick John and unemployed members of the disbanded Defense Force. Political parties and trade unions are free to organize. Labor unions are small but enjoy the right to strike. Women have full rights under the law and are active in the political system; former prime minister Mary Eugenia Charles was the Caribbean's first woman to become a head of government.

DEVELOPMENT

Dominica's agrarian economy is heavily dependent on earnings from banana exports to Great Britain. To strengthen the economy, attempts are being made to diversify agricultural production, to develop a tourist industry, and to promote light manufacturing.

FREEDOM

Freedom House, an international human-rights organization, listed Dominica as "free." It also noted that "the rights of the native Caribs may not be fully respected." The example set by former prime minister Mary Eugenia Charles led to greater participation by women in the island's political life.

HEALTH/WELFARE

With the assistance of external donors, Dominica has rebuilt many primary schools destroyed in Hurricane Hugo. A major restructuring of the public health administration has improved the quality of health care, even in the previously neglected rural areas.

ACHIEVEMENTS

Traditional handcrafts—especially intricately woven baskets, mats, and hats—have been preserved in Dominica. School children are taught the techniques to pass on this dimension of Dominican culture.

Dominican Republic

GEOGRAPHY

Area in Square Miles (Kilometers):
18,712 (48,464) (about twice
the size of New Hampshire)
Capital (Population): Santo
Domingo (3,166,000)
Environmental Concerns: water
shortages; soil erosion; damage
to coral reefs; deforestation;
damage from Hurricane Georges
Geographical Features: rugged
highlands and mountains with
fertile valleys interspersed
Climate: tropical maritime

PEOPLE

Population

Total: 8,130,000
Annual Growth Rate: 1.62%
Rural/Urban Population Ratio:
37/63
Major Language: Spanish
Ethnic Makeup: 73% mixed;
16% white; 11% black
Religions: 95% Roman Catholic;
5% others

Health

Life Expectancy at Birth: 68
years (male); 72 years (female)
Infant Mortality Rate (Ratio):
42.5/1,000
Average Caloric Intake: 106%
of FAO minimum
Physicians Available (Ratio):
1/1,052

Education

Adult Literacy Rate: 82%
Compulsory (Ages): 7–14

COMMUNICATION

Telephones: 1 per 14 people
Daily Newspaper Circulation:
34 per 1,000 people
Televisions: 1 per 11 people

TRANSPORTATION

Highways in Miles (Kilometers): 7,825
(12,600)
Railroads in Miles (Kilometers): 470 (757)
Usable Airfields: 36
Motor Vehicles in Use: 200,000

GOVERNMENT

Type: republic
Independence Date: February 27, 1844
(from Haiti)
Head of State/Government: President
Leonel Fernádez Reyna is both head of
state and head of government
Political Parties: Dominican Revolution-
ary Party; Social Christian Reformist
Party; Dominican Liberation Party; Inde-
pendent Revolutionary Party; others

Suffrage: universal and compulsory at 18,
or at any age if married; members of the
armed forces or the police cannot vote

MILITARY

Military Expenditures (% of GDP): 1.1%
Current Disputes: none

ECONOMY

Currency ($ U.S. Equivalent): 16,19
Dominican pesos = $1
Per Capita Income/GDP: $5,000/$39.8
billion
GDP Growth Rate: 7%
Inflation Rate: 6%
Unemployment Rate: 16%
Labor Force: 2,300,000–2,600,000
Natural Resources: nickel; bauxite; gold;
silver

Agriculture: sugarcane; coffee; cotton;
cocoa; tobacco; rice; beans; potatoes;
corn; bananas; livestock
Industry: toruism; sugar processing;
ferronickel and gold mining; textiles;
cement; tobacco
Exports: $997 million (primary partners
United States, European Union, Canada)
Imports: $3.6 billion (primary partners
United States, European Union,
Venezuela)

http://lcweb2.loc.gov/frd/cs/dotoc.html
http://www.wmbe.doe.gov/
international/dominicanrepublic.html

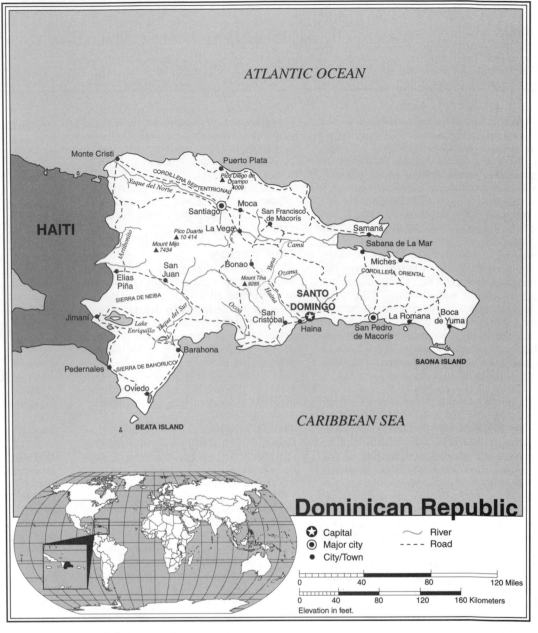

ATLANTIC OCEAN

HAITI

Monte Cristi
Puerto Plata
CORDILLERA SEPTENTRIONAL
Pico Diego de
Ocampo
4009
Yaque del Norte
Moca
Santiago
San Francisco
de Macorís
La Vega
Samaná
Sabana de La Mar
Pico Duarte
10 414
Mount Mijo
7434
Camú
Miches
CORDILLERA ORIENTAL
San
Juan
Bonao
Mount Tina
9285
Yuna
Ozama
Elias
Piña
Artibonito
Haina
SIERRA DE NEIBA
Ocoa
SANTO
DOMINGO
Jimani
Lake
Enriquillo
Yaque del Sur
San
Cristóbal
La Romana
Boca
de Yuma
Haina
San Pedro
de Macorís
Barahona
SAONA ISLAND
Pedernales
SIERRA DE BAHORUCO
Oviedo
CARIBBEAN SEA
BEATA ISLAND

Dominican Republic

⊛ Capital
◉ Major city
● City/Town
〜 River
- - - - Road

0   40   80   120 Miles
0   40   80   120   160 Kilometers
Elevation in feet.

The founding of Santo Domingo, the oldest European city in the Americas **1496**

Independence from Spain is declared **1821**

Haitian control **1822–1844**

Independence as a separate state **1844**

The era of General Rafael Trujillo **1930–1961**

Civil war and U.S. intervention **1965**

The International Monetary Fund approves $78 million in a stand-by loan **1980s**

1990s

Leonel Fernández is elected president

Diplomatic relations are restored with Cuba

In 1998, Hurricane Georges slams into the nation, killing many and causing $1.3 billion in damage

DOMINICAN REPUBLIC: RACIAL STRIFE

Occupying the eastern two thirds of the island of Hispaniola (Haiti comprises the western third), the Dominican Republic historically has feared its neighbor to the west. Much of the fear has its origins in race. From 1822 until 1844, the Dominican Republic—currently 73 percent mixed, or mulatto—was ruled by a brutal black Haitian regime. One authority noted that the Dominican Republic's freedom from Haiti has always been precarious: "Fear of reconquest by the smaller but more heavily populated (and, one might add, black) neighbor has affected Dominican psychology more than any other factor."

In the 1930s, for example, President Rafael Trujillo posed as the defender of Catholic values and European culture against the "barbarous" hordes of Haiti. Trujillo ordered the massacre of from 12,000 to 20,000 Haitians who had settled in the Dominican Republic in search of work. For years, the Dominican government had encouraged Haitian sugarcane cutters to cross the border to work on the U.S.–owned sugar plantations. But with the world economic depression in the 1930s and a fall in sugar prices and production, many Haitians did not return to their part of the island; in fact, additional thousands continued to stream across the border. The response of the Dominican government was wholesale slaughter.

Since 1952, a series of five-year agreements have been reached between the two governments to regularize the supply of Haitian cane cutters. An estimated 20,000 cross each year into the Dominican Republic legally, and an additional 60,000 enter illegally. Living and working conditions are very poor for these Haitians, and the migrants have no legal status and no rights. Planters prefer the Haitian workers because they are "cheaper and more docile" than Dominican laborers, who expect reasonable food, adequate housing, electric lights, and transportation to the fields. Today, as in the 1930s, economic troubles have gripped the Dominican Republic; the president has promised across-the-board sacrifices.

There is a subtle social discrimination against darker-skinned Dominicans, although this has not proved to be an insurmountable obstacle, as many hold elected political office. Discrimination is in part historical, in part cultural, and must be set against a backdrop of sharp prejudice against Haitians. This prejudice is also directed against the minority in the Dominican population who are of Haitian descent. For example, during the contested presidential election of 1994, President Joaquín Balaguer Ricardo introduced the issue of race when questions were raised about his opponent's rumored Haitian origins. President Leonel Fernández has worked hard for better relations with Haitians, but the bitter memories and policies of the past have undercut his efforts.

WOMEN'S RIGHTS

Women in the Dominican Republic have enjoyed political rights since 1941. While in office, President Balaguer, in an unprecedented move, named women governors for eight of the country's 29 provinces. Sexual discrimination is prohibited by law, but women have not shared equal social or economic status or opportunity with men. Divorce, however, is easily obtainable, and women can hold property in their own names. A 1996 profile of the nation's population and health noted that 27 percent of Dominican households were headed by women. In urban areas, the percentage rose to 31 percent.

AN AIR OF CRISIS

Progress toward a political scene free of corruption and racism has been fitful. The 1994 presidential election was marred by what multinational observers called massive fraud. The opposition claimed that Balaguer not only "stole the election" but also employed racist, anti-Haitian rhetoric that "inflamed stereotypes of Haitians in the Dominican Republic." Widespread unrest in the wake of the election, together with pressure from the Roman Catholic Church, the Organization of American States, and the United States, resulted in the "Pact for Democracy," which forced Balaguer to serve a shortened two-year term as president. New elections in 1996 returned Leonel Fernández to the presidency. Fernández has claimed that Balaguer left the country in a state of "bankruptcy . . . and devastation." Indeed, economic problems have generated an unending series of labor disputes. More than a quarter of the workforce are unemployed. Despite his checkered record, Balaguer, now in his 90s, is expected to run once again for the presidency as the candidate of the Social Christian Reform Party in elections scheduled for the year 2000.

DEVELOPMENT

Balaguer's economic policies initially cut inflation from 100% in 1990 to 3% in 1993, but inflation was again in double digits by 1996. GDP is one of the lowest in the region, and more than 25% of the workforce are unemployed. President Fernández, in an attempt to stimulate trade, resumed diplomatic relations with Cuba.

FREEDOM

Democracy was shaken by massive electoral fraud, political turmoil, and racist rhetoric in 1994 and 1995. New elections in 1996 were more peaceful, but political maneuvering and an economy in crisis have maintained an undercurrent of unrest.

HEALTH/WELFARE

Sociologist Laura Raynolds notes that a restructuring of labor that moved thousands of women into nontraditional agriculture and manufacturing for export has reduced them to a "cheap and disciplined" workforce. Their work is undervalued to enhance profits. In that the majority of these workers are mothers, there has been a redefinition of family identity and work.

ACHIEVEMENTS

The National Theater of the Dominican Republic is a professional showcase of Caribbean arts. It is located on the Plaza de la Cultura along with the Museum of the Dominican Man, the Gallery of Modern Art, and the National Library. The theater has become the cultural heart of the city of Santo Domingo.

Grenada

GEOGRAPHY
Area in Square Miles (Kilometers): 133 (340) (about twice the size of Washington, D.C.)
Capital (Population): St. George's (4,500)
Geographical Features: volcanic in origin, with central mountains
Climate: tropical

PEOPLE

Population
Total: 97,000
Annual Growth Rate: 0.87%
Rural/Urban Population Ratio: 64/36
Major Languages: English; French patois
Ethnic Makeup: mainly black
Religions: largely Roman Catholic; Church of England; other Protestant sects

Health
Life Expectancy at Birth: 69 years (male); 74 years (female)
Infant Mortality Rate (Ratio): 11.1/1,000
Average Caloric Intake: 87% of FAO minimum
Physicians Available (Ratio): 1/1,517

Education
Adult Literacy Rate: 98%
Compulsory (Ages): 6–14; free

COMMUNICATION
Telephones: 1 per 3.9 people
Televisions: 1 per 3 people

TRANSPORTATION
Highways in Miles (Kilometers): 646 (1,040)
Railroads in Miles (Kilometers): none
Usable Airfields: 3

GOVERNMENT
Type: parliamentary democracy
Independence Date: February 7, 1974 (from the United Kingdom)
Head of State/Government: Queen Elizabeth II; Prime Minister Keith Mitchell
Political Parties: New National Party; Grenada United Labour Party; The National Party; National Democratic Congress; Maurice Bishop Patriotic Movement; Democratic Labour Party
Suffrage: universal at 18

MILITARY
Current Disputes: none

ECONOMY
Currency ($ U.S. Equivalent): 2.7 East Caribbean dollars = $1
Per Capita Income/GDP: $3,500/$340 million
GDP Growth Rate: 5%
Inflation Rate: 1.4%
Unemployment Rate: 20%
Labor Force: 36,000
Natural Resources: timber; tropical fruit; deepwater harbors

Agriculture: bananas; cocoa; nutmeg; mace; citrus fruits; avocados; root crops; sugarcane; corn; vegetables
Industry: food and beverages; spice processing; textiles; light assembly operations; tourism; construction
Exports: $22 million (primary partners CARICOM, United Kingdom, United States)
Imports: $166.5 million (primary partners United States, CARICOM, United Kingdom)

http://www.cia.gov/cia/publications/factbook/gj.html

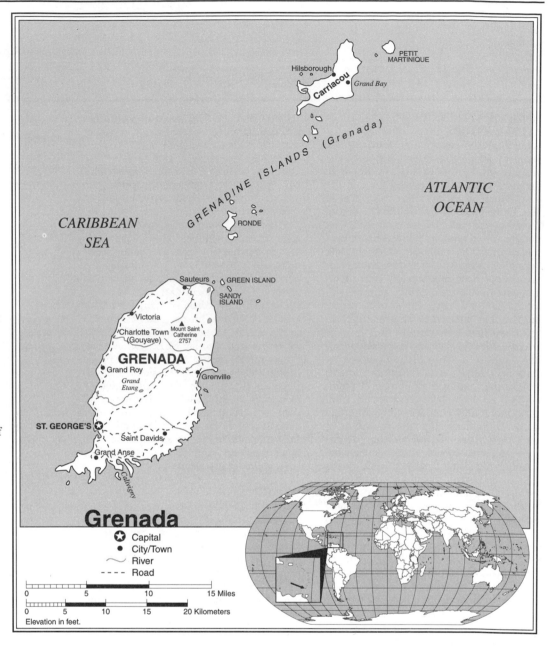

Grenada

⭐ Capital
● City/Town
〰 River
---- Road

0   5   10   15 Miles
0   5   10   15   20 Kilometers
Elevation in feet.

Grenada is discovered by Christopher Columbus
1498

England acquires the island from France by treaty
1763

Slavery is abolished
1834

Member of the West Indies Federation
1958–1962

Independence from Great Britain
1974

A coup brings Maurice Bishop to power
1979

Prime Minister Maurice Bishop is assassinated; U.S. troops land
1980s

1990s

Former mathematics professor Keith Mitchell is elected prime minister in 1995

Prime Minister Mitchell visits Cuba to discuss trade

A proposal to name the new airport after Maurice Bishop proves divisive

GRENADA: A FRESH BEGINNING

On his third voyage to the New World in 1498, Christopher Columbus sighted Grenada, which he named Concepción. The origin of the name Grenada cannot be clearly established, although it is believed that the Spanish renamed the island for the Spanish city of Granada. Because of a fierce aboriginal population of Carib Indians, the island remained uncolonized for 100 years.

Grenada, like most of the Caribbean, is ethnically mixed. Its culture draws on several traditions. The island's French past is preserved among some people who still speak patois (a French dialect). There are few whites on the island, save for a small group of Portuguese who immigrated earlier in the century. The primary cultural identification is with Great Britain, from which Grenada won its independence in 1974.

Grenada's political history has been tumultuous. The corruption and violent tactics of Grenada's first prime minister, Eric Gairy, resulted in his removal in a bloodless coup in 1979. Even though this action marked the first extra-constitutional change of government in the Commonwealth Caribbean (former British colonies), most Grenadians supported the coup, led by Maurice Bishop and his New Joint Endeavor for Welfare, Education, and Liberation (JEWEL) movement. Prime Minister Bishop, like Jamaica's Michael Manley before him, attempted to break out of European cultural and institutional molds and mobilize Grenadians behind him.

Bishop's social policies laid the foundation for basic health care for all Grenadians. With the departure of Cuban medical doctors in 1983, however, the lack of trained personnel created a significant health-care problem. Moreover, although medical-care facilities exist, these are not always in good repair, and equipment is aging and not reliable. Methods of recording births, deaths, and diseases lack systemization, so it is risky to rely on local statistics to estimate the health needs of the population. There has also been some erosion from Bishop's campaign to accord women equal pay, status, and treatment. Two women were elected to Parliament, but skilled employment for women tends to be concentrated in the lowest-paid sector.

On October 19, 1983, Bishop and several of his senior ministers were killed during the course of a military coup. Six days later, the United States, with the token assistance of soldiers and police from states of the Eastern Caribbean, invaded Grenada, restored the 1974 Constitution, and prepared the way for new elections (held in December 1984).

According to one scholar, the invasion was a "lesson in a peacemaker's role in rebuilding a nation. Although Grenada has a history of parliamentary democracy, an atmosphere of civility, fertile soil, clean drinking water, and no slums, continued aid has not appreciably raised the standard of living and the young are resentful and restless."

Grenada's international airport, the focus of much controversy, has pumped new blood into the tourist industry. Moves have also been made by the Grenadian government to promote private-sector business and to diminish the role of the government in the economy. Large amounts of foreign aid, especially from the United States, have helped to repair the infrastructure.

In recent years, foreign governments such as Kuwait, attracted by the power of Grenada's vote in the United Nations, have committed millions of dollars to Grenada's infrastructure. Some of these partnerships, particularly that involving Japan's access to Caribbean fish stocks, may have severe consequences for Grenadians in the future.

Significant problems remain, however. Unemployment has not decreased; it remains at 20 percent of the workforce. Not surprisingly, the island is experiencing a rising crime rate.

Prime Minister Keith Mitchell of the New National Party has promised to create more jobs in the private sector and to cut taxes to stimulate investment in small, high-technology businesses. He also stated that government would become smaller and leaner. To ease his task, the Grenadian economy has experienced a modest recovery, which had begun in 1993. Privatization has continued, attracting foreign capital. As is the case in much of the Caribbean, tourism has become an important source of revenue and employment in Grenada, with a rapid expansion of the service sector. Despite the decline of agricultural exports, Grenada has maintained its position as the world's second-largest exporter of nutmeg. In 1997, the events of 1983 were relived by Grenadians when the proposal to name the airport at Point Saline for the slain Maurice Bishop generated much controversy.

DEVELOPMENT

Prime Minister Mitchell has moved to end what Grenadians call "barter trade" and the government calls "smuggling." For years, Grenadian fishermen have exchanged their fish in Martinique for beer, cigarettes, and appliances. The cash-strapped treasury desperately needs the tariff revenues and has used drug interdiction as a means to end the contraband trade.

FREEDOM

Grenadians are guaranteed full freedom of the press and speech. Newspapers, most of which are published by political parties, freely criticize the government without penalty.

HEALTH/WELFARE

Grenada still lacks effective legislation for regulation of working conditions, wages, and occupational-safety and health standards. Discrimination is prohibited by law, but women are often paid less than men for the same work.

ACHIEVEMENTS

A series of public consultations have been held with respect to the reestablishment of local government in the villages. Some 52 village councils work with the government in an effort to set policies that are both responsive and equitable.

Haiti (Republic of Haiti)

GEOGRAPHY

Area in Square Miles (Kilometers):
10,714 (27,750) (about the
size of Maryland)
Capital (Population): Port-au-
Prince (1,461,000)
Environmental Concerns: extensive
deforestation; soil erosion;
inadequate potable water
Geographical Features: mostly
rough and mountainous
Climate: tropical; semiarid
where mountains in east cut
off tradewinds

PEOPLE

Population
Total: 6,884,300
Annual Growth Rate: 1.5%
Rural/Urban Population Ratio:
68/32
Major Languages: French; Creole
Ethnic Makeup: 95% black; 5%
mulatto and white
Religions: 80% Roman Catholic
(of which the overwhelming
majority also practice
Vodun); 16% Protestant;
4% others

Health
Life Expectancy at Birth: 50
years (male); 54 years (female)
Infant Mortality Rate (Ratio):
97.6/1,000
Average Caloric Intake: 96% of
FAO minimum
Physicians Available (Ratio):
1/10,041

Education
Adult Literacy Rate: 45%
Compulsory (Ages): 6–12

COMMUNICATION

Telephones: 1 per 119 people
Daily Newspaper Circulation: 6
per 1,000 people
Televisions: 1 per 208 people

TRANSPORTATION

Highways in Miles (Kilometers): 2,588
(4,160)
Railroads in Miles (Kilometers): privately
owned industrial line
Usable Airfields: 13
Motor Vehicles in Use: 53,000

GOVERNMENT

Type: republic
Independence Date: January 1, 1804 (from
France)
Head of State/Government: President
René Garcia Préval; Prime Minister
Jacques-Eduard Alexis

Political Parties: National Front for
Change and Democracy; National Congress of Democratic Movements; Movement for the Installation of Democracy
in Haiti; National Progressive Revolutionary Party; Lavalas Family; Haitian
Christian Democratic Party; others
Suffrage: universal at 18

MILITARY

Current Disputes: claims U.S.–administered
Navassa Island

ECONOMY

Currency ($ U.S. Equivalent): 17.54
gourde = $1
Per Capita Income/GDP: $1,300/$8.9
billion
GDP Growth Rate: 3%
Inflation Rate: 8%
Unemployment Rate: 60%
Labor Force: 3,600,000; unskilled labor
abundant
Natural Resources: none
Agriculture: coffee; mangoes; sugarcane;
rice; corn; sorghum; wood
Industry: sugar refining; flour milling;
textiles; cement; tourism; light assembly
based on imported parts
Exports: $110 million (primary partners
United States, European Union)
Imports: $486 million (primary partners
United States, European Union)

 http://lcweb2.loc.gov/frd/cs/httoc.html

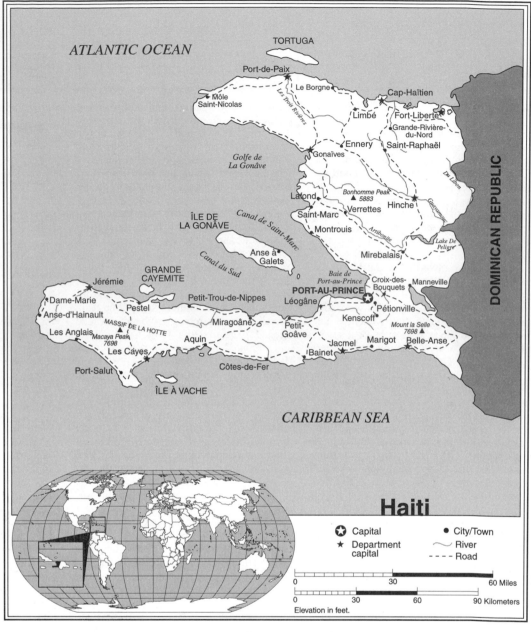

The island is discovered by Christopher Columbus; named Hispaniola
1492

The western portion of Hispaniola is ceded to France
1697

Independence from France
1804

The era of President François Duvalier
1957–1971

Jean-Claude Duvalier is named president-for-life
1971

Jean-Claude Duvalier flees into exile
1986

1990s

A military coup ousts President Jean-Bertrand Aristide; Aristide returns to power in 1994

Political paralysis between 1997 and 1999

Presidental elections are scheduled for 2000

HAITI

Haiti, which occupies the western third of the island of Hispaniola (the Dominican Republic comprises the other two thirds), was the first nation in Latin America to win independence from its mother country—in this instance, France. It is the poorest country in the Western Hemisphere and one of the least developed in the world. Agriculture, which employs about 70 percent of the population, is pressed beyond the limits of the available land; the result has been catastrophic deforestation and erosion. While only roughly 30 percent of the land is suitable for planting, 50 percent is actually under cultivation. Haitians are woefully poor, suffer from poor health and lack of education, and seldom find work. Haiti's urban unemployment is estimated at 40 to 50 percent. Even when employment is found, wages are miserable, and there is no significant labor movement to intercede on behalf of the workers.

A persistent theme in Haiti's history has been a bitter rivalry between a small mulatto elite, consisting of 3 to 4 percent of the population, and the black majority. When François Duvalier, a black country doctor, was president (1957–1971), his avowed aim was to create a "new equilibrium" in the country—by which he meant a major shift in power from the established, predominantly mulatto, elite to a new, black middle class. Much of Haitian culture explicitly rejects Western civilization, which is identified with the mulattos. The Creole language of the masses and their practice of Vodun (voodoo), a combination of African spiritualism and Christianity, has not only insulated the population from the "culturally alien" regimes in power but has also given Haitians a common point of identity.

Haitian intellectuals have raised sharp questions about the nation's culture. Modernizers would like to see the triumph of the French language over Creole and Roman Catholicism over Vodun. Others argue that significant change in Haiti can come only from within, from what is authentically Haitian. The refusal of Haitian governments to recognize Creole as the official language has only added to the determination of the mulatto elite and the black middle class to exclude the rest of the population from effective participation in political life.

For most of its history, Haiti has been run by a series of harsh authoritarian regimes. The ouster in 1986 of President-for-Life Jean-Claude Duvalier promised a more democratic opening as the new ruling National Governing Council announced as its primary goal the transition to a freely elected government. Political prisoners were freed; the dreaded secret police, the Tontons Macoute, were disbanded; and the press was unmuzzled.

The vacuum left by Duvalier's departure was filled by a succession of governments that were either controlled or heavily influenced by the military. Significant change was heralded in 1990 with the election to power of an outspoken Roman Catholic priest, Jean-Bertrand Aristide. By the end of 1991, he had moved against the military and had formulated a foreign policy that sought to move Haiti closer to the nations of Latin America and the Caribbean. Aristide's promotion of the "church of the poor," which combined local beliefs with standard Catholic instruction, earned him the enmity of both conservative Church leaders and Vodun priests. The radical language of his Lavalas (Floodtide) movement, which promised sweeping economic and social changes, made business leaders and rural landowners uneasy.

Perhaps not surprisingly in this coup-ridden nation, the army ousted President Aristide in 1991. It took tough economic sanctions and the threat of an imminent U.S. invasion to force the junta to relinquish power. Aristide, with the support of U.S. troops, was returned to power in 1994. Once an uneasy stability was restored to the country, U.S. troops left the peacekeeping to UN soldiers.

Although there was a period of public euphoria over Aristide's return, the assessment of the *Guardian,* a British newspaper, was somber: Crime rates rose precipitously, political violence continued, and Aristide's enemies were still in Haiti—and armed. Haitians, "sensing a vacuum," took the law "into their own hands."

René Préval, who had served briefly as Aristide's prime minister, was himself elected to the presidency in 1996. According to *Caribbean Week,* Préval has been caught between "a fiercely independent Parliament [and] an externally-imposed structural adjustment programme...." Préval, presiding over a divided party, was unable to have his choices for cabinet posts approved by the Legislature, which left Haiti without an effective government from 1997 until a new prime minister, Jacques-Eduard Alexis, was named in March 1999. Presidential elections were scheduled for December 2000. In the meantime, there has been little economic progress, and the suffering of millions continues.

DEVELOPMENT

The task of rebuilding Haiti following a devastating trade embargo and the ouster of the military is daunting. Two thirds of the Haitian population are unemployed, and a third depend on aid programs for food and health care.

FREEDOM

The Economist noted that unless "a rule of law can be made to hold, and a civilian government made to function reliably, all other plans for Haiti will be just so much wasted paper."

HEALTH/WELFARE

Until 30 years ago, Haiti was self-sufficient in food production. It must now import about a third of its food needs. Nevertheless, the country has a rapidly expanding population, with a doubling time of 35 years overall, far above the Caribbean average of 52 years.

ACHIEVEMENTS

In the late 1940s, Haitian "primitive" art created a sensation in Paris and other art centers. Although the force of the movement has now been spent, it still represents a unique, colorful, and imaginative art form.

Jamaica

GEOGRAPHY

Area in Square Miles (Kilometers):
4,244 (10,991) (slightly
smaller than Connecticut)

Capital (Population): Kingston
(104,000)

Environmental Concerns:
deforestation; polluted coastal
waters; damage to coral
reefs; air pollution

Geographical Features: mostly
mountains, with a narrow,
discontinuous coastal plain

Climate: tropical; temperate
interior

PEOPLE

Population

Total: 2,653,000

Annual Growth Rate: 0.64%

Rural/Urban Population Ratio:
46/54

Major Languages: English;
Jamaican Creole

Ethnic Makeup: 90% black; 7%
mixed; 3% East Indian,
white, Chinese and others

Religions: 56% Protestant; 5%
Roman Catholic; 39% others,
including some spiritualistic
groups

Health

Life Expectancy at Birth: 73
years (male); 78 years
(female)

Infant Mortality Rate (Ratio):
14/1,000

Average Caloric Intake: 119%
of FAO minimum

Physicians Available (Ratio):
1/6,043

Education

Adult Literacy Rate: 85%

Compulsory (Ages): 6–12; free

COMMUNICATION

Telephones: 1 per 8.7 people

Televisions: 1 per 7 people

TRANSPORTATION

Highways in Miles (Kilometers): 11,613
(18,700)

Railroads in Miles (Kilometers): 230 (370)

Usable Airfields: 36

Motor Vehicles in Use: 126,000

GOVERNMENT

Type: parliamentary democracy

Independence Date: August 6, 1962
(from the United Kingdom)

Head of State/Government: Queen
Elizabeth II; Prime Minister Percival
J. Patterson

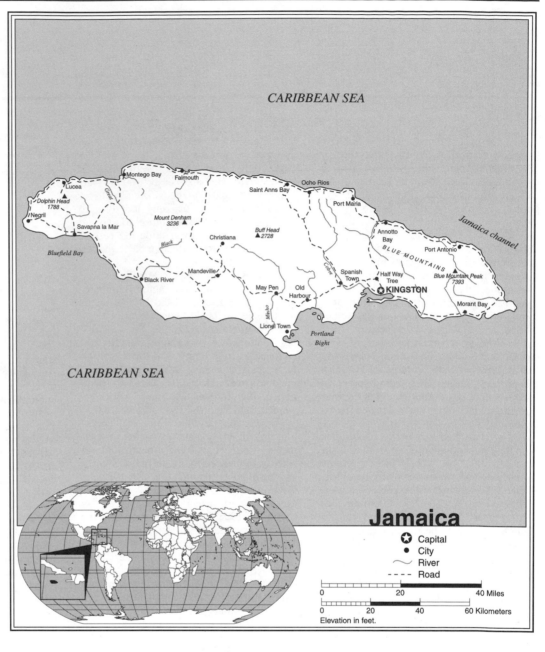

Jamaica

- ✪ Capital
- ● City
- ∿ River
- - - - Road

Political Parties: People's National Party;
Jamaica Labour Party; National
Democratic Movement

Suffrage: universal at 18

MILITARY

Current Disputes: none

ECONOMY

Currency ($ U.S. Equivalent): 40.80
Jamaican dollars = $1

Per Capita Income/GDP: $3,300/$8.8
billion

GDP Growth Rate: –2%

Inflation Rate: 9.9%

Unemployment Rate: 16.5%

Labor Force: 1,140,000

Natural Resources: bauxite; gypsum;
limestone

Agriculture: sugarcane; bananas; coffee;
citrus fruits; potatoes; vegetables;
poultry; goats; milk

Industry: tourism; bauxite; textiles; food
processing; light manufactures

Exports: $1.7 billion (primary partners
United States, European Union, Canada)

Imports: $2.8 billion (primary partners
United States, European Union,
CARICOM)

 http://www.cia.gov/cia/publications/
factbook/jm.html

The first Spanish settlement **1509**	Jamaica is seized by the English **1655**	An earthquake destroys Port Royal **1692**	Universal suffrage is proclaimed **1944**	Independence from Great Britain **1962**	1990s

Violent crime and strong-armed police responses plague the island	Percival J. Patterson is elected prime minister	Prime Minister Patterson visits Cuba; closer economic relations are established between the two countries

JAMAICA:
"OUT OF MANY, ONE PEOPLE"

In 1962, Jamaica and Trinidad and Tobago were the first of the English-speaking Caribbean islands to gain their independence. A central problem since that time has been the limited ability of Jamaicans to forge a sense of nation. "Out of many, one people" is a popular slogan in Jamaica, but it belies an essential division of the population along lines of both race and class. The elite, consisting of a small white population and Creoles (Afro-Europeans), still think of themselves as "English." Local loyalties notwithstanding, Englishness permeates much of Jamaican life, from language to sports. According to former prime minister Michael Manley: "The problem in Jamaica is how do you get the Jamaican to divorce his mind from the paralysis of his history, which was all bitter colonial frustration, so that he sees his society in terms of this is what crippled me?"

Manley's first government (1975–1980) was one of the few in the Caribbean to incorporate the masses of the people into a political process. He was aware that in a country such as Jamaica—where the majority of the population were poor, ill educated, and lacked essential services—the promise to provide basic needs would win him widespread support. Programs to provide Jamaicans with basic health care and education were expanded, as were services. Many products were subjected to price controls or were subsidized to make them available to the majority of the people. Cuban medical teams and teachers were brought to Jamaica to fill the manpower gaps until local people could be trained.

However, Jamaica's fragile economy could not support Manley's policies, and he was eventually opposed by the entrenched elite and voted out of office. But in 1989, Manley was returned to office,

with a new image as a moderate, willing to compromise and aware of the need for foreign-capital investment. Manley retired in 1992 and was replaced as prime minister by Percival J. Patterson, who promised to accelerate Jamaica's transition to a free-market economy. The government instituted a policy of divestment of state-owned enterprises.

The challenges remain. Crime and violence continue to be major social problems in Jamaica. The high crime rate threatens not only the lucrative tourist industry but the very foundations of Jamaican society. Prime Minister Patterson has called for a moral reawakening: "All our programs and strategies for economic progress are doomed to failure unless there is a drastic change in social attitudes. . . ." A stagnant economy, persistent inflation, and unemployment and underemployment combine to lessen respect for authority and contribute to the crime problem. The Suppression of Crime Act of 1974 was repealed in 1994, however, in part because lawyers objected to extraordinary police powers of search and detention. The nation continues to walk the narrow line between liberty and license.

As is the case in many developing-world countries where unemployment and disaffection are common, drug use is high in Jamaica. The government is reluctant to enforce drug control, however, for approximately 8,000 rural families depend on the cultivation of ganja (marijuana) to supplement their already marginal incomes.

Some of Jamaica's violence is politically motivated and tends to be associated with election campaigns. Both major parties have supporters who employ violence for political purposes. The legal system has been unable to contain the violence or bring the guilty to justice, because of a pervasive code of silence enforced at the local level.

The Patterson government has moved deliberately in the direction of electoral reform in an attempt to reduce both violence and fraud. Until those reforms are in place, however, the opposition Jamaica Labour Party has decided to boycott by-elections.

On the positive side, human rights are generally respected, and Jamaica's press is basically free. Press freedom is observed in practice within the broad limits of libel laws and the State Secrets Act. Opposition parties publish newspapers and magazines that are highly critical of government policies, and foreign publications are widely available.

Jamaica's labor-union movement is strong and well organized, and it has contributed many leaders to the political process. Unions are among the strongest and best organizations in the country and are closely tied to political parties.

DEVELOPMENT

In 1997, Prime Minister Patterson visited Cuba, where agreements were signed for closer cooperation in the medical sphere and with a focus on biotechnology. Agreement was also reached on tourism issues and stressed cooperation rather than competition.

FREEDOM

Despite the repeal of the controversial Suppression of Crime Act of 1974, the Parliament, in the face of persistent high levels of crime, provided for emergency police powers. Some critics charge that the Parliament in essence re-created the repealed legislation in a different guise.

HEALTH/WELFARE

Jamaica's "Operation Pride" was designed to combine a dynamic program of land divestment by the state with provisions to meet demands for housing. Squatter colonies would be replaced by "proud home owners."

ACHIEVEMENTS

Marcus Garvey was posthumously declared Jamaica's first National Hero in 1964 because of his leading role in the international movement against racism. He called passionately for the recognition of the equal dignity of human beings regardless of race, religion, or national origin. Garvey died in London in 1940.

St. Kitts–Nevis (Federation of St. Kitts and Nevis)

GEOGRAPHY

Area in Square Miles (Kilometers): 101 (261) (about 1.5 times the size of Washington, D.C.)
Capital (Population): Basseterre (12,600)
Geographical Features: volcanic, with mountainous interiors
Climate: subtropical

PEOPLE

Population

Total: 42,900
Annual Growth Rate: 1.3%
Rural/Urban Population Ratio: 66/34
Major Language: English
Ethnic Makeup: mainly of black African descent
Religions: Anglican; other Protestant sects; Roman Catholic

Health

Life Expectancy at Birth: 65 years (male); 71 years (female)
Infant Mortality Rate (Ratio): 17.4/1,000
Average Caloric Intake: n/a
Physicians Available (Ratio): 1/1,057

Education

Adult Literacy Rate: 97%
Compulsory (Ages): 12–13 years between ages 5–18

COMMUNICATION

Telephones: 1 per 2.8 people
Televisions: 1 per 4.7 people

TRANSPORTATION

Highways in Miles (Kilometers): 199 (320)
Railroads in Miles (Kilometers): 36 (58)
Usable Airfields: 2

GOVERNMENT

Type: constituional monarchy within Commonwealth
Independence Date: September 19, 1983 (from the United Kingdom)
Head of State/Government: Queen Elizabeth II; Prime Minister Denzil Douglas
Political Parties: St. Kitts and Nevis Labour Party; People's Action Movement; Nevis Reformation Party; Concerned Citizens Movement
Suffrage: universal at 18

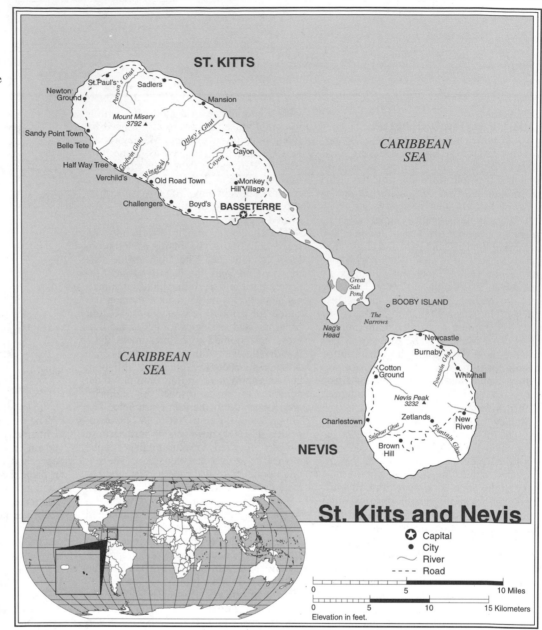

St. Kitts and Nevis

⊛ Capital
● City
〜 River
- - - Road

0   5   10 Miles
0   5   10   15 Kilometers
Elevation in feet.

MILITARY

Current Disputes: Nevis has threatened to secede

ECONOMY

Currency ($ U.S. Equivalent): 2.7 East Caribbean dollars = $1
Per Capita Income/GDP: $6,000/$235 million
GDP Growth Rate: 6.3%
Inflation Rate: 11.3%
Unemployment Rate: 4%
Labor Force: 18,200
Natural Resources: negligible

Agriculture: sugarcane; rice; yams; vegetables; bananas; fish
Industry: sugar processing; tourism; cotton; salt; copra; clothing; footwear; beverages
Exports: $43.7 million (primary partners United States, United Kingdom, CARICOM)
Imports: $129.6 million (primary partners United States, CARICOM, United Kingdom)

 http://www.cia.gov/cia/publications/factbook/sc.html

Elections In 1995 bring Denzil Douglas and the St. Kitts and Nevis Labour Party to power

A referendum on Nevis secession is narrowly defeated

ST. KITTS–NEVIS: ESTRANGED NEIGHBORS

On September 19, 1983, the twin-island state of St. Kitts–Nevis became an independent nation. The country had been a British colony since 1623, when Captain Thomas Warner landed with his wife and eldest son, along with 13 other settlers. The colony fared well, and soon other Caribbean islands were being settled by colonists sent out from St. Kitts (also commonly known as St. Christopher).

The history of this small island nation is the story of the classic duel between the big sea powers of the period—Great Britain, France, and Spain—and the indigenous people—in this case, the Carib Indians. (Although much of the nation's history has centered around St. Kitts, the larger of the two islands, Nevis, only two miles away, has always been considered a part of St. Kitts, and its history is tied into that of the larger island.) The British were the first settlers on the island of St. Kitts but were followed that same year by the French. In a unique compromise, considering the era, the British and French divided the territory in 1627 and lived in peace for a number of decades. A significant reason for this British–French cooperation was the constant pressure from their common enemies: the aggressive Spanish and the fierce Carib Indians.

With the gradual elimination of the mutual threat, Anglo–French tensions again mounted, resulting in a sharp land battle at Frigate Bay on St. Kitts. The new round of hostilities, which reflected events in Europe, would disrupt the Caribbean for much of the next century. Events came to a climactic head in 1782, when the British garrison at Brimstone Hill, commonly known as the "Gibraltar of the West Indies," was overwhelmed by a superior

French force. In honor of the bravery of the defenders, the French commander allowed the British to march from the fortress in full formation. (The expression "peace with honor" has its roots in this historic encounter.) Later in the year, however, the British again seized the upper hand. A naval battle at Frigate Bay was won by British Admiral Hood following a series of brilliant maneuvers. The defeated French admiral, the Count de Grasse, was in turn granted "peace with honor." Thereafter, the islands remained under British rule until their independence in 1983.

AGRICULTURE

Before the British colonized the island, St. Kitts was called *Liamiuga* ("Fertile Isle") by the Carib Indians. The name was, and is, apt, because agriculture plays a big role in the economy of the islands. Almost 90 percent of the nation's economy is based on the export of sugar; the rest derives from the tourist trade.

Because the sugar market is so unstable, the economy of St. Kitts–Nevis fluctuates considerably. Nearly one third of St. Kitts's land (some 16,000 acres) is under cultivation. In a good year, sugar production can exceed 50,000 tons. Although over the years growers have experimented with a number of other crops, they always have come back to sugarcane.

ECONOMIC CHANGE

Unlike such islands as Barbados and Antigua, St. Kitts–Nevis for years chose not to use tourism as a buffer to offset any disastrous fluctuations in sugar prices. On St. Kitts, there was an antitourism attitude that can be traced back to the repressive administration of Prime Minister Robert Bradshaw, a black nationalist who worked to discourage tourism and threatened to nationalize all land holdings.

That changed under the moderate leadership of Kennedy Simmonds and his People's Action Movement, who remained in power from 1980 until ousted in elections in July 1995. The new administration of Denzil Douglas promised to address serious problems that have developed, including drug trafficking, money laundering, and a lack of respect for law and order. In 1997, a 50-man "army" was created to wage war against heavily armed drug traffickers operating in the region. Agriculture Minister Timothy Harris noted that the permanent defense force "was critical to the survival of the sovereignty of the nation."

The future of St. Kitts–Nevis will depend on its ability to broaden its economic base. A potential problem of some magnitude looms, however: The island of Nevis, long in the shadow of the more populous and prosperous St. Kitts, nearly voted to secede in a referendum held in August 1998. The constitution requires a two-thirds majority for secession; 61.7 percent of the population of Nevis voted "Yes." Not surprisingly, the government is working to fashion a new federalism with "appropriate power sharing" between the islands.

DEVELOPMENT

In an attempt to improve an economy that is essentially stagnant, the government of St. Kitts–Nevis, under the auspices of CARICOM, supports the idea of a Caribbean free-trade area. Of particular interest is the inclusion of Cuba in the agreement.

FREEDOM

The election in 1984 of Constance Mitcham to Parliament signaled a new role for women. She was subsequently appointed minister of women's affairs. However, despite her conspicuous success, women still occupy a very small percentage of senior civil-service positions.

HEALTH/WELFARE

Since the economy is so dependent on the sugarcane crop, the overall welfare of the country is at the mercy of the world sugar market. Although a minimum wage exists by law, the amount is less than what a person can reasonably be expected to live on.

ACHIEVEMENTS

St. Kitts–Nevis was the first successful British settlement in the Caribbean. St. Kitts–Nevis was the birthplace of Alexander Hamilton, the first U.S. secretary of the Treasury Department and an American statesman.

St. Lucia

GEOGRAPHY
Area in Square Miles (Kilometers):
238 (619) (about 3 times the
size of Washington, D.C.)
Capital (Population): Castries
(13,600)
Environmental Concerns:
deforestation; soil erosion
Geographical Features:
volcanic and mountainous;
some broad, fertile valleys
Climate: tropical maritime

PEOPLE

Population
Total: 154,000
Annual Growth Rate: 1.09%
Rural/Urban Population Ratio:
63/37
Major Languages: English;
French patois
Ethnic Makeup: 90% black; 6%
mixed; 3% East Indian; 1%
white
Religions: 90% Roman Catholic;
3% Church of England; 7%
other Protestant sects

Health
Life Expectancy at Birth: 68
years (male); 76 years
(female)
Infant Mortality Rate (Ratio):
16.5/1,000
Average Caloric Intake: 99% of
FAO minimum
Physicians Available (Ratio):
1/2,235

Education
Adult Literacy Rate: 67%
Compulsory (Ages): 5–15

COMMUNICATION
Telephones: 1 per 5.4 people
Televisions: 1 per 5.3 people

TRANSPORTATION
Highways in Miles (Kilometers):
451 (1,210)
Railroads in Miles (Kilometers): none
Usable Airfields: 2
Motor Vehicles in Use: 11,800

GOVERNMENT
Type: constitutinal monarchy within
Commonwealth
Independence Date: February 22, 1979
(from the United Kingdom)
Head of State/Government: Queen
Elizabeth II; Prime Minister Kenny D.
Anthony
Political Parties: United Workers Party;
St. Lucia Labour Party; National
Freedom Party
Suffrage: universal at 18

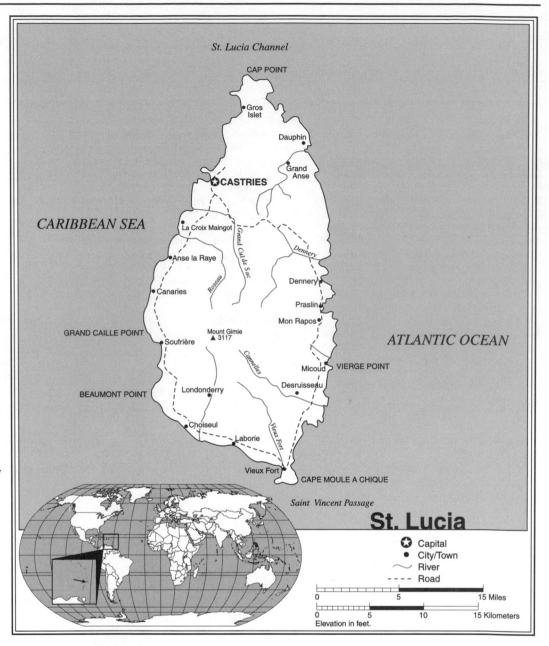

St. Lucia

- ✪ Capital
- ● City/Town
- ～ River
- --- Road

0   5   15 Miles

0   5   10   15 Kilometers
Elevation in feet.

MILITARY
Military Expenditures (% of GDP): 2%
Current Disputes: none

ECONOMY
Currency ($ U.S. Equivalent): 2.7 East
Caribbean dollars = $1
Per Capita Income/GDP: $4,100/$625
million
GDP Growth Rate: 2.2%
Inflation Rate: 1.9%
Unemployment Rate: 15%
Labor Force: 43,800
Natural Resources: forests; sandy
beaches; minerals (pumice); mineral
springs; geothermal potential

Agriculture: bananas; coconuts; vegetables;
citrus fruits; root crops; cocoa
Industry: clothing; assembly of electronic
components; beverages; corrugated
cardboard boxes; tourism; lime process-
ing; coconut processing
Exports: $70.1 million (primary partners
United Kingdom, United States,
CARICOM)
Imports: $292.4 million (primary partners
United States, CARICOM, United
Kingdom)

 http://www.cia.gov/cia/publications/
factbook/st.html

ST. LUCIA: ENGLISH POLITICS, FRENCH CULTURE

The history of St. Lucia gives striking testimony to the fact that the sugar economy, together with the contrasting cultures of various colonial masters, was crucial in shaping the land, social structures, and lifestyles of its people. The island changed hands between the French and the English at least seven times, and the influences of both cultures are still evident today. Ninety percent of the population speaks French patois (dialect), while the educated and the elite prefer English. Indeed, the educated perceive patois as suitable only for proverbs and curses. On St. Lucia and the other patois-speaking islands (Dominica, Grenada), some view the common language as the true reflection of their uniqueness. English, however, is the language of status and opportunity. In terms of religion, most St. Lucians are Roman Catholic.

The original inhabitants of St. Lucia were Arawak Indians who had been forced off the South American mainland by the cannibalistic Carib Indians. Gradually, the Carib also moved onto the Caribbean islands and destroyed most of the Arawak culture. Evidence of that early civilization has been found in rich archaeological sites on St. Lucia.

The date of the European "discovery" of the island is uncertain; it may have occurred in 1499 or 1504 by the navigator and mapmaker Juan de la Cosa, who explored the Windward Islands during the early years of the sixteenth century. The Dutch, French, and English all established small settlements or trading posts on the island in the seventeenth century but were resisted by the Caribs. The first successful settlement dates from 1651, when the French were able to maintain a foothold.

The island's political culture is English. Upon independence from Great Britain in 1979, St. Lucians adopted the British parliamentary system, which includes specific safeguards for the preservation of human rights. Despite several years of political disruption, caused by the jockeying for power of several political parties and affiliated interests, St. Lucian politics is essentially stable.

THE ECONOMY

St. Lucia has an economy that is as diverse as any in the Caribbean. Essentially agricultural, the country has also developed a tourism industry, manufacturing, and related construction activity. A recent "mineral inventory" has located possible gold deposits, but exploitation must await the creation of appropriate mining legislation.

U.S. promises to the region made in the 1980s failed to live up to expectations. Although textiles, clothing, and nontraditional goods exported to the United States increased as a result of the Caribbean Basin Initiative, St. Lucia remained dependent on its exports of bananas. About a third of the island's workforce are involved in banana production, which accounts for 90 percent of St. Lucia's exports. U.S. aid to the region, which topped $226 million in 1985, fell to below $30 million in 1997, leading former St. Lucian prime minister Vaughan Lewis to complain, "We have dropped off the geopolitical map." The North American Free Trade Agreement was clearly of more importance to the United States.

St. Lucia's crucial banana industry suffered significant production losses in 1997, in large part because of drought. Exports were half of the normal volume, and St. Lucia fell short of filling its quota for the European Union. In addition, the United States won a preliminary judgment from the World Trade Organization that acknowledged that St. Lucia and other Caribbean producers received preferential treatment from Europe under the quota system. Reduced quotas would be disastrous to small local producers.

EDUCATION AND EMIGRATION

Education in St. Lucia has traditionally been brief and perfunctory. Few students attend secondary school, and very few (3 percent) ever attend a university. Although the government reports that 95 percent of those eligible attend elementary school, farm and related chores severely reduce attendance figures. In recent years, St. Lucia has channeled more than 20 percent of its expenditures into education and health care. Patient care in the general hospital was made free of charge in 1980.

Population growth is relatively low, but emigration off the island is a significant factor. For years, St. Lucians, together with Dominicans, traveled to French Guiana to work in the gold fields. More recently, however, they have crossed to neighboring Martinique, a French department, in search of work. St. Lucians can also be found working on many other Caribbean islands.

DEVELOPMENT

A pilot project was developed on St. Lucia to help local farmers diversify their crops so they could provide hotels with a consistent and reasonably priced supply of fresh fruits and vegetables.

FREEDOM

The St. Lucian political system is healthy, with opposition parties playing an active role in and out of Parliament. Women participate fully in government and hold prominent positions in the civil service.

HEALTH/WELFARE

The minister of agriculture has linked marginal nutrition and malnutrition in St. Lucia with economic adjustment programs in the Caribbean. He noted that the success achieved earlier in raising standards of living was being eroded by "onerous debt burdens."

ACHIEVEMENTS

St. Lucians have won an impressive two Nobel prizes. Sir W. Arthur Lewis won the prize in 1979 for economics, and in 1993, Derek Walcott won the prize for literature. When asked how the island had produced two Nobel laureates, Wolcott replied: "It's the food."

St. Vincent and the Grenadines

GEOGRAPHY

Area in Square Miles (Kilometers):
131 (340) (about twice the size of Washington, D.C.)
Capital (Population): Kingstown (16,000)
Environmental Concerns: pollution of coastal waters and shorelines by discharges from pleasure boats
Geographical Features: volcanic; mountainous
Climate: tropical

PEOPLE

Population

Total: 120,500
Annual Growth Rate: 0.57%
Rural/Urban Population Ratio: 50/50
Major Languages: English; French patois
Ethnic Makeup: mainly black African descent; remainder mixed, with some white and East Indian and Carib Indian
Religions: Anglican; Methodist; Roman Catholic; Seventh-Day Adventist

Health

Life Expectancy at Birth: 72 years (male); 75 years (female)
Infant Mortality Rate (Ratio): 15.2/1,000
Average Caloric Intake: 91% of FAO minimum
Physicians Available (Ratio): 1/2,708

Education

Adult Literacy Rate: 96%

COMMUNICATION

Telephones: 1 per 6.1 people
Televisions: 1 per 6.8 people

TRANSPORTATION

Highways in Miles (Kilometers): 646 (1,040)
Railroads in Miles (Kilometers): none
Usable Airfields: 6
Motor Vehicles in Use: 8,100

GOVERNMENT

Type: constitutional monarchy within Commonwealth
Independence Date: October 27, 1979 (from the United Kingdom)
Head of State/Government: Queen Elizabeth II; Prime Minister James F. Mitchell
Political Parties: Unity Labour Party; New Democratic Party; United People's Movement; National Reform Party

Suffrage: universal at 18

MILITARY

Current Disputes: none

ECONOMY

Currency ($ U.S. Equivalent): 2.7 East Caribbean dollars = $1
Per Capita Income/GDP: $2,400/$289 million
GDP Growth Rate: 4%
Inflation Rate: 3.6%
Unemployment Rate: 35%–40%
Labor Force: 67,000
Natural Resources: negligible

Agriculture: bananas; arrowroot; coconuts; sweet potatoes; spices; small amount of livestock; fish
Industry: food processing; cement; furniture; clothing; starch; tourism
Exports: $47.3 million (primary partners CARICOM, United Kingdom, United States)
Imports: $158.8 million (primary partners United States, CARICOM, United Kingdom)

 http://www.cia.gov/cia/publications/factbook/vc.html

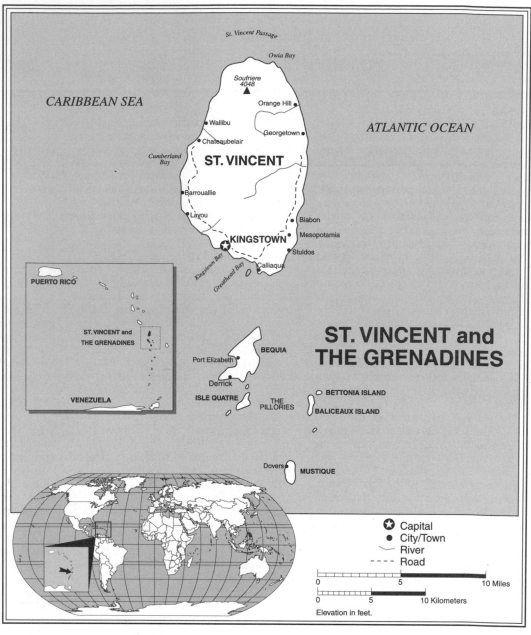

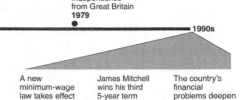

Christopher
Columbus
discovers and
names St. Vincent
1498

Ceded to the
British by France
1763

The Carib War
1795

St. Vincent's La
Soufrière erupts
and kills 2,000
people
1902

Independence
from Great Britain
1979

1990s

A new
minimum-wage
law takes effect

James Mitchell
wins his third
5-year term

The country's
financial
problems deepen

ST. VINCENT AND THE GRENADINES: POOR BUT FREE

Vincentians, like many other West Indians, either identify with or, as viewed from a different perspective, suffer from a deep-seated European orientation. Critics argue that it is an identification that is historical in origin, and that it is negative. For many, the European connection is nothing more than the continuing memory of a master–slave relationship.

St. Vincent is unique in that it was one of the few Caribbean islands where runaway black slaves intermarried with Carib Indians and produced a distinct racial type known as the Garifuna, or black Carib. Toward the end of the eighteenth century, the Garifuna and other native peoples mounted an assault on the island's white British planters. They were assisted by the French from Martinique but were defeated in 1796. As punishment, the Garifuna were deported to what is today Belize, where they formed one of the bases of that nation's population.

In 1834, the black slaves were emancipated, which disrupted the island's economy by decreasing the labor supply. In order to fill this vacuum, Portuguese and East Indian laborers were imported to maintain the agrarian economy. This, however, was not done until later in the nineteenth century—not quickly enough to prevent a lasting blow to the island's economic base.

St. Vincent, along with Dominica, is one of the poorest islands in the West Indies. The current unemployment rate is estimated at between 35 and 40 percent. With more than half the population under age 15, unemployment will continue to be a major problem in the foreseeable future.

Formerly one of the West Indian sugar islands, St. Vincent's main crops are now bananas and arrowroot. The sugar industry was a casualty of low world-market prices and a black-power movement in the 1960s that associated sugar production with memories of slavery. Limited sugar production has been renewed to meet local needs.

THE POLITICS OF POVERTY

Poverty affects everyone in St. Vincent and the Grenadines, except a very few who live in comfort. In the words of one Vincentian, for most people, "life is a study in poverty." In 1969, a report identified malnutrition and gastroenteritis as being responsible for 57 percent of the deaths of children under age five. Those problems persist.

Deep-seated poverty also has an impact on the island's political life. Living on the verge of starvation, Vincentians cannot appreciate an intellectual approach to politics. They find it difficult to wait for the effects of long-term trends or coordinated development. Bread-and-butter issues are what concern them. Accordingly, parties speak little of basic economic and social change, structural shifts in the economy, or the latest economic theories. Politics is reduced to personality contests and rabble-rousing.

Despite its severe economic problems, St. Vincent is a free society. Newspapers are uncensored. Some reports, however, have noted that the government has on occasion granted or withheld advertising on the basis of a paper's editorial position.

Unions enjoy the right of collective bargaining. They represent about 11 percent of the labor force. St. Vincent, which won its independence of Great Britain in 1979, is a parliamentary, constitutional democracy. Political parties have the right to organize.

A NEW POLITICAL SPIRIT

While the country's political life has been calm, relative to some of the other Caribbean islands, there are signs of voter unrest. Prime Minister James Mitchell was reelected in 1999 for an unprecedented fourth five-year term, but his New Democratic Party lost some ground in the Legislature. In addition, two opposition parties, the St. Vincent Labour Party and the Movement for National Unity, merged to create the new Unity Labour Party. In an effort to recover the initiative, Mitchell promised major new investments in the crucial banana industry as well as improvements in St. Vincent's infrastructure and social services. Bananas account for 65 percent of St. Vincent's export earnings; they are shipped to European Union countries as a result of a 1992 agreement that set quotas for Caribbean producers. Because the United States won a preliminary judgment with regard to the EU quotas from the World Trade Organization, there is growing concern about the future of the industry.

DEVELOPMENT

A slump in banana production because of poor weather and low prices forced farmers to produce other crops, including marijuana. In a 1998 sweep, U.S. troops aided St. Vincentian soldiers in eradicating the crop, which spread animosity toward Washington.

FREEDOM

In 1989, the government took a great step forward in terms of wage scales for women by adopting a new minimum-wage law, which provided for equal pay for equal work done by men and women. The law took effect in 1990. Violence against women remains a significant problem.

HEALTH/WELFARE

Minimum wages range from $3.85 *per day* in agriculture to $7.40 in industry. Clearly, the minimum is inadequate, although most workers earn significantly more than the minimum.

ACHIEVEMENTS

A regional cultural organization was launched in 1982 in St. Vincent. Called the East Caribbean Popular Theatre Organisation, its membership extends to Dominica, Grenada, and St. Lucia.

Trinidad and Tobago (Republic of Trinidad and Tobago)

GEOGRAPHY
Area in Square Miles (Kilometers):
1,980 (5,128) (about the size of Delaware)
Capital (Population):
Port-of-Spain (52,500)
Environmental Concerns: water pollution; oil pollution of beaches; deforestation; soil erosion
Geographical Features: mostly plains, with some hills and low mountains
Climate: tropical

PEOPLE

Population
Total: 1,103,000
Annual Growth Rate: –1.35%
Rural/Urban Population Ratio: 28/72
Major Language: English
Ethnic Makeup: 43% black; 40% East Indian; 14% mixed; 1% white; 1% Chinese; 1% others
Religions: 32% Roman Catholic; 24% Hindu; 14% Anglican; 14% other Protestant; 6% Muslim; 10% others

Health
Life Expectancy at Birth: 68 years (male); 73 years (female)
Infant Mortality Rate (Ratio): 18.5/1,000
Average Caloric Intake: 121% of FAO minimum
Physicians Available (Ratio): 1/1,191

Education
Adult Literacy Rate: 98%
Compulsory (Ages): 6–12; free

COMMUNICATION
Telephones: 1 per 6.2 people
Daily Newspaper Circulation: 135 per 1,000 people
Televisions: 1 per 3.2 people

TRANSPORTATION
Highways in Miles (Kilometers): 5,167 (8,320)
Railroads in Miles (Kilometers): minimal agricultural service
Usable Airfields: 6
Motor Vehicles in Use: 153,000

GOVERNMENT
Type: parliamentary democracy
Independence Date: August 31, 1962 (from United Kingdom)
Head of State/Government: President Arthur Napoleon Robinson; Prime Minister Baseo Panday

Political Parties: People's National Movement; National Alliance for Reconstruction; United National Congress; Movement for Social Transformation; National Joint Action Committee; others
Suffrage: universal at 18

MILITARY
Current Disputes: none

ECONOMY
Currency ($ U.S. Equivalent): 6.27 Trinidad and Tobago dollars = $1
Per Capita Income/GDP: $8,000/$8.85 billion
GDP Growth Rate: 4.3%
Inflation Rate: 3.7%
Unemployment Rate: 14%

Labor Force: 541,000
Natural Resources: petroleum; natural gas; asphalt
Agriculture: cocoa; sugarcane; rice; citrus fruits; coffee; vegetables; poultry
Industry: petroleum; chemicals; tourism; food processing; cement; beverages; textiles
Exports: $2.4 billion (primary partners United States, CARICOM, Latin America)
Imports: $3.3 billion (primary partners United States, Latin America, European Union)

 http://www.cia.gov/cia/publications/factbook/td.html

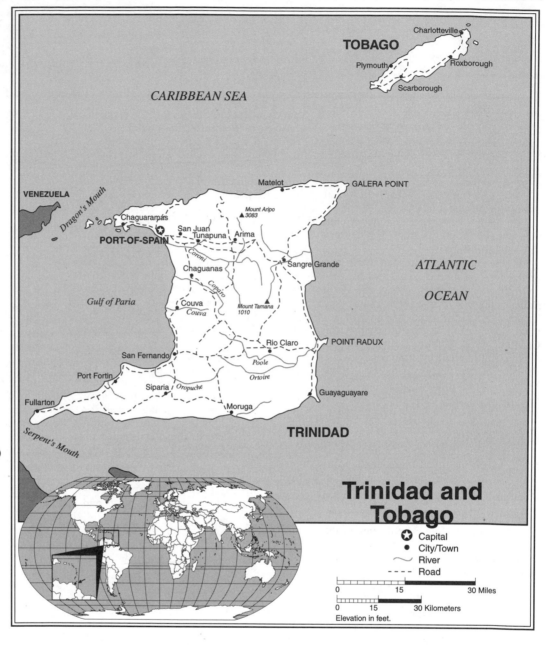

Trinidad and Tobago

- ✪ Capital
- ● City/Town
- River
- --- Road

0   15   30 Miles
0   15   30 Kilometers
Elevation in feet.

The island now called Trinidad is discovered by Columbus and later colonized by Spain
1498

Trinidad is captured by the British
1797

Tobago is added to Trinidad as a colonial unit
1889

Independence from Great Britain
1962

Oil-export earnings slump
1980s

1990s

Basdeo Panday is elected prime minister

Trinidad and Tobago enjoy a trade surplus with Cuba as a result of petroleum exports

Earl Lovelace wins the 1997 Commonwealth Writers' Prize for his novel *Salt*

TRINIDAD AND TOBAGO: A MIDDLE-CLASS SOCIETY

The nation of Trinidad and Tobago, which became independent of Great Britain in 1962, differs sharply from other Caribbean countries in terms of both its wealth and its societal structure. More than one third of its revenues derive from the production of crude oil. Much of the oil wealth has been redistributed and has created a society that is essentially middle class. Health conditions are generally good, education is widely available, and the literacy rate is a very high 98 percent.

The country also enjoys an excellent human-rights record, although there is a good deal of tension between the ruling urban black majority and East Indians, who are rural. The divisions run deep and parallel the situation in Guyana. East Indians feel that they are forced to submerge their culture and conform to the majority. In the words of one East Indian, "Where do Indians fit in when the culture of 40 percent of our people is denied its rightful place and recognition; when most of our people exist on the fringes of society and are considered as possessing nothing more than nuisance value?"

The lyrics of a black calypso artist that state the following are resented by East Indians:

If you are an East Indian
And you want to be an African
Just shave your head just like me
And nobody would guess your
    nationality.

The prosperity of the nation, however, tends to mute these tensions.

Freedom of expression and freedom of the press are constitutionally guaranteed as well as respected in practice. Opposition viewpoints are freely expressed in the nation's Parliament, which is modeled along British lines. There is no political censorship. Opposition parties are usually supported by rural Hindu East Indians; while they have freely participated in elections, some East Indians feel that the government has gerrymandered electoral districts to favor the ruling party.

Violent crime and political unrest, including an attempted coup by black fundamentalist Muslim army officers in 1990, have become a way of life in the nation in recent years. Prime Minister Basdeo Panday, elected in 1996, noted that there were still agendas, "political and otherwise," that divided Trinidadian society. "How much better it will be," he stated, "if all in our society, and particularly those in a position to shape mass consciousness, will seize every opportunity to promote and mobilise the greater strength that comes out of our diversity. . . ."

Trade-union organization is the most extensive among Caribbean nations with ties to Britain and includes about 30 percent of the workforce. In contrast to other West Indian states, unions in Trinidad and Tobago are not government-controlled, nor are they generally affiliated with a political party.

Women are well represented in Parliament, serve as ministers, and hold other high-level civil-service positions. Several groups are vocal advocates for women's rights.

In an attempt to redress imbalances in the nation's agricultural structure, which is characterized by small landholdings— half of which are less than five acres each—the government has initiated a land-redistribution program using state-owned properties and estates sold to the government. The program is designed to establish more efficient medium-size family farms, of five to 20 acres, devoted to cash crops.

TOBAGO

Residents of Tobago have come to believe that their small island is perceived as nothing more than a dependency of Trinidad. It has been variously described as a "weekend resort," a "desert island," and a "tree house"—in contrast to "thriving," "vibrant" Trinidad. Tobagans feel that they receive less than their share of the benefits generated by economic prosperity.

In 1989, the Constitution was reviewed with an eye to introducing language that would grant Tobago the right to secede. The chair of the Tobago House of Assembly argued that, "in any union, both partners should have the right to opt out if they so desire." Others warn that such a provision would ultimately snap the ties that bind two peoples into one. Trinidadian opposition leaders have observed that the areas that have historically supported the ruling party have more and better roads, telephones, and schools than those backing opposition parties.

DEVELOPMENT

The economy has experienced rapid growth thanks to vast reserves of natural gas, which attracted investors from developed countries. The government has also promoted the use of natural gas, instituting a program to encourage consumers to switch from gasoline.

FREEDOM

Freedom of expression on the islands is guaranteed by the Constitution. The independent judiciary, pluralistic political system, and independent and privately owned print media assure that free expression exists in practice as well as in theory.

HEALTH/WELFARE

Legislation passed in 1991 greatly expanded the categories of workers covered by the minimum wage. The same legislation provided for 3 months' maternity leave for household and shop assistants as well as other benefits.

ACHIEVEMENTS

Eric Williams, historian, pamphleteer, and politician, left his mark on Caribbean culture with his scholarly books and his bitterly satirical *Massa Day Done*. V. S. Naipaul is an influential author born in Trinidad. Earl Lovelace is another well-known Trinidadian author.

Annotated Table of Contents for Articles

Regional Articles

Mexico Articles

Central America Article

South America Articles

Caribbean Articles

Topic Guide to Articles

TOPIC AREA	TREATED IN	TOPIC AREA	TREATED IN
Human rights (continued)		**Population Growth**	
		Regional Overview	1. The Real Latin America
South America	13. Colombia: Civil War without End?	*Mexico*	8. Smaller Families to Bring Big Change in Mexico
	14. Ecuador 1972–19978: Indigenous Peoples and the Crisis of the Nation-State	*South America*	11. The Two Brazils
	15. Ecuador's Indigenous People: "We Seek True Participation"	*The Caribbean*	18. Sun, Fun, & a Rum Deal: Perspectives on Development in the Commonwealth Caribbean
The Caribbean	20. Haiti and the Limits to Nation-Building		
Indigenous Peoples		**Poverty**	
Regional Overview	6. Latin America: The Internet and Indigenous Texts	*Regional Overview*	2. Inequality in Latin America
South America	11. The Two Brazils	*Mexico*	8. Smaller Families to Bring Big Change in Mexico
	14. Ecuador 1972–1997: Indigenous Peoples and the Crisis of the Nation-State	*South America*	11. The Two Brazils
	15. Ecuador's Indigenous People: "We Seek True Participation"	**Privatization**	
		Regional Overview	3. Economic Crisis in Latin America: Global Contagion, Local Pain
Leaders, Current		*Mexico*	7. What's Next for Mexico: Potential Surprises from a U.S. Neighbor
Regional Overview	4. Women in Latin America: Unequal Progress toward Equality	**Religion**	
South America	16. The People Give Chavez a Mandate	*South America*	12. A Scholar and Pai-de-Santo Straddles 2 Worlds in Multicultural Brazil
	17. Venezuela's Democracy Teeters	**Social Reform**	
Legal Issues		*Regional Overview*	1. The Real Latin America
Regional Overview	4. Women in Latin America: Unequal Progress toward Equality		2. Inequality in Latin America
	5. Crime in Latin America		4. Women in Latin America: Unequal Progress toward Equality
The Caribbean	20. Haiti and the Limits to Nation-Building	*South America*	11. The Two Brazils
Migration			14. Ecuador 1972–1997: Indigenous Peoples and the Crisis of the Nation-State
Mexico	7. What's Next for Mexico: Potential Surprises from a U.S. Neighbor		15. Ecuador's Indigenous People: "We Seek True Participation"
Military			17. Venezuela's Democracy Teeters
Mexico	7. What's Next for Mexico: Potential Surprises from a U.S. Neighbor	*The Caribbean*	19. A Failed Revolution
The Caribbean	20. Haiti and the Limits to Nation-Building	**Technology**	
Origins		*Regional Overview*	6. Latin America: The Internet and Indigenous Texts
South America	11. The Two Brazils	**Turmoil, Civil**	
	12. A Scholar and Pai-de-Santo Straddles 2 Worlds in Multicultura Brazil	*Mexico*	7. What's Next for Mexico: Potential Surprises from a U.S. Neighbor
	14. Ecuador 1972–1997: Indigenous Peoples and the Crisis of the Nation-State	*South America*	13. Colombia: Civil War without End?
	15. Ecuador's Indigenous People: "We Seek True Participation"	*The Caribbean*	19. A Failed Revolution
Politics		**Women's Issues**	
Regional Overview	4. Women in Latin America: Unequal Progress toward Equality	*Regional Overview*	4. Women in Latin America: Unequal Progress toward Equality
South America	14. Ecuador 1972–1997: Indigenous Peoples and the Crisis of the Nation-State		6. Latin America: The Internet and Indigenous Texts
	16. The People Give Chavez a Mandate		
The Caribbean	20. Haiti and the Limits to Nation-Building		

Article 1   *The World & I*, March 1998

The Real Latin America

Today the average Latin American is better off and more optimistic than during the 1980s, years that saw the failure of socialism and nationalism.

CARLOS A. BALL

Remember Carmen Miranda with the pineapple and bananas on her head, the suave Fernando Lamas, and Desi Arnaz with his funny accent? In a more optimistic and less complicated age, they personified Latin America. But the image has tarnished. Today, when Latin America is mentioned, the picture that usually forms in the American mind has little to do with palm trees and beautiful señoritas but rather with drug trafficking and illegal immigration.

Both mental images reflect but a fragment of a much bigger and complex subcontinent that for over a century has engaged in a love/hate relationship with its rich, northern neighbor. Even the expression "continent" has a different meaning; for Latin Americans, "America" is not the name of a single country but that of the Western Hemisphere, an indivisible continent running from Hudson Bay to Cape Horn. But most Americans are not even aware that Brazil is as big as the continental United States.

In Latin America, the nineteenth century was the heroic era of the fight for independence, the formation of national states, and the abolition of slavery. Most nineteenth-century Latin American constitutions were based on the writings of the great Western thinkers, such as Montesquieu, Locke, and Jefferson, in order "to govern the government."

Juan Bautista Alberdi was the father of the classical liberal Argentine constitution of 1853, perhaps the best of them, which allowed his country to reach a higher standard of living by the turn of the century than Italy and France. Alberdi wrote that "the Constitution of Argentina is the first one that distinguishes the wealth of the Nation from the wealth of the government.... The distribution of wealth works by itself more fairly, the less the state meddles by imposing rules."

Death of classical liberalism

The century of classical liberalism died in the muddy fields of Passchendaele in the First World War, and the Russian Revolution of 1917 was to play an important role by unleashing nationalism, socialism, and state intervention from the Rio Grande to Patagonia. Under military regimes and populist democratic governments alike, the demarcation between the governmental sphere and the private, economic sphere slowly dissolved. Power, both political and economic, was concentrated more than ever in fewer hands, and decisionmaking became a centralized and politicized process.

The Latin American military dictators, as well as the democratic governments that succeeded them, set about nationalizing mines, oil, fishing, telecommunications, transport, and energy, along with industries the politicians referred to as "basic and strategic." Central planners enjoyed the enthusiastic support of the UN's Economic Commission for Latin America, the Inter-American Development Bank founded by U.S. President Eisenhower, and other multilateral organizations that have done more harm than good. Those are the same organizations that still provide well-paying, tax-free jobs in Washington to former Latin bureaucrats.

In Venezuela, state takeovers of private enterprises began in the 1950s under Gen. Marcos Pérez Jiménez, as the British-owned telephone company and railroads were nationalized. In 1961 Venezuela enacted a socialist constitution that generously guarantees health, housing, education, employment, and even paid vacations to its citizens.

Succeeding governments, by trying to do everything, have failed miserably in their fundamental duty of protecting the lives and property of the people, while politicians squandered opportunities in those areas where the country enjoys extraordinary comparative advantages, by placing them beyond the reach of private entrepreneurs. In 1976, President Carlos Andrés Pérez dealt the Venezuelan economy a mortal blow by nationalizing the oil industry.

Venezuela, because of its oil wealth and the old Spanish laws that give ownership of the subsoil to the state, has suffered some of the most corrupt governments. Inflation during the first half of 1996 was greater than during the period 1946 to 1973, when the central bank began to lose its independence. In the last 14 years the bolivar has suffered a devaluation of 11,574 percent (from 4.30 to the dollar in 1983 to the current 502). Inflation is the pseudolegal way by which the authorities shamelessly rob the population. As a result, 79 percent of Venezuelans are today living in poverty, walking on top of immense mineral wealth mismanaged by the country's self-serving politicians.

A corrupt judiciary

Another surprising mishap of the new democratic era has been the evolvement of a politicized and corrupt judiciary, which was not usually the case even under the old military rulers, who often gave the most honest and respected people judicial appointments.

Winning elections has often meant giving away much more than budgetary constraints allow, and the easy way to do so is by printing money. Thus, both judicial independence and central banks' autonomy were often the victims of new democratic governments. We then find in the Latin America of the 1970s and '80s a great paradox: the spread of democracy but also a deterioration of the rule of law and of sound currency, two prerequisites for economic development.

In the early 1970s, no one better described the scapegoat Latin philosophy of the day than Uruguayan writer Eduardo Galeano. He insisted that Latin America's shortcomings were not the result of its own mistakes and counterproductive economic policies but, rather, of Yankee imperialism.

Galeano wrote:

The division of labor means that some countries specialize in winning and others in losing. The region's work as a servant continues. It serves outside needs as a source and reserve of oil and iron, copper and meat, fruit and coffee, raw materials and food for the rich countries, which gain from consuming them much more than Latin America gains from producing them.

It was left to economists Raúl Prebish of Argentina and Fernando Henrique Cardoso (current president of Brazil) to transform Galeano's lyrical language into a full-bodied interventionist system.

The consequences of those ideas were not slow to appear. After United Fruit, Standard Oil, U.S. Steel, and other multinationals were expelled, replacing both their foreign and native born professional executives with apparatchiks and appointing political cronies to the boards of corporations taken over by the government, impoverishment was swift and dramatic. Cuba, Venezuela, and Uruguay, three of the formerly most prosperous Latin nations, have been badly damaged by socialism.

During the Cold War, Washington was not too interested in violations of private property or the rule of law south of the border, as long as the presidential palace made the appropriate noises against Fidel Castro and denounced the Soviet backing of guerrilla movements. Washington made no distinction between old-style *caudillos,* modern dictators, and the more recent democratic rulers. As long as they identified with the West, they were rewarded generously with economic aid that was shared out among the local nomenklatura, helping it to remain in power, and never reached the hands of the poor.

Bad rap for Pinochet

This scene changed dramatically with the end of the Cold War and with the ultimate failure of the world press in bad-mouthing the Chilean economic success. No regime, not even Castro's Cuba, suffered from a worse press than Pinochet's Chile. The so-called Chicago boys appointed by General Pinochet to run the economy did what had to be done: liberalize the economy, privatize social security, and reform the labor laws.

At about the same time, the traditional Latin American way of silencing leaders of the opposition by inviting them to step up and join the politically powerful clique on its sumptuous platform put so much weight on those structures that they started to collapse. Insufficient public funds were available to continue buying popular support. Then, pressure for political and economic reform surged throughout most of Latin America.

In Mexico and Argentina, some dismantling of the unwieldy state apparatus has taken place; unfortunately, most of the benefits of privatization went into the hands of economic groups close to the corridors of power. Also, virtually everywhere, the IMF's requirements are satisfied by increasing taxes rather than by reducing the size of overblown state bureaucracies. The substitution of public monopolies for private oligopolies has led to some improvements. Assets are handled more responsibly when they belong to someone, but prices for goods and services have also risen considerably, which has tarnished the reputation of the so-called neoliberal policies.

What Latin American politicians have yet to understand is that privatization's real contribution to economic development has absolutely nothing to do with the sale price obtained for the state-owned assets but depends entirely on the radical opening of new sectors to free competition. A higher price is obtained when some of the old state monopoly conditions are passed on to the new owners, but open competition is the only way to ensure that scarce resources are used efficiently to improve the standard of living and create new wealth.

Chile, as Alvaro Bardón explains in his article, was the first country in Latin America to start along the road of market reforms and has advanced the most. The Chilean process has suffered relatively little from corruption, and its main success, the privatization of its state pension fund, is being copied all over the continent.

In Peru, the success of President Alberto Fujimori's economic policies assured his reelection in 1995 with 64 percent of the vote and a majority of 52 percent in Congress. Fujimori has sold state companies valued at over $5 billion and has promised to double this figure by 1999. According to a recent World Bank study, the indigenous majority, until recently completely forgotten, has benefited most from these policies. But now it seems that Fujimori has been infected by the old zeal of Latin caudillos to cling indefinitely to power, as if the country would grind to a halt without him. In Peru, there is a growing climate of intimidation and authoritarianism, with the judicial system one of the weakest institutions.

In 1997, Argentina led the continent not only in economic growth (8 percent) but also in the fight against inflation (-0.1 percent). President Carlos Menem's former finance minister, Domingo Cavallo, wiped out inflation by setting the peso's value at one dollar and changing the law so the central bank could only print one peso when its reserves went up by one dollar. But, Menem has issued 300 presidential decrees, more than all previous presidents put together going back to 1853, which is a demonstration of the strange sort of democracy prevailing today in Latin America.

Indeed, 1997 was the best year for Latin America in the last quarter century, with economic growth reaching an average of 5.3 percent and inflation hovering around 10.5 percent. The Dominican Republic made second place in economic growth (7.5), followed by Peru (7), Mexico (7), and Chile (6.5).

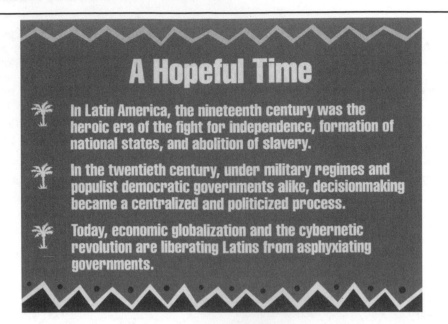

A Hopeful Time

🌴 In Latin America, the nineteenth century was the heroic era of the fight for independence, formation of national states, and abolition of slavery.

🌴 In the twentieth century, under military regimes and populist democratic governments alike, decisionmaking became a centralized and politicized process.

🌴 Today, economic globalization and the cybernetic revolution are liberating Latins from asphyxiating governments.

This economic renaissance is good news for the United States, which in 1996 sold $51.8 billion in goods to Latin America, twice its exports to the European Community.

The U.S. is backing off

But as market reforms and entrepreneurial success are beginning to transform Latin America, the economic leadership of the United States diminishes. U.S. protectionist textile interests blocked the extension of NAFTA benefits to poor Central American and Caribbean countries, and soon afterward "fast track" authority was denied to President Clinton.

The U.S. government, instead of leading the way by unilaterally opening its own market and showing how that benefits the people, is immersed in a byzantine discussion of "level playing fields," bad-mouthing *maquilas* and child labor practices (knowing that those children either work or don't eat) and pushing a green diplomatic agenda under "sustainable development," a code phrase that clearly means zero growth.

The war on drugs has not only been a total failure but is becoming a barrier to capitalism in Latin America. Free markets do not function without rule of law and secure property rights, institutions that never were very strong and now are threatened by a war that corrupts policemen, judges, bureaucrats, and military officers.

Washington chooses to ignore that it took Latin Americans some 130 years, after the wars of independence, to get the soldiers back to their barracks. Now the American embassies want them on the streets and in the countryside, trampling over civil liberties because the U.S. government cannot keep its own people from abusing drugs.

Milton Friedman said it best: "We are not trying to prohibit the use of narcotics at tremendous cost. The particular consequence that I find most indefensible is the havoc wreaked on residents of Colombia, Peru, and other countries because we cannot enforce our own laws."

In the [March 1998] issue of THE WORLD & I, William Perry looks at Brazil, the nation of 165 million Portuguese-speaking people that Stefan Zweig, Austrian poet and essayist, called in 1940 "the country of the future." Brazil has indeed fascinated travelers since Amerigo Vespucci visited it in 1503, four years before the name America appeared for the first time on a map.

It is difficult to think of two countries more different than Brazil and Chile, in their geography, history, or people. Latins joke about Brazil being the eternal country of the future but never reaching it. Chile, on the other hand, is on the verge of becoming a rich, industrialized nation despite its small population and awkward geography. The joke is that if a Chilean falls asleep lying east to west, his head will freeze and his feet will get wet. But the enormous success of the Chilean free-market policies is no joke, as Alvaro Bardón makes very clear in his essay.

Our Latin American trip ends near home, in Mexico. Mexican dictator Porfirio Díaz (1877–80 and 1884–1911) is supposed to have sobbed: "Poor Mexico, so far from God and so close to the United States." With 65 percent of the Latin population living in the United States having come originally from Mexico, it is by far the best known of all Latin American countries. If not as big as Brazil or as successful as Chile, Mexico is finally beginning to take advantage of being next door to the richest market in the world. Roberto Salinas-León brings us up to date on "Crisis and Confidence in Mexico."

Today, as we near the new millennium, the average Latin American is better off and more optimistic than during "the lost decade" of the 1980s. Those years saw the culminating failure of socialism and nationalism. Now, economic globalization and the cybernetic revolution are liberating Latins from asphyxiating governments.

As brains and skills become their countries' main resources, Latin politicians find it increasingly difficult to nationalize and expropriate the nations' wealth. Instead, they will be forced to create a competitive and attractive environment, with low taxes, few regulations, personal security, and respect for property rights and the rule of law. The absence of these institutions for most of the twentieth century set Latin America apart from the industrialized world. With the likely rebirth of their civil society, Latin Americans are starting to reach for the united continent of freedom envisioned by Simón Bolívar.

Carlos A. Ball is a Venezuelan journalist and editor of Agencia Inter-americana de Prensa Económica (AIPE), a news organization serving Spanish-language newspapers in the United States and 14 Latin American countries.

Article 2

Dissent, Summer 1999

Inequality in Latin America

Forrest D. Colburn

EVERY YEAR the Inter-American Development Bank (IDB) publishes a monograph titled *Economic and Social Progress in Latin America.* Most years the reports address a particular theme, some of them of narrow interest. Reading them can be tedious; they are written by economists who favor a matter-of-fact style. But the reports invariably contain a wealth of information. Especially compelling is the 1998–1999 report, a monumental study of inequality in Latin America, entailing a staggering amount of work. But the report is especially useful because it addresses issues that have been overshadowed by a flurry of attention to the region's financial markets: the stability of currencies, the interest rates set by central banks, the movement of capital, debt-repayment schedules, and, above all, the rise and fall of stock markets.

For the overwhelming majority of Latin Americans, "economic issues" are immediate and family-centered. Who works, where, and with what remuneration? Mostly, remuneration is low. The countries of Latin America suffer from extreme income inequality. The largest and most populous country—Brazil has one of the widest income gaps in the world: the wealthiest 10 percent of the population amass almost 50 percent of national income, while the poorest 50 percent of the population scrape together little more than 10 percent.

The most inequitable countries, besides Brazil, are Chile, Guatemala, Ecuador, Mexico, Panama, and Paraguay. By regional standards, Costa Rica and Uruguay have less inequity. For the region at large: the wealthiest 5 percent of the population receive 25 percent of national income; the wealthiest 10 percent receive 40 percent. By contrast, the poorest 30 percent of the population receive only 7.5 percent of total income, less than anywhere else in the world.

These bald statistics are arrived at from an analysis of household surveys from fourteen countries accounting for more than 80 percent of the region's population. The surveys were done between 1994 and 1996. Sample sizes were large: in Peru, for example, 16,744 households were queried, providing data about 88,863 Peruvians. Data from these surveys were compared to data from earlier surveys, leading to the unhappy conclusion that inequality in Latin America worsened considerably in the 1980s and has remained stagnant at high levels in the 1990s. Finally, comparisons with other parts of the world are facilitated by international data bases prepared by such organizations as the World Bank and the International Monetary Fund (IMF).

The IDB report not only goes to unprecedented lengths to measure inequality rigorously but also documents its deadly implication: widespread poverty. The income level of more than 150 million Latin Americans—roughly one-third of the population—is under U.S. $2 a day (corrected for differences of purchasing power of the different currencies). And $2 is the meager sum regarded as the minimum needed to cover basic consumption needs. Thus, although the World Bank and the IMF judge per capita incomes in Latin America to be high enough to warrant the region's being labeled "middle-income," a third of the population barely subsists.

The economists who wrote the study acknowledge that there is inequality everywhere. But they argue that Latin America has *excess* inequality. Other regions with similar levels of "development" have substantially less poverty. If Latin America had the income distribution suited to its level of development by international standards, the incidence of poverty would be half of what it actually is today. Per capita income levels of Eastern European countries are not appreciably different from those of Latin America, but only 7 percent of their population is poor. Admittedly, the communist history of Eastern Europe strains the comparison. But comparisons with other regions lead to a similar conclusion. For example, if income in Latin America were distributed as it is in the countries of Southeast Asia, poverty would be reduced by four-fifths.

ACTUALLY, income distribution in Latin America is even worse than calculated by the IDB study. The household surveys measure only income from labor, not capital (such as rental properties and other kinds of investments). Still, the measurement of income from labor (and other data from the household surveys) provides insight into the Latin American rich. The rich are numerous; a class, not a clan, of tight-knit families. They are well educated, working as professionals and managers of companies (in which they may or may not have equity). Wives tend to work, and to earn a good income. Families are small, with an average of just 1.4 children.

The poor have poor educations. Twenty-three percent of Latin Americans are "uneducated." The average Latin American over twenty-five years of age has only 4.8 years of education. Three-fourths of Latin Americans over twenty-five years of age have either no education or, more likely today, only a few years in a primary (elementary) school. The poor never make it to school or attend school only briefly. The households of the poor are large; the poorest 30 percent of Latin Americans have an average of 6.3 members in their household. The poor have more children, an average of 3.3. And households are more likely to include additional adult dependents (such as grandparents). Hence, per capita income is lower for poor families not only because earnings are less, but also because they have more individuals to support.

Most of the poor still live in the countryside. Only in Brazil, Chile, and Venezuela do more than half of all households of the poorest 30 percent live in urban areas. The urban slums of the poor can be even more depressing—and dangerous—than the forsaken rural settlements, but, it is notable that the majority of the poor continue to live in the countryside. In contrast, nine out of ten families in the two highest income deciles live in cities.

Left unexamined in the report is the daily life of the poor. But how can one convey a sense for what it means to be poor for 150 million people? My own scattered conversations with the poor lead me to believe that any attempt has to include more than a description of misery and wretchedness. Poverty entails, too, emotional pressures—for example, of fear and worry. Sometimes there is despair, humiliation, or rage. Poverty is profoundly threatening. It takes a constant toll on one's equilibrium and frequently, too, on family ties. Finally, the burden of poverty is different, and greater, in Latin America, because the munificence of the few is a constant reminder that life could be more bountiful. Moreover, the wealthy, as employers, are frequently demanding, miserly, and insensitive. At the same time, the poor have their "weapons of the weak": false compliance, dissimulation, foot dragging, and sabotage. There is a never-ending struggle—what James Scott has called "the small arms fire of class war." The social landscape is treacherous.

Why is Latin America so inequitable? The authors of the Development Bank study offer two theories, but neither is persuasive. One explanation is that Latin America is at an early stage of economic development where, for example, a scarcity of capital leads to high returns, which are a cause of income inequality. But as capital becomes more abundant, its returns fall vis-à-vis labor, helping to improve income distribution.

Similarly, the present low levels of schooling entail high returns for the few who are educated. With continued economic growth, the expansion of education, and other good things, the distribution of income should improve. This line of reasoning sounds plausible. But empirical studies have shown that when countries, like the Philippines, begin with inequality, after several decades of economic growth they remain highly inegalitarian. This outcome also fits the experience of Latin America. At the beginning of the twentieth century, Latin America was inegalitarian. After a century of economic growth, it is still inegalitarian. Why should another half century or even another century lead—by itself—to a reversal?

Another explanation for Latin America's inequality—and by extension of the poverty of so many Latin Americans—is the region's endowment of natural resources. This explanation is surprising. But evidence is marshaled to show that countries with large amounts of agricultural land per capita are substantially more unequal than countries with little land per capita. Similarly, countries that rely upon large exports of primary commodities are also substantially more unequal than countries with lower primary commodity exports. But it is hard to believe that abundance is a burden or that there is something pernicious about either tropical fruits or coffee. What is missing from the analysis is an appreciation of the politics of inequality.

Neither of the two explanations is pushed very far. The bankers and economists of the Inter-American Development Bank aren't really interested in explaining the causes of inequality in Latin America. In any case, solutions do not leap from their analysis. Latin America's severe income inequality is connected to its level of development and to the characteristics of its natural resource endowment. That would seem to provide a twofold reason for doing nothing: the first implies waiting and the second resignation.

BUT THE IDB is an activist organization, committed to fostering "development." Resignation is not allowed. Income inequality must be redressed. And redress is to come from the state: "Income distribution in Latin American countries will depend heavily on government in the next century."

The authors' logic is curious. In explaining the causes of inequality, they look to distant, impersonal, exogenous variables: the "stage of development" and natural resource endowment. Issues of authority and power are slighted. Those who have long held the reins of power in the economy and the state are not held accountable. But if the serious problem of inequality—and the poverty it begets—is to be redressed, then, yes, we need to look at the management of the economy and the state.

During the recession that battered Latin America in the 1980s, the worst since the 1930s, "international development organizations" had considerable leverage over policy design and implementation in Latin America. There were four powerful institutions, all based in Washington, D.C.: the World Bank, the IMF, the IDB, and the United States Agency for International Development (AID). In what came to be known as the "Washington Consensus," there was a pitch for Latin American governments to attain macro-economic stability, reining in the government deficits that had fueled inflation.

Government spending was slashed and, to a lesser extent, taxes were raised. The same four institutions promoted economic "liberalization," ending government intervention in the economy to leave markets "free." Since many government interventions, such as maintaining unprofitable state enterprises or offering subsidies to consumers, added to budget deficits, "liberalization," was seen as crucial to fiscal responsibility. Trade policy was also "liberalized," as were controls on foreign investment. These latter measures were said to contribute handsomely to economic growth.

Beaten down by debt and inflation, Latin American governments were receptive to a new paradigm. The old statist model was thoroughly discredited in the 1980s. In country after country, when there was a change of political regime—and sometimes even before—central bankers and finance ministers followed the prescriptions of the "international donor community." And, poof, they worked: macro-economic stability (a euphemism for low rates of inflation) was attained throughout the region, even in countries, like Brazil, Bolivia, and Nicaragua, that had been wracked by hyper-inflation.

But fiscal restraint and economic "liberalization" appear to have been oversold: many people, in and out of government, came to believe that these policies would be a panacea for all economic woes, including the poverty afflicting a third of Latin Americans. Throughout the 1990s, Latin American countries have enjoyed moderate rates of economic growth. Nonetheless, income distribution has not improved. The poor remain poor.

So international organizations now call for a "second generation" of reforms to address pressing social needs: education, health care, and income generation for the poor. Public opinion surveys suggest that Latin Americans are supportive of these reforms. For example, at least four out of five think that government has a responsibility to "reduce the differences between the rich and the poor." An even higher percentage of Latin Americans thinks that government ought to accept responsibility for "providing health care to the sick" as well as "a decent standard of living" for old people and the unemployed. A philosophical endorsement of ambitious government efforts to provide redress for the poor comes from an essay by Mario Vargas Llosa titled "América Latina y la opción liberal." He makes a forceful argument that liberal democracy and capitalism are only defensible if there is equal opportunity for all. Especially important, he suggests, is equality before the law and in education.

International development organizations make a well-reasoned case for social reform in Latin America. And the majority of Latin Americans appear to endorse at least the idea of these reforms. But despite occasional rhetoric to the contrary, little is being done to provide social services—education in particular—that might help the poor improve their position. The so-called "second generation reforms" are not forthcoming. No doubt, government and economic elites are distracted by the continuing struggle to maintain macro-economic stability. No doubt, the challenge of meeting the needs of the poor is daunting; a Herculean effort is necessary and no government

has an abundance of political capital. But it is also true that there isn't much empathy for the poor; the political will to redress inequality hardly exists.

In the world's richest countries (which tend to have a more equitable distribution of income), government spending represents around 40 percent of gross domestic product (GDP). In contrast, Latin America, with the world's worst distribution of income, is also the region where governments are smallest. Government spending represents about 20 percent of GDP. The scope of government is limited by difficulties in taxing those who have something that might be taxed. Income tax rates in Latin America are the lowest in the world. The IDB suggests that "Low collection rates for income and other taxes in Latin America reflect the limited institutional capacity of public administration to enforce the law." That interpretation has merit, but it needs to be complemented by an understanding of the political constraints produced by economic inequality.

To be sure, throughout Latin America there are programs to aid the poor. But most often they pale before the challenge. And when efforts are ambitious, they are usually driven by political calculation. For example, with only a year to go before standing for reelection as president of Peru—an opportunity made possible only by rewriting the constitution—Alberto Fujimori suddenly embarked upon a dramatic expansion of social spending. Fujimori profited politically by having the media portray him, wearing a poncho, visiting remote Andean communities to inaugurate schools or other "public works." The political manipulation of social spending, much of it financed by the sale of state assets, was blatant. It was, as is said in Latin America, "un show." Mexico's *Programa Nacional de Solidaridad* has been similarly criticized.

The IDB report highlights the importance of improving access to education for reducing inequality in Latin America. It is true that slowly the poor are becoming better educated. Illiteracy is being eradicated and the average number of years of schooling is slowly being increased. But the real dynamism in Latin American education is in the growth of professional training for the sons and daughters of the elite. Many of today's professionals are children whose parents already enjoyed a comfortable status in agriculture, industry, commerce, or construction. Here is a story the report doesn't tell. The upper class of Latin America has a remarkable gift for self-preservation and has been quick to realize that in our era the most valuable—and the safest—capital is human capital. Meeting the need for quality higher education are many new private universities, found throughout the major cities of the region. They are good, they are expensive, and they are most definitely not agencies of equality.

FORREST D. COLBURN is completing a book about Latin America at "the end of history."

Article 3   *Current History,* March 1999

> **"The late 1990s were supposed to be the years in which the long period of austerity and adjustment to world market norms would pay off for the majority of Latin America's people. The post-Russia crisis has shaken this faith. Like [Brazilian President Fernando Henrique] Cardoso, many Latin Americans again wonder if the region is the innocent victim of irrational forces."**

Economic Crisis in Latin America: Global Contagion, Local Pain

JAMES E. MAHON, JR.

At a small luncheon on January 4 in honor of his second inauguration, Brazilian President Fernando Henrique Cardoso spoke extemporaneously to a crowd that included four other regional leaders and about a hundred VIPs from Brazilian business and diplomatic circles. Criticizing "asymmetric globalization," Cardoso argued that free financial markets imply a "protectionism of the strongest" in which "perverse processes" can "turn markets into casinos." Although globalization is "a fact of our times," he said, and although "it is useless to oppose it, it would be irresponsible not to seek ways to guarantee economic and social growth." Only nine days later, what Cardoso would have called "perverse processes" forced an unscheduled depreciation of the Brazilian currency and created a new round of worries about the regional economy.

Although the regional fallout from Brazil's financial crisis may turn out to be less severe than the August 1998 Russian debt default, many Latin American countries continue to suffer from important weaknesses, especially the growth of fiscal and current account deficits. At a time when global investors have become selective about emerging markets, these deficits will make new inflows of portfolio capital scarce and expensive in large part because the region now needs them badly. This implies another round of domestic "adjustment," which will entail additional burdens on debtors and the poor in a region whose income distribution is the most unequal in the world. Political opposition to liberal economic policies may also grow even as financial markets, and governments' dependence on them, seem to foreclose other policy options.

JAMES E. MAHON, JR., *is an associate professor of political science at Williams College and author of* Mobile Capital and Latin American Development *(University Park: Penn State Press, 1996).*

FLOATING RATES, FLEEING CAPITAL

Global economic conditions have affected Latin American economies in several ways. First, the recession in Asia has further depressed commodity prices, especially for copper and oil, which has hurt export prices across the region. Second, Asian firms, many desperate to cover debts and operating with sharply devalued currencies, have become more formidable competitors for Latin American manufacturers in home and third-country markets. Finally and most important, financial crisis in Asia and Russia triggered the big stampede out of Latin American securities, mainly in the third quarter of 1998.

The first two phenomena have negatively affected trade balances, and thus current account balances, which provide one measure of the need for capital inflows. According to preliminary estimates by the IMF and the UN Economic Commission for Latin America and the Caribbean (ECLAC), the regional current account deficit (that is, trade in merchandise and in services, including interest payments) rose from just over 3 percent of GDP in 1997 to more than 4 percent in 1998. The largest deficits were in Bolivia and Ecuador (both around 9 percent), Chile (just under 7 percent), Colombia (6.6 percent), and Peru (6.5 percent). Brazil's deficit declined slightly, due to the government's austerity efforts, to equal the regional average. The steep drop in oil prices helped double Mexico's deficit to 3.5 percent and turned Venezuela's 1997 surplus into a small deficit. The oil decline, of course, has also had a strong negative impact on government budgets in oil-exporting countries.

The third phenomenon—flight of capital from emerging markets—has had various effects. Equity markets in Latin America had their worst year since 1987. Latin American funds were the weakest of all stock fund categories tracked by Lipper, Inc., for 1998, with average losses of over 38 percent. (Emerging market funds worldwide lost almost 27 percent, with those specializing in the Asia-Pacific region falling

9 percent.) More important, the withdrawal of foreign money forced up local interest rates as governments sought to defend the "credibility" of their currency regimes and avoid massive, Indonesia-style depreciation. This took place even in countries (for example, Chile, Colombia, and Mexico) whose floating exchange-rate regimes gave them more flexibility in choosing a response.

Devaluations of fixed or programmed exchange rates (the latter included Brazil's) were avoided until the Brazilian crisis in January of this year. But the rise in interest rates has also raised government borrowing costs at the same time as slowing economies have reduced tax revenues—thus knocking budgets further out of balance. Conditions improved in the last quarter of 1998, thanks in large part to the IMF agreement with Brazil negotiated in October and November. Yet even before the Brazilian shock of mid-January, interest rates were much higher than they were before August.

In 1998 governments in Latin America were not yet ready to embrace policies unfriendly to international capital.

THE AUSTERITY CURE

Combined, the deterioration of the current account and the continued reluctance of global investors create gloomy prospects for Latin America for 1999. Risk averse international investors may now be inclined to shy away from precisely those countries whose needs for external financing are greatest—and whose needs they were willing to meet until August 1998. As the IMF noted in its interim December 1998 *World Economic Outlook,* "the spillovers from Russia were felt with most severity in those Latin American countries perceived as having the largest financing needs . . . Asian emerging markets were less affected, since their external financing needs were regarded as relatively small in view of large current account surpluses." Looking toward the coming year, Charles Clough, chief investment strategist for Merrill Lynch, said in *The New York Times* on December 6 that "the theme for 1999 is that money will gravitate toward economies and markets that are running current account surpluses and are not heavily dependent on inflows of foreign capital."

What will fill the gap? There will be more lending by multilateral official sources other than the IMF: the World Bank and the Inter-American Development Bank. The latter doubled its lending in 1998 and is preparing to do so again in 1999. Beyond this, there are some reasons for optimism. The Russian crisis has forced global speculators to retreat from extreme levels of leverage, which means that the markets may be more selective and that Brazil's problems may not pull down every country in the region. Investors may then notice that current account deficits have been shrinking since late 1998 in several countries, Chile and Peru among them.

Moreover, many Latin American companies with strong balance sheets began the year trading at less than eight times their projected 1999 earnings—a fraction of the bubble-inflated ratios among United States blue-chip stocks. Global conditions could change favorably, too. An Asian recovery or a euro bloom would firm up commodity prices. And although emerging markets have often followed Wall Street in its downward swings, their present weakness might insulate them (though probably not Mexico) from a correction in American stock markets. Such a correction would bring on a recession in the United States, but it would first push down American interest rates and the value of the dollar. These conditions might permit Latin American interest rates to decline substantially.

However, these outside remedies are uncertain or, where not uncertain, probably insufficient. Most likely, Latin American governments will continue to mollify international capital by taking its prescribed medicine internally—that is, first, another dose of "adjustment," meaning fiscal austerity and the persistence of high interest rates, and second, new openings to foreign direct investments through accelerated and extended privatizations of state assets, or through the sale of locally owned private firms at bargain prices. Why this mix of policies?

FORCED TO CHOOSE

Despite the coalescence of some left intellectuals and politicians around an *alternativa* latinoamericana or Latin American alternative, there remains a widespread perception that there is little choice about major economic policies, at least under the present circumstances of moderate indebtedness and rising fiscal and current account deficits.[1] Instead, the crisis has pushed the region's governments to adopt policies even more in line with the preferences of international financial markets.

Consider the recent events in Venezuela. Hugo Chávez, the newly elected president, entered 1998 as the worst nightmare of his country's economic and financial establishment: not only was he a vitriolic opponent of the traditional political parties, he had also advocated, among other "populist" measures, a moratorium on foreign debt payments. During the presidential campaign he equivocated on economic policy as his opponents called him a fascist, a Stalinist, and another Castro. Some of the nervous rich took their families and a lot of their assets to Miami. Yet at the same time, many international investors were voicing confidence that, given the country's difficult situation, Chávez would have to "come to terms" with the IMF and international finance. Some Wall Street hands, citing the examples of other "populists" who changed their spots upon election (Argentina's Carlos Saúl Menem, Peru's Alberto Fujimori, and Venezuela's Carlos Andrés Pérez himself), counseled investors to buy on the preelection panic and sell when Chávez came around. And they were right. After his December 6 election, Chávez rejected devaluation and exchange controls (both of which had been tried by his predecessor) while promising spending cuts, a revival of the widely hated value-added tax,

---

1 See Lucy Conger, "A Fourth Way? The Latin American Alternative to Neoliberalism," *Current History,* November 1998.

stricter tax enforcement, and a welcome mat for foreign investment. Prices of Venezuelan bonds rose.

Controls on capital flows are another area in which financial market preferences have been adopted. The Asian meltdown led many well-known liberal economists to part company with the orthodox camp on capital controls, repeatedly pointing to Chile as an example of their wise use. But just as they were doing so the Chilean government, under pressure from market conditions, first reduced and then, during the September chaos, eliminated the most important barrier, the *encaje* (an obligatory, non-interest-bearing deposit equal to a set proportion of a capital inflow that was held at the central bank). Although the authorities say they intend to raise it again as conditions allow, and thus it may again serve (however effectively) to moderate currency fluctuations, their responses to financial contagion have been in the direction of more orthodoxy, not less.

Finally, consider the approval of Mexico's controversial bank-bailout legislation. The bill proposed to make tradable sovereign debt obligations, totaling $65 billion, out of the IOUs the government had given bankers in exchange for their bad loans during the crisis of 1994–1995. Building on suspicions that fraud and cronyism were being rewarded with taxpayers' money, the opposition Party of the Democratic Revolution turned this bill, and banking generally, into a mount-the-barricades issue for the Mexican left. The obvious unpopularity of a public dole for rich and sometimes shady bankers stalled negotiations on the bill until late September, when talks resumed after several weeks in which Mexican markets were roiled by the global storms. As Felipe Calderón, leader of the opposition National Action Party, told the October 7 *Financial Times,* "I see an international panorama that is serious and very delicate and it's better to hurry up and put things in order."

Hence, while the terms of the debate may have shifted somewhat in the wake of the Asian and Russian crisis, in 1998 governments in Latin America were not yet ready to embrace policies unfriendly to international capital.

THE ORTHODOX CURES

Let us consider the current adjustment policies in more detail. We can begin with the last policy response noted: accelerating privatization in the pursuit of fiscal and current account balance. Brazil is likely to be the largest privatizer in the coming year, since it still has considerable good state-owned assets to sell and because its large projected debt-amortization costs demand that something be done quickly. According to UN estimates, Brazil could gain between $40 billion and $50 billion from sales of state assets in 1999. Across the region, privatizations will likely include firms in electrical generation and distribution, airports, banking, and telecommunications. There may also be strong pressure to look at important natural resource companies, perhaps those producing coal in Colombia or aluminum in Venezuela, or even parts of Ecuador's state oil operations.

The trend toward greater foreign ownership will be accentuated by purchases of local private firms by bargain-hunting multinationals. As Doreen Hemlock reports in the Fort Lauderdale, Florida, *Sun-Sentinel* of January 4, "global companies

with a foot in the Latin region are taking advantage of today's tough times to boost their market share at discount prices. They are snapping up low-priced stock and buying debt-strapped rivals at a discount." Latin American economies will probably be significantly more foreign-owned at the end of 1999 than they were at its beginning.

Since privatization will not suffice, additional fiscal stringency is also in the cards. Public-sector deficits are a major determinant of a country's ongoing financing needs (and thus of bond market opinion), so resolute action to cut spending and increase tax revenue can often calm the markets at relatively little cost to the real economy (or, if conditions are right and markets respond enthusiastically, at no net cost at all, as President Bill Clinton has found out).

But as Brazil has shown, the fiscal road to adjustment is slow and slippery because of the political implications of taxing and spending. Mexico has followed it most ably, with three major budget cuts in 1998 and an austere budget approved for 1999. Brazil, Ecuador, and Venezuela, with the largest projected deficits, now face some rough patches. Like most countries, they do not have pro-austerity legislative majorities in place. Anxious investors can find a lot to worry about in the open democratic politics of fiscal policy. Every step in the progress of Brazilian budget legislation and every revelation of the country's fractious federalism has been enough to spook markets around the world.

As was noted, the dominant policy response to international financial contagion has been tight money. Part of the reason is that presidents can raise short-term rates immediately in reaction to market slumps without consulting anyone outside a small circle of technocrats. But although this option is quick and clean, in recent Latin American experience it has generally taken punishing levels of interest rates to persuade nervous investors. This has immediate effects in the real economy. In October 1997 and September 1998, for example, Brazilian debtors, generally in floating-rate contracts, saw their obligations triple almost overnight. Credit scarcity choked off growth in interest-rate-sensitive sectors.

Large currency devaluations used to be part of adjustment packages, but Latin American countries have shied away from them recently. Why? Until a few years ago, received wisdom held that countries faced this trade-off: either slow the economy with tight money or cause some inflation, through rising import prices, with currency depreciation. This reasoning would imply that exporters and import-competing firms favor depreciation because it improves their competitiveness, even though it may later require fiscal or interest-rate adjustments to forestall an inflation-depreciation spiral. By the same token, government budgets could gain from depreciation where state-owned firms sell oil into the world market in dollars (for example, Ecuador, Mexico, and Venezuela) since depreciation would reduce government expenditures denominated in the local currency while not affecting revenues earned from the sale of oil.

But this picture gets complicated when a variety of financial connections link the domestic and the international economy. Holders of domestic-currency bonds dislike depreciation because it erodes the value of their asset in terms of dollars (or another reference currency). Domestic firms owing debts in dollars fear depreciation insofar as their revenues are in local currency, since these are thereby reduced relative to expenses. (They may hedge against it but where markets are poorly developed this may be expensive.) Holders of dollar-denominated bonds may not mind it unless they see in it a willingness to violate the trust of all creditors. In general, however, the old formulas of the gold-standard era usually apply: financial interests want currency stability while manufacturers and exporters prefer to keep credit loose and the economy growing.

The difference today is that financial interests now have a stronger hold on more of these economies. The Mexican crisis showed that a sudden depreciation of the currency scares the markets so much that stratospheric interest rates are required to stop a downward spiral. Mexico and Asia showed the dangers of systemic crisis arising from a devaluation's damage to big domestic firms with unhedged foreign debts. Hence Latin American governments have been more receptive to insistent voices coming from the IMF and Wall Street.

As Brazil has lately shown, the tight-money policy concentrates the initial damage among highly indebted or interest-rate-sensitive businesses with few international financial ties, as well as among the consumer-debt-loving urban salaried class. The greatest and most persistent damage is to employment. According to ECLAC, regional unemployment reached 7.9 percent in 1998, well above the 6.3 percent that was seen in 1994 just before the Mexican crisis forced an increase in interest rates.

One consequence of long periods of tight money is to make the political divide between debtor and creditor, and between domestically focused industry and internationally connected finance, more salient than that between capital and labor. In Brazil, for example, the leader of the Federation of Industries of São Paulo State, the country's most powerful employers' organization, sought in December 1998 an unprecedented alliance with the radical labor confederation, the Unified Workers' Central, against the "monetarist" policies of the Cardoso government.

The debtor-creditor conflict may get even worse if tight money leads to a banking crisis. At high real interest rates, banks opt increasingly for the easy profits of high-coupon government debt and the private sector becomes starved for credit. Banks' existing portfolios deteriorate. Old fixed-rate assets will become losers, while floating-rate contracts will squeeze the borrowers and lead to a rise in defaults. Banking systems are only as solid as the people and firms making the interest payments, and not many borrowers can remain solid if real interest rates exceed 15 or 20 percent for a year. In 1998, banks in Colombia and Ecuador saw their portfolios weaken considerably. The crisis set back the recuperation of Mexico's ailing banks, too, and it has already begun to affect Brazil's in 1999.

What kind of capitalism do we get when interest rates suddenly double or triple, bringing bankruptcy and unemployment, because global asset-holders have taken fright of events on the other side of the world?

Some political consequences of a banking crisis can be seen in recent Mexican experience. Massive defaults on consumer and business loans create the potential for organized action on the part of debtors, as in the movement called El Barzón (The Yoke). Seeing their numbers, debtors become aware of the larger causes behind their plight and they lose their shame. If the crisis requires government intervention, further polarization may ensue as taxpayers—who under the now common consumption taxes include everybody, even the poorest—are forced to bail out rich and sometimes dishonest bankers.

A final, more subtle issue relates to the magnitude of the interest-rate spikes that have been imposed on these countries. Over the last few years, with liberal economic policies firmly in place, Latin Americans have been urged to pursue a second, more fundamental kind of reform, aimed at strengthening institutions and deepening the rule of law. It is true that the rule of law can bring predictability to economic life. It makes contracts easily enforceable, secures property rights, and reduces the arbitrariness of the state. It is thus a necessary ingredient for a rational and just capitalism.

Necessary, but maybe not sufficient. In another part of his luncheon speech, President Cardoso argued that "the market ought to reward effort, work, technical innovation, and the entrepreneurial spirit, and not speculation." But what kind of capitalism do we get when interest rates suddenly double or triple, bringing bankruptcy and unemployment, because global asset-holders have taken fright of events on the other side of the world?

ASYMMETRY AS A FACT OF LIFE

Over the course of the 1980s, most Latin American opinion leaders accepted the idea that the largest portion of blame for the decade's debt crisis lay with the bad policies pursued by their governments. By the mid-1990s the bad policies were mostly remedied, and in the last few years many Latin American governments have become accustomed to receiving praise for their achievements in free-market reform. Indeed, after the Asian crisis broke, Mexico's response in 1995 to its crisis was taken as a model for others to emulate. The late 1990s were supposed to be the years in which the long period of austerity and adjustment to world market norms would pay off for the majority of Latin America's people.

The post-Russia crisis has shaken this faith. Like President Cardoso, many Latin Americans again wonder if the region is the innocent victim of irrational forces. Not that problems are absent: the commodity price declines are real, as are the daunting schedule of Brazilian debt amortization and the slow, narrowly confined progress on legal and institutional reform. But

Latin Americans are now less ready to agree that these sins are enough to make them deserve the financial purgatory of recession, unemployment, bank bailouts, and denationalization of the productive structure.

What can they do? The crisis has helped to clarify a few of the structural problems associated with Latin America's insertion into the world economy, and with the world economy itself.

For the region, four problems stand out. First, a still significant dependence on commodity exports; second, a tendency for the import bill to increase quickly with GDP growth; third, in most but not all countries, weak tax structures with high rates of evasion; and fourth, national savings that are probably too low and are relatively globalized in their disposition. The first makes export receipts and thus the current account balance (and in some places the fiscal balance) vulnerable to the wild price swings of these goods. The second tends to make growth dependent to an unusual degree on capital inflows, while the third means that government finance often shares this dependence. And the fourth implies that a great proportion of Latin American countries' national savings has a global view, and thus is as unstable as foreign capital in the event of a crisis.

Of these problems, only two have straightforward solutions. For commodity price shocks, stabilization funds (as Chile has in place for copper) save hard currency during commodity booms in order to spend it during busts. And tax evasion could be reduced. In addition, policymakers should use periods of rapid growth and capital inflow to build net fiscal surpluses and large defensive stocks of foreign exchange reserves, which would help insulate the economy from an unpredictable and unforgiving global financial environment. Capital controls are best applied when flows are abundant; they should be eased, as in Chile, when they are scarce. While the events of the past year have provided a good argument for reducing dependence on foreign finance, there are obvious problems with a government unilaterally doing so immediately after it has sold (and encouraged local firms to sell) many billions of dollars of debt into the world market.

Until good times return, "asymmetric globalization" will be a painful fact of life. Some governments are discussing the abolition of their central banks and the adoption of the United States dollar. This would soothe investor worries about exchange rate risk, but it would also mean renouncing the benefits of a local lender of last resort and a monetary policy that helps moderate global shocks. Other countries will have to accept that they need to regain the "confidence" of international financing by following another old recipe: making bankers and other asset-holders lots of money for a long time.

This leads us to the world economy. Keep in mind the Merrill Lynch strategist quoted earlier, who wanted to see current account surpluses before committing funds in 1999. Insofar as this reasoning holds sway, the present situation resembles that of the 1930s, when a joke then popular in Eastern Europe compared international bankers to people who are happy to lend you an umbrella as long as it is not raining. Well, it's raining again in Latin America, and a lot of people are getting wet.

Article 4

Current History, March 1999

> "The status of women in Latin America is generally improving. Women's basic opportunities have increased from a few decades ago, which can be seen in better health, higher levels of educational attainment, and greater access to economic resources.... Some governments have [also] made major advances in the areas of legal reform, violence against women, and education. Still, many new laws and policies are not enforced or implemented, leaving an immense variation in women's status between and within countries."

Women in Latin America: Unequal Progress toward Equality

Mala Htun

Mala Htun

As the century draws to an end, the basic elements of democracy, such as free elections and the rule of law, have been consolidated in virtually every Latin American country. But the extension of democratic rights and liberties to all citizens remains an unfinished task. Improving the rights of women, who make up just more than half the region's population, represents a fundamental and immediate challenge.

Women form one-third of Latin America's labor force, constitute more than half of university students in many countries, and hold 16 percent of the seats in national legislatures.[1] Governments have created state agencies on women, changed discriminatory laws, and introduced new public policies designed to improve women's lives. Yet, many new laws and policies are poorly implemented and funded, or target only small groups of women. Women's status varies greatly between and within countries according to socioeconomic status, regional origin, and skin color. In short, progress toward gender equality in Latin America is uneven.

A NEW TREND IN POLITICS . . .

Women's political representation in Latin America has increased gradually since the 1970s, but it is still low relative to women's share of the electorate and their participation as active party members. Historically, women tended to rise to power at the margins. Their opportunities to participate in decision making were greater at lower levels of the organizational hierarchy, in less prestigious government ministries, and outside major cities. Many women leaders gained power as the wives, daughters, or sisters of prominent men.

The 1990s brought some changes to these traditional patterns. Women in Argentina, Costa Rica, and Guatemala headed political party lists in national elections. A woman was named president of Peru's Congress, and there are women at the helm of powerful ministries, such as justice in Chile and foreign affairs in Mexico.

Governments are taking dramatic steps to boost women's presence in decision making. Under pressure from women politicians and women's movements, Argentina, Bolivia, Brazil, Costa Rica, the Dominican Republic, Ecuador, Peru, and Venezuela have adopted national laws requiring political parties to reserve 20 to 40 percent of candidacies for women.

Whether quotas actually improve women's presence in power depends on each country's political parties and its electoral system. Quotas work best in a closed-list electoral system under which voters cast ballots for a party list, not for individual candidates, and the party leadership controls the placement of candidates on the list. In this system candidates have an incentive to cooperate to maximize votes for their party. In Argentina, where a closed-list system is in place and a quota law was passed in 1991, women occupy 28 percent of the seats in Congress, the highest percentage in the region.

There must also be effective enforcement mechanisms to ensure that political parties comply with the quota. In Argentina in 1993, when male party leaders failed to apply the

Surveys show that approximately 50 percent of all Latin American women have suffered violence at the hands of their husbands or partners.

women's quota to the placement of candidates on party lists, women challenged the lists in court, where they were declared invalid.

In Brazil, applying the women's quota has proved more problematic because of the country's open-list electoral system and undisciplined parties. In the national elections of October 1998, Brazilian parties uniformly failed to comply with the 25 percent women's quota. Brazil's open-list electoral system provokes competition for votes among candidates from the same party. Because they are relative newcomers, women lose out to their male colleagues in the struggle for money and resources. Thus, despite the quota, the number of women in the Brazilian Congress actually decreased following the October election.

Women legislators have also been able to exercise power more effectively by uniting into broad, multipartisan alliances. Organized around specific women's issues, political alliances have secured the approval of new laws on domestic violence, sex crimes, and workplace discrimination in Argentina, the Dominican Republic, Mexico, and Peru.

. . . BUT AN UNCHANGED LEGAL CULTURE

Latin American countries have adopted major reforms to grant women equal rights in family and constitutional law, to recognize domestic violence as a crime, and to outlaw sex discrimination. In the region's labor codes, women have long enjoyed mandatory maternity leave and they cannot be dismissed from their jobs for becoming pregnant. All Latin American countries have ratified the United Nations Convention on the Elimination of All Forms of Discrimination against Women, and most have ratified the Inter-American Convention to Prevent, Punish, and Eradicate Violence against Women.

However, in many countries laws remain in force that are antithetical to gender equality. Women in all countries except Chile, Cuba, Mexico, and Venezuela are prohibited from certain types of employment, including working at night, holding dangerous or unhealthy jobs, lifting heavy objects, working in mines, and distilling or manufacturing alcohol.

In many countries, rape is considered a crime against custom, not against a person. This means that the goal of the law is to protect good customs, not the person who is raped. In some countries rape and other sex crimes can only be committed against "honest women."

With the exception of Cuba, abortion is considered a crime in all Latin American countries. Many permit "therapeutic abortion," or abortions performed to save the life of the mother, and some countries also permit abortions if the pregnancy results from rape. However, legal abortions are rarely performed in public health facilities. Middle- and upper-class women who can afford private doctors and clinics have safe access to legal abortions, but poor women do not.

---

[1] For comprehensive data on the status of women in Latin America, see the Latin American Faculty of Social Science (FLACSO), *Latin American Women: Compared Figures* (Santiago: FLACSO, 1995). Data on women in parliaments around the world is available at the Inter-Parliamentary Union website at http://www.ipu.org/wmn-e/classif.htm.

Although few women are prosecuted for having abortions, criminalization pushes the practice underground. The millions of women who undergo abortion every year in Latin America must do so in unregulated and often dangerous circumstances. Clandestine abortions put women at risk of infection, hemorrhage, damage to the uterus or cervix, and adverse reactions to drugs. Botched abortions account for a high proportion of maternal mortality in the region today.

Even where laws reflect principles of gender equality, discriminatory practices persist. The central problem with women's legal rights in Latin America is not the lack of legislation and regulation, but the inconsistent application of the law. Women's movements today are focusing on increasing a woman's knowledge of her rights and training lawyers and judges to be sensitive to gender prejudice. A promising trend is the growing number of women with legal training and the entrance of more women into the legal profession; in many countries almost half the students enrolled in law school are women. Women now make up 45 percent of trial court judges in the region as a whole but merely 20 percent of appeals court and almost no supreme court judges.

Fifteen Latin American countries have human rights ombudsman offices, and six of these (Colombia, Costa Rica, El Salvador, Guatemala, Mexico, and Peru) have a specific institution charged with working with women. These "women's rights ombudsman" agencies receive complaints about human rights violations, investigate cases, work to train and sensitize judges and law enforcement personnel, and have challenged the constitutionality of discriminatory laws in court. Improving women's legal rights in the region requires not only changing old laws but also transforming the legal culture.

ATTACKING VIOLENCE AGAINST WOMEN

Domestic or intra-family violence against women is widespread in Latin America.[2] Surveys show that approximately 50 percent of all Latin American women have suffered violence at the hands of their husbands or partners. The problem is compounded by women's unequal economic and social positions. Since women have fewer opportunities than men in the labor market, receive lower wages, and are subject to family and social pressures, leaving an abusive relationship appears unviable, both to women victims and to their male abusers. A 1997 study conducted by the Inter-American Development Bank in Nicaragua found that 41 percent of non-wage-earning women are victims of violence, compared with 10 percent of women holding salaried jobs outside the home.

By 1997, 12 Latin American countries had adopted new laws to define the crime of domestic violence, map out policy measures, and offer judges and prosecutors greater power to issue protective orders. Following models created by feminist non-governmental organizations (NGOS), governments have established shelters, launched educational campaigns, and set up

centers to counsel women who have been victims of violence and to offer legal advice. Inadequate resources have, however, led to poor enforcement of new laws and incomplete implementation of preventive and treatment programs. Moreover, most efforts have focused on urban areas, leaving rural women with little recourse.

The most important policy change has been the establishment of women's police stations. First created in Brazil in 1985, the stations are staffed by women police officers trained to handle cases of domestic violence and rape. Today hundreds of women's police stations can be found throughout Latin America.

Women's police stations have helped communities recognize domestic violence as criminal behavior that constitutes a violation of human rights. And with the establishment of the stations, the reporting of domestic violence and rape has grown. However, the rates at which violent offenders are investigated, prosecuted, and sentenced remain low.

Studies from Brazil show that only about one-third of the complaints received by women's police stations lead to an investigation, and far fewer than this to prosecution. In Chile, only one in five domestic violence suits ends in a judgment, and only one in twenty of these results in conviction of the offender. In Ecuador in the early 1990s, the state prosecuted 10 percent of those arrested for sexual violence, with little more than half of these convicted. Although victims of violence feel increasingly empowered to seek help, perpetrators continue to enjoy impunity.

A major problem is securing medical evidence acceptable to law enforcement authorities. Many victims find it difficult to obtain medical examinations because of the scarcity of officially recognized facilities, few female personnel at those facilities, and demeaning treatment. Women's police stations, unfortunately, are often inadequately funded and poorly organized; working at these stations is also considered to be a low-prestige position within the police force.

NEGLECTED HEALTH ISSUES

Latin American women's basic health has improved from a generation ago: female average life expectancy was 54 years in the 1950s, 64 years in the 1970s, and is now 71 years. Still, there are major gaps in the area of reproductive and sexual health, and in some countries there have been alarming increases in rates of breast and cervical cancer, heart disease, and AIDS.

The 1994 United Nations Conference on Population and Development in Cairo urged governments to approach women's health in an integral manner. The integral approach represents a major advance over past policies, which tended to treat women exclusively in their roles as mothers and reproducers.

Brazil has been a pioneer in the integral approach. In 1984 the government introduced a Program for Integral Assistance to Women's Health that had been designed according to the recommendations of experts and activists from the women's movement. However, the program remains unimplemented in the vast majority of cities and states around the country. The Brazilian example reveals that women's health programs often lack sufficient funding and the political will to seriously implement them.

---

[2] See Lori L. Heise et al., *Violence Against Women: The Hidden Health Burden* (Washington, D.C.: World Bank, Discussion Paper 255, 1994); Inter-American Development Bank, *Domestic Violence* (Washington, D.C., 1997); and Dorothy Thomas, *Criminal Injustice: Violence Against Women in Brazil* (New York: Human Rights Watch, 1991).

Women's access to prenatal care and obstetric services has increased in most countries, leading to lower rates of maternal mortality since the 1970s, although the variation among countries is substantial. In general, the coverage and quality of health care remain inadequate, a situation reflected in the low frequency of screening for cervical cancer. In most of the region, cervical cancer is the most common form of cancer death in women. Cervical cancer is preventable by regular pap smears and effective laboratory analysis, but few women have access to prevention and treatment options. In Mexico, for example, a 1997 survey of 4,000 women found that 42 percent were unaware of the purpose of a pap smear, and that 97 percent had never had one. In Peru, one study in 1997 estimated that merely 7 percent of Peruvian women had had a pap smear taken.

Limited access to health care is also reflected in high unmet demand for modern contraceptives. Government-run family planning programs frequently have limited coverage, so many women have no access to safe and reliable contraception, or they self-medicate, without good information and at some risk. As a result, illegal abortions are frequent and many poor women suffer complications because of dangerous and unsanitary conditions. In many countries, women's NGOS, such as Sì Mujer in Nicaragua and SOS Corpo in Brazil, have begun to fill the gap left by inadequate state action in family planning and women's health.

Sterilization is among the most widely used methods of family planning in Latin America, except in countries such as Argentina and Chile, where it is illegal or access is restricted. High rates of sterilization are common in most developing countries: the percentage of contraceptive users who are sterilized is two times higher in developing countries than in developed countries (22 verus 11 percent). Latin America is not an exception. In 1990, the percentage of women contraceptive users who were sterilized was 38 percent in Mexico, 44 percent in Brazil, and 69 percent in El Salvador. Data from Brazil show that there is a high correlation between low levels of economic development and the frequency of sterilization: in 1991 there was a much higher proportion of sterilized female contraceptive users in the poorer northeast (63 percent) than in the wealthier city of São Paulo (36 percent). Sterilization is seen as the cheapest option for women who have little money to buy other methods or who lack information about their options and proper usage.

Many women are sterilized without receiving prior information about the procedure or without giving their consent. A recent study from Mexico found that one-quarter of women who had been sterilized were not informed beforehand that the procedure is irreversible. Nationwide family planning targets in Peru have created incentives for public health officials to pressure women into sterilization, leading to widespread abuses that have been documented by women's organizations, members of the Peruvian Congress, and the Roman Catholic Church.

In Argentina and Chile, improved economic conditions have led to improvements in women's general health. But the governments of these two countries continue to neglect reproductive health, which contributes to high abortion rates. Although the procedure is considered a crime, in 1990 there were an estimated 4.5 abortions per 100 women aged 15 to 49 in Chile, compared with 2.7 in the United States, 2.3 in Mexico, and 1.2 in Canada. Abortion rates are high in Chile because of a lack of information about contraceptive methods. In Mexico, Colombia, and Brazil, state activity in family planning has lowered the abortion rate. Many Latin American governments do little concerning reproductive health and sexuality because they are reluctant to confront the Roman Catholic Church. The consequences of this inaction are grave for women's health.

In many countries laws remain in force that are antithetical to gender equality.

WOMEN'S WORK?

One of the most salient trends in Latin America over the past several decades has been the increasing participation of women in the economy. Women make up one-third of the region's labor force, but they continue to participate on unequal terms with men.

Women are generally clustered into lower-status and lower-paying jobs from which promotions are rare. In Brazil, for example, 50 percent of women work in occupations that employ only 5 percent of the male labor force; conversely, 50 percent of men work in areas where only 5 percent of the female labor force is employed. More than 80 percent of tailors, primary school teachers, secretaries, telephone or telegraph operators, nurses, and receptionists are women.

As a result, women earn less than men. Women's average wages were between 20 and 40 percent lower than men's in 1992 (a gap comparable to that found in Western Europe and North America). Since the 1970s, however, income differentials between men and women have generally decreased, particularly in urban areas. And the gap is smaller for younger women than for older women. In 9 out of 12 countries surveyed by the United Nations Economic Commission on Latin America and the Caribbean, women 25 to 34 years of age earned between 80 and 90 percent of men's income in 1992.

The problem of pregnancy discrimination is widespread in the region. In theory, laws in Latin America demand that employers protect the rights of pregnant women and new mothers to care for their babies and retain their jobs. Labor laws designed to protect women include mandatory maternity leave, protection from being fired for becoming pregnant, prohibitions in some countries against the administration of pregnancy tests, and requirements that businesses with a certain number of women workers provide day-care services on the premises and allow women to take breaks to nurse their babies. Many countries forbid companies from firing workers during their maternity leave, and others protect new mothers from dismissal for an established period of time following their return to work. Women are often allowed to take a paid leave to care for young children who are sick.

In practice, however, employers, in order to cut costs, go to great lengths to avoid situations where the law is applied.

Some companies are reluctant to employ women full time and resort to strategies such as subcontracting, part-time employment, and paying for piecework done at home. Others deliberately pay women less than men to compensate for the perceived higher costs of employing women.

Even when child-care facilities do exist, many women find that commuting to work with children in tow is time-consuming and unpleasant for the child, and prefer instead to use child care that is close to home. Most mothers working outside the home rely on family members or domestic employees to care for their children.

Some businesses require a pregnancy test or a sterilization certificate as a condition of employment, or fire women workers once they become pregnant. Pregnancy tests are widespread in the maquiladoras and factories in the export processing zones of Mexico, Central America, and the Dominican Republic, even though national laws prohibit them.

EDUCATION: NOT SEPARATE, BUT NOT EQUAL

Women's enrollment in schools and in institutions of higher education has advanced in the region, but there are substantial variations among countries in women's access to the educational system, women's levels of educational attainment, and women's choices in school. Although Latin Americans have become steadily more literate since the 1970s, female illiteracy tends to be higher than men's; women's illiteracy is most acute in rural areas and among older populations.

In 1995, 48 percent of primary level students and 52 percent of secondary level students in Latin America were female. Yet there is tremendous variation among countries. In Guatemala, primary school education is obligatory, but only 45 percent of school-age girls are enrolled.

The percentage of women enrolled in universities in the region has climbed steadily: in 1970, women made up 35 percent of enrolled university students; in 1980, 43 percent; and in 1995, 49 percent. In terms of gender equity, enrollment rates offer some encouragement, but need to be carefully examined among other trends. Women are enrolled at higher rates than men in several countries, and women tend to repeat fewer grades than men. However, because of labor-market discrimination, women are in practice required to have higher levels of education than men—in one case four more years of schooling—in order to compete in the workforce on equal terms.

School dropout rates are highly correlated with poverty and maternity. Families who take children out of school generally cite the lack of economic resources as the reason. Forced to pick between keeping a son or a daughter in school, families generally choose the son on the assumption that he will be a more profitable investment for the family's future. Adolescent pregnancies also keep women from completing their education.

Certain areas of study remain predominantly masculine or feminine. Women are underrepresented in fields related to science and technology, but overrepresented in lower-paying occupations such as education, nursing, and library science.

However, women's presence in schools of business administration and, as noted, law is growing steadily.

School textbooks and curriculum content tend to reproduce gender stereotypes. Women appear less frequently than men in images and references in textbooks. When they do appear, they are frequently depicted in stereotypical roles, cooking or cleaning in the home.

Women's studies programs are becoming more numerous, and have consolidated into a reputable field of study and research. Brazil was one of the first countries in the region to develop women's studies programs and today there are more than 20 university centers around the country dedicated to the field. However, few courses about women are offered to undergraduates, even though this is a crucial mechanism for teaching future generations about women's rights and equal opportunities.

THE BALANCE SHEET

The status of women in Latin America is generally improving. Women's basic opportunities have increased from a few decades ago, which can be seen in better health, higher levels of educational attainment, and greater access to economic resources. International conventions and agreements related to women's rights have proliferated in the 1990s, intensifying the pressure on local governments to take steps to improve women's status. Most have responded at least symbolically to this pressure by formulating national plans concerning women, announcing new public policies, and creating special mechanisms to represent women's interests in public decision making. When pressured by women's movements and women politicians, some governments have made major advances in the areas of legal reform, violence against women, and education. Still, many new laws and policies are not enforced or implemented, leaving an immense variation in women's status between and within countries.

Relative to their numbers and potential, women are an underorganized social constituency and political force. Women's movements have become more numerous and diverse since the 1970s but lack the national political presence of other interest- and identity-based organizations such as labor movements and church groups. The socioeconomic, political, and ideological differences that exist among women often serve as barriers to women's organization. But when women find ways to mobilize despite their differences, they are able to push local governments and civil societies to take more action to promote gender equality.

MALA HTUN *is a Ph.D. candidate in political science at Harvard University. This article draws on "Women's Rights and Opportunities in Latin America: Problems and Prospects," an issue brief published by the Washington, D.C.-based Inter-American Dialogue and the International Center for Research on Women in April 1998.*

Article 5

Dissent, Summer 1998

Crime in Latin America

Forrest D. Colburn

SAN JOSE, COSTA RICA: The telephone rang; Danilo said, "Hello."

"This is Bam-Bam. I hear you have lost something."

"Yes, my car was stolen."

"If you authorize me, *if you authorize me,* I will look for it, providing that you pay me a reward of $2,500 if I am successful in finding it."

Danilo agreed. Three days later Bam-Bam called and told him that his car had been found and that Danilo must bring $2,500 in cash to a specified location. Danilo had two friends, Noel and John, who had recovered their stolen cars after paying a "ransom." But he was still surprised by Bam-Bam's audacity when they met:

"Before you pay me, let us inspect the car to make sure there is no damage."

There was no damage; Danilo handed over the cash.

"Before you go, let me give you some tips on how to protect your car against future theft—although I personally guarantee that your car will not be stolen in the next six months." Prominent among his tips was the installation of an alarm, which Bam-Bam said could be done at a local shop where, he concluded, "You can tell them Bam-Bam sent you and you will get a 30 percent discount."

It was true; Danilo got a 30 percent discount.

Bam-Bam, a handsome young man with a ponytail, was finally arrested and given a modest prison sentence. His "business" had soured only because he became such a celebrated figure—to the point of being asked for his autograph on the streets of San José—that the authorities had to act.

Although Danilo could find some humor in his costly encounter with Bam-Bam, other "kidnappings" in Latin America are not so benign. Stefano drove up to the still-charming Mexican city of Taxco and was abducted at gunpoint. His captors took him to a nearby mountain and chained him to a tree, keeping a machine gun aimed at his throat, feeding him cans of tuna fish. His family was asked to pay two million dollars for his release. The family asked for a more manageable sum. The kidnappers sliced off a section of his left ear, which they sent to the family. A telephone call threatened that a finger would be next, then a hand, and so forth. Stefano's father, Alberto, contacted the authorities. The governor of the state of Guerrero paid a visit of consolation, but the police were of no help, unable even to tap the phone line. A ransom was finally agreed upon, and Alberto divided the money (nearly all borrowed), as he was instructed, into two piles: half the sum in pesos and the other half in dollars. Twenty-two days after being abducted, Stefano was released, an emotional wreck.

Stefano's saga is far from an isolated case. This past year there have been, according to the governor, over a hundred *reported* kidnappings in the state of Guerrero. Other states and the Federal District, home of Mexico City, also report a surge in kidnappings and other violent crimes. Indeed, Mexico City is now one of the most dangerous cities in the world. The wave of kidnappings is notable because this crime is rare in most wealthy countries, where good police work makes it all but impossible for perpetrators to avoid capture. Kidnappings, whether of late-model Toyotas or children, are so common in contemporary Latin America at least in part because of the absence of competent police.

In many Latin American countries, from Mexico to Argentina, there is, in fact, the suspicion that the police collaborate or even participate in such violent crimes as kidnappings, as well as more prosaic robberies. Shortly after Stefano's release, the chief of the neighboring state of Morelos and two of his aides were arrested as they prepared to dump a corpse along a road in Guerrero—the tortured body of a seventeen-year-old member of a kidnapping gang. Mexico's attorney general's office opened an investigation into the Morelos police, declaring that "it appears these individuals are involved in the protection of gangs dedicated to kidnappings and to narcotics trafficking." Guerrero is likely no different; the police there just take offense at their state being used as a "body dump."

ALTHOUGH DATA on crime are often problematic, figures published by the World Bank confirm anecdotal evidence that crime is a serious—and growing—problem in Latin America. Colombia's murder rate is nine times as high as that of the United States. Guatemala and El Salvador's rates are fourteen times as high. In ten of the thirteen countries in Latin America that keep credible records, crime has increased substantially in the last ten to fifteen years. For example, in Panama and Peru homicides have multiplied by a factor of five. And in countries like Honduras and Ecuador, where kidnappings and extortion were rare, such crimes are now common.

A recent World Bank study titled "Institutional Obstacles for Doing Business" surveyed 3,600 entrepreneurs in 69 countries. Latin American respondents had the highest rate of concern about theft and other kinds of crime: 90 percent of respondents stated that crime is a serious problem. Moreover,

80 percent of respondents in Latin America reported that they did not feel confident that the state authorities protected them and their property from criminals. They reported, too, that personal safety and the security of property had decreased over the last decade. When presented with a long list of potential obstacles to their activities, business leaders in Latin America reported that their gravest problems are: (1) corruption, (2) inadequate infrastructure, and (3) theft and other crimes. If one defines corruption as nothing more than "theft and other crimes" by public officials, then the dimensions of the problem are truly staggering. Correspondingly, those interviewed in Latin America expressed little confidence in the region's judiciary system.

Crime in Latin America is widespread, a plague on all classes, including the poor. In the slums of Caracas, Venezuela, armed robbers take the shoes from the feet of pedestrians. Those who resist are murdered. (The murder rate in Caracas has increased fivefold in ten years.) In my rural neighborhood of Dulce Nombre in Costa Rica, even the local church was burglarized; the priest's microphone and vestments were stolen (the neighborhood reaction: "The thieves will pass directly to hell").

How can this surge in crime be explained? Didn't the 1980s and early 1990s bring an end to thirty years of ideological conflict, of militarism, civil wars, and authoritarianism? Hasn't there been an embrace of democracy and economic reform in Latin America? Isn't the region supposed to be off to a good start, finally, on the right road? It is understandable, surely, that there is still poverty, difficult to eradicate even with the best of economic models and with high rates of economic growth. But why is there such a dramatic increase in crime throughout the region, in countries as different from one another as Mexico, Costa Rica, Peru, and Argentina? Are there parallels with Russia and South Africa, two countries that have also recently made sweeping political and economic transitions and that also suffer from an increase in crime, much of it violent?

Ann Bernstein, a South African long involved in the struggle against apartheid and now director of the Center for Development and Enterprise in Johannesburg, has a number of explanations for why crime has dramatically increased in South Africa: (1) apartheid created criminals and fostered crime; (2) the movement away from authoritarian rule left weakened institutions unable to fight crime—a poorly trained and ill-paid police force, and judicial and penal systems sorely in need of reform; and (3) democracy, with its attendant liberalization, creates an "opening" for all sorts of activities, including criminal activity.

Her explanations for South Africa are suggestive also for Latin America. Guerrilla movements, civil wars, and military governments all led to violence. Some guerrillas and some members of the "security apparatus" have continued to do the only thing they know how to do—use a gun. The rule of law was weak in the region's military governments, and those regimes have bequeathed to today's democracies antiquated laws, poorly trained police forces, and weak judiciary systems. Perhaps, too, the greater freedoms afforded by democracy, and the attendant constraints on coercion, have been exploited by those tempted by the quick gains of crime.

This set of explanations is intuitively plausible. But how does one explain the rise in crime even in those countries with a history of democracy; namely, Costa Rica, Colombia, and Venezuela (and perhaps, too, the Dominican Republic)? Alternative explanations are offered. Perhaps fault lies with the "neoliberal" economic model, which has curbed the role of the state and increased, in turn, the role of markets. Despite the gain of greater macroeconomic stability, especially in the control of inflation, there have been costs: battered social programs, rising unemployment, heightened income inequality, and the championing of a crass materialism. So, the reasoning goes, if you can't get wealthy through privatization of state assets or through buying shares in a shopping mall, you will be tempted to rob someone.

Others argue that what is decisive about the neoliberal model is not its economic import, but the extent to which "state capacity" has been undermined, or at least neglected. Although it may be advisable to scale back the state's role in the economy, that should not be taken to mean—as it frequently has—that a weak state is desirable. What is needed is a "lean but strong" state, capable of fulfilling the traditional responsibilities of government, including, prominently, the provision of public order.

A different explanation for the rise in crime is based on culture: the collapse of the family; dislocations from mass migration and rapid population growth; the lack of civic education; the secularization of society; and, among other similarly diffuse forces, the spread of anti-civic norms from the United States, with its "gangsta rap," gangs, drug culture, and rampant consumerism. It seems facile to connect the introduction of MTV music videos with rising crime. But there are ingrained norms and practices in many parts of Latin America that do work against the rule of law and that may provide an amoral staging ground for criminal activity. In Argentina people joke that the national sport is tax evasion. In Brazil there is an expression, "For my friends, everything; for my enemies, the law!" In Ecuador the saying is, "The law is for the poncho [that is, the impoverished Indians who wear them]." Corruption in many public institutions, ministries, agencies, even police forces, is endemic. For example, a study conducted in 1996 by Mexico's Secretariat of Administrative Development and Oversight, based on anonymous interviews with police and on payroll information, indicated that police, who earn less than $350 a month, spend four times their wages. The majority of rank-and-file police interviewed said that if they did not rob ordinary citizens and steal from—as well as collaborate with—criminals, they would be unable to support their families. Those interviewed added that they were not overly concerned with the image they projected; their priority was money.

WHAT IS to be done? Before assuming office as mayor of Mexico City, Cuauhtémoc Cárdenas of the center-left Democratic Revolutionary Party (PRD) announced that security would be his top priority. A former mayor of Mexico City said that trying to do anything in Mexico City was like trying to service a jet in midflight and, in fact, success has to date eluded Cárdenas. But he is one of the few ranking public officials in the region to recognize publicly the importance of crime. The pernicious effect of crime on economic development is mostly ignored, as is the extent to which democracy's legitimacy depends on its ability to solve problems. Greater attention to crime is needed throughout the region; public officials need to think hard about how the surge in crime can be reversed.

It would be easier to proceed if we knew just why crime has risen in the last ten to fifteen years in Latin America. But there are competing explanations and no way to prove their relative merits. And, in any case, the prominent theories suggest Herculean projects: ending poverty or transforming the culture. The only viable short-run policy seems to be effective law enforcement. Citizens don't engage in crime for two reasons: (1) the coercive power of the state and (2) the moral authority of the state. The first has been weakened in Latin America by the transition from authoritarianism to democracy

and the second has yet to be established by the new democracies. Building the moral authority of the state is an ambitious and long-term endeavor. So the burden for now falls on making the coercive power more consistent, fair, and effective.

Given the sorry condition of many of the police forces and judicial systems in the region, this task cannot be accomplished just by adding to the ranks of the police; and it is dangerous to augment their ranks with personnel from the armed forces, as has been tried in Mexico and Brazil. Police forces have to be completely rebuilt and judicial systems overhauled—these are among the first reforms that democratic rulers must seek.

FORREST D. COLBURN's most recent book is *The Vogue of Revolution in Poor Countries.*

Article 6

Cultural Survival Quarterly, Winter 1998

Latin America

The Internet and Indigenous Texts

by Guillermo Delgado-P. and Marc Becker

In an age of global communication and computer technology, indigenous peoples have slowly gained access to electronic communication. With all of the hype surrounding cyberspace and hyperspaces as we enter a new millennium, we need to examine how indigenous peoples use and are impacted by this technology. Is there still a possibility that marginalized indigenous territories within Latin America are successfully and effectively utilizing this technology to make their voices heard?

Anthropologists' fears that electronic communication would inevitably have a negative impact on indigenous peoples, who gained access to Western culture's consumer commodities, have been discredited. Our images of Western culture contaminating untouched and pristine indigenous cultures have been irremediably crushed. Globalization has caused the demise of whatever pristine elements or environments remained, as well as these naive images of indigenous peoples.

Native activists and scholars have observed that patterns of economic inequality which exist elsewhere have been reproduced in access to electronic media. A noticeable crevice based on the accumulation (or lack) of wealth reproduces Latin America's historical discrepancies found in the interaction between non-indigenous peoples and 'peoples without histories,' as indigenous societies have often been considered. Rather than creating a space for the democratization of society, electronic communication systems reinforce traditional hierarchical social structures. This dynamic reproduces a socio-economic interpretative approach that helps explain the manner in which wealth has been accumulated and distributed over the last five centuries, reproducing a hierarchy between 'core' or developed nations, and 'peripheral' or undeveloped nations. This paradigm also highlights how economic relations in Latin America isolate and discriminate against indigenous communities by placing them, geographically speaking, on the periphery.

Following this core-periphery paradigm, indigenous peoples who live in proximity to the core have been touched by its magic and consciously participate in world politics through their access to the web or the never-ending Internet information lists. Alternatively, those societies separated from the core suf-

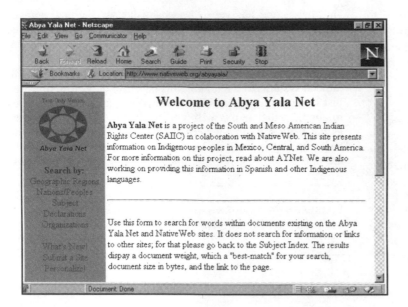

fer the consequences of being 'delinked' despite their wish to enter into the dynamics of information exchanges in cyberspace. Unfortunately, a lack of money and computer technology stifles such desires.

Although personal computers (PCs) have reached indigenous peoples, the use and distribution of this technology reproduces a picture similar to what happened after Alexander Bell invented the telephone. In Latin America, during the Alliance for Progress program in the 1960s, a sociologist considered the phone to be an indicator of a person's class and social status in society. The assumption was that those individuals or family units connected to a phone line belonged to the middle class!

So far, indigenous peoples' experience with electronic communication has followed a similar dynamic. Despite early developments which indicated that computer networks might prove to be a democratizing influence, it now threatens to become another tool which the elite use to dominate society and exclude indigenous peoples from political discourse. Today, those with access to telephone lines and PCs are indeed experiencing certain privileges, and those without access are becoming increasingly marginalized. Unless there are broad structural changes, these networks may fail in their attempt to induce positive changes within society.

In this short article, we restrict our analysis to the use of interactive electronic conferencing via PCs, primarily as a means of enabling indigenous peoples, who live in remote areas and share common concerns, to exchange information regarding their similar problems of relating to nation-states. We will illustrate the relationship between computer ownership and economic disenfranchisement. Such comparisons allow us to analyze the use of PCs which have been implemented to educate the general public on human rights for indigenous peoples. Electronic bulletins presumably allow for a more democratic participation in society since it is the indigenous peoples who become subjects of their own electronic transmissions.

These bulletins allow a degree of equal access to the public unparalleled by any other medium. Although not all indigenous peoples are active participants on the Internet, leaders and their representatives (or non-indigenous co-workers acting in solidarity and in direct consultation with indigenous peoples), are at the center of this endeavor.

North and South

While electronic communication has been in use since WWII, it was not until the late 1970s that a few universities established closed-circuit computer networks. The 1980s introduced the widespread use of PCs which led to a continual rise in computer access and a drop in associated costs. As a direct result of the uneven distribution of computers, electronic networks, and infrastructure, tribes and indigenous organizations in North America began to use PCs before their counterparts in the southern part of the Americas (or for that matter, throughout the rest of the world). This is largely due to the active presence of native intellectuals at North American universities in academic centers that are devoted to the study, research, and promotion of indigenous cultures. This experience has not been repeated in Latin America, where, with few exceptions, indigenous peoples are not allowed to house research centers at national universities.

The expanded use of the Internet in universities, government offices, and businesses during the early 1990s helped indigenous organizations circulate an increasing amount of information regarding the relationships between nation-states and indigenous peoples. In the North, those messages generally dealt with news related to sovereignty issues and the interaction between indigenous representatives and the nation-state. Archiving retrievable information on specific problems, tribes, treatises, and cultural issues allowed for the emergence of a truly dynamic cyberspace. For the first time, indigenous peoples accessed information that enhanced their knowledge about the complexity of indigenous life. They could read messages and learn from one another through the system.

With greater use of the Internet by indigenous peoples, ethnic identities became much more important. People who did not formally belong to an indigenous group rediscovered their ethnic heritage and others claiming Indian heritage began populating the newsgroups and mailing lists. Many people used the Internet to raise questions concerning their personal and collective identities and to share their histories. Before the Internet, these histories were only accessible through restricted classified systems at university or public libraries. In other words, the information came home and in exchange, people started to share their own oral histories regarding their indigenous experiences.

Columbus' quincentennial initiated a reunion of indigenous peoples of the North and the South. This reunion symbolized an awareness of 'indigenousness' and their shared colonial experiences. They were able to exchange information pertaining to a continental saga set within the framework of the nation-state, globalization, and human rights. People started to build exchanges and organized meetings with the purpose of furthering decolonization. Indigenous collective entities continued to struggle for the preservation of their livelihoods and territories against the reckless incursion of transnational corporations. For indigenous peoples, the debate was, and still is the struggle over colonialism, neocolonialism, and liberation.

PCs and Economic Inequality

Internet access has become a specialty; one must be trained before navigating the Internet and computers are not always openly available to indigenous peoples. Computer technology has been taught in a manner which makes indigenous peoples recall the way their languages work. Most of these languages work on an agglutinative principle; a root word provides the base and an infinite number of suffixes are added according to the situation. Computer technology, listservs, newsgroups, and websites work in this way as well.

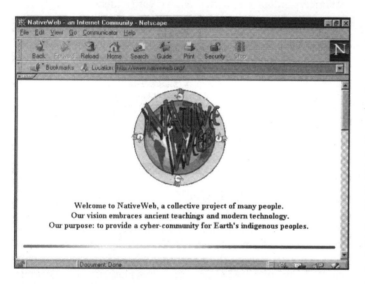

Welcome to NativeWeb, a collective project of many people.
Our vision embraces ancient teachings and modern technology.
Our purpose: to provide a cyber-community for Earth's indigenous peoples.

After the electronic 'brouhaha' of the early 1990s, access to information has slowed and tends to be routine rather than sporadic, as participants regulate their contributions. Rapid PC technological change has provoked short circuits. Floppies, as well as early PC consoles quickly became outdated. Today, specialization emerges as participants look for their own 'cybertribes.' Mailing lists start to crisscross and overlapping purposes inundate users with unwanted information. To address this problem, specialized lists which focus on specific areas and themes have emerged as an alternative to an overwhelming amount of generic information on 'Indians.' Participants have started to build networks in order to more effectively manage their time on-line. The Internet has become so specialized that participants tend to stick together. Internet participants express their opinions freely which produces a sense of equality in the process of exchanging information. Several interesting cases will highlight the extent to which the Internet has allowed the flow of information.

Cases in Latin America

In Guatemala, the Powers that Be brandished internal security arguments to curtail the use of the Internet. As indigenous organizations gained computer knowledge to press for their cultural rights, traditional sectors of the government tried to control this flow of information. Due to this tense situation, Maya on-line activists have been labeled 'hackers,' providing us with an important example of the limits and potential of communication technology in third world countries. Adaptation of computer technology to meet local needs, however, helps redefine cultural and national identities. Not only have computer technological issues been solved, but programs have been adapted to the specifics of indigenous reality.

The Maya project is one of the most serious attempts at creating a space on the Internet for the 22 indigenous cultures which still exist in Guatemala. The Maya are working to retrieve all the information that pertains to their culture starting with programs of linguistic restoration, as well as documents that may shed light on the legitimacy of their ancient territorial claims. The Maya of Guatemala constitute one of the best examples where Western computer technology, appropriately used by the Maya themselves, has been co-opted to promote their demands within the nation-state. Unless the military regains their Cold War dictatorial power as it often appears evident, the Guatemalan example could be one where PC technology mediates a true democratization process.

Although the Kuna nation of Panama is numerically small, it also has strong young organizations which make serious use of computer technology. Demonstrating ethnic assertiveness for many years, the Kuna, especially through their organization Kunas Unidos de Napguana or 'United Kunas of Napguana,' have served as the frame of reference regarding ethnic identity. The Internet has helped the Kuna become strong international advocates of environmental issues. Some of their members have been able to establish strong collaborative relationships with environmental organizations. Environmentalists have invited their leaders to serve as consultants for international agencies, to develop plans that defend the environment, and to work for human rights for indigenous peoples. Kuna representatives have become leading figures in debates concerning biodiversity, indigenous property rights, and DNA collection. The use of electronic media has been extremely important to them in defending their interests and questioning government decisions.

Radical changes in the way politics have worked under the PRI-dominated political system in Mexico have also opened space for a more active voice for indigenous peoples. Starting with the Zapatista Uprising of 1994, the use of computer technology and the Internet played an essential role in the diffusion of information. Although indigenous peoples themselves are rarely visible on the Internet, some indigenous individuals have been able to train themselves on the use of computer technology.

Indigenous peoples in Mexico continue to live under a system of profound poverty which leaves organizing and gaining access to computer systems in the hands of the non-indigenous majority. A few positive beginnings have failed, such as the formation of the International Office of the Indigenous Press (AIPIN) in 1992. This was one of the first organizations of indigenous journalists, based in Latin America, Europe, and the U.S., that tried to coordinate an international network. Unfortunately, they did not have strong economic support. The venture received outside financial aid, but was unable to become a functional unit. AIPIN accumulated exorbitant phone bills and was eventually forced to sell their computers in order to pay off debts. Although this idea was essentially a good one, the lack of expertise defeated the cause and by 1997, AIPIN became a one-person struggle.

The Mapuche in Chile working with the Council of All Lands, the Aymara in Bolivia and Peru, the pan-Indian CONAIE coalition in Ecuador, and occasionally, the ONIC in Colombia, sporadically participate in building computer networks. As one heads south, access to satellites, computers, and phone lines becomes an important issue for indigenous peoples. If sociologists previously thought that possession of phone lines entitled individuals or families to qualify for middle class status, this theory can now be applied to the economically disenfranchised indigenous peoples of the Andean area and the Amazon basin. In these areas, indigenous peoples remain dependent as their ability to use computer technology remains limited. It is difficult for economically viable indigenous groups to acquire a personal computer. Those organizations with computers do not actively send information concerning their situations or contribute their own perspectives as indigenous peoples on important issues.

Obstacles to the Internet

Both in the Amazon and the Andes, indigenous peoples exist in a state of dependency, domination, and control. Until this is overturned, demands cannot be clearly heard on the Internet. Also, the Andean area has traditionally trusted the short wave radio as the primary means of communication between indigenous peoples. Since the short wave radio is still an important and economically accessible system of communication, they have been less interested in current computer technology which continues to be very expensive.

In the Amazon basin, the CPI (Comissão Pro-Indio) of São Paulo has functioned as a hub which coordinates the reception and transmission of indigenous news. CIMI (the Conselho Indigenista Missionãrio or Indianist Missionary Council) supports indigenous efforts but retains an outsiders' perspective, common in Brazil, that views indigenous peoples as child-like. There are few indigenous individuals who have entered journalism and even fewer who have the economic power to communicate their ideas through the Internet. Although indigenous peoples occasionally utilize written forms of journalism, it has been difficult to move from this form to the electronic media. Non-indigenous persons (often anthropologists or missionaries) continue to mediate these systems which produce an image of an absentee indigenous voice that is reduced to a level of informant without agency.

In the U.S. and Canada, indigenous networks have received extensive technical support from universities and others who offered help as a way of collaborating with indigenous peoples. Examples include the establishment of GLAIN (Great Lakes

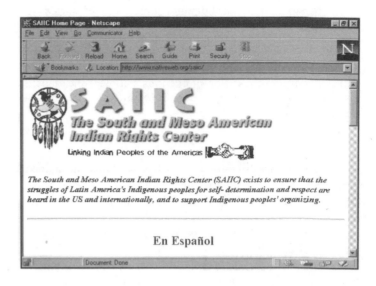

American Indian Network), NativeNet (under the direction of Gary Trujillo in Boston), NativeWeb (which universities in Kansas and New York hosted before acquiring its own domain), and SAIIC-L (hosted as saiic.indio on 'PeaceNet' in San Francisco). In Latin America, however, such collaboration is rare and often does not work.

The general public is more informed about indigenous issues in areas where PCs are a household item, such as in the U.S. or Europe, than in the areas where most indigenous peoples live. One reason is that some indigenous organizations in Latin America orient the information they disseminate to English speakers (often with the help of volunteer translators) hoping that in return, people in developed countries will financially contribute to indigenous causes. A second reason is the establishment of computer networks by indigenous peoples who live outside their traditional areas. This is the case with 'Inkarri,' an Information Center on Indigenous Issues sponsored by the Basque county of Vitoria-Gasteiz (northern Spain) and under the direction of an indigenous journalist. Inkarri's mission is to achieve a high level of professional journalism. Inkarri is probably the first website that emerged as a result of a constant exchange of information between Internet participants in the Andean region of South America, the U.S., and Europe. A similar Internet site has been functioning in Geneva, Switzerland under the name of 'Pueblo Indio.' As in the case of Inkarri, a team of indigenous peoples, as well as non-indigenous volunteers, concentrate their efforts on Andean issues and are in charge of this project. Whereas Pueblo Indio broadcasts in Spanish, Inkarri uses Spanish, Euzkera, and English.

The availability of information on the Internet has not resulted in a large or significant indigenous participation. Collaborative efforts between indigenous peoples and non-indigenous volunteers generate forms of 'cyberbrokerage' and solution-search strategies. These collaborative efforts often advocate for the reformation of policies at higher levels of decision making (for example, the World Bank and the International Monetary Fund) when such policies affect indigenous peoples. Indigenous peoples have gained access to resources

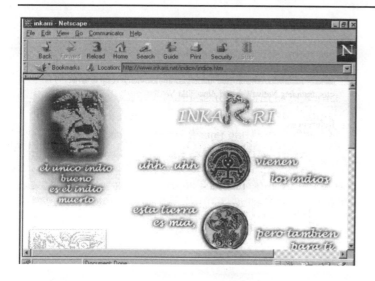

which Western technology provides, but concrete progress in their quality of life continues to lag behind.

Needless to say, while the periphery remains a producer of information despite its 'hackers,' the availability of information remains paramount. Decisions that affect indigenous peoples continue to be made at institutions where power is a game. The idea that messages and urgent actions need to be translated into English so that they can have concrete repercussions is also a problem. For example, a section of the NativeWeb site called 'Abya Yala Net' focuses on indigenous issues in Latin America. The site is mostly in English and functions primarily as a research and information tool for activists in the North rather than as an organizing tool for indigenous organizations in the South.

Representing Indigenous Women

While indigenous men are often content with their ability to participate in cyberspace, the same is not true for indigenous women. Indigenous websites have, for the most part, failed to include indigenous women. While women have gained stronger representation in indigenous organizations, their opportunities to work with electronic equipment have been circumscribed. Thus, women's voices on the Internet are very limited and access to resources that would facilitate their training continue to be scarce. Although indigenous women have successfully adopted the electronic calculator as a tool in the Andean marketplace and have learned to produce short-wave radio programs, indigenous women have not come close to mastering computer technology. Several indigenous women talk about restoring full use of indigenous languages, writing new grammar books and dictionaries, compiling information on medicinal plants, circulating health information, talking about gender relations, upbringing, family, and denouncing the nation-state's historical disregard for their problems. The Internet could play an important role in achieving all these goals.

Female participation in indigenous organizations has increased and we hope that their future level of participation on the Internet will match that of men's. Compared to the North,

where indigenous women's agencies have attained a visible presence, the South needs more opportunities where women become active participants in the decision-making processes in their communities. Most international aid continues to fall into male hands and indigenous women suffer a high level of discrimination due to their gender, economic poverty, and ethnicity, often called the 'triple burden.'

Activism on the Internet

Finally, consciousness-raising activities have been promoted through the use of electronic bulletins where indigenous, as well as non-indigenous advocates and activists, merge together to defend vanishing cultures, disappearing languages, receding ecosystems, and a world view that contributes to the restoration of human peace. Because this technology is interactive, access to, and retrieval of information from the Internet can be used to trigger, support, and encourage continuous democratic social change that benefits the last echelon of Latin America's marginalized indigenous peoples.

The sporadic and careful introduction of solar panels and computer access in some communities has encouraged better systems of wealth redistribution within nation-states. The same could be true for wealthier communities which have learned to share with those in need. Rather than being placed in a position to react to on-line information, indigenous peoples can establish interactive relations focused on solving problems. The solution does not remain only in the dissemination of information, but in the interactive resolution of concrete problems. Gender, language, and better monitoring systems could provide high returns for indigenous, as well as non-indigenous peoples. Through broader structural changes, computer networks can lessen exploitative and oppressive conditions and lead to a more democratic and empowered situation for indigenous peoples.

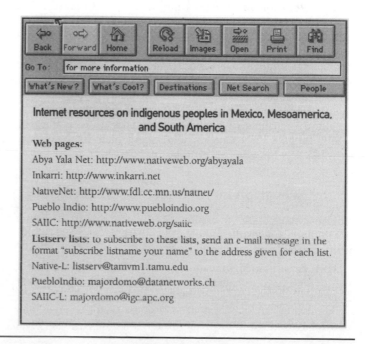

Internet resources on indigenous peoples in Mexico, Mesoamerica, and South America

Web pages:

Abya Yala Net: http://www.nativeweb.org/abyayala

Inkarri: http://www.inkarri.net

NativeNet: http://www.fdl.cc.mn.us/natnet/

Pueblo Indio: http://www.puebloindio.org

SAIIC: http://www.nativeweb.org/saiic

Listserv lists: to subscribe to these lists, send an e-mail message in the format "subscribe listname your name" to the address given for each list.

Native-L: listserv@tamvm1.tamu.edu

PuebloIndio: majordomo@datanetworks.ch

SAIIC-L: majordomo@igc.apc.org

Guillermo Delgado-P. is an anthropologist and teaches Latin American and Latino Studies at the University of California at Santa Cruz. He is the Technical Advisor of the Abya Yala Fund based in Oakland, California, an all indigenous non-profit organization that supports the self-development of indigenous peoples.

Marc Becker (mbecker@ilstu.edu) is a Visiting Assistant Professor of Latin American History at Illinois State University. He is author of Mariãtegui and Latin American Marxist Theory and has recently completed his dissertation entitled "Class and Ethnicity in the Canton of Cayambe: The Roots of Ecuador's Modern Indian Movement." He has helped launch and develop a variety of Internet sites, including NativeWeb and Abya Yala Net.

References

Gwyn, Robert J. 1983. "Rural Radio in Bolivia: A Case Study." Journal of Communication. *Vol. 33:* 79–87.

Nehemkis, Peter. 1964. Latin America: Myth and Reality. Westport: Greenwood.

O'Connor, Alan. 1991. "Between Culture and Organization: The Radio Studios of Cotopaxi, Ecuador." Department of Communication. Ohio State University.

O'Donnell, Susan and Guillermo Delgado-P. 1995. "Using the Internet to Strengthen the Indigenous Nations of the Americas." Media Development. *Vol. XLII (3):* 36–39.

Article 7   *The Futurist*, October 1999

What's Next for Mexico:

Potential Surprises from a U.S. Neighbor

Mexico's future could reflect a **flourishing democracy** or an **ungovernable slide into chaos**. A noted scholar assesses five scenarios for the near-term future.

By Michael J. Mazarr

The aim of this article is not to forecast the future, but to furnish a sense of the range of outcomes that could develop as Mexico undergoes the transition to a knowledge era. The five detailed scenarios examined here are intended to help government and business planners consider the implications of Mexico's possible futures, even if we may not be able to specify a single likely outcome. Individuals and organizations with a stake in Mexico's future are invited to use these snapshots of hypothetical futures to keep track of events, judge their character, understand their likely course, and plan accordingly.

Scenario One: Democratic Mexico

Mexico's democratic transition accelerates robust economic growth and expands the middle class; these developments have positive effects on other trends.

This scenario is significant for its differences in kind rather than degree from the status quo. It assumes that democratization and liberalization accelerate, economic growth improves, a vibrant small and medium-sized business sector emerges, and Mexicans continue to thrive at the intersection of global-local

trends, where the citizens of so many other countries feel bewildered and alienated. The indispensability of a good economic performance to this scenario means that (in contrast to the next three scenarios) it can be understood as a fast-growth scenario.

Another way of putting it is that the "Democratic Mexico" scenario represents the achievement of virtuous cycles and the avoidance of vicious ones.

For this scenario to take hold, millions of new job seekers over the next decade will have to find meaningful employment, expanding the tax-paying, savings-enhancing middle class. Mexican institutions will gain increasing control over society, allowing for more economic progress, more faith in government, and in turn ever more effective institutions. Greater access to information will allow people to counteract, rather than succumb to, the sensationalistic impulses of the media. Mexico's service sector will be strengthened, in both the domestic and the export arenas.

In the broadest sense, then, this scenario represents a world in which Mexico's democratic transition works to alleviate social ills—in the way that advocates of democracy hope—rather than to exacerbate them through demagoguery and corruption, as some pessimists fear.

This scenario does not assume that a magic wand will wave away Mexico's challenges. Unemployment and inequity would remain major social problems; tensions associated with globalization would persist; corruption and drug trafficking would continue. However, "Democratic Mexico" does assume that nearly all major social and economic indicators begin to move in the right direction and at a pace notably better than the status quo.

Preconditions for "Democratic Mexico"

Along with strong economic growth, an essential precondition for this scenario is increasingly corruption-free and credible institutions—from the Congress to the police, the courts, and the military. These institutions should be able to get a better handle on the three daggers pointing at the heart of Mexican progress: crime, corruption, and narcotrafficking. The country must also close the gap between social and economic development and political institutions, and it must improve the legal foundation for the economy.

Regionally, this scenario witnesses improved relations between Mexico and its neighbors. A strong economic performance and the emergence of a larger middle class will reduce the pressure for illegal immigration to the United States, swell the market for U.S. exports, and otherwise establish Mexico as a stable, reliable partner.

Is "Democratic Mexico" Emerging? Signs to Look For

■ Elections at all levels become more open and competitive, and major parties accept the results. Political participation throughout society—demonstrations, campaigning, referenda, and the like—increase.

■ Congress acquires growing powers and exercises an oversight role over the executive. The principle of reelection is introduced into the legislature and, eventually, all levels of government.

■ Public opinion polls show slight but notable growth in public confidence in governmental institutions and optimism about the future.

■ Economic growth tops 6% to 7% or greater; no major financial crises occur. Official unemployment remains below 5%. The middle class grows to 30% or more of the population.

■ Civil society grows healthier, with more people volunteering and stronger nongovernmental organizations. Innovative business practices begin to influence society. The educational system shows signs of improvement at all levels.

■ Police become more professional. The levels of crime, especially violent crime, plateau and begin to decline. Illegal immigration to the United States declines. Regional cooperation on immigration, environmental, and drug issues grows.

Scenario Two: Muddling Through

"Muddling Through" is the scenario closest to the status quo. In this world things do not get notably worse, but neither do

any breakthroughs occur in such areas as economic reform or democratization.

It is a mildly optimistic scenario that assumes that major social collapse, attacks on reforms, or other disastrous events do not come to pass. The modest economic recovery since the 1994 collapse of the peso continues: More jobs are created, the financial sector grows healthier, foreign investment continues, and privatization proceeds. Politically, it expects Mexico's nascent democracy to remain intact, functioning well enough to prevent social gridlock.

But "Muddling Through" offers many reasons for worry, because it also assumes that Mexico does not take major steps to solve its numerous challenges. Incremental progress continues in such areas as environmental protection and weeding out corruption, but how long incrementalism can hold off social unrest is an open question. This scenario assumes that seven or eight years from now the degree of rule of law, social crime, penetration of government and the military by drug-related corruption, and other measures of stable governance remain much as they are today.

The implication is that underlying forces—the power of narcotraffickers, levels of public disaffection, corporate frustration with lax economic regulations—have been moving in a profoundly disturbing direction and will ultimately cause mischief, even though Mexico's institutions do not seem to have changed. This is an important example of how dependent Mexico is on positive progress: Even the mildly negative scenario of stagnation has the potential of declining into social instability.

Meanwhile, relations with the United States bounce along on the same roller coaster of friendly rhetoric and sudden controversy that they have been on since 1994. From drug smuggling to immigration to financial reform, the "Muddling Through" scenario assumes that the major issues in the relationships neither improve nor deteriorate. Similarly, Mexico's relations with its other neighbors and potential trading partners (such as the European Union) show little change.

Signs to Look for in a "Muddling Through" Scenario

■ Most aspects of economic reform and privatization continue at more or less the same rate as today. Economic growth runs at 4.5% to 5%.

■ Some halting progress is realized through autonomy of the central bank and transparency of financial transactions. Bank failures occur occasionally, but in broad terms the effort to enhance bank capitalization and address problem loans moves forward.

■ Politically, the turbulence of recent years continues with no major breakthrough: No opposition candidate wins the presidency, nor does the Institutional Revolutionary Party (PRI) return to old-style national dominance.

■ Disputes and brinksmanship continue between the PRI presidency and the opposition Congress, but both sides recognize the danger of gridlock, and some key legislation is passed.

■ Elections remain fairly free and honest as they have been in recent rounds. Violence in Chiapas continues, without exploding on the national scene.

Profile of Two Neighbors: Similarities and Differences

	United States	Mexico
Government type	Federal Republic	Federal Republic
Date of Constitution	1789	1917
Population, 1998	273 million	101 million
Population, 2015 (est.)	352 million	126 million
Percentage urban	75%	74%
Largest city	New York	Mexico City
Population, 1995	16.3 million	16.5 million
Percentage of national total	6.5%	16.3%
Population, 2015 (est.)	17.6 million	19.1 million
Percentage of national total	5.0%	15.2%
Life Expectancy at Birth	76.1	71.6
Exchange rate	$0.105/1 Mexican peso	9.5 pesos/U.S. $1
Gross Domestic Product	$7.6 trillion	$777.3 billion
Per capita GDP	$28,600	$8,100
Area	3.6 million sq. mi.	761,400 sq. mi.

Sources: *The World Almanac, 1999*; U.S. Census Bureau; U.N. Population Information Network.

■ Environmental protection improves very gradually, with the lack of major investments remaining a substantial barrier to more dramatic advances.

■ Narcotrafficking continues at current or perhaps slightly increased levels.

Scenario Three: Losing Ground

"Losing Ground" represents the victory of stagnation and the beginning of a slow reversal of recent economic, legal, and environmental progress. This scenario assumes that fundamental conflicts in Mexican society—mercantilism vs. liberalism, authoritarianism vs. democracy, equality vs. oligarchy—are not resolved to the extent that they are in the two previous scenarios.

In this scenario, action gets bogged down in political and economic disputes, producing a stalemated society. Incomplete economic reform leaves the domestic industrial sector in a precarious position. Unemployment, savings rates, and the role of small and medium-sized firms show little or no gain. Mediocre economic performance, including stagnant oil production, leaves the government with insufficient revenues for the social investments that are crucial to Mexico's future, especially in the areas of health and education.

The "Losing Ground" scenario would be most likely if Mexico's democratic process proves harmful rather than helpful to solving major social problems. For instance, persistent standoffs between the legislative and executive branches could produce policy gridlock; partisan debate could destroy the potential for meaningful action on social equity and environmental protection; and big-money interests could subvert the popular will on many issues. Thus, contrary to the hopes of reformers, Mexico's halfway democracy might delay rather than accelerate the development of a truly "Democratic Mexico."

There are always expectations attached to emerging democracy and a liberal economic system; there are also major social strains below the surface of such issues as inequity and corruption. Therefore, a scenario in which Mexico stumbles along without major progress and begins a long, slow cycle of de-

cline is almost certain to lead to instability. At some point, the weight of unfulfilled expectations could become too great for the system to bear, and the "Losing Ground" scenario would generate a widespread reaction and renewal of old politics, or encroaching social chaos.

Beyond Mexico's borders, this scenario would likely play out in a gradual heightening of tensions with the United States, as a host of important bilateral issues went unattended, such as immigration, drug smuggling, and U.S. appeals for a stronger rule of law and business protections in Mexico. Meanwhile, Mexico's plans for broader economic ties with Latin America, Europe, and Asia, as well as its larger hopes for regional cooperation on cross-border issues, would make little progress.

The danger of "Losing Ground" is that it could not last forever: It may be a halfway point to something much worse—the scenario of "Old Wine in New Bottles" or "Ungovernability."

Early Warnings of a "Losing Ground" Scenario

■ Mexico makes little or no progress on major economic reforms, especially financial sector accountability and transparency. The central bank's recent trend toward greater independence and influence is interrupted.

■ Economic growth plateaus in the unspectacular range of 3% to 4%. This growth level provides half a million jobs annually—not enough to match the need generated by demographic trends. As a result, unemployment rises to 10% or more.

■ Major elections generate protests of irregularities. Voting and nonvoting forms of political participation decline. Citizens become more disaffected with the political and economic system. Media sensationalism continues to undermine hope for the future.

■ Congress does not approve presidential budgets in a timely fashion; repeated budgetary stalemates wrack the legislature. Constant standoffs with the executive branch often paralyze government decision making. Corruption scandals continue at all levels of government. Congress remains an adjunct player to the executive's dominant role in government. Public confidence in government remains low.

■ Bank failures accelerate. Domestic capital is unavailable for business. The small and medium-sized business sector shows no improvement, and its share of GDP and exports does not increase.

■ Little growth occurs in the middle class. Inequity persists and even grows as the new wealth coming into the country is not shared. The educational system fails to improve, finding itself unable to reach needy populations or to raise their achievement levels.

■ Investments in environmental protection are delayed or canceled. Measures of air and water quality do not improve. A water crisis continues to threaten Mexico City.

■ Immigration and drug smuggling remain major irritants to Mexican-U.S. relations. Levels of crime remain high.

Scenario Four: Old Wine in New Bottles

This scenario describes a turning back of the clock on economic and political reform, a resurgence of some form of authoritarian rule, and a halt in privatization. Political reform is stifled and economic liberalization reversed, all with an eye toward recreating a "perfect dictatorship."

Politically, democratic contests for offices at all levels give way to the old style of Mexican politics: rigged campaigns, stuffed ballot boxes, bribed voters, and a presidency with final oversight on any election result in the country. Opposition parties are generally shut out of crucial election victories. Violent intimidation of regime opponents is revived.

If such a scenario does occur, the now-extended process of political opening and economic reform will probably ensure that it will occur violently; many elements of Mexican society will react angrily to being stripped of their new rights. A brief period of the "Old Wine" scenario could be followed by widespread social upheaval, or "Ungovernability."

On the other hand, a monolithic party attempting to reinstitute old methods of rule would find a number of allies in Mexican society, particularly if it cloaks its grab for power with the language of revolution, equality, and nationalism. This scenario could emerge as nationalistic and class-based reaction to the pressures of globalization. The agenda might include income redistribution, resistance to U.S. dictates, improved government-led health and educational systems, and stronger environmental protection.

A variation of this scenario could involve an unprecedented role for the military in a recentralized government structure. Most observers view an outright military takeover as unlikely, but a partnership between the increasingly powerful military and old-style politicians is not out of the question, and it could give this scenario a repressive tinge.

The "Old Wine" scenario suggests a substantial rise in tensions with the United States. The revisionist movement in Mexico is likely to welcome such tensions as a spur to its rule, and its probable actions—economic protectionism and antidemocratic repression—will certainly provoke sharp rebukes from the United States and many Latin American states. The deteriorating cycle of hostility could put the North American Free Trade Agreement (NAFTA) at risk.

Signals of an "Old Wine In New Bottles" Scenario

■ Old-guard candidates dominate the Institutional Revolutionary Party and the Party of the Democratic Revolution, winning massive victories in the 80% to 90% range. Democratic processes are interrupted, amid complaints from the press and warnings from outside human-rights groups and the Catholic Church. Harassment of regime opponents expands.

■ Mexican business discards new management models and reverts to old patterns of hierarchical control. Privatization is halted and reversed. Financial and banking reform is shelved. Unofficial figures for unemployment top 10%.

■ The commitment to free trade wanes in favor of protectionism and industrial policy, imperiling NAFTA. Exports stagnate and then decline.

■ Crime worsens, generating new calls for social order. Illegal immigration to the United States increases. Nationalist, anti-American rhetoric grows. Regional cooperation essentially comes to a halt.

■ Corruption scandals are widespread. Reports of military corruption and ties to narcotraffickers rise. Evidence of a closer alliance between the old-guard politicians and the military emerges, including the influence of high-level military officers and the placement of top generals in key civilian posts.

Scenario Five: Ungovernability

This extreme scenario contemplates the worst of all possible outcomes: the degeneration of Mexican society into violent chaos, which could take a number of different forms.

The "Ungovernability" scenario demands an immense trigger—an economic depression, a massive wave of social violence—to become reality. Many of the subscenarios described below might have their roots in the insurgencies now under way, which could, over time, more dramatically damage Mexico's social fabric than they have done so far. Here are some likely forms of chaos:

■ **The dark age of neo-medievalism.** Central authority in Mexico, and indeed all forms of authority, wanes rapidly, and social chaos gains ground. Political authority is fragmented into local or regional pieces, or into a complicated patchwork of rule involving government, business, the military, drug barons, and other actors. Democracy is under assault everywhere, and coordinated action on issues such as inequity and environmental degradation comes to a halt. There is no centrally directed process of reform and liberalization as there is today.

■ **Capitalism gets vicious.** Rapacious and unaccountable corporations emerge as a key social actor. Once a broad process of social disintegration begins, companies respond by taking control of certain parts of the country, beginning in the north, and imposing their own vision of social order. Concerns for social equity, labor rights, and environmental protection decline along with democratic accountability for business.

The "Vicious Capitalism" subscenario assumes that the collapse of order would magnify the desperate selfishness of corporations. Their role could then become threatening to democracy, liberalization, and long-term social order.

■ **A social revolution from the bottom up.** Poverty and inequity worsen substantially, leading to a traditional rebellion of a poor and disenfranchised majority against the power centers of the country. A search for security amid the knowledge era's tidal waves of change could result in a classic revolution that installs a coherent new central government.

It is worth stressing that this subscenario is unlikely. Mexico's relatively recent program of economic and political liberalization has opened a wide safety valve, furnishing Mexicans with the hope of a better future through reform, exports, education, national savings, and all the other benefits of development.

■ **The drug lords rule through Colombianization.** Mexico becomes a narcostate, based on the Colombian model. This subscenario assumes that current trends continue and that substantial portions of Mexican society come to be dominated by drug gangs. The implications of such a scenario are depressingly familiar: widespread social violence, the corrupting influences of drug gangs reaching into the upper echelons of Mexican government and turning the entire state machinery to their benefit, and the assassination or intimidation of anyone who stands in the way.

Of all the subscenarios of "Ungovernability," this one appears to be the furthest developed. Drug shipments into the United States have reached an unprecedented volume. Mexico has begun to generate its own drug kingpins. And violence is regularly directed at journalists and government officials attempting to expose the trend.

The Colombianization of Mexico need not involve a collapse of social order. One can imagine a version of this scenario in which crime rates within Mexico City actually decline as the drug bosses win public sympathy. Moreover, the narcostate is likely to involve a tight network of actual drug barons along with businessmen, government officials, and military leaders, so that economic development can actually proceed at a good pace in many areas of the country.

But immense hostility would inevitably arise abroad, especially in the United States and many nations of Central and South America. Washington might revoke NAFTA and take extreme measures to halt all legal and illegal immigration. Given Mexico's economic dependence on the United States, such moves will destabilize Mexican society and lead to social chaos and even civil war.

Indicators of the "Ungovernability" Scenario

The specific combination of indicators that occurs will depend on which subscenario begins to emerge. Among those to look for are:

Social violence by guerrillas, vigilante groups, criminal gangs, narcotraffickers, paramilitary groups, and military and police forces increases substantially.

Political participation is discredited and declines. Decentralization in government decision making accelerates in a rapid but haphazard fashion.

Mexicans become alienated, disenchanted with society and politics, and less trusting.

Illegal immigration to the United States surges, along with requests for political asylum. Foreign investment and tourism plummet. Those foreign investors who remain must deal with regional bosses and other non-governmental authorities.

There are growing reports of government corruption and loss of control over large areas of the country. Protests against the government are staged by workers, the poor, and Indians in the south and southeast. Rebel groups increase their operations and begin targeting the capital and other key cities.

Economic growth stagnates and declines, nationally or in specific regions, due to declining investment. Unemployment rises. Corporate leaders are increasingly tied to government corruption schemes and narcotraffickers. Corporations undertake repressive activities in order to "rule" parts of the country.

Mexico's relations with all its neighbors suffer as outside actors attempt to press for reform, social control, and political freedom.

Prospects for Mexico

Of the five scenarios proposed, three ("Muddling Through," "Losing Ground," and "Old Wine in New Bottles") are moderate extrapolations from the status quo in either a promising or a discouraging direction. The remaining two ("Democratic Mexico" and "Ungovernability") represent positive and negative extremes.

It is important to note that the scenarios are not completely independent; they could emerge serially, one after another. In a sense, the major risk in Mexico over the next decade is that "Losing Ground" will mutate into "Old Wine in New Bottles," which would generate "Ungovernability;" short-term indicators for the first two scenarios, then, might be clues to the long-term emergence of the third, even though society-wide chaos remains unlikely.

On balance, there are reasons to be guardedly optimistic about Mexico's prospects over the next decade. A number of major trends, such as the expansion of democracy and the emergence of environmentally friendly technologies, provide grounds for such optimism. But the strongest reason for optimism is the fact that the Mexican people have become empowered by the technologies and information of the new era, giving them the ability to influence which scenario occurs. In the knowledge era more than ever before, people are not the prisoners of trends, but their authors.

Still, it is crucial not to underestimate the scope of the challenge that Mexico faces, or the intensity of its social transformation, or the embryonic nature of the institutions it so badly needs to see it through.

In reality there are two Mexicos. One is relatively prosperous, educated, and urbane. The other is poor, rural, and often disconnected from the positive trends under way. This persistent fact calls into question the empowering character of the knowledge era. Today, only the fairly small middle class could be said to have the power to shape the trends of the new era to their benefit. Improved social equality may be a precondition for achieving the promise of the knowledge era. Likewise, the persistence of crime and corruption keeps alive a very real danger of widespread social instability.

About the Author

Michael J. Mazarr is an adjunct fellow at the Center for Strategic and International Studies, 1800 K Street, N.W., Washington, D.C. 20006. Telephone 1-202-887-0200; Web site www.csis.org. CSIS, a private, tax-exempt institution, does not take specific policy positions; accordingly, all views expressed should be understood to be solely those of the author.

This article is based on his book *Mexico 2005: The Challenges of the New Millennium* (The CSIS Press, 1999), which is available from the Futurist Bookstore for $21.95 ($19.95 for Society members), cat. no. B-2282.

Article 8   *The New York Times*, June 8, 1999

Smaller Families to Bring Big Change in Mexico

By Sam Dillon

MEXICO CITY, June 7—Like many old-style Mexican matriarchs, Emma Castro Amador bore so many children that she can't keep their birthdays straight. Sometimes she even loses track of whether Oscar, her 10th, came before David, her 11th, or vice versa.

"But I never regret having so many," said Mrs. Castro, 59, who had 14 children in 25 years.

Mrs. Castro's offspring, however, have a different view. In a generational divide repeated in millions of Mexican families, all 14 say they are determined to limit their families to two or three children.

"Small families live better," says Gloria Muñoz Castro, Mrs. Castro's eldest daughter, echoing the jingle, broadcast incessantly on television here after the Government reversed its stance in 1974, and put a brake on exploding growth. Gloria has two children and says she will have no more.

Next year, Mexico's population is projected to reach 100 million, and the contrast between Mrs. Castro's family and those of her children illustrates the extraordinary changes under way in the country's family and population patterns, which hold important consequences for the rest of North America.

Because Mexican women like the elder Mrs. Castro traditionally had so many children, the population has quintupled since 1940, and will continue to surge at about one million people a year for nearly three decades. But because of people like her daughter, many forecasters predict that slowing fertility rates will mean that the country's population will virtually stop growing by 2045.

The tremendous reduction in fertility, from 7 children per woman in 1965, to 2.5 today, [is] slightly below worldwide rates. The drop is resulting in a significant decline in the number of dependent children supported by each worker. It may also offer Mexico what population experts call a "demographic bonus," the opportunity to generate higher savings rates and domestic investments that can raise this country's standard of living and bring rapid development if the bonus is managed shrewdly.

"The drop in fertility is a spectacular change that has meant a revolution in mental attitudes," said Dr. Rodolfo Tuirán Gutiérrez, secretary general of the Government-run National Population Council. "It's opening a demographic window of opportunity for Mexico."

Around the world, fertility rates have fallen from an average of 4.95 children per woman in the 1960–1965 period to 2.96 children in the first half of the 1990's.

But fast-growing populations are like speeding locomotives that cannot brake slowly, and even though Mexican birth rates fell dramatically, the population has kept surging.

For now, unemployment will remain high, since even when the economy is robust it cannot provide jobs for the 1.3 million new workers who enter the job market each year. Many of the jobless will continue to emigrate to the United States; during the next decade, some 3.5 million Mexicans are projected to travel to the United States to work and establish residence.

When Emma Castro was born in 1940, Mexico's population was 19.6 million, little changed from what it had been in 1910, at the outset of the Mexican Revolution. She married at 15 after a one-day courtship, and bore her first son the following year. For the next 25 years she bore one child, on average, every 21 months.

Her experience was typical. In 1956, the year Mrs. Castro bore her first son, an American anthropologist, Oscar Lewis, began collecting an oral history of a poor Mexico City family, later published as "The Children of Sanchez." When Mr. Lewis first interviewed the patriarch, Jesús Sánchez, he had 4 children, but when Mexican reporters interviewed him 14 years later, Mr. [Sánchez]Hernández had 16 more.

Government policy encouraged rapid growth, partly for historical reasons. Mexicans believed that the 19th century seizure of Mexican territories stretching from Texas to California by the United States would have been impossible had they not been so sparsely populated.

But in the late 1960's, as Mexico's postwar economic boom began to slow, the sheer force of the population figures began to alarm experts. In 1970, Mexico's population hit 48 million, and in an influential study several prominent Mexican demographers warned that unless policies changed it would more than triple by the year 2000, to 148 million.

Faced with the challenge to national stability those projections implied, President Luis Echeverra Álvarez in 1974 reversed course, establishing a National Population Council to control population growth and a network of Government clinics to help couples plan their families.

The reversal came as women's attitudes about birth control were already changing; ignoring the Government and the Roman Catholic hierarchy, many women in the 1960's and early 1970's were buying contraceptives on the black market. As a result, the Government's new offer of family planning services began satisfying a repressed demand, and Mexican families began changing dramatically, almost overnight.

"We were determined to have just two," said Mrs. Castro's eldest daughter, Gloria, who married in 1977. "We didn't want to spend all our money just to feed and clothe children."

Several of Gloria's married siblings and in-laws have no children. Eira Hernández Ramírez, a 39-year-old sister-in-law with no children, explained: "Food is expensive, the oil is running out, water is scarce. The future's just too bleak."

But though Mexican birth rates have plummeted, the population has continued to expand. While none of Emma Castro's 14 children have borne even a quarter as many children as she did, they have produced 23 grandchildren so far. Millions of others in their generation have formed new families, too. That is why the population surged from 66.8 million in 1980 to 81 million in 1990 and is projected to reach the 100 million mark next year.

For more than two decades, the economy has failed to keep up with the exploding population. Jean Maninat, director of the Mexico office of the International Labor Organization, said that about 1.3 million new workers join Mexico's job market each year.

"That's the population pressure," Mr. Maninat said. "And despite the Government's efforts to generate investments, never in any year has the economy created that many jobs."

In good years, the expanding economy and new investments can create 900,000 or perhaps one million new jobs, leaving about 300,000 new job-seekers unemployed. In 1995, a recession year, Mexico lost 500,000 jobs, meaning that together with the 1.3 million new job-seekers, the ranks of the unemployed grew by a total of 1.8 million in a single year.

A vast army of Mexicans are in the informal sector, the platoons of windshield washers who converge on cars at street corners and battalions of chewing-gum vendors who clog downtown sidewalks.

Still others have emigrated to the United States. During the 1960's, only about 27,000 workers left Mexico each year to establish permanent residence in America, according to Mexican Government figures. In the three decades since, the flow has multiplied by 10; it is currently about 277,000 a year, according to the binational study.

For the next 10 years or so, population growth is expected to continue to generate mass emigration and millions of new unemployed. But as the effects of the dropoff in fertility rates continue to make themselves felt, the number of people who join the job market each year is projected to fall to about 650,000 in 2010, Government demographers estimate.

If the economy continues to grow, then the number of Mexicans who emigrate to the United States each year, legally and illegally, could begin to decline, according [to] a 1977 Binational Study on Migration. Some demographers believe, however, that because wages in the United States are often 10 times the pay for the same work in Mexico, Mexicans will continue to emigrate even when jobs are available here.

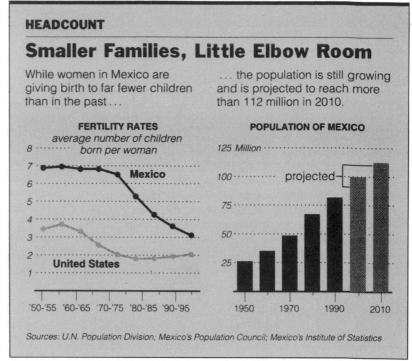

HEADCOUNT

Smaller Families, Little Elbow Room

While women in Mexico are giving birth to far fewer children than in the past...

... the population is still growing and is projected to reach more than 112 million in 2010.

FERTILITY RATES
average number of children born per woman

Mexico

United States

'50-'55 '60-'65 '70-'75 '80-'85 '90-'95

POPULATION OF MEXICO

125 Million

projected

1950 1970 1990 2010

Sources: U.N. Population Division; Mexico's Population Council; Mexico's Institute of Statistics

The New York Times

The slowing growth is bringing Mexico good news of another kind. In 1970, for every 100 Mexican workers there were 100 dependents, mostly children and a few retired people. As the children have grown up and entered the work force, this "dependency ratio" has declined, to about 60 dependents for each 100 workers. By the year 2020, the burden of nonworking dependents should decline still further, to about 40 per 100 workers.

"There's a moment in the evolution of populations when they have the absolute best structure for development, and that's the structure Mexico is developing right now," said Eduardo Arriaga, an Argentine demographer who is a lecturer at Georgetown University.

This demographic bonus gives Mexico the opportunity to increase domestic savings and with sensible economic management, could result in higher per capita economic growth.

The bonus phase of Mexico's demographic transition is expected to last for 30 years. By then, the population will be, on average, far older than it is today, and millions of Mexicans will need retirement care.

The costs of caring for the elderly will be higher, because currently most retired Mexicans live with their children. But the characteristically large Mexican family is shrinking, increasing numbers of Mexicans live alone, and in the future the elderly may not be able to count on home care provided by their children.

"The Mexican family is being transformed in crucial ways," said Carlos Welti, a demographer at the National Autonomous University. "Throughout our history, an important social safety network has been the extended family, uncles, cousins. In the future, fewer will have these relationships."

Article 9   *The Chronicle of Higher Education*, May 7, 1999

INTERNATIONAL

A New Kind of University Grows in the Salvadoran Countryside

Central America's first rural institution aims to stanch the flow of students to the city

BY PAUL JEFFREY

ALDEITA, EL SALVADOR

THE CAMPUS of Monseñor Oscar Arnulfo Romero University used to be a cow pasture. Were it not for the fence around the grounds, it still would be.

Although this is probably not where you'd expect to find an institution of higher education, the setting is appropriate for what is Central America's first rural university. Located in the north of El Salvador, the private institution is named for the martyred Archbishop of San Salvador, who was gunned down by government-linked assassins in 1980. The university aims to serve the rural poor of this tortured country, whom Romero loved deeply.

"Monseñor Romero's great ideal was to promote a better life for the peasants, for people who have few resources and opportunities," says Eduardo Alas, Roman Catholic Bishop of Chalatenango province. "It was his longing."

SLOWING THE BRAIN DRAIN

Bishop Alas and several other civic leaders in the province established this university in 1993 as a contribution to the reconstruction of Chalatenango, the scene of some of the worst violence in El Salvador's 12-year civil war, which ended in 1992. They also saw the institution as a way to slow the brain drain caused by students who travel to San Salvador, the capital, for their postsecondary education, often never to return.

Some 500 students are now enrolled at Romero University, which offers five-year professional degrees, called *licenciaturas*, in agricultural engineering, education, and law. It also offers technical degrees in agricultural and veterinary sciences, which take 30 months to complete.

About 1,600 students graduate from high school every year in Chalatenango, but until the university came along, continuing their education meant moving to San Salvador. "All the traditional academic opportunities are in the capital," says Román Mejía, vice-rector of Romero. "Out here in the countryside, there's nothing."

AN EXPENSIVE PROPOSITION

If local students don't find local options for study or work, he points out, many of them leave. He cites a recent study in California, which found that 14.8 per cent of the Salvadorans in Los Angeles came from Chalatenango, which has only 3.5 per cent of El Salvador's population. "If we can't offer educational opportunities that allow people to get involved with the rural economy, they feel pressured to migrate to where they can find work."

The university has 11 classrooms, a library, and a biology laboratory. More facilities are planned when more money becomes available, Mr. Mejía says.

Starting a university from scratch proved to be an expensive proposition. Because much of Chalatenango was under rebel control during the civil war, the university's founders at first sought help from some former guerrilla commanders, who had become politicians. But leaders of the former Farabundo Martí National Liberation Front, or F.M.L.N., said they would participate only if they could control the institution's finances and select the faculty members. The founders rejected the condition.

Then Bishop Alas entered the picture. His diocese provided funds to help purchase land for the 16-acre campus, which is outside the village of Aldeita—a parish created by Archbishop Romero just four days before he was murdered.

The diocese thinks it will get a return on its investment. The university's acting rector, the Rev. Gabriel Rodríguez, says the institution hopes to eventually add a philosophy department, which would allow Catholic seminarians to complete some of their studies here. To obtain such training in rural Chalatenango would help prospective priests "live the reality of the countryside," says Father Rodríguez, who is Aldeita's parish priest.

The university offers educational opportunities to many people who otherwise would go without. They include single mothers, of whom there are several among the students.

Romero already has developed a reputation as academically tough. "Just because you're the son of someone important doesn't help you here," says Wendy Carranza, an agronomy student. "It's a university where, God willing, you'll graduate because you've learned something."

CRACKDOWN ON DIPLOMA MILLS

In the early 1990s, several universities in the capital opened rural branch campuses. But those operations were not well financed. Father Rodríguez calls some of them no more than "diploma mills, set up to take advantage of the student market in the countryside." A recent government crackdown has thinned their number significantly.

Alfredo Lobo, a member of the group that founded Romero University, says it seeks to offer an education that helps develop professionals with a social conscience "that corresponds to the environment." In legal studies, for example, rural lawyers are needed to help peasants legally register their land under the government's land-reform provisions. "Many times the lands they possess haven't been legalized, because there's no one to help them do that," Mr. Lobo says. "Lawyers traditionally seek out the big cities, but here we're forming a social conscience in them."

Mr. Mejía, who served as vice-minister of education in the 1980s, says Romero's leaders also recognize the importance of technical training. "At times we err by graduating only *licenciados* and engineers. We also have to graduate technicians," who, he says, can help to meet important national needs.

Romero University recently asked the Ministry of Education for permission to offer three more technical degrees—in accounting, business administration, and computer studies—but was turned down because it lacks the infrastructure to support such programs. There are no phone lines, for example, to connect campus computers to the Internet. The university operates with only a cellular phone.

A FINANCIAL STRUGGLE

Mr. Mejía says Romero hopes to overcome some of the physical restraints on expansion, but recognizes that it needs money to do so. The university has received some significant donations—computers from bishops in Italy, laboratory equipment from Carmelite nuns—but it needs to develop a stronger financial base before it can expand. Its only current source of revenue is tuition, which costs each student $34 a month.

Although it is struggling financially, the university recently took over management of a massive government reforestation project on the nearby Guazapa volcano. It also is involved in a major research project to investigate a form of hydroponics in which plants are grown in moistened, pulverized volcanic rock—a resource that this region doesn't lack.

In addition to the usual challenges faced by a fledgling university in search of competent faculty members and funds with

which to pay them, Romero also has had to contend with a nasty political struggle sparked by rumors that the government wanted to shut down the university, ostensibly because the institution did not meet government standards.

When those reports began to circulate, in 1997, the university's supporters in El Salvador and abroad contacted Catholic leaders and mobilized old networks to put pressure on the Salvadoran government. According to Adalberto Campos, an economist who serves as the Ministry of Education's director of higher education, hundreds of letters arrived at the ministry and at the Salvadoran Embassy in Washington. El Salvador's president, Armando Calderón Sol, was even questioned by a U.S. Senator about why his government was picking on Romero University.

"The government doesn't want the school to succeed, precisely because we used the name of Monseñor Romero," says Carmen de Mejía, wife of the vice-rector and herself an official of the university. The current government, she contends, is made up of followers of Roberto D'Aubuisson, late leader of the right-wing Arena party, who was identified by a United Nations–sponsored investigation as being responsible for planning the assassination of Monseñor Romero. "So the people in the Education Ministry don't look upon us with great joy—that's obvious," she says. "Yet, because of the international pressure, the ministry wasn't able to have its way with us."

Mr. Campos acknowledges the impact that the campaign had. "We knew that they had support outside the country," he says. "It was obvious, and we had to take it into account."

He blames the trouble on Salvadoran news-media reports that some private universities, including Romero, were about to be shut down, when no decisions had yet been made. Romero's backers, he says, reacted naturally. "They accused us of using the media to attack them, rather than dealing with them directly. But we never gave out names of schools with problems."

The university's deficiencies were real, Mr. Campos says. "You should have seen the place when they got started—it was just a shack beside the road. It had a deplorable infrastructure. It didn't have any equipment. It didn't fill the basic requirements to be a university."

But, he adds, it did have the distinction "of not being a school that gave away diplomas. That helped its cause. Because of that, we didn't try to close it, but gave it the opportunity to solve its problems."

Mr. Mejía, the vice-rector, says the university, no longer distracted by its skirmish with the government, can now concentrate on improving the education it offers from its home amid the pastures.

"We're a new institution, so we have to struggle," he says. "But we have big dreams for our university, and for our province."

Article 10   *Bolivian Times,* April 29, 1999

Erosion Eats Away Bolivia

By Mike Ceaser

Over-harvesting of wood for fuel, overgrazing by domestic stock: Bolivians are allowing their country to be literally washed away by a series of dangerous practices. The remaining land is less productive, and eventually, good for nothing.

Bolivia may not have a seacoast, but countless tons of the nation flow seaward each year.

That flow carries away the land's topsoil and leaves behind hunger, poverty and desertified land. Experts calculate that nearly half of Bolivia's land is undergoing erosion-caused desertification, affecting three-quarters of the population.

Nature and mankind have combined to create Bolivia's tremendous erosion problem. Nature provided a hilly topography and high rainfall, to which mankind has added deforestation, overgrazing and unsustainable agricultural practices. The erosion causes widespread desertification, clogs rivers with silt and even makes railroad lines impassable.

In Bolivia, desertification is severest in the valleys of the Andes Mountain Range and on the altiplano. The problem extends along the Andes from Chile and Argentina to Ecuador and also affects areas of northern Brazil.

According to the United Nations (UN), 900 million people worldwide are affected by desertification, and since 1950 11 percent of the planet's vegetated surface, or 1.2 billion hectares, "has suffered moderate to extreme degradation." The UN estimates the annual lost income at US$42 billion and says the desertification rate is accelerating.

Rain, rain, go away

When loggers or colonists cut away the forest or cattle gobble up grassland, the land loses its protection from rain's impact. Instead of flowing softly down tree trunks and grass stems and then percolating into underground water banks, the raindrops smash into the soil with great force. Without plant roots to anchor it, the topsoil flows into suddenly swollen streams, which tear more earth away from their banks. The wind carries away more of the unprotected soil and the desert land left behind no longer grows crops nor can it support human and animal life.

"The soils become unproductive and no species of plant or animal grows," said forestry engineer Ricardo Cox, national small donations coordinator for the League for Environmental Defense (LIDEMA). "They make the erosion irreversible."

Since the rain no longer replenishes underground water banks, the land's wet and dry seasons become more marked and extreme.

"The rivers grow instantaneously, and the rest of the year there's no water," Cox said.

Turning rivers into mud

Erosion's impacts do not end with the wasteland left behind. The sudden rush of water causes valley flooding and the silt-filled rivers suffer ecological changes and can even disappear under their own silt load.

Bolivia's prime example is the Pilcomayo River, whose upper reaches have been turned into a watery desert by a poisonous combination of erosion and mining pollution. Meanwhile, the Pilcomayo's lower reaches, where it forms the Paraguay-Argentina border, are disappearing under the river's load of silt, causing it to recede about 5km per year.

Plants also return moisture to the atmosphere through transpiration and, it is believed, attract clouds and rainfall to themselves. So desertification causes tremendous environmental changes far beyond the land it destroys.

Environmental impact expert René Méndez has studied desertification in the area around Sucre. In some areas, such as

Huayacan, Chqsca, where the soil is very weak, the erosion rate reaches 150 tons of soil per hectare per year.

"It's a very strong erosion, very serious," Méndez said.

The common cause of erosion in the area, he said, is deforestation, either for firewood, to make railroad ties, or for charcoal for metal foundries. The deforestation began soon after the mining boom in Potosí, when tremendous numbers of trees were consumed for energy and construction. And many farmers, with access to seemingly limitless land and interested in quick profits, did not bother controlling erosion on their land.

Rediscovering the old ways

Humanity's impact today contrasts dramatically with those of pre-Columbian farmers, such as the Andean Mollos culture, which used terraced farming techniques. The terraces, built like huge steps on mountain sides, slowed flowing water and conserved topsoil. Mollos-style terraces can still be seen on Andean hillsides, where they "continue functioning well to control erosion," Cox of *Lidema* said, and have minimized erosion in some valleys on the Andes' eastern side.

In contrast, Cox said, some modern farmers plow furrows with the gradient—creating channels that quicken erosion.

Lidema sponsors many micro-projects aimed at combating desertification. They include creating a sustainable management plan for a Cochabamba watershed and another for an altiplano 'forest.' Programs in Los Yungas, LP, and the Department of Potosí have installed micro-hydroelectric plants and solar panels to generate electricity and so reduce the amount of firewood that campesinos cut. Other altiplano projects are rebuilding terraces and allowing vegetation to regenerate in Potosí and are planting salt-tolerant plants in La Paz.

"The idea is that these types of technologies be widely popularized," Cox said.

Marc-Andre Franché, program assistant for the United Nations anti-desertification program in Bolivia, ties desertification to poverty and underdevelopment.

"We've realized that desertification can't be stopped without an integrated development strategy," he said.

The thola story

One illustration of why that is true is the thola, an altiplano bush used as cooking fuel. According to UN data, 3.3 million tons of thola are harvested each year, deforesting 165,000ha annually.

"It's because people are poor and don't have other alternative energy sources," Franché said.

But he said solutions must be appropriate, or they won't work. In one program, simply drilling holes in campesino ov-ens to allow in more oxygen improved burning efficiency by 30 percent.

"But in another area of the country, if you provide people with ovens that produce more heat, they might not be able to cook their food like before and it might change their whole food chain," Franché said.

Franché said the Bolivian Government is gathering information and ideas for a plan to combat desertification. Bolivia is a signatory of the 1994 "International Convention to Fight Desertification and Drought" and is a member of two international work groups, one with Argentina and Paraguay to address desertification in Chaco—in Bolivia's Southeast—and another with Chile, Ecuador, Peru and Argentina for the Andes Range.

While desertification occurs in rural areas, environmental demands from urban areas for water, firewood and agricultural products can contribute to the process. And desertification can affect cities—for example by causing dust storms.

"Desertification and degradation of land is not only a rural issue; it's a rural-urban issue," Franché said.

He also said that desertification is worsened by climate change—the global warming caused by industrial pollutants—and in turn worsens the changes by reducing vegetation.

"More than anything, the Europeans and North Americans are causing it, and we have to pay the price," agreed Enrique Sucre, technical director for the organization Alternatives for Suburban and Rural Development in Sucre.

Solutions frustrated

But without large-scale prevention of overgrazing and control of slash and burn agriculture, Bolivia's desertification will be difficult to halt.

In 1997 Méndez and five other environmentalists studied methods for managing the watersheds of two rivers in the Department of Chuiquisaca.

Méndez's group recommended several actions to fight desertification and improve the local residents' quality of life. They included controlling overgrazing, fencing off areas to enable plants to recover, improving soils by eliminating pests, such as nematodes, and building bike trails to give residents transportation routes during the months when rivers dry up.

But far from the government funding a pilot program, Méndez said the researchers had to hire a lawyer just to force the government to pay their salaries.

"It receives no priority from the government," he said, "not even an effort to find financing."

If nothing's done, Méndez predicted, "the desertification will continue and become catastrophic. The people will have to migrate. The fauna will migrate. Some will die. Some will migrate."

Article 11   *The Wilson Quarterly,* Winter 1999

The Two Brazils

"We progress at night when the politicians sleep," goes an old Brazilian saying. Today, after more than a decade of political and economic change, Brazil's landless, its evangelicals, its indigenous peoples, and others have emerged into the daylight. Brazil's future lies as much in their hands, our author writes, as in those of the politicians and bankers.

by Kenneth Maxwell

Only a year ago, Brazilians were full of confidence that their country was poised to surge into the 21st century, that perhaps it was finally on the road to becoming the great power many had long imagined it would be. In 1994, Finance Minister Fernando Henrique Cardoso, a former Marxist professor of sociology turned neoliberal reformer, had masterminded a sweeping currency reform—the Real Plan—which joined other liberalizing measures and thrust Brazil, with the world's eighth largest economy, into the forefront of the global trend toward open markets and free trade. Not only were Brazilians prospering but their decade-old democracy had found solid footing. Later in 1994, Cardoso was rewarded for his efforts as finance minister with the presidency, becoming Brazil's second directly elected civilian chief executive since the military surrendered power in 1985.

Then came the global economic crisis, beginning with the currency collapses in Southeast Asia in 1997, escalating with the Russian defaults last August, and landing with a crash on Brazil shortly after. Having failed, despite its many other successes, to get its fiscal house in order, Brazil found itself dangerously dependent on infusions of foreign capital to finance its trade and government deficits, struggling to stay afloat even as nervous investors fled with their dollars.

Cardoso, who won a second term in October in the midst of the crisis, was forced to take drastic measures to cut government spending, increase taxes, and reduce indebtedness. In return, Brazil won a $41.5 billion bailout orchestrated by the International Monetary Fund (IMF)—and the guarantee of more painful measures to come, as well as a recession that promises to be long and deep. Cardoso, who was, in his Marxist days, a high priest of dependency theory—the notion that the developed capitalist nations would forever hold the less developed economies in thrall—must have wondered if he had been so wrong after all.

Yet Brazil's decade of political and economic success has changed the country in certain irreversible ways. And the changes will, paradoxically, complicate its recovery. Prosperity, the opening up of political life, and the expansion of educational opportunities brought with them a deeper political engagement by the population, and the emergence of unions, political parties, and a variety of grassroots organizations. To a degree that is unprecedented in the country's history, Brazilians have found their political voice, and they have begun to rethink what it means to be Brazilian.

The IMF-mandated policies thus risk bringing about headlong confrontation between the Brazil of bankers and businessmen and a new Brazil of political and social activism. One thing is certain: the Brazilian government can no longer rule by dictate or from the top down, whatever it may have promised the IMF.

How successfully these two Brazils work out their collective future will be one of the most dramatic stories of coming months, and not only for Brazil. Failure in this South American giant will profoundly affect the reforms under way throughout Latin America as well as the assumptions on which the new international economic order has been founded. It is precisely for this reason that U.S. treasury secretary Robert Rubin declared that Brazil is "too big to be allowed to fail."

Brazil for many foreigners is still the land of the bossa nova and "The Girl from Ipanema," but Brazilians themselves are becoming irritated with their country's willful folkloric self-image as forever young, bronzed, and beach bound, oblivious to the past and giddily committed to a future as ephemeral as the country's torrid *telenovelas*. Antonio Carlos Jobim, author of that great lyrical celebration of Ipanema beach and the graceful passing beauty of its denizens, once said that Brazil is "not for beginners." And he was right.

Brazilians still want to have fun, to be sure, and no one is proposing the abolition of Carnival. Yet as Brazil has embraced democracy over the past decade, bringing new voices into the political and social arenas, Brazilians are beginning to recognize that getting to the future involves understanding the past.

This new concern with history is reflected in the recent vogue for restoring colonial architecture—some of the most extraordinary examples in the Americas—which was once allowed to rot or was simply swept away to make room for modern buildings. In Bahia and São Luis in Maranhão, splendid baroque churches and 18th-century townhouses have been magnificently restored; old forts and ruins of Jesuit missions along the southern frontier have become popular tourist attractions. But these buildings are artifacts of the traditional Brazilian history, while the past that Brazil is rediscovering is replete with contradictions.

Brazil's transition to national independence in 1822, unlike that of its Spanish American neighbors, preserved great continuity in institutions—the military, the law, and administration. It was led, after all, by the eldest son of the Portuguese monarch, who promptly named himself Emperor Pedro I. Portuguese America, unlike its Spanish-speaking neighbors, also avoided fragmentation into numerous new republics. Independent Brazil emerged as a monarchy with its huge territory intact. The state as it developed was, as a consequence, highly centralizing, and the national mythology it spawned depicted the country as a product almost exclusively of the coastal Portuguese and the imperial inheritance.

But today Brazilians are learning a new history. It brings into focus the unruly Brazil of the escaped slaves who held out for decades in the backlands of what is today the state of Alagoas against the Portuguese in the 17th century; the bloody uprisings in the Amazon, Pernambuco, and the southern borderlands of Rio Grande do Sul against the Brazilian empire in the early 19th century; and the extraordinary messianic communities of the semiarid interior of Bahia brutally suppressed a century ago and immortalized by the great Brazilian essayist Euclides da Cunha in his *Rebellion in the Backlands,* and more

recently by the Peruvian novelist Mario Vargas Llosa in his *War at the End of the World.* The historian Laura de Mello e Sousa calls this the Brazil of the "unclassified ones"—the majority of the Brazilian population, neither white nor black, neither slave master nor slave in origin, not landowners but squatters and small holders, not only Portuguese but Italians, Germans, Japanese, Arabs, and Jews, as well as mestizos, mulattos, Indians, and Africans, not only bankers but small entrepreneurs and shopkeepers, not just bishops but African *orixás* and Pentecostal pastors.

The recognition of the "unclassified ones" has been accompanied by the emergence of movements among the landless, the indigenous peoples, industrial workers, Protestants, and others. African Brazilians are perhaps the most important group now finding a political voice.* For centuries, they retained a resilient pluralistic religious and cultural presence at the core of Brazilian society, but one barely recognized in the corridors of elite power until very recently. São Paulo elected its first black mayor, Celso Pitta, in 1996, and President Cardoso brought Edson Arantes do Nascimento, universally known as Pelé, the great Brazilian soccer star, into his cabinet as minister of sport. The new vice governor of Rio de Janeiro, Benedita da Silva, is an African Brazilian born in a Rio favela (shantytown). As more Afro-Brazilians have moved into the middle class, black faces have also appeared more regularly in advertisements and the press.

Brazil's rediscovery of history challenges above all the peculiar legacy that has since the 18th century allowed the country's rulers to graft the imperative of authoritarianism onto their vision of the future. It was this mindset that made the French positivists so attractive to the military officers who overthrew the monarchy in 1889, and to the generals who seized control in 1964. It is perfectly summed up in the motto emblazoned across Brazil's national flag: *Ordem e Progresso* (Order and Progress). Democracy in Brazil has all too often been seen as the enemy of progress, the harbinger of anarchy, disunion, and backwardness. That, it seems clear, will no longer do.

Brazil's transformation grows in part out of its recent prosperity. When I first came to Rio de Janeiro as a student in the mid-1960s, the country was still largely rural, with short life expectancy, large families, low per capita income, and a high illiteracy rate. By the 1990s, Brazil, with a population of more than 160 million, had become one of the world's largest economies, with a per capita income of more than $5,000. Family size had dropped dramatically, from six children per family in the 1970s to 2.5 in the mid-1990s. It had become a largely urban country. Brazil's two million cars in 1970 had grown in number to 26 million, its TV sets from four million to 31

---

* Racial self-definition is a complex matter in Brazil, where a very wide range of racial categories between black and white has traditionally been recognized. The count of "African Brazilians" varies from a high of 120 million, using a U.S. definition that includes all persons with some degree of African ancestry, to Brazil's official 1991 census estimate, which lists only seven million blacks (*prêtos*) and classifies 62 million Brazilians as browns (*pardos*). Essentially in stark contrast to the traditional U.S. classification, being black in Brazil means having no white ancestors. Brazil was the foremost recipient of African slaves in the Western Hemisphere.

million. Infant mortality had decreased from 118 per 1,000 in 1970 to 17 per 1,000, and illiteracy has greatly diminished.

Today the Brazilian states of São Paulo and Rio Grande do Sul, if they stood alone, would be numbered among the richest 45 nations on earth. The economy of Rio Grande do Sul, the southernmost state, abutting Argentina and Uruguay, was built on European immigration and cattle. The state of São Paulo has a gross national product larger than Argentina's, and São Paulo City is a megalopolis with a population of 15 million and a vibrant financial, cultural, and business life; the state-supported university of São Paulo is a world-class institution. Like several of Brazil's larger cities, São Paulo has a lively press; dailies such as the *Folha de São Paulo,* the grand old *Estado de São Paulo,* and the business-oriented *Gazeta Mercantil* are as articulate, critical, and influential as any quality newspaper in Europe or North America. Brazil also boasts one of the world's most successful television networks, TVGlobo, and one of its most aggressive publishing empires, Editora Abril, proprietor of the mass-circulation newsweekly *Veja,* which reaches more than four million readers, all of them full-fledged members of the emerging global consumer order.

A large segment of the population, perhaps 40 million people, however, remains in poverty, with incomes below $50 a month. Brazil's income disparities are among the worst in the world. The most impoverished 20 percent of Brazilians receive a mere two percent of the national wealth, while the richest 20 percent receive 60 percent. Festering shantytowns surround the large urban centers, and Rio's favelas are especially notorious for crime and violence. This is the Brazil of half-starved children playing outside makeshift shacks in dusty northeastern villages and smudge-faced urchins knocked out by glue sniffing, huddled together under benches in São Paulo's principal downtown squares. But extreme poverty is now concentrated in the semiarid Northeast of Brazil, where drought and disease have long been curses of biblical dimensions. Both were greatly aggravated in 1998 by the effects of El Niño. Brazilians are proud to call themselves a racial as well as a political democracy, and are irritated when scholars and activists point out that poverty is disproportionately concentrated among the Afro-Brazilian population. In fact, whites on average earn two-and-a-half times as much as blacks. As veteran Brazil watcher Ronald Schneider notes, out of 14,000 priests, 378 bishops and archbishops, and seven cardinals, the Brazilian Catholic Church has only 200 nonwhite priests. Similar disproportions can be seen in Brazil's diplomatic service and military officer corps.

Nevertheless, the poor have seen their lives improve over the past decade, with large numbers of people moving up from the bottom ranks of society into the emerging middle class. The credit for this change belongs to Cardoso's Real Plan, introduced in 1994 while he was finance minister under President Itamar Franco. Confronted with economic chaos and feverish inflation, Cardoso created a new currency, the real, linked to the U.S. dollar, with its value pegged to permit only minimal depreciation. Inflation plunged from more than 2000 percent annually to single digits, with instant tonic effects felt throughout the country.

Suddenly, as the currency stabilized, Brazilians had money to spend for refrigerators, televisions, and clothing. Analysts looking at consumer trends over the past six years reckon that some 19 million people have moved from basic subsistence into the lower level of the Brazilian middle class, which today embraces some 58 million people. Those who remained poor benefited as well, finding more money in their pockets for meat, chicken, eggs, corn, and beans. Their income increased by 30 percent during 1995–96 alone.

In earlier decades, poverty pushed millions of Brazilians from the hinterlands into São Paulo and Rio de Janeiro and out into the frontier on the western fringes of the Amazon basin. During the 1990s, prosperity allowed many of the smaller cities in the interior of Brazil to flourish, attracting some five million mostly middle-class people searching for a better quality of life.

The spread of prosperity and population over the face of Brazil have made it both a more homogenous and a more complex society. For four-and-a-half centuries, most of Brazil's population remained around key seaports close to the zones where sugar, cotton, cacao, coffee, and other major export commodities are grown. Brazil's first historian, Friar Vicente do Salvador, writing in 1627, said that the Portuguese settlers and their African slaves "scratched at the seacoast like crabs." The first Europeans to penetrate the vast interior were intrepid missionaries, explorers, and ruthless Portuguese frontiersmen traveling up the Amazon River and the tributaries that run south into the La Plata basin. This huge geographical area, larger than the contiguous United States, remained for centuries a hollow frontier, incorporating vast unexplored territories and many thousands of indigenous peoples unknown to the Portuguese governors and viceroys who ruled until 1808, or to the Portuguese monarchs who held court in Rio de Janeiro between 1808 and 1821, or to the Brazilian emperors Pedro I and Pedro II, who succeeded them after the declaration of Brazil's independence from Portugal in 1822, or to the generals and civilian politicians who established the United States of Brazil in 1889.

Yet slowly and inexorably the hollow frontier was filled in, as cattle ranchers moved inland from the coast and squatters established themselves between the plantation-dominated littoral and the backlands. These independent-minded mixed-race families lived largely outside the juridical formulas that elsewhere defined and contained both Portuguese masters and African slaves, but they helped root Brazilian society in the Brazilian landscape.

In the 18th century, the first great modern gold rush brought European settlers, slaves, and, belatedly, government, into the mountainous interior of what is today the state of Minas Gerais. Today the spectacular churches and mountain towns they constructed are among Brazil's most precious colonial heritage; here the magnificently carved figures of the Apostles by the crippled mulatto sculptor Aleijadinho stand as marvels of this age of extravagance and piety. In the 19th century, large-scale coffee bean plantations were developed in São Paulo and Paraná in the south, reviving the demand for African slaves. After the abolition of slavery in 1888, immigrant laborers poured in from Italy and southern Germany, joined in the 1920s by newcomers from Japan. By the early 20th century, a cotton textile industry was established in São Paulo, augmented in the 1960s by steel and automobile industries, creating an industrial urban working class and a powerful business elite.

Both civilian and military rulers saw the development of the interior as the means to Brazil's future greatness. In the late 1950s, President Juscelino Kubitschek forced through the extraordinary plans for the futuristic new capital and federal district of Brasília, set down like a spaceship on the largely uninhabited high plateau of Goiana in the center-west of the country. Modernistic bowls, towers, and upturned cups contained the Congress and its functionaries, dwarfed against a backdrop of enormous sky and red earth. Soon thereafter, the generals who ousted Kubitschek's successor, President João Goulart, and established one of Latin America's longest-lived military regimes (1964–85), embarked on a series of grandiose schemes to develop the Amazon. Ignoring the established river-based lifelines, they drove roads straight through the tropical rainforest and built huge dams to tame the Amazon's tributaries and flood the river plains, often with disastrous ecological consequences. The highways brought with them economic exploitation and its predictable companions, greedy speculators and corrupt and callous bureaucrats, as well as a plague of infectious diseases. The forced contact with the outside world was disastrous for the remaining 250,000 Brazilian Indians, the majority living in the Amazon forests. The long-isolated Yanomami were hard hit with malaria as 10,000 prospectors invaded their territory in the late 1980s.

The military regime also poured money into the expansion of higher education, substituting more pragmatic American approaches for the old French-influenced disciplines that had produced Cardoso and other scholars. But this only created a new generation enamored of democracy as well as technology. Purging and exiling Cardoso (who was seen as a dangerous Marxist despite the fact that he was the son and grandson of generals) and other professors from the University of São Paulo and other major institutions also had paradoxical consequences. It provoked U.S. foundations, notably the Ford Foundation, to invest heavily in a parallel system of private research centers in Brazil that would later provide a haven and political base for the democratic opposition.

Meanwhile, the exiles were welcomed on American campuses. Cardoso, who lived in Chile, and later in France, became a visiting professor at the University of California, Berkeley, and Stanford University, and spent two years at the Institute for Advanced Study in Princeton, New Jersey, working closely with that wise and brilliant pragmatist, the veteran economist and proponent of reform by "muddling through," Albert O. Hirschman. When he returned to Brazil in 1970, Cardoso, like many of the other upper-middle-class exiles of his generation, had become thoroughly cosmopolitan, skeptical of Marxism, well connected in the wider world, and thoroughly knowledgeable about the workings of the U.S. political and economic systems.

Momentous changes were also taking place at the grassroots within Brazil. Throughout the late 1970s and early 1980s, trade unions that had been founded in the 1930s during the dictatorship of Getúlio Vargas on an Italian fascist model as syndicates dependent on the state, shook off government control. Most formidable was the metalworkers' union in São Paulo. The unions nourished the emergence of a new Workers' Party (PT) in 1980 and a National Trade Union Confederation in 1983. Together they provided a base for the charismatic Luis Inácio da Silva, popularly known as Lula, who rose through union ranks from the shop floor and awakened hopes that he would become a Brazilian Lech Walesa. He has run three times unsuccessfully for the presidency, most recently in October 1998.

The Workers' Party thrives nevertheless, especially in the industrialized south of Brazil, and in the 1998 election gained control of the important governorship of Rio Grande do Sul with the election of PT candidate Olívio Dutra. But the organization of workers was not restricted to the industrial zones. Threatened by the encroachment of cattle ranchers and loggers, rubber tappers on the Amazon frontier began to mobilize in the 1980s to protect their livelihood. Like the metalworkers in São Paulo, these poor workmen produced a formidable grassroots leader from among their ranks, Chico Mendes. His rubber tappers' organization linked up with Brazilian social activists and international environmental groups to pressure the Brazilian government for recognition of their grievances and to carve out ecological reserves to protect the forests on which their way of life depended. They also developed critical networks of international supporters in Europe and the United States who were able to pressure international lending agencies such as the Inter-American Development Bank and the World Bank into incorporating ecological concerns into their decisions about loans to Brazil.

The indigenous communities, facing a life-and-death struggle for survival as the outside world pressed in on their remaining refuges in the Amazon basin, also found a voice during the 1980s. With the support of international organizations such as the Cambridge, Massachusetts-based Survival International, tribes such as the Kayapó and Xavante pressed for recognition and protection against the freelance gold prospectors who were invading their forests and polluting their rivers with deadly mercury. A Xavante chief, Marío Jaruna was elected as federal deputy and Ailton Kremak of the Kayapó became well known in Brasília and among the international human rights networks.

While the hierarchy of the Catholic Church was divided on its approach to political activism, grassroots clergy strongly influenced by liberation theology provided organizational support to Brazil's many new reform movements. Protestant fundamentalists have also emerged as a force in the Brazilian social and religious landscape. Small, impeccable, white Pentecostal meeting houses now dot the landscape. The Universal Church of the Kingdom of God, founded in 1977 by a Pentecostal pastor, Edir Macedo, claims more than 3.5 million members and receives more than $700 million in annual donations. It owns Brazil's third largest TV network and 30 radio stations. As it is often said in Brazil: "Catholics opted for the poor; the poor opted for the evangelicals."

Many Protestant converts come from the lower levels of the new urban middle class. Protestant evangelicals practice a faith of personal salvation and promote a frugal lifestyle emphasizing thrift and family. They are seen as a conservative force; at the local level, however, their organizations have quickly shifted to municipal activism, seeking improved water supplies and better services, which has propelled them increasingly into politics. The evangelicals have a caucus of 35 deputies in the Brazilian Congress, and an evangelical bishop in Rio de Janeiro, Carlos Rodrigues, received a huge vote in the recent congressional elections. The new governor of the state of Rio, Anthony Garotinho, is also an evangelical. Responding to the Evangelical challenge, the Catholic church in Brazil is now encouraging a powerful charismatic movement that is galvanizing many of the faithful in Brazil's cities. The charismatics, like the evangelicals, place a strong emphasis on family values, but they, like the Catholic hierarchy, are also critical of the harshness of Brazil's capitalist system.

Most threatening to Brazil's political elite and to its large rural landowners in particular has been the emergence of a powerful rural movement of the landless. Founded in Rio Grande do Sul in the mid-1980s, the Movimento dos Trabalhadores Rurais Sem Terra (Movement of Landless Rural Workers, MST) now has some 500,000 members, including all sorts of people from the margins of Brazilian society: the unemployed, migrant agricultural workers, the illiterate, slum dwellers, all people the traditional Left believed it was impossible to organize, stimulated by Brazil's total failure for centuries to break the power of the great *latifundios* and bring about any meaningful land distribution. Less than one percent of farms, all over 500 acres in dimension, account for 40 percent of all occupied farmlands in Brazil. The movement was also energized by the expulsion of many small holders from their plots, especially in Rio Grande do Sul, Paraná, and Santa Catarina, by the mechanization of large-scale soya and wheat production in the 1980s. The MST is now the largest and best-organized social movement in Latin America, with successful cooperatives, a Web site, and extensive international contacts. Its members often take the law into their own hands, invading properties and setting up squatter settlements, sacking warehouses to obtain food, and challenging landowners. Almost as often they provoke violent reactions from *fazendeiros* (large landowners), local police, and hired gunmen.

What the MST seeks is access to land and the breakup of the large estates, many of which remain undeveloped and unproductive, or are held for tax purposes or to draw government subsidies. Its ideology is an eclectic mix of revolutionary socialism and Catholic activism, as befits an organization built in large part by itinerant priests. Its most prominent leader is an economist named João Pedro Stédile, who did post-graduate work in Mexico and takes inspiration from the Mexican Zapatistas. He argues that the Brazilian elite is too "subservient to foreign interests"—an obvious swipe at the IMF and the forces of global capitalism as well

as the former *dependentista* now lodged in the futuristic presidential palace in Brasília.

Finally there is the Brazilian environmental movement, composed of some 800 organizations stirred into being by the uncontrolled destruction of the Amazon rain forest, ecological disasters in the grotesquely polluted chemical complex at Cubatão in São Paulo state, and rampant encroachment on the remnants of the once lush Atlantic forests.

In 1998 forest fires in the Amazon region, aggravated by the impact of El Niño, were the worst on record, but the Cardoso administration did little to respond until the extent of the catastrophe became difficult to hide. The devastating drought in the Northeast, another predicatable consequence of El Niño, also received scant attention until famished peasants organized by the MST raided warehouses and occupied bank agencies and police stations. This finally caught the attention of the indifferent bureaucrats in the surreal world of Brasília, preoccupied with the purchase of expensive Oriental carpets for their offices so that "foreign visitors could be more elegantly received," as a spokesman for the minister of communication explained to the *New York Times*. Not surprisingly, all these movements strike a raw chord with the "owners of power," as the brilliant Brazilian lawyer and social critic Raymundo Faoro so aptly put it. Owing to the overseas support the environmental movement receives, the Brazilian military views it as a pawn of foreign interests, part of a thinly disguised effort by the United States to take the Amazon away from Brazil. The military intelligence network closely monitors the activities of the MST, and Cardoso's ministers dismiss the movement as "enemies of modernity." It was similar attitudes that a hundred years ago led to the repression and slaughter in the backlands so brilliantly immortalized by Euclides da Cunha and Vargas Llosa.

The great 20th-century Brazilian historian Sergio Buarque de Hollanda defined a Brazilian as a "cordial" individual, and Brazilians are like their president, people of great and infectious charm. But where politics and social conflicts meet, their country can be a very violent place. It has many martyrs to prove it, among them Chico Mendes, gunned down in 1988 by cattle ranchers threatened by his rubber tappers' movement. More than a thousand labor leaders and grassroots peasant activists have been assassinated in Brazil since the mid-1980s. In much of the country the murderers of activists act with impunity. In November 1998, Miguel Pereira de Melo, the crusading Brazilian photojournalist, was killed by gunmen. He had recorded the 1996 massacre of landless peasants by military police and was about to testify at the trial of those officers.

The subtler obstacles to pluralism may prove the hardest to overcome. Reform will require changing an oligarchic style of politics and an entrenched bureaucracy that have both skillfully deflected challenges for centuries. Indeed, the deals made to bring about the transition from military to civilian rule during the 1980s guaranteed the persistence in power of many old-line politicians, including preeminently the powerful Bahia political boss, former state governor, and current president of the Senate, Antonio Carlos Magalhães. ACM, as he is universally known, is a gregarious, tough, and single-minded political operator who proudly professes his admiration for Napoleon. Today he is more influential than ever, a pivotal figure in the coalition that supports President Cardoso—an odd but very Brazilian twist of fate since Cardoso was precisely the sort of upper-class intellectual that Magalhães and other power brokers under the military regimes of the past most distrusted.

The bosses and bureaucrats have plenty to protect. The welfare and pension system, for example, does virtually nothing for the poorer workers but vastly benefits state functionaries. In 1996, Brazil had 29 four-star generals on active duty and 5,000 people drawing generous pension checks at the four-star level, including far-flung relatives of dead and retired officers.

Brazil's formal political structure also makes reform excruciatingly difficult. It has 27 state governors and more than 5,500 municipal mayors (*prefeitos*), many of whom have run up massive deficits which by tradition the federal government is expected to cover. The 1988 constitution obliges the central government to transfer a large share of tax revenues to the state governments and municipalities but without a commensurate shift of responsibility for government programs. The idea was to devolve power and encourage democracy. The result was to strengthen parochial interests and the local political bosses. These problems were aggravated by the Real Plan's success, since, during the years of high inflation, government deficits had miraculously disappeared as delayed payments wiped out obligations. But after 1994 such flimflams no longer worked, as money retained its value. The opening of the economy and the stabilization of the currency had some perverse effects as well. Many industrial workers were displaced as imports flooded the consumer market. Not only did the service sector expand, but many industrial workers were forced into the informal sector. Subsequently, unemployment increased dramatically.

Cardoso hoped to pass a half-dozen ambitious reform measures during his first term—from cutting public payrolls to rewriting tax laws—and, not surprisingly, all fell victim to constant dilution and delays. His major success, altering the constitution to allow for his own re-election, was bought at the high cost of also allowing state and local political bosses to run for re-election. They promptly opened the spending spigots to ensure victory at the polls, swelling public-sector debt to more than $300 billion in early 1998 and leaving Brazil pitifully vulnerable when the international crisis hit.

President Cardoso will find it difficult to deliver on his promises to the IMF. Arrayed against him will be both the old corporatist interests, eager to protect the past and their own privileges, and the newly assertive groups such as the MST, which disagree with the path chosen for the future.

Cardoso's popularity, though great enough to secure him a clear majority in last October's election, is based almost entirely on the success of the Real Plan. He views himself as a man of the Center-Left, an adherent of the new "third way" of Bill Clinton and Tony Blair, but is perceived by the public as being a political leader decisively of the Center-Right, the friend of bankers, industrialists, civil servants, and politicians rather than workers and the landless. As the realities of IMF-imposed austerity begin to hit home—Brazil's economy was already shrinking by the end of 1998—Cardoso may find his popular support waning. He has consciously steered away from the heady rhetoric of populism, avoided demagoguery, and preferred persuasion and compromise to executive decree, but the next year may well test his resolve.

Lula lost the 1998 election in part because he chose to attack the Real Plan. But the 1998 elections also saw the emergence of middle-class Workers' Party leaders who spoke a language closer to that of the new social democrats of Europe, consciously avoiding the radical rhetoric of the shop floor. These Workers' Party representatives in Congress are likely to provide solid opposition to Cardoso's IMF-inspired policies over the next year. The center-left political allies within Cardoso's own political family also risk being alienated by his orthodox economic retrenchment, which will cut deeply into the social programs Brazil so desperately needs. Nor will the president find support from powerful governors among whom he will find fewer friends than during his first term, especially since they will be forced to bear the brunt of the budget cuts. Particularly troublesome will be the newly elected governor of the important state of Minas Gerais, the former president Itamar Franco, under whom, as finance minister, Cardoso implemented the Real Plan. The erratic Franco is still deeply resentful that Cardoso and not he got all the credit. Nor will the protests of landless rural workers go away. Stédile in particular makes no secret of his desire to "finish off the neoliberal model."

It is ironic that in the charged international economic climate in which Fernando Henrique Cardoso begins his second term as president, the protection of the Real Plan, by plunging Brazil into recession, now poses the greatest threat to the benefits it brought to many Brazilians. Yet posing one of the greatest challenges to the IMF-mandated program to satisfy the international markets are groups and forces within Brazil that barely existed before political and economic liberalization began a decade ago. The travails of the Brazilian economy—no matter where they lead—should not obscure the significant success story the rise of these new voices represents.

KENNETH MAXWELL *holds the Rockefeller Chair in Inter-American Studies at the Council on Foreign Relations.*

Article 12   *The Chronicle of Higher Education*, March 27, 1998

A Scholar and Pai-de-Santo Straddles 2 Worlds in Multicultural Brazil

by Carolyn J. Mooney

SALVADOR DA BAHIA, BRAZIL

IN THIS CITY where African roots run deep, the Candomblé religion shows its public face with joy. Glimpses of the faith, whose devotees worship African Yoruba divinities, are everywhere—in the lush gardens of Candomblé houses found even in the grittiest neighborhoods, in the white clothes worn by the most observant practitioners on Fridays, in the strings of beads (their colors and patterns correspond with different deities) that hang in local markets. Brazilians of all faiths toss flowers and perfume into the ocean each year to placate Iemanjá, goddess of the seas. During Carnival, groups called *afoxés* parade through the city wearing the colors of their patron deities. And then there's the festival of *Bonfim*, huge and colorful and steeped in Candomblé tradition.

But it takes patience and time to see Candomblé's private face. Julio Santana Braga knows that as well as anyone else. A respected anthropologist of Afro-Brazilian religions, he spent years studying the repression of Candomblé houses of worship by the Brazilian police in the first half of the century. Now he heads his own.

Since 1990 he has been a Candomblé priest—a *pai-de-santo,* or father of the saints. And he remains an active scholar, straddling Candomblé's religious and scholarly worlds.

"I've reconciled the two," says Mr. Braga, a man with blazing dark eyes, a small triangle of a beard, a quick tongue, and a fondness for his cellular phone. "I know exactly where to stop."

Like Candomblé, Mr. Braga's home is elusive at first. It lies behind high white walls above a winding dirt road far from the city's center. The blue doors open onto a driveway leading up to a handsome gold-stucco house. A group of television journalists is just leaving as a visitor pulls up.

Mr. Braga shrugs. "I'm considered exotic," he says. "That's why people come."

Candomblé is the Brazilian strain of the religion that is rooted in the beliefs of the Yoruba people of West Africa. Known as Santería in Cuba and Vodoo in Haiti, it's especially strong in Brazil's northeast, where many people are of African descent. Many initiates also consider themselves Roman Catholic. It isn't unusual for devotees to layer one set of beliefs over another, a phenomenon that was apparent during Pope John Paul II's visit to Cuba.

The syncretism dates back centuries, when African-born slaves worshipped the Yoruba deities known as *orixás* (pronounced "o-ri-shas") as Catholic saints, to avoid persecution. Hence Iemanjá was worshipped as the Virgin Mary, and Ogum, the deity of war, was equated with St. Anthony.

The practice of Candomblé involves elaborate initiation rituals, a tradition of animal sacrifice and other offerings, and ceremonies that feature drumming, chanting, dancing, and feasting. The *pai-* or *mãe-desanto* (female priests are known as mothers of the saints) acts as an intermediary between initiates and *orixás* at such ceremonies. Through the frenetic dancing and music used to summon the *orixás,* some people fall into a trance, believing themselves to be possessed by a particular deity.

Mr. Braga has studied Afro-Brazilian religions both here and in Africa. Among his mentors here was the French scholar Pierre Verger, a pioneer in the study of Candomblé. Mr. Braga earned his doctorate at the *Université Nationale de Zaire.* He spent much of his academic career at the Federal University of Bahia, where he was director of the Center for Afro-Oriental Studies. Since retiring, in 1994, he has been a visiting professor at the nearby *Universidade Estadual de Feira de Santana.*

For Mr. Braga, the history of Candomblé is linked to the history of Brazil's black-rights movement. "At the turn of the century, Brazilian society wanted to create a European model," he explains. "It rejected everything African, and Candomblé was the most visual manifestation of Africa."

Police mounted a war on the religion in the 1920s, shutting down Candomblé houses and jailing people. "But the rejection made the religion stronger. It gave it the strength of resistance."

As Brazilian society became more racially mixed, there was more willingness to acknowledge its African roots. An Afro-Brazilian congress, held in 1937, and writers including Jorge Amado helped form a more inclusive notion of Brazilian culture.

In *Tent of Miracles,* Amado's rich novel about life in Salvador, an editorial writer for the local paper often expressed his disgust for the city's African flavor. "An observer judging Bahia by its carnival could hardly help equating it with Africa," he observed. Where, he wondered, were the police? What were they doing "to show that civilization does veritably exist in this fair city?" How long, he asked, "can our Latin heritage endure if we continue to let this scandalous African exhibition go on—the drumming, the lines of mestizas of every shade from rich creole to off-white mulatta, the mesmerizing samba beat, these charms, these spells, this sorcery?"

By the 1970s, the black-rights movement had led to the formation of cultural groups like Oludum, the popular drum corps. But even today, race remains a complicated issue in multicultural Brazil.

"Who is black?" Mr. Braga demands. "Who decides?" He moves to the edge of his seat. "A lot of people would say I'm not black or white. But I say I'm black."

And what makes him black?

"The desire to be black."

MR. BRAGA ESTIMATES that the number of Candomblé houses in Salvador has grown over recent decades, to about 2,000. While plenty of Brazilians remain wary of the religion, which some associate with black magic, it has become integrated into the society, and its following among white people is growing.

Mr. Braga often presides over ceremonies held at a *terreiro,* a house of worship located off his property. Other ceremonies are held in a complex adjoining his home, where a low white building with a row of blue doors houses small rooms devoted to specific *orixás.* In the room of Mr. Braga's patron *orixá,* Iansa, is an altar surrounded by small statues. Fronds, bowls, and other offerings are arranged around a small animal skin on the floor. The complex also includes a communal kitchen with a chicken coop, for preparing ritual meals. Tropical plants grow in clusters on the lawn, including the sharp-leafed *espado de Ogum,* or sword of Ogum, used in Candomblé rites.

As a *pai-de-santo,* Mr. Braga consults with people about their personal problems. But, as a spiritual confidant, "I'm not free to describe it all. An ordinary anthropologist can go much further than me."

On the other hand—the thought of it makes him smile—he admits to taking an almost perverse pleasure in the struggles that other scholars face in seeking to understand a world he knows through practice. "I'm capable of analyzing their errors," he says. "I know they suffer, but I can't help them. I have limits."

Mr. Braga is writing a book that will describe his work as a scholar-priest. But it won't be a tell-all of life from the inside. "There are things," he says, "that are not necessary to tell."

THE FESTIVAL of *Bonfim* holds nothing back. It's taking place back in the city this same week. Thousands of people, of all faiths and classes, have gathered downtown to join a procession that will end 10 kilometers away, at the popular Catholic Church of *Bonfim.* There, women in traditional white dresses will ritually wash the church steps.

The church won't be open, though, since *Bonfim* isn't an official Catholic observance. Like so much else here, the festival is a blend of cultures. *Nosso Senhor do Bonfim* (Our Lord of Bonfim) is worshiped as both Jesus Christ and *Oxalá,* lord of creation, most powerful of Candomblé spirits.

Anyone can join; you just file into line behind bands playing the *Bonfim* anthem and horse-drawn carriages decked in flowers. The crowd shuffles through the hot city streets, hips swinging, banners waving. When the church's twin domes finally come into sight, the procession squeezes together so tightly that the surging crowd pushes you up the last hill.

And now all of Salvador spills out before you: The houses spill down the cliffs overlooking All Saints' Bay, and the crowd spills out into the side streets, where makeshift bars are set up, and the revelers spill bottles of water over sweating bodies that spill out of tight, revealing clothing.

Even years ago, during the height of repression against Candomblé, the people of Salvador celebrated *Bonfim.*

Not that anyone could have stopped them.

Article 13

The World & I, March 1999

Colombia: Civil War Without End?

by Mark Holston

Colombia over the years has become for Americans almost synonymous with illegal drugs—especially cocaine and, more recently, heroin. But the country's bloody 30-year-old civil war is one major reason the government has been unable to shut off the drug spigot that's connected to the eager nostrils and veins of millions of U.S. drug abusers.

It is by no means clear, however, that the racking conflict will end anytime soon.

Some are boldly confident of a felicitous future: "Two innate abilities have helped us to elude our calamitous fate," writes Nobel Prize-winning novelist Gabriel García Marquéz of his fellow Colombians. "One is a talent for creativity, the supreme expression of human intelligence. The other is a fierce commitment to self-improvement."

However, considering what Colombia has been through in the past three decades of no-holds-barred warfare between government forces, several armed insurgencies, and right-wing paramilitary groups, many citizens of this South American nation of 38 million might question whether their "calamitous fate" has indeed been avoided.

But as the first tentative steps toward formalizing a peace process began in a remote jungle outpost in early January, few

Penchant for Self-destruction?

✳ A civil war that has bedeviled Colombia for three decades rages on today.

✳ Rebel forces control huge swaths of the country and tie down the government's law enforcement and military resources, allowing the U.S.-bound drug trade to flourish.

✳ The nation has awesome economic assets, but they are being wasted due to the war effort and the need to care for a million peasants displaced by the fighting.

✳ The new administration of President Andrés Pastrana, who has started peace talks with the rebels and who has the trust of international lending groups, offers a chance to end the conflict.

doubted the necessity of Marquéz's recipe for national salvation if Colombia's penchant for self-destruction is to be reversed.

Among the daunting questions that face Latin America's third-most-populous nation are:

• Will talks between the government of recently elected President Andrés Pastrana and the Revolutionary Armed Forces of Colombia (FARC), the largest of several guerrilla groups waging war against the government, end the armed conflict that has claimed an estimated 35,000 lives and displaced a million peasants?

• If successful, how will the peace process influence the country's ability to stem the tide of illegal drugs that have made it the world's biggest supplier of illicit narcotics?

• Will an end to armed conflict help bring about fundamental economic and social changes likely to produce a more prosperous and secure life for the majority of Colombians?

• How can the United States assist Colombia in the peace process, and how will America benefit from a resolution of the armed conflict?

These and other questions haunt Colombians of every economic and social class. From the richest to the poorest, they have been victimized by a conflict that has cultivated a culture of violence and given rise to a spate of problems.

HUMAN TOLL CUTS
ACROSS CLASS LINES

Félix Ambuila is well into his long workday even before the neighborhood roosters begin to stir. The soft-spoken, muscular 51-year-old baker and his wife, Marlén, shape mounds of fresh dough into a variety of *pan dulce* (sweet bread) creations, pastries, and hard rolls.

The baking sheets are slipped carefully into the gas-fired oven that's been provided by the Center for Peace, Justice, and Transformation of Conflicts (JUSTAPAZ), a project of the Mennonite Church.

An hour later, a few of the couple's four children will be camped on a dusty street corner in the poor, remote Bogotá barrio of Palermo Sur, hoping to sell enough bread to keep the family together for another day.

According to Bonnie Klassen, a Canadian Mennonite social worker who coordinates the church's outreach efforts in the Bogotá area, the Ambuila family, and thousands of others like them, are the uncounted victims of the country's civil unrest. Driven from their homes in the countryside by the fighting, hundreds—no one knows the exact number—arrive every day on the doorstep of Colombia's largest cities to take their place at the bottom of the social and economic pecking order.

"The Ambuilas are fortunate in that they've kept their family unit intact," Klassen says. "But we see children who've been traumatized by the murder of their parents, and women whose husbands have been killed or jailed. Life for them is very tough in the cities, but they keep coming—they have no choice."

Even those whose personal wealth affords a wide array of choices live under constant threat of violence if they remain in Colombia. A woman of means who passes a quiet but apprehensive hour in the luxurious confines of Club Colombia, the marble-encased private retreat of Cali's privileged elite, is in constant cell phone contact with family members and her security detail.

She anxiously monitors the whereabouts of her two high school-age children, eager for their return from a private school to the heavily guarded family estate. During one week in November, two members of the woman's extended family were kidnapped, victims of a national crime spree that has grown as fighting in the countryside has intensified.

BATTLE OF BULLETS VS. PROPAGANDA

From his richly appointed office on the top floor of the Bolsa de Bogotá, the capital city's stock exchange, Augusto Acosta ticks off a long list of his country's considerable economic assets: its strategic location at the gateway to South America, with coasts on both the Atlantic and Pacific Oceans; a well-trained, highly educated workforce; diversified regional economies based in major population centers like Medellín, Cali, and Bogotá; an impressive transportation and communications infrastructure; and a wealth of natural resources, including expansive petroleum and coal reserves.

What a shame, says the Fordham University-educated bolsa director, that Colombia's considerable potential is being undermined by the current unresolved armed conflict. Foreign investment—led by the United States, which is Colombia's No. 1 trading partner—is sure to find the country hard to resist once the armed conflict is ended, Acosta believes.

For the time being, however, the former vice minister of defense admits that the guerrillas have won the propaganda war.

"In Europe and the United States, many have been led to believe that the Colombian military is the only party guilty of human rights violations," he says. "And that's because we haven't been very successful at letting people know what the real situation is in Colombia."

While the country's high command is attempting to resolve the image problem through, among other things, a Web site

The Andean Bloc

Throughout the region, questions abound about the prospects for economic, social, and political stability in the four other Andean Group nations.

Venezuela: This Caribbean-fronting nation of 25 million that borders Colombia to the east is in the midst of a tumultuous political honeymoon during the first months of recently elected President Hugo Chavez's administration.

The former army officer, who led an unsuccessful coup attempt in 1992, emerged as a champion of the country's disenfranchised masses, promising to root out corruption and radically overhaul Venezuela's ineffective governmental institutions.

While his populist rhetoric has raised concerns throughout the hemisphere as to whether he will install an authoritarian-leaning regime, some observers believe the charismatic leader will become more pragmatic over time and will not pursue the full scope of the revolutionary agenda he advocated during the election campaign.

Ecuador: After several years of political discord and revolving-door presidencies, Ecuador has a new constitution and chief executive. Moreover, it has struck an agreement to resolve the long-standing border dispute with neighboring Peru that since the 1940s resulted in periodic armed conflict between the two countries.

Geographically the smallest of the Andean countries, Ecuador, bolstered by sizable petroleum reserves, has seen steady economic growth in recent years and greater employment opportunities for its 12 million citizens.

Peru: The big question in this nation of 25 million that in recent years has worked to strengthen economic ties with Pacific Rim countries is whether the current president, Alberto Fujimori, will run again.

The former college professor championed capitalist economic reforms that improved Peru's economic outlook and helped or-

---

(www.cgfm.co) that presents the military's position on its human rights record, its success in combating the insurgencies in the field has been hindered by a lack of adequate equipment, trained personnel, and innovative tactics.

"A few Blackhawk helicopters would make a lot of difference here," Acosta notes.

He says they would be especially useful in seeking out and attacking cocaine—and heroin-processing operations and interdicting shipments of illegal drugs within the country. And anything the military does to strengthen its combat capabilities may help persuade the guerrilla factions to lay down their arms.

For its part, while talking peace, FARC flexed its military muscle in the two-month period leading up to the start of negotiations, mounting a string of last-minute attacks that captured isolated government garrisons, sabotaged oil pipelines, and disrupted traffic on the major highway near Cali.

During the same period, right-wing paramilitary gangs demonstrated their growing power by launching murderous attacks on villages believed to be sympathetic to the guerrilla movement.

U.S. ROLE IN RESOLVING THE CONFLICT

"There's no question that our relationship with Colombia is immensely better today than it was before the election last summer of President Pastrana," says Michael May, director of the MERCOSUR South America project of the Washington, D.C.-based Center for Strategic and International Studies. MERCOSUR is a trade bloc that includes Argentina, Bolivia, Brazil, Paraguay, and Uruguay.

"During the corruption-plagued Samper administration, the formal relationship between Bogotà and Washington was all but nonexistent. But," he cautions, "the U.S. government has to come to grips with a Colombia policy, and I don't think one has yet been formulated."

May is a former resident of Bogotà who now works to increase the focus of U.S. policymakers on the MERCOSUR nations as well as Venezuela and Colombia. He believes the

No. 1 policy goal of the United States in Colombia is to strive for a stable, democratic government and a free-market economic system.

Under Pastrana, May thinks, Colombia is making strides toward achieving those goals. Following such a program, he postulates, would curtail the disruptive threat of the drug traffickers and guerrilla groups, because a strong central government would reinstitute sovereignty over outlying regions of the country and foster economic opportunities.

In doing so, chronic unemployment could be reduced and an array of social problems, including endemic violence and involvement in the drug trade, could be addressed in a more meaningful way.

The United States has failed to take a strong leadership position vis-à-vis Colombia and other nations in the region, May contends, by not getting congressional approval of "fast-track" trade legislation.

"What's happening in Latin America," he adds, "is an integration of economic systems, and the fact is that the United States is becoming less influential in the region.

"Those countries are not just going to sit around and wait while the United States decides whether or not to engage," May contends. "They're going to forge ahead with what they believe to be important, whether it's MERCOSUR or the Andean Group [trade bloc]."

In addition to Clinton's impeachment distracting from the creation of effective foreign policy, the U.S. government's skepticism toward Colombia has been exacerbated by that nation's image problem and Pastrana administration policy initiatives that have been viewed with suspicion by conservative members of the U.S. Congress. The Colombian government's decision, for instance, to cede control to the guerrillas of a vast expanse of territory in the country's thinly populated southeast raised some congressional eyebrows.

"The abdication of a portion of national territory doesn't make sense to many here in D.C.," says the CSIS's May. "Any

chestrate the successful campaign to defeat the Shining Path, the country's rural Marxist insurgency.

But he has been accused of using an overly cozy relationship with the military to carry out what many consider a constitutional coup, consolidating his control and using his executive powers to tighten up on individual and media freedoms.

Bolivia: This landlocked, poor, and largely indigenous nation of 8 million is one of the region's current success stories.

New President Hugo Banzer, the former military dictator who ruled the country in the early to late 1970s, is earning high marks as a born-again democrat.

Banzer's administration is working closely with the United States to combat drug trafficking and coca production, estimated to represent one-third of the world's total. Bolivia is second only to Peru in cultivation of the illicit crop, and second only to Colombia in production of refined cocaine.

Like Colombia, all four nations are challenged by such fundamental concerns as growing their economies, providing better economic opportunities for their citizens, and providing a social safety net for those citizens who are victims of the region's high unemployment rate.

government that doesn't govern runs the risk of losing credibility and legitimacy."

Seeking to strengthen Colombia's hand in the peace negotiations by bolstering the effectiveness of the country's 250,000-member armed forces, the Clinton administration is funneling military trainers and much-needed equipment into the country, including the promise of coveted Blackhawks.

Secretary of Defense William Cohen, attending a meeting last November of the hemisphere's defense ministers in the Colombian port city of Cartagena, stressed the importance of restructuring the military so it can be more effective in combating the country's narcoterrorists and drug traffickers.

Since many guerrilla groups have become deeply involved in the illicit narcotics trade, if the army redoubles its efforts in the war on drugs, the efforts will ultimately improve the overall military picture as well. Up to 200 U.S. military personnel are already in the country on training missions, and more may be on the way.

PROSPECTS FOR PEACE TIED TO ECONOMY

"Colombia's problems are not easy to solve, and I can't say whether this government will be able to solve them," says Scott Jeffery Jr., the country's Colgate-Palmolive general manager.

But the 38-year-old, Colombian-born business leader believes the Pastrana administration is on the right track.

"With the current government, we have the best chance of trying to solve the problems," he says, "because the international community is supporting the government's peace process, and international financial institutions want to help improve Colombia's economy."

The government is improving the nation's economic health, the Cali-based executive believes, which is essential to weaning Colombians away from the cycle of violence that has plagued the country since 1948. A political assassination in Bogotá that year, dubbed the Bogotazo, sparked the decade-long orgy of internecine strife known simply as *La Violencia,* which claimed close to 300,000 lives.

Although the casualty rate has decreased in subsequent decades, armed conflict has seldom abated. Moreover, the combination of illicit drug production and guerrilla warfare has disrupted the once-strong traditional agricultural base, requiring the country to import food products that were once cash-earning export crops.

"The peace process will take some time," Jeffery speculates. "If we're lucky, the current government will be able to set the groundwork, by the end of its four-year term, to have the following government finalize the process.

"In the meantime, just the movement toward real peace will bring some tangible benefits, including humanizing the country's internal struggle, which will continue but in a more moderate, nonviolent form and, hopefully, with an increase in respect for human rights by all parties."

That's a prospect equally appealing to Félix Ambuila and his family, who live for the day when they'll be able to return to their Cauca Valley home and resume the simple routine of daily life that was shattered by ever-increasing death threats, abductions, and assassinations.

Weary of war and eager to share in their country's economic promise, the Ambuilas, like millions of Colombians, only want a chance to begin again.

Mark Holston is a contributing editor to **Hispanic, Americas, Seis Continentes,** *and other publications specializing in Latin American issues. The assistance of Avianca Airlines and Inter-Continental Hotels in making this story possible is acknowledged.*

Article 14

Cultural Survival Quarterly, Summer 1997

Ecuador 1972–1997:

Indigenous Peoples and the Crisis of the Nation–State

by Pablo Ortíz-T

translated by Bret Gustafson

The indigenous uprisings during the Festival of Inti Raymi in 1990 and 1994 exposed a weakly masked ideological project: the 19th century liberal construction of a project to convert the Indian subject to a white-mestizo citizen. This underlying liberal ideology in Ecuador saw the "Indian" as a passive and animalized 'other' that must be liberated. When the "peculiar character of the Indian has been modified," as liberal theorist Abelardo Moncayo wrote at the turn of the century, "one can achieve Ecuadorian citizenship."

The massive movement of indigenous peoples during the last 25 years has dissolved this ideology which was once an important part of the political system. In addition, indigenous resurgence has contributed to the disintegration (initiated in recent decades from various sides: the developing State, the agrarian reform, the urban migration, indigenous organizations) of the "Indian object." This Indian was to receive a "token" Ecuadorian citizenship but was still deprived of recognition, without legality or legitimacy, and would still require political mediators. In reality, a political shift has occurred, the model and formation of white-mestizo citizenship, elaborated by the national State and civil society, have been thrown into question.

In this sense, recent changes in Ecuador's democratic transition have been substantial. The relationship between indigenous peoples and the State political system is completely distinct today from what it was in the past, despite the short term results of recent ethnic conflict in Ecuador. According to Andrés Guerrero, the "Confederation of Indigenous Nationalities of Ecuador, CONAIE, is not merely a new apparatus of mediation and function of the Ecuadorian Federation of Indians (FEI is an indigenous organization that served, through the Spanish speaking mestizo population, to channel demands of the indigenous population

Photo: Courtesy of Centro de Estudios y Difusion Social, CEDIS

An indigenous leader speaks in Guaranda, Sierra Central, Ecuador during an indigenous uprising in June, 1990.

within the national political context). CONAIE and the current indigenous organizations are not simply mediating instruments for neocolonial political subjects." This fact, adds Guerrero, is demonstrated in the acts of mobilizing, organizing, and sustaining large indigenous movements, autonomous from political parties and labor unions. This movement has created a new social agent, linking and promoting demands previously unheard of and unmentionable: a reinterpretation of history from the indigenous point of view, articulated with demands of autonomy, self-government, and self-determination.

The indigenous masses have abandoned the patterns of national history and cleared a space for new kinds of struggles. Particularly, the national indigenous uprisings in 1990 and 1994, and the regional uprisings during the same period, have forced the State into an unforeseen political practice. This new practice is replete with recently created symbols and expansive spaces in the political system: dialogue and direct negotiation between citizens who demand recognition of their ethnic collectivity as indigenous peoples, and the citizen-elites of the white-mestizo government (in the case of the regimes of Rodrigo Borja in 1990 and 1992, and Sixto Durán Ballén in 1994).

The indigenous uprisings of the 1990s, and the construction of a unique and recognized indigenous discourse have exposed and widened the cracks and fissures in Ecuador's goals of modernity, civilization, and progress built on exclusion of Ecuador's "other." In essence, the demands of indigenous organizations imply a radical reform of the nation-State, as expressed by Luís Macas.

In this context, the disintegration of local power, the historical formation formerly in charge of the semi-private administration of the indigenous population, has generated a power vacuum in the rural areas at the county and parish levels. In contrast to what occurred until the 1960s, the hacienda owners today no longer govern indigenous subjects on plantations, rather, as efficient capitalists, they manage a salaried work force. In addition, the loose instrument of power (hacienda, Church, state officials, private inter-ethnic ties) once ruled by the hacienda, no longer reigns supreme.

Community relations between white-mestizos and indigenous people has been secularized in many ways. These relations are no longer restricted to the private and daily life, nor restricted to regional politics. When these ties exist (in many communities they have disappeared), economic and symbolic ethnic relations appear more and more as simple contractual ties. Hence secularization develops in the form of anonymous labor or mercantile exchanges.

The oil-led growth and "modernization" of Ecuador has paralleled the disintegration of this local-state infrastructure that functioned as a hinge between the central State and the indigenous population. State-led development projects and instruments treated the indigenous peoples of Ecuador not as neocolonial subjects or a mass of population needing a system of administration, but rather as agents of production, as peasants. This situation has had tangible repercussions in recent decades, the indigenous peoples (free communities, cooperative ex-*huasipungueros*, or indigenous peasants, and urban Indians) have become more autonomous. Indians are reaffirming and reinventing their identity and establishing for the first time a direct mediating position with the State. This affirmation entails at least two aspects: it implies a reduction in white-mestizo power and population in rural areas and communities, and a broad process of indigenous organization.

The seats of power were abandoned in Ecuador's countryside as the local white "ethnic administration" disintegrated. The seats have been rapidly filled in various ways and through various economic, symbolic, and political strategies. The indigenous communities and their *cabildos* have reinvented the huge festivals that were once presided over by *hacienda patrones*. They have fortified and increased their communal territories, pushing limits onto former haciendas now taken over after long, local struggles. A number of higher level political groupings have appeared that organize cabildos into regional federations and national organizations (Ecuarunari, CONFENAIE, CONAIE). According to Andrés Guerrero, these have surpassed the mere function of a supra-regional political presence and have presented a serious challenge to the symbolic power of the nation-State.

It's no coincidence that, as the indigenous movement has raised the flags of resurgence, the governments of Ecuador, especially from 1982 to 1997, have been obligated to make a few legal adjustments. For example, the partial reform of Article 1 of the Constitution, in which the "pluricultural" not "plurinational" definition of the State has been recognized. Likewise, an Office of Indigenous Affairs was created in 1993, which was linked to Ecuador's legislative branch. Also, there was an attempt to create an Ethnic Ministry near the end of 1996, during the government of the deposed Bucaram. It appears that the motives of these hurried measures of the State

are trying to balance the need to respond to indigenous demands, as well as to diminish the organizing force of indigenous organizations.

Nonetheless, it is symptomatic that the State is avoiding, at all costs (as is public opinion), debating the political reorganization of the country, even when talking of decentralization. Even more interesting is that neither lawmakers nor intellectuals (some of them sincerely preoccupied with the need to theorize a scientific reorganization) seriously consider ethnicity as a relevant variable for the process of territorial organization and decentralization. Moreover, when demands for the formation of ethnic political entities were proposed, within the confines of the National State, lawmakers ignored and rejected them.

Pablo Ortíz-T. *is a sociologist with a M.A. in Political Science, a minor in Comparative Politics and specializes in Development Management. He currently is professor at the Pontificia Universidad Católica de Ecuador (PUCE), and consultant to FTPP and the FAO. He has worked in participatory research and communication with first and second tier peasant and indigenous organizations.*
Bret Gustafson *is a Fellow at the Center for Cultural Survival and a Ph.D. candidate in Anthropology at Harvard University*

Bibliography

Almeida, José et.al. 1993. "Sismo Étnico en el Ecuador." *Varias perspectivas.* Quito: Cedime-Abya-Yala.

Conaghan, Catherine. 1989. "Capitalist, Technocrats and Politicians: Economic Policy-Making and Democracy in the Central Andes." In *Working Paper #109.* The Helen Kellog Institute, University of Notre Dame.

Guerrero, Andrés. 1994. *La semántica de la dominación. El concertaje de indios.* Quito: Edcs. Libri Mundi.

Ibarra, Hernán. 1992. *Indios y Cholos: Orígenes de la clase trabajadora ecuatoriana.* Quito: Edit. El Conejo.

Isaacs, Anita. 1996. "Ecuador: Democracy Standing the Test of Time?" In *Constructing Democratic Governance: South America in the 1990s.* Eds. Jorge I. Dominguez & Abraham F. Lowental. Baltimore: Johns Hopkins University Press.

Korovkin, Tanya. 1993. *Los Indígenas, los campesinos y el Estado: el crecimiento del Movimiento Comunitario en la Sierra Ecuatoriana.* Canada: Flacso-Universidad de Waterloo.

León, Jorge. 1994. *De Campesinos a Ciudadanos diferentes.* Quito: Cedime-Abya Yala.

Macas, Luís, et.al. 1992. *Indios.* Quito: Ildis-Abya Yala. 2da. edición.

Malloy, James y Abugattas, Luís. 1990. "Business and the Boys. The Politics of Neoliberalism in the Central Andes." *Latin American Research Review.* Vol. XXV, no. 2,

Menéndez, Carrión. 1994. "Ciudadanía." In *Léxico Político Ecuatoriano.* Quito: Ildis.

Rosero, Fernando. 1990. *Levantamiento Indígena, tierra y precios.* Quito: Cedis.

Wray, Alberto et.al. 1993. *Derecho, pueblos indígenas y reforma del 1993 Estado.* Quito: Abya Yala.

Yashar, Deborah J. 1996. "Indigenous Protest and Democracy in Latin America." In *Constructing Democratic Governance: South America in the 1990s.* Eds. Jorge I. Dominguez & Abraham E Lowental. Baltimore: Johns Hopkins University Press.

Article 15

Cultural Survival Quarterly, Summer 1997

Ecuador's Indigenous People:
"We Seek True Participation"

by Pablo Ortíz-T

translated by Bret Gustafson

Dr. Luis Macas, 1996.
Photo: Courtesy of Centro de Estudios y Difusion Social, CEDIS

This article is based on an interview with Luís Macas, a Quichua from the highlands of Ecuador and currently the National Deputy in the Congress of Ecuador. He is ex-president and leader of the Confederation of Indigenous Nationalities of Ecuador (CONAIE).

In order to speak about the last 25 years of the indigenous movement in Ecuador, we should locate ourselves within the wider context and the historical situation. In order to understand the dynamics of our movement, we must look at the causes. In these causes we find the accumulation of exploitation and oppression which we have suffered for more than 500 years, given that even in these days Indians are still the poorest and most marginalized of this society.

"We believe that the most recent events of the 1990s had fundamental origins in the defense and recovery of land and territory, and a clear unity strengthened by a revitalization of ethnic identity of Indian peoples. In addition, we responded to the ideological limits of the political system that surrounds us, as well as the incapacity of democratic governments to incorporate and respond to our demands.

"We see that after more than 500 years of the European invasion and 150 years of the republican regime, Indian rights are still not recognized. The conquest has not ended, rather it continues into our times. New forms of subjugation, exploitation, and oppression are being systematically reproduced, leading to injustice in the lives of our people. The looting of our natural resources, the destruction of our cultures, the ecological imbalance, the burden of the foreign debt—in other words, the domination and subjection of our people has not ended. With few exceptions, the governments of Latin America have not applied authentic and democratic land reform. Our people's struggles for land are repressed, our cultural values disparaged,

and an alienating culture is imposed upon us that silences our own cultural expressions. For these reasons we have searched for the road to unity among the different indigenous peoples of Ecuador. Now, we have the hope of constructing new societies where the ethnic and cultural rights of the indigenous nationalities will be respected and recognized."

Our Objectives

"The important task is to seek the construction of an alternative social project that responds both to our history and to the interests of all of Ecuador. We want to exercise the legitimate right of self-determination which we believe to be a fundamental goal in achieving our liberation. The consolidation of this objective will not only be the exclusive task of Indian Peoples, but it will be a social compromise that we should make, among all of the sectors of society who are convinced of the need for a pluralist, democratic society where justice and peace are guaranteed.

"At this time, the living conditions of our people are extremely miserable. There is an accelerated erosion of our productive means, malnutrition, acculturation, unemployment—in other words, a general social disintegration is occurring. The fundamental problem is the scarcity of land which has led to the migration of Indians to the cities, where we are left to the most menial of jobs, mistreated, and underpaid.

"The State has developed policies which have not solved the structural problems of our society The programs applied in the rural area have served only to further the needs of capitalist modernization in agro-industries. The series of agrarian transformations of the 1960s and 1970s, only served to suppress the feudal forms of production which were obstacles to development; they were a tool to calm the indigenous insurrection. These reforms never affected the interests of the large ranchers and farmers, given that the best lands are still concentrated in very few hands, three million people have only

4% of the cultivable land (plots are smaller than 5 hectares). On the other hand, about 200,000 people control about 50% of the land (landholdings are 100 hectares or more).

"The projects of colonization in the Amazon and the coastal regions have not been favorable for our peoples; the situation has worsened. Through the system of colonization, the theft of natural resources has been legitimized, as well as the appropriation of natural resources by large businesses. Little by little, we are pushed further and further into the corners of the forest without the chance for a dignified existence.

"In the face of this structural and historical situation, the indigenous people of Ecuador have responded with different forms of struggle and resistance including rebellions, mobilizations, uprisings, and most importantly, the organization and the unity of our people. Likewise we have responded with the affirmation of our culture and identity in relation to our languages, customs, beliefs, and traditions, as our own forms of consciousness and resistance in the face of domination.

"Not one of the democratic governments in Ecuador has brought a significant or favorable change for the popular sectors of the country. We think, on the contrary, that the situation is worsening. The conditions of life have deteriorated, inflationary processes continue, and the people are still in conditions of extreme poverty."

Land and Self-Determination

"Among our primary demands, which are not new, is the right to land and territory. We do not think there will be a solution to the problems of indigenous people if there is no solution to the problem of land. The essential task for us is the recovery of land. Land is of course the indispensable condition for life, for the existence of a people, and for our development. Without this basic element, it is impossible to have conditions for educating children, lead healthy lives, and reproduce our cultures.

"With respect to the State, it should understand and apply the universal human rights for indigenous people. Likewise, our demands include the reform of Article 1 of the Constitution of the State, recognizing the country as a multicultural State, since we consider ourselves indigenous nationalities that make up part of this multicultural State. The reform of the Constitution would imply the reconstruction of the State as multicultural, pluralist, and democratic; not solely to grant the rights of indigenous people, but all of Ecuadorian society together.

"This demand is directed at the same time as the constitutional reordering and the creation of laws and judicial instruments that will give us the right to self-government. This consists of creating a system of self-government that allows us legal control over the administration of the internal affairs of our communities within the framework of the national State.

"Since we are Ecuadorians, during recent years we have also demanded support from the State to finance our self-initiated programs to develop infrastructure, basic social services, grants of small loans, and technical assistance to aid in improving productivity and the sale of our products. Indigenous people's labor, of course, supplies the majority of the food produced in the country.

These are the most important aspects of our struggle during recent years. We are not demanding anything outrageous, strange, or new. We only ask for justice, and for understanding and compliance on the part of the State."

Our Contributions to Democracy

"With the Indian uprising in June of 1990, the March of the Organizations of Indigenous Peoples of Pastaza (OPIP) in April and May of 1992, and the mobilizations of the indigenous communities in June of 1994 in opposition to the Law of Agricultural Development, the indigenous movement has been a protagonist of the most authentic forms of protest within a process of struggle and resistance. We will continue to pursue this struggle in order to achieve land, liberty, and dignity.

"These historic events have led us to confront a number of challenges and responsibilities. We realize that we are a social and political force with significant influence. We have won a space within society and we seek true democratic participation, as we represent the aspirations of Ecuador's poor. We have and will continue to call for justice. We will not allow ourselves to be divided, nor will we allow outside influences within our movement that do not respond to the true and legitimate demands of the indigenous people."

Photo: Courtesy of Centro de Estudios y Difusion Social, CEDIS
Otavaleños in Ecuador during an uprising, June 1990.

Pablo Ortíz-T. is a sociologist with a M.A. in Political Science, a minor in Comparative Politics and specalizes in Development Management. He currently is professor at the Pontificia Universidad Católica de Ecuador (PUCE), and consultant to FTPP and the FAO. He has worked in participatory research and communication with first- and second-tier peasant and indigenous organizations.

Bret Gustafson is a Fellow at the Center for Cultural Survival and a Ph.D. candidate in Anthropology at Harvard University.

The People Give Chavez a Mandate

After the resounding victory by the Polo Patriótico in the elections for the Constituent Assembly on Sunday, Polo leaders and President Chavez began reassessing their strategy, as their overwhelming victory suggested a change. Chief among the new strategy appeared to be a change in heart over the dissolution of Congress and the Supreme Court. Given the complete domination of the Assembly by the Polo, it was deemed unnecessary to create a confrontation given that more elegant solutions exist, such as the election of a new Congress and Court within the new Constitution, which could now be done without any opposition. While the issue is not yet resolved at the time of the writing of this report, this appeared to be the President's inclination. This position was reinforced by some of the most sensible statements made by any Government official of the Chavez Government, when Minister of Finance Rojas warned that the dissolution of established powers would create a serious obstacle to the country's plans to issue new debt in the second half of the year. President Chavez himself tried to be conciliatory on Sunday, but on Wednesday said Congress and the Court would not be dissolved as long as they did not interfere with the Assembly.

The landslide victory is seen as having both positive and negative aspects. On the positive side, President Chavez received a very strong mandate that will require him to deliver on many of his promises. Additionally, the overwhelming majority by the Polo Patriótico should make the process much more efficient as the discussion will be limited as long as the Polo's heterogeneous forces do not deviate from the President's agenda. The much-dreaded discussion of what would be considered a majority for the approval of the Constitution or the rules of order for debate will certainly be avoided. Finally, if the Assembly is presided by the more sensible personalities of the Polo Patriótico, such as Luis Miquilena, then the new Constitution might even be reasonable.

On the negative side, the same overwhelming control of the Assembly by the Polo increases the risk that the new Constitution might contain undesirable elements. The various groups in the Polo Patriótico have different plans for the new Constitution. While the President is in control, he will have to negotiate and yield on some issues. Some of the more radical members of the President's coalitions have already begun to talk about their ideas, such as the inclusion in the Constitution of what the country's economic framework should be and the creation of the "moral power", whatever that may mean.

The President himself has said that he will introduce a preliminary version of the new Constitution to the Assembly as soon as it is installed. The draft that has been circulated appears reasonable, but lacks the detail where concerns may be raised. Thus, markets will have to wait until the actual process of writing the new Constitution gets under way to gauge whether the more radical groups of the Polo Patriótico will have or not an influence on the final document.

In general, we feel about this in the same way that we feel about President Chavez and his current Cabinet. The President so far has been aggressive on words but moderate on action, but his current Cabinet gives us little hope that a reasonable economic program will be proposed. The same goes for the new Constitution, while the President and his closest advisers will push for a more moderate document, we suspect the radical forces in the Polo will not want to miss the possibility to push the country to the left, in the way they have dreamt for many decades. But even the more moderate scenario is worrisome; clearly President Chavez would like to increase the militarization of the country, a trend with which we can't possibly sympathize. Given an increased level of militarization with the landslide victory on Sunday, President Chavez has now acquired an inordinate amount of power in a country where the President has traditionally concentrated too much power in his hands. Only the decentralization process stands on the way of the President's total control of power, one should thus watch any attempt to weaken such a process within the new Constitution.

Given the success of the election for the Constituent Assembly, we expect it to redefine Congress sufficiently to require a new Congressional election late this year or early in the year 2000. Redefining the federal structure of the country, in order to elect new Governors, would be much more difficult, but can not be ruled out given the total control of the Assembly by the President.

Finally, the President's mandate is so strong that he has lost his best target, the old, corrupt political system. Oil prices will be the best and worse of the President's allies. If prices remain strong, he should be able to contain the deterioration of the economy, if prices go down it is unlikely that a continued contraction of the economy can take place without an erosion in the President's popularity. In any case, at some point down the line the electorate will ask the President to deliver on his many promises to magically improve their purchasing power and eradicate corruption in the country. He has yet to start working on any of the two.

When 56% equals 96%

It is somewhat embarrassing for analysts (including us) when we are so far off in our predictions, as was the case of the election for the Constituent Assembly. The truth is that while we all appreciated the complexity of the election process, what we did not understand was the fact that it could lead to such control of the Assembly with a reduced number of votes. Indeed, a close study of the election results shows that the Polo Patriótico managed to obtain total control of the Assembly with approximately 56.0% of the total number of possible votes. With 98.2% of the votes counted, a total of 5,003,741 voters participated in last Sunday's election, which implies an abstention of 53.62%. Each of the voters had up to ten choices at the national level or 50,037,410 votes. The Polo Patriótico candidates obtained a total of 28,010,223 votes, giving them 56.0% of the total number possible (We had predicted 55.3). Thus, it appears if the Polo Patriótico might even have given up some positions, as they might have obtained one more delegate to the Assembly, had they fielded 24 candidates.

There is no question that the Polo Patriótico executed its strategy extremely well. First of all, they mobilized their hard-core vote by providing transportation where it was required. Second, their advertising campaign to promote the voters to cast their ballot for their full slate completely overwhelmed the campaign by independent candidates, since the opposition made no concerted effort to campaign against the Polo. By limiting the number of their candidates to the number of positions, except at the national level, the Polo was able to concentrate their votes, while the opposition completely diluted itself. To top it all off, abstention in classes A and B of the population was extremely high, with some of the residential areas of Caracas registering as much as 65% abstention.

Some of the details of the final results are quite interesting. Former President Carlos Andrés Perez, who was elected easily to the Senate in November, not only did not qualify in the top four spots in his native state of Tachira, but he would have required twice the number of votes to become a delegate. Former Presidential candidate Claudio Fermín received 1.35 million votes to become the top vote getter among independent candidates. MAS President Felipe Mujica, who ran outside the Polo when he was excluded from the official slate, barely managed to obtain 15% of the votes obtained by MAS Secretary General Leopoldo Puchi who is probably less well known. In states where the machinery of the opposition was supposed to rule over the Polo Patriótico such as Carabobo, Miranda, Monagas and Apure, the Polo obtained all of the delegates. Even the Polo had expected to [win] no more than half of the delegates in these states. Finally, the Polo Patriótico actually received fewer votes than the opposition in a total of eight states.

Thus a new chapter of Venezuela's electoral history was written at this election. Given the success of the Polo's strategy we expect them to promote a similar scheme for future elections, the question is whether the opposition will repeat its misstep or will it try to get organized next time.

The Cat and the Mouse

Venezuela's old political guard got its second burial on Sunday, June 25th. Chavez, who had been playing with this dead mouse throughout his campaign (i.e. his tenure so far) exhumed AD's and Copei's bodies from the ground, held them high for people to see, beat them up, and pronounced them dead, again. The President proved that even though you only die once, you can have a long funeral and certainly, many burials.

The beauty of Chavez' plan (the political plan) is that he created confrontation, and stirred interest in the Constituent process, by picking on defenseless enemies. Nonetheless, on last Wednesday's speech, President Chavez revealed how he plans to strike the 'real' opposition. Not Congress, not the Supreme Court, nor the independents, but the governors. Decentralized power appears to be the only standing obstacle between Chavez and total concentration of power, particularly considering Chavez' plans to reorganize the territorial distribution of the country.

Aiming to have it his way, Chavez has proposed two things to the yet-to-be installed Assembly. First, Chavez invited the Assembly to draft a new constitution in three months, instead of the six that were originally approved, giving it only enough time to consider Chavez' unique, and Bolivar-inspired, proposal. And second, Chavez placed his post at the Assembly's will, in a menacing ploy that seeks to invite all other elected public servants to do the same.

Herein is likely to lay Chavez' first hunting trap. The Assembly, as per the Polo Patriótico's view, is of original nature, meaning that it wields absolute power. By placing their posts at the Assembly's will, the Polo Patriótico members would just be showing their respect for the Assembly that Chavez appears to dominate in full. Chavez might pressure the Assembly to call for a broad ratification of public servants if constituted powers fall out of line over the next three months.

The second hunting trap is the one that we deem most dangerous. We believe that the Assembly, as per Chavez' disposition, will call for general elections after the new Constitution is approved. If recent history serves as a guide, and if the new territorial arrangement is approved, governor elections are likely to be swept by the Polo Patriótco, doing away with the last stronghold of power different from Chavez in the country.

We fear that further concentration of power will lead to excess. This latest round of cat and mouse might prove more interesting than the last. Lacking strength, the mouse must outsmart the cat if it wants to live. AD and Copei proved dumb mice, will the governors?

What now for the markets?

The news that the Polo Patriótico is reconsidering its threat to dissolve both Congress and the Supreme Court might be the most positive development of the last week for Venezuelan markets. We had considered this possibility to be the darkest cloud in the horizon. While the decision has yet to be made, all indications at this time are that it will not happen as long as Congress and the Court keep a low profile and do not interfere with the Assembly. While we are sure that Congress is willing to go about its business without conflicts, we can not be certain about the position of the Supreme Court. The Court and its President have repeatedly said that the Assembly is a derivation of Constituted power. While Chavez keeps saying that, the argument may prove to be simply academic if the decision of the Assembly does not threaten any of the Constituted powers in the end.

Given this scenario, there is room for some upside in the equity markets if, as expected, Luis Miquilena is named to preside the Assembly. This would indicate a moderate stance on the part of the President, which should be reflected on the new Constitution. In addition to this, rumors began circulating again this week that President Chavez has begun contacting prominent economists in an effort to do something about the economy. Since equity prices are cheap, only the debit tax seems to stand on the way of a strong rally if deliberations by the Assembly are reasonable. Our top picks in the equity market are Sivensa, Electricidad de Caracas, Manpa, Fondo de Valores Inmobiliarios, Vencemos and Mercantil Servicios Financieros.

Debt markets have not been affected by the noise of last Sunday's election as strong oil prices reaffirm the country's ability to fulfill its obligations. A moderate rally may happen as the Assembly develops. Some members of the Assembly have begun making suggestions that may unnerve the markets, the only question at this time is whether the President will manage to quiet dissenting forces. Only time will tell.

For more information call: Miguel Octavo, Ricardo Larrazabal, José Roberto Vázquez or Allan Brewer
Phone: (582) 207.2511

Article 17   *The Christian Science Monitor*, August 30, 1999

Venezuela's democracy teeters

There are likely to be more confrontations like last week's between 'old' and 'new' powers.

By Howard LaFranchi
Staff writer of The Chritian Science Monitor

CARACAS, VENEZUELA—Before Hugo Chavez was elected Venezuela's president last December, he promised to clean out the country's Congress, gut and reform the judicial system, and deliver a new constitution.

Since taking office in February, Mr. Chavez has been true to his word, supporters say. But to his critics, the former army colonel and failed coup leader is rapidly dismantling one of Latin America's oldest democracies.

The nation is in the midst of a constitutional crisis that erupted last week as the newly elected 131-member constitutional assembly stripped the sitting Congress of most of its power. A day earlier, the president of the Supreme Court resigned in protest of what she called lost judicial independence. On Friday, the National Guard used water cannons and tear gas to stop members of Congress from reconvening in defiance of the constitutional assembly's actions.

One tactic the Congress may use is to withhold funding from the new assembly and refuse to approve presidential trips abroad. But some assembly members planned to meet yesterday and revoke all of Congress's remaining powers and declare an "executive emergency."

With two branches of Venezuela's democracy teetering, the United States and other nations are expressing concern about the changes under way. But for many Venezuelans, who continue to overwhelmingly support the red-bereted Chavez, what is happening here is democracy at work.

"The president is doing what he promised in his campaign and what we elected him to do, so how is that antidemocratic?" asks Anibal Silva, a watchmaker who lost his job five years ago in Venezuela's economic slump.

"There aren't many Venezuelans who don't agree that Congress and the courts are filthy and corrupt," he adds.

Some observers say events in Venezuela serve as a warning of what can happen when democracies, even when relatively mature and established, fail to demonstrate that they operate for the common good. When powers like the legislative branch or the judiciary are perceived to be corrupt and only serving the interests of a few, the voting public not only might fail to

> **'The president is doing . . . what we elected him to do, so how is that antidemocratic?'**
> —Aníbal Silva, watchmaker

react when those powers are threatened—but might also encourage their downfall.

Ask almost any Venezuelan if Chavez's failed 1992 coup is succeeding in 1999, and you are likely to get an answer that plays like a broken record: The traditional political parties that have ruled the country since democracy was reestablished in 1958 are responsible for turning the world's third-largest oil exporter into a nation of paupers while keeping the wealth for themselves.

"The only way to achieve the reform Venezuelans want is to get the Congress out of the way, because with so many personal interests at stake [members of Congress] would be acting at every turn to sabotage the process," says Luis Centeno, a civil lawyer here. "The success of one side means the demise of the other, so it's unreasonable to think some kind of cohabitation could work."

To what extent Venezuela's four-decade-old democracy is actually threatened remains open to debate. In a televised speech last Thursday, Chavez called the reform process "the liveliest of the century," and he insisted that rather than dying, "democracy is being born." But his remarks failed to match those of Supreme Court President Cecilia Sosa, who resigned Tuesday.

THE new assembly is expected to try half of the country's judicial officials for corruption. Lamenting what she called the "disintegration" of "the last control on constitutionality and legality," Ms. Sosa concluded: "The court simply committed suicide to avoid being assassinated. The result is the same—it is dead."

Those words acted like a wakeup call to members of Congress, who had earlier voted themselves a long recess into October to make way for the constitutional assembly. After the assembly on Wednesday declared a state of emergency, opposition members of Congress tried on Friday to convene and challenge the assembly's actions.

The result outside the historic white capital in central Caracas was a tense shoving match between Chavez supporters and congressional advocates. Chavez called the confrontation a "macabre show" designed to sully Venezuela's reputation.

The streets around the capital were quiet yesterday, while leaders from the assembly and the congressional opposition searched for a way out of the impasse. But the coming months before the assembly delivers a new constitution early next year are likely to include more confrontations between "old" and "new" powers, observers here say.

"It's a good thing to pull out a decaying molar, but it's going to hurt," says Adolfo Salguiero, a lawyer and political columnist for "El Universal," a Caracas daily. "In the same way, an institutional reform that reaches to the roots is going to hurt some people's interests, and some of them are going to react."

Still, Mr. Salguciro—who describes himself as "hardly a friend of the government"—acknowledges that an ample percentage of the population supports the Chavez "peaceful social revolution." And while he agrees with analysts who call the assembly's actions "tampering with the judiciary," he says he's not sure how reforms the voters have demanded could be accomplished otherwise.

What bothers Salgueiro is the threat of a concentration of powers implicit in the assembly's actions, and the repeated contradictions from within the Chavez government. The group including Chavez says the reforms can be carried out while upholding democratic principles. But another group from Venezuela's old extreme left would be in favor of suspending democratic guarantees if that proved necessary to complete the reform. "So far the more democratic-minded are leading the process," he says, "but that could change."

Article 18

Focus, Winter 1997

Sun, Fun & a Rum Deal: Perspectives on Development in the Commonwealth Caribbean

Robert B. Potter and Sally Lloyd-Evans

European and North American perceptions of the Caribbean Sea and its many islands seem to revolve around the "sun, fun and rum" equation at best, or "sand, sea and sex" at worst. This is not surprising given the promotion of the Caribbean as a major holiday destination by tour operators, the media, international agencies and national governments alike. Such an image is reinforced by advertisements and publication of a quarterly lifestyle magazine under the title *Caribbean World,* which provides articles on these "seductive" islands, the visits of the rich and famous, and fashion tips for the beach.

Other views of the region are dominated by images of the exotic, and as geographer David Lowenthal stressed in his book *West Indian Societies* (1972), there is the false homog-

TABLE 1

Gross Domestic Product Per Capita and Urban Development in the Caribbean
(Caribbean Members of the British Commonwealth)

Country	Gross Domestic Product per Capita $US 1991*	Percentage of Total Population Urban 1990**	Percentage Growth of Urban Population per annum 1990–95 (estimated)**
Anguilla	6,778	—	—
Antigua/Barbuda	6,591	30.8	2.9
Bahamas	—	57.5	2.14
Barbados	6,572	42.2	2.12
British Virgin Islands	10,479	—	—
Cayman Islands	28,270	100.00	1.27
Dominica	2,491	—	—
Grenada	2,319	—	—
Jamaica	1,442	49.4	2.55
Montserrat	5,387	11.5	3.34
St. Kitts and Nevis	3,974	45.0	2.81
St. Lucia	2,730	43.8	2.67
St. Vincent and the Grenadines	2,630	18.4	3.90
Trinidad and Tobago	4,266	63.9	2.56
Turks and Caicos	5,975	48.2	2.53
Guyana	454	32.2	3.24

Sources: * Caribbean Development Bank, 1992; ** United Nations, 1990.

enization which is born of a unified cricket team, and a sea parading as a landmass. The vibrant culture of the Caribbean, as portrayed through its music, evokes images of a carefree, fun-loving society, but the reality is somewhat different. Beneath a contemporary surface shaped by the dictates of international tourism, the realities of political struggle, oppression and the daily round of poverty are all too clear to see.

Although the wider Caribbean region is home to 35 million residents, it is also the vacation playground for over eight million North American and European tourists a year, accounting for an estimated three percent of total world tourism. The majority of tourists are attracted by the promise of a brief visit to paradise, where their every need will be catered to in secluded luxury resorts. Only a minority of visitors venture out of this contrived environment to observe the reality of the lives of the people who serve them rum punch with a smile. Fewer still are witness to the underlying cultural, economic and societal complexities which make each island unique in detail, while at the same time sharing many common features and challenges. The Caribbean is seen by many as lacking its own unique cultural identity, and as not possessing a coherent self-image. A parallel economic view suggests that the Caribbean should become a series of service stations for tourism, export processing, and offshore (tax-avoiding) banking.

The Caribbean region has always been highly fractioned and is culturally pluralistic, home to many ethnic and cultural groups (see box, "Caribbean History in Brief"). This diversity belies the common heritage that colonial development imposed, making the present day Caribbean a European creation. According to the acclaimed Trinidad writer V. S. Naipaul, the Caribbean can be described as Europe's "Other Sea," the Mediterranean of the New World. Indeed, the Caribbean was one of the regions which economist Andre Gunder Frank specifically cited in outlining his ideas on dependency theory, in which he argued that the longer a developing country was part of the European economic system, the more underdeveloped it would become. From a cultural point of view, the writer C. L. R. James made a similar point when he wrote of a Caribbean still in the process of being born.

Colonial cultures tend to be hybrid-syncretic, that is, admixtures of diverse elements. This is the result of centuries of cultural penetration, control and manipulation by outsiders. In the Caribbean, these outside-imposed forces were extreme and resulted in a high level of westernization, evident today in the areas of cricket, literature, and ideology. Politically, for the majority of the islands in the decades since gaining independence from their European rulers, governments have generally been led by center-right political parties. In this respect, the islands can be seen as capitalist states, peripheral to the US/European capitalist core. Culturally, though, the Caribbean is a product of an amazingly complex mixture of European, African, Asian and American influences, representing one of the true socio-cultural melting pots of the world.

The following pages present the reader with an examination of socio-economic change in the region, together with the common bonds and differences that characterize the Caribbean islands. We suggest that the region is open to misrepresentation by outsiders, and we identify the importance of basic needs in the wake of this, the western hemisphere's longest history of slavery and colonialism, in the Caribbean Sea. Although our discussion focuses on the Commonwealth Caribbean—those islands once or still under British rule and influence—the maps and tables include all significant Caribbean islands.

The basic characteristics of Caribbean states: commonalities and diversity in development

In addition to the historical bonds of slavery and colonialism, the second major commonality shared by Caribbean states is poverty: by world standards, the Caribbean islands are poor. Within the Commonwealth Caribbean, the Windward Islands, including St. Lucia, St. Vincent and the Grenadines, Grenada and Dominica, are generally regarded as being the poorest. In a global context however, Haiti ranks as one of the poorest countries in the world. These facts can be seen in the data shown graphically on the map. In the early 1990s, the Gross Domestic Product (GDP) per capita of the Windward Islands stood somewhere between US $2,300 and 2,700 as shown in Table 1, "Gross Domestic Product and Urban Development." In much of the region, rural households still lack electricity, and a large proportion of the population is living without access to the basic needs of adequate shelter, health-care and employment.

Although difficult to estimate, unemployment in Caribbean countries currently ranges from 20 to 50 percent of the male workforce, and is much higher among women and the young. The jobs that are available, such as those in the tourist industry, tend to pay wages insufficient to support a family. Women who assemble electronic goods for export, or who labor on plantation estates, for example, typically earn less than US $5 a day. As a result most households rely on multiple-income earning strategies in order to, as they say in the region, "make do." Others are forced to earn a living by whatever means possible within the informal—small-scale and unregulated—sector of the local economy.

The Caribbean's struggle has been dominated by the fact that the islands entered the world economy, not as independent communities, but as plantation economies, similar to the situation that prevailed in the American South before the American Civil War (1860–1865). Cash crops such as sugar, bananas and cocoa have been exported since the seventeenth century to serve foreign markets, and this set the pattern, with each island having its own single-crop economy. Control of agriculture by distant landowners led to the neglect of crops for consumption by island residents, a problem which has gotten worse in recent years. The economies of the Windward Islands, for example, rely on the export of bananas through multinational distributors such as Geest Ltd. Cash crop exports make up between 60 and 85 percent of the area's total exports and account for between 20 and 40 percent of its GDP. Without the capacity to feed themselves, the islands are heavily dependent on imports, particularly of food. For the Windwards, data show that the total value of imports is approximately two times greater than the value of exports. In 1973 economist Norman Girvan observed that Caribbean nations produce what they consume (producing bananas, sugar and coconuts and consuming all manner of foods and consumer goods).

Industry is in its infancy on most islands, currently accounting for less than 10 percent of Caribbean GDP. One exception to this is Trinidad and Tobago, industrially more advanced because of its role as an oil producer. Tourism has been one of the few growth industries in the Caribbean, and for many has become the main source of hard currency earnings, account for 50 to 70 percent of the area's foreign exchange earnings. As the main source of hard currency for Jamaica, tourist spending there has exceeded US $400 million annually since 1985. Other smaller islands have become even more dependent; for example, a quarter of the labor force in Antigua-Barbuda is employed in tourism. As is the case with agriculture, foreign investment dominates the tourism industry; over half the hotels of both Barbados and Jamaica are in foreign hands. Much of the money spent by tourists leaves the Caribbean—it is not reinvested locally. In addition to the profits flowing back to North American and European interests, the social effect in the islands has been the creation of predominantly white, rich enclaves, set within an overall background of poverty.

Even with careful consideration, it is unlikely that tourism, heralded as the current development strategy, will make any significant contribution to improving the basic needs of the majority of the population. Much evidence exists to show how the flow of workers to the tourist sector dampens the availability of labor for farming, and as a result may lead directly to the abandonment of farmland. This clear antipathy between agriculture and tourism in the minds of Caribbean residents is starkly apparent in a wide variety of contexts.

In Grenada, external debt amounted to US $69.4 million in 1989, almost half of that nation's Gross National Product (GNP); and in St. Vincent it amounted to 38 percent of GNP. Jamaica, which has experienced the greatest problems associated with international debt and International Monetary Fund (IMF) restructuring policies, has a total external debt of US $3,569 million, a figure which is 141.2 percent of its GNP. In other words, the country owes one-and-a-half times as much as it makes. The twin-island state of Trinidad and Tobago is following the path of Jamaica with its current level of debt accounting for 54 percent of GNP. During the 1980s, Caribbean economies became weaker and more vulnerable to fluctuations in the international arena, as well as to natural disasters. Caribbean citizens are now poorer in relative terms than they were in 1980. A 1991 report from the U.S. Agency for International Development (USAID) recorded that widespread malnutrition, illiteracy, deficient educational, training and health conditions, and inadequate housing all threaten to erode the foundations of the Caribbean, and limit prospects for growth in the long term.

Contemporary patterns of production and economic change in the Caribbean

Since independence, Commonwealth Caribbean states have followed a passive path toward development. The smaller islands of the eastern Caribbean have unquestioningly adopted the same policies as their larger More Developed Country (MDC) neighbors such as Jamaica, Trinidad/Tobago and Barbados: an evolutionary, not revolutionary, development strategy.

Thus, despite a lot of talk about the need for greater self-sufficiency and the better use of domestic resources, very little has actually been accomplished. It is far easier to plan for new hotels than it is to meet basic needs, which would require income and land redistribution, together with growth. As long as Caribbean countries remain dependent on the outside world, due to debt repayments and high levels of imports, the region has little chance of acting on a radical program for basic needs. That would require a complete overhaul of present economic and social systems. Instead, international attention is focused on "assisting" the islands in their debt repayments by providing strategies for economic growth. Structural adjustment programs imposed by the World Bank and International Monetary Fund have led to reduced public employment and social spending, and deregulation. These developments have adversely affected the poor and benefited the rich. Grenada and Cuba, however, stand as notable exceptions, both countries having followed paths towards self-reliance and self-sufficiency.

In the 1970s, outside experts from the World Bank advocated crop agricultural diversification—more varied crops—as the region's best hope for economic growth. Also actively promoted during this era were the abundance of cheap labor, particularly among young women, and the growth of export processing zones—producing goods cheaply for overseas markets. Since 1990 tourism appears to have become the favorite approach, giving little consideration to the vulnerability of the human and natural ecosystems of these islands. The government of Trinidad and Tobago is being encouraged to sell large coastal strips of Tobago to foreign hotel chains in order to improve the economy. It may not be long before southern Tobago starts to resemble St. Lawrence Gap in Barbados, or Grand Anse Beach in Grenada, overdeveloped and commercialized. The Jalousie Plantation near the twin volcanic Pitons in St. Lucia was sold to Lord Glenconner (also known as Colin Tennant) in 1989, and his development of a 320-acre luxury resort and watersports complex was permitted, despite vociferous environmental outcry. In the eyes of many, Barbados has come to exemplify the development of tourism without a clear environmental balance sheet being maintained.

As a corollary of these internationally oriented policies, relatively little attention has been given to agriculture for domestic purposes. The 300-year-old plantation system, associated with persistent poverty and psychological dependency, still dominates today through export of a few staple crops. The decline of plantation-produced sugar and the introduction of the replacement staple, banana, has given rise to a number of land redistribution plans in St. Vincent and St. Lucia. Since the end of slavery well over a century ago, a substantial smallholder farming sector has developed in many islands. Indeed, local small-scale farmers are making significant contributions to the domestic food supply in Trinidad and Jamaica, principally by growing vegetables. In Trinidad, following emancipation, the offering of land to indentured laborers in place of their return passage to India has resulted in a substantial smallscale, informal farming sector. However it is generally recognized that agricultural activity has decreased in the region as a whole, and food imports currently account for around 30 percent of all imports to the region. Around 1990, Trinidad and Tobago and Jamaica each imported approximately 290,000 metric tons of cereals.

Farming has been neglected in favor of light manufacturing partly on the advice of St. Lucia-born, Nobel-prize winning economist Sir Arthur Lewis, involving what he termed indus-trialization by invitation. Lewis argued that Caribbean economies would develop by following a program of industrial modernization, a favorite global model in the 1950s and 1960s. He suggested that governments should attract investment by foreign companies in light manufacturing plants by promoting advantages such as cheap labor. A local model was provided by Barbados and its Operation Beehive, launched in 1969 and partly based on Puerto Rico's earlier Operation Bootstrap. Since that time, many foreign companies have invested in the Caribbean, mainly adding to the growing sector of export processing zones (EPZs) and free trade zones (FTZs), where garments, electrical items, and other goods are assembled in sweatshop-like establishments. A more recent growth area is in the data-processing industry, with major airlines and financial companies relocating to the region. American Airlines, for instance, set up a data-entry operation in Barbados as early as 1984 and this is now a wholly-owned subsidiary company, Caribbean Data Services Inc. There are currently five data entry firms operating on the Harbour Industrial Estate. There are 25 such firms operating in Jamaica, although many are locally owned. Approximately 90 percent of the employees are women.

The benefits accrued from these developments are difficult to interpret and depend on the observer's economic and political persuasions. The World Bank, on the one hand, states that EPZs will create large numbers of much-needed jobs in the region, and provide additional sources of foreign exchange. The World Bank also argues that such developments will increase urban productivity, and points to the economic success

---

TABLE 2

Average Wage Rates in Selected Countries, Including Caribbean States

Country	Average Wage Rate in US$ Per Hour
Antigua and Barbuda	1.25
Barbados	1.20–2.50
China	0.13
Costa Rica	1.20
Dominica	0.70
Dominican Republic	0.50
Grenada	0.73
Hong Kong	0.80
Malaysia	0.50
Montserrat	1.00
St. Kitts and Nevis	1.00
St. Lucia	0.75
St. Vincent and the Grenadines	0.93
Sri Lanka	0.20
Thailand	0.30

Source: Wen, Y-K and J. Sengupta. 1991 (eds). *Increasing the International Competitiveness of Exports from Caribbean Countries.* Washington, D.C.: World Bank.

of the Asian Tigers such as Hong Kong or Taiwan, or Newly Industrializing Countries, which include Brazil and Mexico. However, it is notable that average wage rates are much lower in Asia, as shown by the World Bank data in Table 2, "Average Wage Rates in Selected Countries."

Another argument is that EPZs have simply replaced sugar as the means of perpetuating development by external control of an island's resources and money. According to this viewpoint, putting together a data processing and manufacturing industry may cost more in subsidies and foregone taxes than in gains. In many cases, EPZ investors are exempt from paying import duties, and are free to remove their profits from host countries. Secondly, this kind of industry favors the employment of young, single women who earn low wages. Anthropologist Carla Freeman has recently referred to this as "high tech in high heels." These jobs do not create the increased purchasing power that an island's economy requires, nor the substantial number of jobs needed. Many women work 10 hours days in cramped and unhealthy conditions performing repetitive tasks. It is well documented that the conditions under which these women toil are reminiscent of earlier forms of colonialism. In 1990, it was estimated that some 20,000 women worked in 750 garment factories in the English-speaking Caribbean, producing mainly for the United States market. These workers earned wages sometimes as low as US $20 per week; a 1988 study revealed weekly wages as low as US $15 in Jamaica. The average worker is a 22-year-old rural migrant who is the sole supporter of two or more children. Over and above her wages she enjoys very little in the way of family benefits or social security. The exploitation of many Caribbean women and the poor social conditions in which they are employed do not represent desirable forms of development, but rather new forms of slavery and servitude.

Multinational corporations promote the interests of elite groups, diverting attention away from the needs of the poor. In a well-documented case, two foreign firms actually persuaded the government of St. Vincent and the Grenadines to break its own minimum wage legislation with a "training rate" at 30 percent less than the minimum statutory wage then in force. Factory workers on St. Lucia hope to acquire skills which will enable them to emigrate to metropolitan countries. Unfortunately for many women the alternative to these low wages is unemployment. Development policies aimed at meeting basic needs must consider women, who have all too often been excluded from the development process. Within the Caribbean, it is women who hold society together, with a full-time job in addition to having the responsibility for their family's well-being. Edith Clark's 1976 book, *My Mother Who Fathered Me,* reflects this issue in her autobiographical story that takes place on Jamaica.

Increasing outside control and globalization (the internationalization of economic activities and cultures) can also be seen in the other growth sector of the economy, tourism. As much as 70 percent of all tourist expenditure in the Caribbean leaves the islands for the foreign bank accounts of hotel owners. The environmental impacts of tourism are only now being made part of the costs/benefits equation. In Barbados, it has been estimated that 80 percent or more of the coral reefs off the west coast are dead. On the main coastal road, the view is blocked by condos and resort hotels. The governments of the smaller islands such as Dominica and St. Vincent want to encourage more ecologically sensitive and sustainable forms of tourism development and much is hoped of ecotourism in promoting the natural bounty of countries. Another negative aspect is the impact of tourism upon these fledgling independent cultures: the importation of foreign lifestyles and tastes, the labor requirements for increased servitude, and the expanded presence of prostitution, drugs and crime.

Patterns of consumption and globalization as they relate to the Caribbean

All of these developments can be seen as part of the global process of divergence, in respect of the sphere of production, and the control of capital. Since the 1970s world recession, the locational and production decisions of transnational firms have become increasingly dominant. Just as the tendency toward Fordist (assembly line) production has characterized the Newly Industrializing Countries (NICs), and flexible (small, short-run) systems of production and accumulation in developed countries, so related contrasts are discernible in the Caribbean region. This all boils down to the fact that the places and spaces of the Caribbean are increasingly coming to be highly differentiated between the urban and the rural, the rich and the poor, the developed and the less developed. The following discussion will illuminate this much-reduced summary.

Present-day Caribbean societies are strongly urban in character (see Table 1, "GDP and Urban Development"). These densely-settled areas within farming-oriented countries originated during the mercantile and colonial periods well after the first settlements, which were established along the coasts as points of colonial administration and commercial control.

The growth of densely-settled areas has intensified in the present post-colonial era as tourism and industrialization have taken over from farming. Plantopolis—the settlement pattern that dominated during the era of the plantation system—has given way to the present-day Caribbean metropolis, with its residential and tourist-focused suburbs. By the year 2000, the Caribbean's population will show an overall urbanization level of 64.6 percent, higher than the world as a whole at 51.3 percent. In fact, by 2025 it is predicted that the Caribbean will be almost as highly urbanized as the more developed regions of the world.

As in other world regions, present-day towns and cities in the Caribbean are nodes and centers from which the complex processes of global economic, social and environmental change flow outward to affect the more rural areas. These cities are key agents in globalization, which simultaneously is leading to a global homogenization, yet also to the emergence of growing differences between and within world regions. Tourism and the mass media are influencing the Caribbean in this divided fashion.

Caribbean islanders want what tourists have. This is the so-called "international demonstration effect": locals take up affluent North American and European tastes, lifestyles and patterns of consumption. Is this imitation flattering, or is it neo-dependency, as Caribbean locals abandon their culture for that of Los Angeles, USA or Manchester, England? Workers who would rather aspire to the modern culture brought in by foreign visitors see farming as a low-status and backward occupation. It is likely that people will crave new things in advance of the jobs needed to pay for those things. Given the limited resources available to these small countries, a totally inappropriate level of imitative lifestyle may be taking place. If demand for such goods and services rises faster than their production locally, the result will have to be a rise in imports as well as quick growth in the informal sector of the economy, in order to meet the challenge.

The mass media, television in particular, affect the aspirations of those who watch. Island viewing of such North American soap operas as "Dallas," "Dynasty," "The Young and the Restless" and the appallingly vacuous "Baywatch"—the latter with an estimated weekly global viewing audience of over 2 billion people—may have significant impacts on material, if not spiritual, aspirations. Identifying with, and desiring, the lifestyles portrayed in such serials by those with annual incomes of US $1,300 is likely to be particularly frustrating. The rapid spread of cable television in the Caribbean is intensifying this process. In certain high-income residential areas of Trinidad's Port of Spain, such as Ellerslie Park and West Moorings, up to 25 percent of households now have cable television. The 1990 Census for Barbados showed that ownership of television sets is nearly universal, while a surprisingly high proportion of households, even those on low incomes, have a video cassette recorder/player.

Changing too are dietary habits and food preferences, leading to the so-called industrial palate: a larger proportion of food is consumed by non-producers. Of course, this change is closely related to the international demonstration effect and the activities of multinational food companies as witnessed in the ubiquitous spread of fast food chains within the region (as shown in the accompanying photos.) By now most capital cities in the region, even small ones like Kingstown on St. Vincent, have their highstreet Kentucky Fried Chicken (KFC). An interesting exception is offered by Barbados, where after a great deal of debate and controversy, a McDonald's outlet was opened on the south coast in 1990. However, Barbadians have for some time shown a strong preference for white meat as opposed to red, and a little over a year later, the outlet closed down.

These socio-cultural shifts are on a path of convergence with the patterns of consumption found in the rich developed countries. At the same time as divergence characterizes those changes relating to production and ownership of capital, so a pattern of similarity and convergence characterizes demand and consumption. It is the combination of these two sets of forces that helps explain why places around the world are, at one and the same time, becoming more similar, and yet more differentiated.

But of course this process is highly uneven, both in time and space. Good examples are provided by the development of supermarkets, shopping malls and high-status residential areas. Modern Euro-American styles are increasingly popular, side-by-side with the traditional, small-scale neighborhood.

Supermarkets have become an important part of urban and tourist areas on many of the larger Caribbean islands. In Trinidad, for instance, American-style shopping malls attract large numbers of the nation's young to spend an entire day shopping, eating fast foods, and watching large-screen cable television. In particular, West Mall in the suburbs of Port of Spain, and Gulf City located just outside San Fernando, are diffusers of imported American culture to both the young and the wealthy. By contrast, the informal retail sector still provides goods and services to the majority of those in the lower-income communities of eastern Port of Spain. A recent move by the International Monetary Fund to lift all bans on imported goods has served to increase the disparity between the rich and poor in Trinidad.

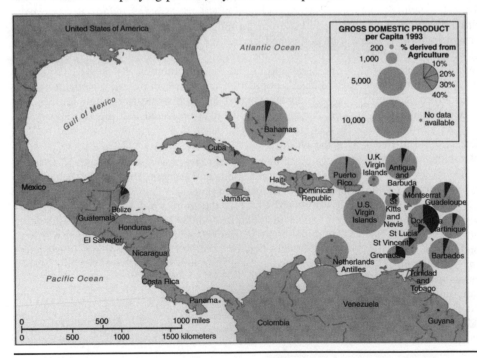

In Barbados, 97 percent of total retail floor space is located within the western and southern coastal urban strip. Ten new retail centers, owned and operated by members of the white business community, have been developed within this urban-suburban tourist zone to provide goods and services for tourists, expatriates and members of local elite groups. In the rural areas, the traditional informal rum shop and grocery remains the main point of retail supply, together with a few superette chains such as Basx, Ricks and Budg-Buy, run by members of the black community. However, multinational capital can be seen adorning the basic rum shop, as shown in the Pepsi-decorated photograph of a small neighborhood shop.

Similarly, while in many parts of the Caribbean modern middle- and upper-class residential areas have been developed, relatively few houses have been provided for those on lower incomes. In

St. Vincent, for example, a substantial number of people live on the upper part of the beach, facing the full fetch of the Atlantic as shown in the photo of Byera. In the Windward Islands, with the exception of St. Lucia where 357 homes were provided during the 1960s, houses built by state agencies were sold at prices only affordable to middle-income residents. Similar situations are found throughout the Caribbean.

These same processes, that together create a widening gap between rich and poor, can be discerned at the wider scale of the development of wedges of high-status housing within cities. These may be seen as basically akin to those envisaged by land economist Homer Hoyt in his sectoral model of urban structure. This has been well-documented in the case of large Latin American cities such as Lima, Caracas and Bogota, and has been graphically represented in a general model of Latin American city structure. There is considerable evidence that within many Caribbean cities, affluent groups are moving out of the central area, forming high-status suburbs, in a basically sectoral or Hoytian-manner. This is true, for example, of the strong suburbanization taking place towards the south-east of Kingston in St. Vincent and the Grenadines. It is also occurring in a northerly and south-easterly direction out of Bridgetown in Barbados. In Trinidad, middle- to high-income groups have moved towards the valleys which lie to the north and north-west, and have also leap-frogged to the eastern extremity of the city, across the large swath of low-income areas in the central and eastern sections.

Conclusions: variety versus uniformity in the Caribbean and elsewhere

It is the juxtaposition of the processes of divergence and convergence that is giving rise to distinctive, locality-based development and change in the contemporary Caribbean, as elsewhere in the developing world. Places are becoming highly varied in terms of their patterns of economic production. And, while a Euro-US pattern of consumption is becoming the norm for the Caribbean as a whole, the participation of different social groups in this process is also highly uneven. The poor remain dependent upon traditional facili-

CARIBBEAN HISTORY IN BRIEF: A Mix of Many Peoples

For at least 3000 years B.P. (Before Present) various peoples, including the Ciboney, Arawak and Carib, migrated across the Caribbean's islands from the South American mainland. By the time of Christopher Columbus' first voyage in 1492, the Caribs were dominant. In 1493 Pope Alexander VI divided the New World between Spain and Portugal, assigning all of the Caribbean to Spain; by 1504 Columbus had made a total of four voyages, naming and claiming most all of the major islands.

However, Carib and Spanish dominance were temporary. From the 16th into the 19th centuries, the Caribbean islands were fought over by, and changed hands among, the Dutch, Danes, Swedes, English, French, Irish, and Spanish. An estimated two to five million Africans were imported as slaves to work the vast sugar plantations, making possible the Triangular Trade. On the first leg of the triangle, ships carrying cloth, whisky, and cheap manufactured goods voyaged from northern Europe and the northeastern U.S. to the west coast of Africa. There, these goods were exchanged for slaves who had been collected for Portuguese and Dutch traders. On the second leg, shiploads of slaves were brought to the Caribbean for sale to the plantation owners. To close the triangle, ships would return to Europe and the Yankee states with loads of sugar, rum and other tropical products.

Although this system built great fortunes for some and an adequate living for many more, an abhorrence for human slavery was also gradually developing. The human cost eventually outweighed the economic benefits and between 1838 and 1886, European countries and the U.S. abolished slavery. Plantation owners partially replaced their black workforce with indentured laborers from India, and some from China. Over the next 100 years, European dominance was eclipsed by three trends: the growth of U.S. power in the region, population movement and communication among the islands as a result of the two world wars, and a compelling desire for independence by those on many islands, from the largest to the very small. Today each island has its own unique mix of skin colors and cultures from Europe, India, China and Africa. Sometimes the ethnic roots of a building type or a particular meal are clearly West African, or Dutch, or French; but often, they have blended to become—Caribbean.

Geographic complexity and confusion

Spatially, the Caribbean consists of three groupings: the islands—tips of submerged mountains—that stretch from Florida to the coast of Venezuela; three nations on the South American mainland south of Venezuela: Guyana, French Guiana and Suriname; and the Central American country of Belize. All share a common history of European colonization, plantation-based economy, slavery, and an Afro-European heritage.

Geographic misunderstanding has led to a confusion of names for the 7000-odd islands and reefs of the region. For example, Columbus believed that he had reached India, naming the people he met Indians. That he had in fact found new continents was soon realized, but the name stuck and spread eventually to include all of the pre-European inhabitants of North, Central, and South America. Geographically the damage was ameliorated by amending the region's name to the West Indies, when the Caribbees, or Caribbean—land of the Caribs—wouldn't suffice. The ramifications of this mistake intensified with the 19th century arrival of indentured workers from India, who became known as East Indians, to differentiate them from the locals.

The complexity does not end there, of course. Some of Columbus' contemporaries believed that he had found a legendary island, Antillia, and so the area also came to be known as the Antilles. The Greater Antilles are the larger islands; the Lesser Antilles are the smaller ones. The Lesser Antilles are further subdivided, according to the requirements of sailing and politics, into the Leeward and Windward Islands. Windward means the direction from which the wind is coming, leeward is the direction toward which it is blowing. The trade winds blow across the islands from an easterly direction. So it was that the northern British-held islands became the Leewards because they lay to leeward of Barbados; and the southern arc of islands became the Windwards because they lay to windward of the Spanish-held mainland. A third group, those islands just off the South American mainland, makes up the rest of the Lesser Antilles.

TABLE 3

CARIBBEAN LANDS; INDEPENDENT AND DEPENDENT

Name	Population in 1996	Political Status
Anguilla	8,000	U.K. dependency
Antigua and Barbuda	100,000	Independent of U.K. in 1981
Bahamas	300,000	Independent of U.K. in 1973
Barbados	300,000	Independent of U.K. in 1966
Belize	200,000	Independent of U.K. in 1981
British Virgin Islands	12,000	U.K. dependency
Cayman Islands	36,000	U.K. dependency
Cuba	11 million	Independent of U.K. in 1902
Dominica	100,000	Independent of U.K. in 1978
Dominican Republic	8.1 million	Independent of Spain in 1844
Guyane (French Guiana)	73,000	French dependency
Grenada	100,000	Independent of U.K. in 1974
Guadeloupe	400,000	French *region*
Guyana	700,000	Independent of U.K. in 1966
Haiti	7.3 million	Independent of France in 1804
Jamaica	2.6 million	Independent of U.K. in 1962
Martinique	400,000	French *region*
Montserrat	100,000	U.K. dependency
Netherlands Antilles	200,000	(Aruba—independent; Bonaire
Puerto Rico	3.8 million	U.S. citizens 1917; U.S. Commonwealth 1952
St. Kitts and Nevis	40,000	Independent of U.K. in 1983
St. Lucia	100,000	Independent of U.K. in 1979
St. Vincent and Grenadines	100,000	Independent of U.K. in 1979
Trinidad and Tobago	1.3 million	Independent of U.K. in 1962
Turks and Caicos	17,000	U.K. dependency
U.S. Virgin Islands	108,000	U.S. terriroty 1917; U.S. citizens 1927

Population data: 1996 *World Population Data Sheet*. Population Reference Bureau, Washington, D.C. popref@prb.org http://www.prb.org/prb/

ties, and members of the elite participate more fully in the up-market, modern and exogenous sectors of the island economy. This process is all too frequently etched in terms of color and gender as well as class.

The path toward development in the small states of the Caribbean remains a hard one. Small states may face many difficulties in reducing their reliance on large metropolitan powers. The use of indigenous resources, requirements and ways of doing things is necessary for real development. A move toward forms of tourism, industrial and other types of development which are more sustainable, and both locally and environmentally sensitive, is of paramount importance. Otherwise, the real position for much of the Caribbean will not be "sun, fun and rum"; rather, it will remain as it has been for centuries: plenty of sun, some fun, and all too frequently, a rum deal.

Acknowledgements

Congratulations on the birth of Sally Lloyd-Evans' son, Sam, who arrived during the final editing of this article.

References and additional reading

Clark, E. 1976. *My Mother Who Fathered Me: A Study of the Family in Selected Communities in Jamaica*. New York: Routledge, Chapman and Hall.

Lowenthal, D. 1972. *West Indian Societies*. London: Oxford University Press.

McAfee, K. 1991. *Storm Signals: Structural Adjustment and Development Alternatives in the Caribbean*. London: Zed Books.

Potter, R. B. 1989 (ed). *Urbanization, Planning and Development in the Caribbean*. London and New York: Mansell Publishers.

Potter, R. B. and D. Conway. 1977 (eds). *Self-Help Housing, the Poor, and the State in the Caribbean*. Knoxville: University of Tennessee Press, and Jamaica, Barbados and Trinidad & Tobago: The University Press of the West Indies.

Thomas, C. Y. 1988. *The Poor and the Powerless: Economic Policy and Change in the Caribbean*. London: Latin American Bureau.

Article 19

The World & I, June 1999

A Failed Revolution

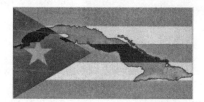

Visitors to Cuba encounter a country suspended in time—the late 1950s.

MARK FALCOFF

Though the causes and consequences of Castro's revolution in Cuba have provoked enduring controversy, one point is above dispute: It was (and is) the most radical upheaval in Latin American history. Indeed, in many ways it is the region's only really "successful" social revolution, in that it alone fully destroyed an entire social order and managed to install a new one.

True, there have been other revolutionary or quasi-revolutionary projects in Latin America in the twentieth century—in Argentina and Chile, in Bolivia, Mexico, and more recently in Nicaragua—but alongside Cuba's they seem pallid and incomplete, and justifiably so. For Cuba alone has abolished private property and utterly liquidated civil society. More than that: Fidel Castro has succeeded where so many other Latin American revolutionary leaders have failed. He has created a regime that depends wholly and completely upon his every will and wish, so much so, indeed, that it is difficult to imagine how his country will fare after he is gone.

Not really a failure

In these narrow terms, then, Cuba's revolution has not been a failure at all. Paradoxically, however, these are not the goals that Castro proposed to his people before or immediately after his seizure of power. Originally, Cubans were promised "bread and freedom—without terror" and, in even more expansive moments, "a standard of living higher than Sweden's."

Once Castro linked Cuba to the fortunes of the Soviet empire, such outcomes were frankly impossible, and consolations were sought elsewhere. The Cuban revolution was to be judged by equality of result at home and "proletarian internationalism" abroad.

That is, Cubans were to enjoy the benefits of a Soviet-style socialist system, which would provide not abundance but free medical care, free education, and free or low-cost housing. Meanwhile, rationing would assure that no one went hungry.

Cuba would also become a different kind of international actor—a "banana republic" no more but rather an important nation with global interests and ambitions, with diplomats, troops, and "security specialists," or at least doctors and teachers, spread across the globe. Above all, Cuba would be independent for the first time—in this case defined as free of U.S. interference in its internal affairs.

For many years, these more modest goals seem to have been attained, and countless foreign visitors—even some as far from communist sympathies as former U.S. Defense Secretary Robert McNamara—have freely praised the island for its "achievements" in health and education. There was some question about the quality of Cuba's health services, or the content of its educational curricula, but apparently nobody could deny the bald figures of literacy, life expectancy, or infant mortality.

Today, however, it is apparent that these things were not the result of a more productive economic and social system but a curious arrangement with its ally and patron, the Soviet Union. Thanks to an accident of geopolitics and ideology, Moscow was led to treat Cuba as a favored client rather than—as in the case of East Germany, Poland, or Czechoslovakia—a colony to be pillaged for raw materials and industrial goods. Whether in the form of preferential prices for Cuban sugar (sometimes at four times that of the world market) or subsidized energy or foodstuffs, it was the generosity of the Soviet Union—not the genius of Fidel Castro—that made Cuba "work."

Stuck in a time warp

Visitors to Cuba today all come back with the same story: a country strangely stuck in a time warp, magically suspended in the late 1950s. For a country that received the equivalent of 10 Marshall Plans (in 1947 dollars) from the Soviet Union, there is surprisingly little to show for it—not even a road system in proper repair. In a way this is logical, because the Soviet economic model that Cuba adopted in 1960–61 was designed to seize and appropriate wealth, not to create it. Thus, despite massive transfers over four decades, Cuba today is poorer than at any time in its "revolutionary" history, indeed perhaps than at any time in the twentieth century.

The depth of Cuba's economic crisis can best be gauged by two crucial changes made over the last decade. The first is legalization of the dollar, which has become the island's virtual currency of choice. As a result, Cuba is now two countries: one with access to greenbacks, the other without. One, by far the smaller of the two, has the living standard of an ordinary Latin American country; its population is limited to government officials, army officers, functionaries of the Communist Party, and those Cubans lucky enough to have relatives abroad. The other—encompassing as much as 80 percent of the Cuban population—has a living standard approaching that of Haiti or one of the sub-Saharan African countries.

The second crucial change is the rapid development of tourism as the island's principal growth industry, particularly since the collapse in the world price of sugar (formerly its leading export) and the deterioration of Cuba's outdated mills and refineries. Since 1991, vast resources have been poured into the tourist sector, thanks to changes in the law permitting joint ventures among European, Canadian, and Latin American companies and Cuban state enterprises, which are controlled by the armed forces.

According to some estimates, the country will gross close to $2 billion this year from foreign visitors. Given the perilous state of the local economy, however, most of the inputs (including food) will have to be imported. Consequently, Cuba will probably net at best $500 million. In effect, tourism may earn enough to shore up the regime and buy the loyalty of the army and police; what it cannot do is replace the Soviet subsidy for the population as a whole, since that would require gross earnings in the neighborhood of $24–30 billion. (Mexico, a country with a far more sophisticated menu of attractions, last year grossed $7.6 billion.)

WIDE WORLD

Making history: After 40 years of fighting the Catholic Church, President Fidel Castro welcomed Pope John Paul II to Cuba in January 1998.

Was the Revolution Compromised?

★ Originally, Cubans were promised bread and freedom—without terror.

★ Castro envisioned a standard of living higher than Sweden's.

★ But once Cuba's fortunes were linked to those of the Soviet empire, such outcomes were impossible, and consolations were sought elsewhere.

★ The mantra became that the revolution was to be judged by equality of result at home and "proletarian internationalism" abroad.

★ For a country that received the equivalent of 10 Marshall Plans (in 1947 dollars) from the Soviet Union, there is surprisingly little to show—not even a road system in proper repair.

Revolutionary 'achievements'

Where does this leave the revolution, then, and its "achievements"? In theory, all Cubans continue to be entitled to any kind of medical attention they require, up to and including sophisticated surgery. Today, however, clinics lack medicine, syringes, bandages, sometimes even electric power. Patients who present themselves for surgery have to bring their own sheets and sometimes some of the elements used in the procedure (which only those lucky enough to have relatives in Miami can do). Surgeons complain about lack of adequate soap with which to wash their hands. Vital replacement parts for machinery used in kidney dialysis are lacking.

Meanwhile, the Cuban government has created an agency called SERVIMED with its own Web page targeted to foreign clients, inviting them to come to the island for medical procedures at a fraction of the price they would pay at home. There are no shortages at SERVIMED, which has the best doctors and offers the most expeditious service. As well it should, since "medical tourism" has become one of the country's leading foreign-exchange earners.

Cuba's vaunted educational system is still in place, but apart from its relentless ideological content, increasingly it is producing graduates whose skills are not marketable. With the collapse of the island's economy and the loss of its global reach, employment possibilities for economists, engineers, scientists, and teachers have shrunk, and many now look to the burgeoning tourist sector, where salaries and tips are earned in dollars, as their only hope. A popular Cuban joke has it that a nuclear physicist ended up in an insane asylum, his diagnosis: delusions of grandeur. The reason? He claimed to be a hotel clerk! Visitors to the island report, in fact, that the maxi-

JOHN HARRINGTON/THE WORLD & I

Going nowhere fast: Except for revolutionary slogans, Cuba has not changed in 40 years.

mum aspiration of many young people in Cuba is to be either a tourist or a foreigner.

The revolution's telling impact has been felt in the most basic area, the food supply. In 1958, Cuba's population was one of the best-fed in Latin America, with the average daily per capita consumption of calories (2,730) just behind those of Argentina (3,100) and Uruguay (2,960). Today it languishes at about the same level as Haiti and Bolivia, two of the more poorly nourished countries in the hemisphere. The reasons are twofold.

In the first place, the Soviet Union no longer provides imports at subsidized prices. And in the second, Cuban agriculture, socialized along Soviet lines, is hugely unproductive. The country's production of roots and tubers (potatoes, yams) has hardly changed at all since 1958, even though the population has almost doubled. The average per capita annual consumption of rice—the staple of the Cuban diet—has dropped from 53.5 kilograms in 1956 to 36.8 in 1997.

Livestock presents an even gloomier picture: In 1956 the average annual consumption of meat was 62.5 kilograms (97.9 for Havana). Today meat has virtually disappeared from Cuban tables. Not surprisingly, many diseases associated with malnutrition have appeared in Cuba for the first time in modern history, including dengue fever and another exotic ailment that causes blindness.

Castro's Cuba has never provided adequate housing for its people. In this it does not differ from other Latin American governments. Of course, the latter have never claimed that this was their particular obligation. The matter, moreover, is not merely one of a housing deficit; visitors return from Havana remarking upon the dramatic deterioration of the housing stocks Castro inherited. Despite special financial assistance from UNESCO, much of Havana's Old City is literally falling apart, and the only building going on these days is luxury hotels in the tourist ghetto of Varadero—an area restricted to foreigners.

Independence compromised

Even the revolution's other putative achievement—independence from the United States—is now drastically compromised. To be sure, during its three decades of alliance with the Soviet Union, Cuba ceased to depend upon American markets, finance, machinery, equipment, technology, foodstuffs, consumer items, or culture. But since 1991, it has found a new lifeline in remittances from Cubans resident in the United States, variously estimated at between $400 and $800 million a year. And whereas formerly Cuban diplomats bragged that they had successfully circumvented the U.S. trade embargo (We don't need the United States!), today they spend every working hour trying to pressure Washington into lifting it, as if the revolution is somehow incomplete without U.S. recognition.

Meanwhile, Castro continues his anti-U.S. tirades. The walls of Havana and other Cuban cities are covered with huge murals depicting Uncle Sam as a voracious monster, constantly held at bay by small bands of courageous Cubans. A more extreme version of old-fashioned Cuban nationalism has replaced communism as the regime's principal rationale. Over the longer term this may produce a devastating reaction. One distinguished Cuban writer recently observed that a whole generation of Cuban youth may come to associate poverty, repression, and hunger with Castro's ideological banners. "In the future," he suggested, "Cuba may well become not only the most radically capitalist society in Latin America but the most pro-American."

There is probably little need to insist upon the price the Cuban revolution has exacted from the island's people in ordinary civic and human rights, since even Castro's Western apologists are willing to cede the point. Nonetheless, it may not be inappropriate to cite the latest report of Human Rights Watch (1999). Despite Pope John Paul's visit last year, "Cuba's stepped-up prosecutions and harassment of dissidents, along with its refusal to grant amnesty to hundreds of remaining political prisoners or reform its criminal code, marked a disheartening return to heavy-handed repression."

Boxed in at present

Cuba—a country that once boasted 58 daily newspapers and 129 magazines—is today reduced to two or three government organs. Lately the regime has enacted a law making it illegal for independent journalists to practice their trade. A nation that once boasted of a lively and varied (if sometimes troubled) political life now insists upon the rule of a single party. Recently, four dissidents were put on trial for advocating peaceful dialogue and gradual political change.

It is doubtful that such things would justify a revolution that actually "worked" in economic and social terms. But Cuba today must excuse systematic repression by citing "rights" that are recognized for its citizens on paper but unrealized (and unrealizable) in practice.

More serious still, by destroying Cuba's civil society (independent professional organizations, interest groups, political parties) Castro has made certain that the task of reconstruction will be more difficult once he has departed the scene. This point is perhaps the most crucial of all. Without a small business sector, Cuba does not possess the demographic base of a middle class, and by systematically jailing or exiling opponents, Castro is systematically eliminating a future democratic political class.

The purpose, of course, is to create an abyss so wide and deep that Cubans will shrink from any course of political change. In this the dictator has been reasonably successful. Anecdotal evidence suggests that while there is widespread dissatisfaction throughout the island with his rule, many Cubans, particularly older Cubans, cling to Castro for fear of an undefined alternative. But change is coming, whether Castro wills it or not. In this sense the revolution's greatest failure has been to deprive the Cuban people of what they need most today: the capacity to readily face the future.

Mark Falcoff is a resident scholar at the American Enterprise Institute. He is at work on a book on U.S.-Cuban relations.

Article 20

Current History, March 1999

> "The international effort to consolidate democracy and promote development in Haiti following the 1994 intervention has been comprehensive and ambitious ... Ultimately, [however,] the building of democracy and long-term socioeconomic development must be a domestic project driven by Haitian political leaders."

Haiti and the Limits to Nation-Building

JAMES R. MORRELL, RACHEL NEILD, AND HUGH BYRNE

On September 19, 1994, the United States military led an international intervention in Haiti to force out a military junta, restore the elected government of President Jean-Bertrand Aristide, and establish the foundations for democracy and socioeconomic development. For the Clinton administration, the intervention's political stakes were high. The American public was opposed to the use of troops in the aftermath of Somalia, where only a few months earlier, in March, an American humanitarian intervention had ended in the deaths of 18 American soldiers and a hasty withdrawal. And in Congress, conservatives were opposed to any attempt to restore the leftist Aristide.

Long-term prospects for the United States and the broader international community were uncertain. Could the United States carry out the security side of the intervention with limited human and political costs and lay the groundwork for long-term development in Haiti? Could the international community help deepen democracy in a nation that had barely known it; build a democratic state where only a predatory one had existed; and construct a viable economy in the poorest nation in the hemisphere? And could Haitians hold credible elections that winners and losers alike would respect?

In September 1994, the difficulties and challenges were clear. But hopes were nonetheless high that a large-scale se-

curity, humanitarian, and development program could transform the desperately poor Caribbean nation.

Nearly five years later there is little consensus about the success or failure of the international effort in Haiti. The debate has been highly polarized and the results are, at best, mixed. While the time that has passed is not sufficient to make final judgments on long-term development efforts, it is possible to assess progress to date, draw some lessons from Haiti for future international ventures, and point to the steps that could be taken to make improvements that would benefit Haiti's people.

THE INITIAL ASSESSMENT

In important respects, the international action in Haiti was successful. The military intervention was almost flawless. The majority of the 20,000-plus international force withdrew by 1995, and, incrementally, the international military and police presence has declined, leaving a limited UN civilian police mission and a United Nations/Organization of American States human rights mission. The Haitian armed forces have been disbanded and a new civilian police force—the Haitian National Police—has been created. The human rights situation has improved dramatically.

The country experienced its first democratic transfer of power from one elected civilian president to another with the accession of President René Préval in 1996. A series of local, departmental, and national elections was held. And the government has maintained economic stability—bringing down inflation, ensuring fiscal discipline, and taking initial steps to divest state-owned companies that aid donors say could be run more efficiently by the private sector.

JAMES R. MORRELL *is research director of the Center for International Policy in Washington, D.C. He was a member of President Jean-Bertrand Aristide's negotiating team at the Governors Island conference in 1993.* RACHEL NEILD *and* HUGH BYRNE *are senior associates with the Washington Office on Latin America.*

Despite these advances, Haiti's economic and political landscape looks extremely bleak. Real wages fell by 14 percent in 1997 after dropping 17 percent in 1996. The assembly sector, which was to be the engine of growth for the economy, lost 3,500 jobs in 1997.[1] The economy grew by about 1 percent in 1997. Two-thirds of Haitians continue to live in poverty and almost half consume less than 75 percent of the recommended daily caloric intake.

Politically, the enthusiasm that accompanied the election of Aristide as president in 1990 and his restoration in 1994 has evaporated. The fracturing of Lavalas, the grassroots movement that had brought Aristide to power, the inability to hold credible elections, a political impasse between President Préval and the legislature, and the general economic deterioration have demobilized Haitians. For the mass of Haiti's people, democracy has failed.

The international community is enormously frustrated with these developments. The Clinton administration's efforts to break through the political impasse, as well as warnings from leaders of international financial institutions (the World Bank, International Monetary Fund, and Inter-American Development Bank) that funds originally planned for Haiti will go to other nations, have fallen on deaf ears. Three and a half billion dollars committed to Haiti since 1994 has yielded little. What happened? And where does responsibility lie for Haiti's desperate situation? In flawed donor strategies and programs, in Haitian politics and practices, or both?

ORDER WITHOUT LAW

The reform of public security is perhaps the international community's major success. Within weeks of the September 1994 intervention, American and Haitian officials formed an interim public security force comprised of former Haitian armed forces personnel who had been vetted to remove human rights violators. In January 1995 a major effort began to recruit and train a completely new police force. With assistance from the United States, UN, Canada, France, and others, the civilian Haitian National Police (HNP) was created and deployed throughout the country within 18 months.

It is not surprising, given this timetable, that the HNP has suffered from problems that include human rights violations, the emergence of rogue units, some politically motivated arrests, and increasing police corruption linked to the drug trade. Still, Haitian government and police leaders are punishing police abuse and appear committed to creating a professional force.

Haiti today thus has the foundations of a professional and civilian police. A number of factors account for the rapidity and the relative success of the police reform, including the mandate intervention forces were given "to establish a secure and stable environment" yet not to undertake policing tasks themselves, and the Haitian government's reluctance to rely for long on military personnel in the interim public security force. There was also consensus between Haitian and United States officials about the need to create a civilian police force and an extremely high level of involvement from the international community in police reform. The vital Haitian input was

President Préval's appointment of officials with ability and integrity to top HNP positions.

Despite this relatively rosy picture, Haiti's police reform remains fragile. The political crisis generates insecurity and police responses are often perceived as partisan. While current HNP leaders appear committed to ending these problems, there is no guarantee that new police leaders will continue their efforts. International donors remain deeply immersed in police development and provide a further check on problems. But police assistance and the international police presence are shrinking and it remains to be seen whether the HNP can withstand the barrage of political instability, crime, and a dysfunctional judicial system.

The judiciary's dysfunction stems from years of mismanagement, corruption, and distortion. Under the military government, criminal courts in many jurisdictions had not heard cases for three years; the military had also appointed paramilitary cronies as judges and, in 1993, assassinated the minister of justice, Guy Malary.

Despite this desperate situation, judicial reform took a backseat following the intervention. The fear generated by Malary's assassination and the lack of competent successors hamstrung judicial reform. International concerns increased as the HNP was deployed and found itself severely handicapped by the absence of its key partner in law enforcement. The results of donor efforts to date are limited. In September 1997 the National Coalition for Haitian Rights, a nongovernmental organization, noted that the government of Haiti had "failed to set priorities [and] coordinate police, prison and legal reform activities"; that international donors "have often competed for influence over judicial reform rather than coordinating resources; and [that] the consultants hired by the US and other donors . . . have failed to design and implement programs appropriate for Haiti's legal context." Although a judicial reform law was finally passed in mid-1998, it has yet to be implemented.

HUMANITARIAN AID: THE GOOD AND THE BAD

Although the humanitarian element of the international effort in Haiti has been hailed as a great success, it has also been severely criticized. Its two major components were job creation–infrastructure rehabilitation programs and food aid.

A 1998 World Bank study of 10 major job creation–infrastructure rehabilitation programs concluded that they had generated short-term employment through labor intensive public works and had rehabilitated targeted infrastructure; however, the report found that the hoped-for institutional development and long-term durability of the projects were open to question. From 1993 to 1997, $207 million was spent to employ about 500,000 workers for an average of two months; the workers earned a total of approximately $72 (about 30 percent of urban annual GDP, and about 50 percent of rural annual per capita GDP). The projects reportedly attracted farmers away from their fields and reduced agricultural production. It was also claimed that the relatively high wages paid increased labor costs in rural areas and interfered with long-term community development based on volunteer work.

As with the job creation program, food aid addressed the desperate humanitarian needs of many Haitians and helped stabilize the political environment. In 1995 food aid had reached an estimated 1.3 million direct beneficiaries, or 16 percent of the population. Another recent World Bank study found a "clear consensus that food distribution and other relief efforts from 1991–1995 significantly reduced the negative impact of the embargo" (economic sanctions had been imposed on Haiti by the Organization of American States and later the UN following the 1991 coup). But the same study noted that food aid programs can create dependency and shift the production behavior of households; they also create the possibility of market distortions and the danger that lower food prices may reduce incentives for investment.

PUTTING THE ECONOMY BACK TO WORK

Aristide's restoration to power was accompanied by the 1994 Emergency Economic Recovery Program. The program, which was agreed to by international donors and the Haitian government, stressed macroeconomic stability and privatization more than poverty alleviation. (Some critics believe this agreement was forced on Aristide by the international community as a precondition for his return.) By 1996, the emphasis on traditional adjustment-type policies was balanced by a more comprehensive assessment of Haiti's problems and prescriptions for development with a greater focus on the plight of Haiti's desperately poor majority population.

Critics have also accused the international financial institutions of imposing a strict adjustment program with little regard for the country's realities. But these organizations were willing to "lower the bar" for Haiti because of its dire economic situation and the desire to maintain political stability. Significant international funding continued despite the snail's pace of privatization, and donors worked with the Haitian government to develop a mixed-model privatization plan that maintained the state as a key shareholder. But the rule book was not thrown out completely; the international financial institutions were prepared to stop funding in late 1995 when they believed Haiti was unwilling to carry out a real adjustment program.

The element of the international development recipe for Haiti that did not vary from the structural adjustment model was the emphasis on poverty alleviation through growth; a rebuilt assembly sector was to power the process. However, in 1997 the assembly sector provided only 21,500 jobs, far short of the 44,000 available in that sector before the military junta took over in 1991.

A major weakness of the international effort in Haiti was the absence of an effective rural development strategy. The Haitian government itself, however, did not have a comprehensive vision for rural development. Préval launched a small land redistribution program but it failed to address broader policy issues.

Two-thirds of Haiti's people live in the countryside and depend on the land for their livelihood. Yet only 7 percent of international aid ($250 million of the $3.5 billion committed) was destined directly for agriculture (although other assistance also benefited rural areas, such as funds for road-building, health, and education projects). Some donors argued that agriculture in Haiti was not sustainable or ecologically sound. Even if all donors did not share this view, there was no overall strategy for rural Haiti beyond niche areas such as the cultivation of fruit trees and coffee.

The challenge of rural development in Haiti is daunting. Half the country's land is on slopes inclined at more than 40 percent, rendering mechanical farming difficult if not impossible. Nearly 30 percent of farms are in agriculturally marginal areas. Landholdings are small and oriented toward subsistence farming.

These extremely difficult conditions would argue strongly for a strategy of rural development, if only to prevent worsening rural poverty. Without support to peasants to remain on the land and make farming productive (through increased access to credit, technical support, and other inputs), the result must be continued deterioration and increased migration abroad or into Port-au-Prince, where jobs are scarce.

While the shortcomings of the aid program were significant, they are not the reason for the current lack of movement. Considerable aid has been delivered, but internal divisions among Haitian political actors and their debates on privatization and structural adjustment have blocked the rest. At least $300 million in international assistance has been lost or delayed because of the absence of a functioning government or political disputes over structural reforms demanded by the international donors.

THE POLITICS OF NOT COMPROMISING

Haiti's past provided fertile ground for the political deadlock in which the country finds itself. The Haitian state had functioned historically to transfer surplus extracted from the peasantry to an urban elite, and never provided benefits to the population at large. Weak national institutions did not provide an institutional setting that fostered dialogue. Political parties had been the vehicle of powerful and ambitious individuals and were not accountable to the grass roots. And there was little tradition of resolving political differences through dialogue and compromise. Furthermore, Haiti's unique history as home to the only successful slave revolution, and its consequent struggles against hostile colonial and slave-owning powers, have bred a fiercely nationalistic psyche that tends to portray all foreign overtures toward Haiti as colonialist and hostile.

The current impasse was not, however, an inevitable outgrowth of Haiti's history. After the ouster of the dictator Jean-Claude (Baby Doc) Duvalier, Haitian voters overwhelmingly ratified a new constitution in 1987. All sectors of the progressive movement remain pledged to the constitution. Yet, while the constitution has not been overturned, the fracturing of the Lavalas movement has created a crisis that threatens the possibility of progress in Haiti.

During the struggle against dictatorship between 1986 and 1990, Jean-Bertrand Aristide was one brave voice among many calling for a new Haiti—although no Haitian politician had more appeal with the people. When, in mid-1990, military exhaustion and foreign pressure made possible the transformation of the protest movement into an electoral movement, Aristide, the survivor of at least two assassination attempts by the military, became its standard-bearer. The democratic sector political parties, recognizing Aristide's electoral appeal, accepted him as titular head of the political coalition that helped him win the presidency in late 1990. But fissures appeared even in 1991 before Aristide was ousted by the military and during his subsequent three years in exile.

Following Aristide's return to power after the 1994 intervention, the Lavalas movement began to fracture. When the Lavalas Political Organization (OPL)—one of the formal political parties that formed from the movement—won a landslide victory in the June 1995 legislative elections, separately affiliated former colleagues cried foul. The split extended when a sharp debate broke out over the question of whether Aristide should remain president for three more years or step aside to allow presidential elections in December 1995. His most fervent supporters insisted that he should be allowed to make up the years lost in exile. United Stated diplomats strongly warned Aristide against continuing in office unconstitutionally and many other Lavalas leaders agreed, including Gerard Pierre-Charles, general coordinator of the OPL.

Aristide himself never took a public position during this intraparty debate, but he encouraged supporters: "I hear you. If you want three more years, you won't be disappointed." The remark proved prophetic. As his price for withdrawing, Aristide secured the nomination of a loyalist, René Préval, as president; Aristide himself has remained the power behind the throne. Aristide did not publicly support Préval's candidacy until the end of the campaign and under intense American pressure. He apparently wanted to show the Americans, the Haitian bourgeoisie, his political adversaries, and above all the OPL that without him no one could rule. This message has formed the subtext of the last three years of chaotic politics since the December 1995 elections.

The OPL leaders considered the Lavalas movement their common patrimony. As Pierre-Charles said, "Lavalas belongs to no one . . . It is a child of the people. Even if a candidate, a leader in a difficult moment claims paternity, it is the people who have borne Lavalas in their hearts since time immemorial." The rhetoric could not erase Aristide's role as standard-bearer, and it failed to recognize his considerable, albeit diminished, electoral appeal. Aristide considered most of the newly minted OPL members in the legislature to have won on his coattails. In December 1998 he publicly admonished them that "Lavalas won't give free rides anymore."

The greater significance of the "three more years" debate was to reveal that the Haitian government and most of the political spectrum had divided into broad camps increasingly defined as for or against Aristide. The dispute between the two was latent at the beginning of the Préval administration, and would flare up later.

In early 1996, President Préval and the OPL majority in parliament were unable to agree on a candidate for prime minister as required by the constitution. Negotiations were complicated by the fact that a third negotiator, former President Aristide, always had to be included. Finally, Rosny Smarth,

an OPL member and agronomist, and brother of a priest close to Aristide, was approved as prime minister by parliament.

Préval and Smarth displayed an independence during the early months of their administration. Aristide's external dominance appeared less than anticipated and Préval's style appeared pragmatic and energetic. In 1996, a democratic structure began to establish itself.

It was not long before small "popular" groups mounted "general strikes." Few observed them, but they were widely reported by the media. On December 24, 1996, Rosny Smarth declared, "A systematic destabilization offensive has been launched against the constitutional government." Arguing that the country was in danger of becoming uncontrollable, Préval asked Smarth to leave. Smarth said he would never yield to pressure from the streets and survived a motion of censure in parliament. Préval again asked him to resign.

For the mass of Haiti's people, democracy has failed.

The crisis came to a head with the 1997 legislative and regional elections. Voter turnout in the elections that April was only 5 percent. The election mechanics were severely flawed, if not completely fraudulent. The international community divided, with the UN and the Organization of American States rejecting the results; the Clinton administration, still wishing to show progress in Haiti, reluctantly accepted them. On June 9, 1997, Prime Minister Smarth resigned to protest President Préval's handling of the elections, remarking, "In our country, power is a disease." For more than a year the OPL used its slim parliamentary majority to block any prime ministerial nominee unless Préval agreed to name a new electoral council. The existing council, the OPL argued, was irredeemably biased in favor of Aristide's party, La Fanmi Lavalas (FL). This was a step Préval refused to carry out until July 1998, despite economic stagnation, a growing sense of crisis and insecurity, and a series of high-level visits from United States officials.

Following Préval's nomination of Education Minister Jacques Edouard Alexis as prime minister, tortuous negotiations about the composition of his cabinet continued through the end of 1998. In January 1999, the crisis deepened abruptly when Préval announced that he would not permit parliament to remain in session past January 11, 1999. The January deadline had been set by an electoral law that shortened the term of this parliament from the constitutionally stipulated four years in order to reestablish an electoral calendar (also constitutionally mandated) that had been disrupted by the coup. Préval then announced that he would appoint Alexis as prime minister by presidential decree and hold elections for a new parliament. The OPL and other parties denounced the action as an effort that would overturn the democratic process and give

Préval a free hand to assure an overwhelming FL victory in the elections.

There is wide consensus that the only solution is to hold elections for the entire Chamber of Deputies, a third of the Senate, and many local posts. This political hurdle must be cleared successfully to achieve the political legitimacy without which no government will be able to address Haiti's many economic and social problems.

Where does responsibility lie for Haiti's desperate situation?

THE ELECTORAL CHALLENGE

Unfortunately, Haiti has a poor electoral track record. Even in 1990, arguably Haiti's first credible presidential election, there were massive administrative difficulties and substantial voter intimidation. The more than 1,000 international observers monitoring the presidential and first-round legislative elections dwindled to fewer than 100 for the second legislative round a month later. The chronic difficulty in holding trustworthy elections below the presidential level creates a grave problem under a constitution that deliberately devolves and decentralizes power away from the president.

The 1995 legislative elections were plagued by administrative problems and the perception of electoral council bias in favor of Aristide. After a chaotic second round, voter turnout fell to under 15 percent for a third, make-up round. As was noted, voter turnout for the April 1997 elections was a miserable 5 percent—so low that the failure to count blank ballots as required by the electoral law changed the outcome of two Senate races in favor of Aristide's FL. Only the FL and ultimately Préval accepted the results, leading to the resignation of Smarth and beginning of the present political deadlock.

Despite spending over $50 million on elections for the last 10 years, the international community has failed to establish strong electoral machinery. If Alexis is approved as prime minister, the international community must ensure that the proposed parliamentary elections are thoroughly monitored; only extensive monitoring can lend these elections the credibility needed to prevent further deadlock. Yet even an effort along these lines may not overcome the disillusionment most Haitians have with their political process, or adequately buttress the process against the time-honored tactic of losers who seek to discredit the process itself and delegitimate the winners rather than form a loyal opposition.

A HAITIAN SOLUTION?

The international effort to consolidate democracy and promote development in Haiti following the 1994 intervention has been comprehensive and ambitious. The security component—neutralizing the old forces and creating a new civilian police—created favorable conditions for political and economic development. Humanitarian aid programs provided a bridge to long-term development.

But international aid strategies have lacked a coherent approach to rural development that would offer a viable future to most Haitians. The international financial institutions and bilateral donors have also failed to develop an effective way of dealing with the volatile issue of privatization that might have encouraged investment without exacerbating domestic political conflict. And the demanding electoral calendar the international community established following Aristide's return in 1994 deepened political fissures as parties fought to differentiate themselves and dominate electorally.

International assistance has helped stave off a more disastrous situation, but it has done little to move Haiti to the beginnings of a new era that many hoped to see by now. More participatory processes to develop and implement foreign assistance programs, and more of a public information effort might have allayed some of the problems encountered by the international financial institutions in their efforts.

Until the events of this January, Haiti's political parties had conducted their feuds within constitutional rules. But Préval's decision to bypass parliament threatens the legitimacy of the political process in Haiti. Although a solution to the crisis remains unclear, it is obvious that the organization of free and fair elections in which both winners and losers accept the results poses a tremendous challenge to Haitians and the international community.

Beyond the electoral challenge, the international community has an important and difficult role to play. It must show a willingness to improve development plans where these fall short, and it must work with Haitians to encourage dialogue and compromise—all the while sending a tough bottom-line message that the window of opportunity for obtaining and using international aid is closing.

Ultimately, the building of democracy and long-term socio-economic development must be a domestic project driven by Haitian political leaders. Only if these leaders demonstrate the vision, compelling strategies, and, most important, the ability to compromise politically will international assistance be able to do more than hold back the tide.

Credits

REGIONAL ARTICLES

Page 138 Article 1. This article appeared in *The World & I,* March 1998. Reprinted by permission from *The World & I,* a publication of The Washington Times Corporation. © 1998.

Page 141 Article 2. Reprinted with permission from *Dissent* magazine, Summer 1999, pp. 26-29.

Page 144 Article 3. Reprinted with permission from *Current History* magazine, March 1999. © 1999 by Current History, Inc.

Page 148 Article 4. Reprinted with permission from *Current History* magazine, March 1999. © 1999 by Current History, Inc.

Page 153 Article 5. Reprinted with permission from *Dissent* magazine, Summer 1998, pp. 27-30.

Page 155 Article 6. Reprinted courtesy of Cultural Survival, Inc. (www.cs.org.)

MEXICO

Page 160 Article 7. Originally published in the October 1999 issue of *The Futurist.* Used with permission from The World Future Society, 7910 Woodmont Ave., Suite 450, Bethesda, MD 20814 .wfs.org

Page 165 Article 8. © 1999 by The New York Times Company. Reprinted by permission.

CENTRAL AMERICA

Page 167 Article 9. © 1999, The Chronical of Higher Education. Reprinted with permission.

SOUTH AMERICA

Page 169 Article 10. Reprinted from the *Bolivian Times,* April 29, 1999.

Page 171 Article 11. © 1999 by Kenneth Maxwell and from *The Wilson Quarterly,* Winter 1999.

Page 177 Article 12. © 1998, The Chronical of Higher Education. Reprinted with permission.

Page 178 Article 13. This article appeared in *The World & I,* March 1999. Reprinted by permission from *The World & I,* a publication of The Washington Times Corporation. © 1999.

Page 182 Article 14. Reprinted courtesy of Cultural Survival, Inc. (www.cs.org.)

Page 184 Article 15. Reprinted courtesy of Cultural Survival, Inc.(www.cs.org.)

Page 186 Article 16. From *BBO Weekly Report,* July 30, 1999. BBO Servicios Financieros S.A.C.A. (www.bbo.com.ve)

Page 188 Article 17. This article first appeared in *The Christian Science Monitor* on August 30, 1999 and is reproduced with permission. © 1999 by The Christian Science Publishing Society. All rights reserved.

THE CARIBBEAN

Page 189 Article 18. © 1997 by The American Geographical Society. All rights reserved.

Page 197 Article 19. This article appeared in *The World & I,* June 1999. Reprinted by permission from *The World & I,* a publication of The Washington Times Corporation. © 1999.

Page 201 Article 20. Reprinted with permission from *Current History* magazine, March 1999. © 1999 by Current History, Inc.

Sources for Statistical Reports

U.S. State Department, *Background Notes* (1996–1999).

The World Factbook (1999).

World Statistics in Brief (1999).

World Almanac (1999).

The Statesman's Yearbook (1997–1998).

Demographic Yearbook (1998).

Statistical Yearbook (1999).

World Bank, World Development Report (1997).

Ayers Directory of Publications (1998).

Glossary of Terms and Abbreviations

Agrarian Relating to the land; the cultivation and ownership of land.

Amerindian A general term for any Indian from America.

Andean Pact (Cartagena Agreement) Established on October 16, 1969, to end trade barriers among member nations and to create a common market. Members: Bolivia, Colombia, Ecuador, Peru, and Venezuela.

Antilles A geographical region in the Caribbean made up of the Greater Antilles: Cuba, Hispaniola (Haiti and the Dominican Republic), Jamaica, the Cayman Islands, Puerto Rico, and the Virgin Islands; and the Lesser Antilles: Antigua and Barbuda, Dominica, St. Lucia, St. Vincent and the Grenadines, St. Kitts–Nevis, as well as various French departments and Dutch territories.

Araucanians An Indian people of south-central Chile and adjacent areas of Argentina.

Arawak An Indian people originally found on certain Caribbean islands, who now live chiefly along the coast of Guyana. Also, their language.

Aymara An Indian people and language of Bolivia and Peru.

Bicameral A government made up of two legislative branches.

CACM (Central American Common Market) Established on June 3, 1961, to form a common market in Central America. Members: Costa Rica, El Salvador, Guatemala, and Nicaragua.

Campesino A Spanish word meaning "peasant."

Caudillo Literally, "man on horseback." A term that has come to mean "leader."

Carib An Indian people and their language native to several islands in the Caribbean and some countries in Central America and South America.

CARICOM (Caribbean Community and Common Market) Established on August 1, 1973, to coordinate economic and foreign policies.

CDB (Caribbean Development Bank) Established on October 18, 1969, to promote economic growth and development of member countries in the Caribbean.

The Commonwealth (Originally the British Commonwealth of Nations) An association of nations and dependencies loosely joined by the common tie of having been part of the British Empire.

Compadrazgo The Mexican word meaning "cogodparenthood" or "sponsorship."

Compadres Literally, "friends"; but in Mexico, the term includes neighbors, relatives, fellow migrants, coworkers, and employers.

Contadora Process A Latin American intiative developed by Venezuela, Colombia, Panama, and Mexico to search for a negotiated solution that would secure borders and reduce the foreign military presence in Central America.

Contras A guerrilla army opposed to the Sandinista government of Nicaragua. They were armed and supplied by the United States.

Costeños Coastal dwellers in Central America.

Creole The term has several meanings: a native-born person of European descent or a person of mixed French and black or Spanish and black descent speaking a dialect of French or Spanish.

ECCA (Eastern Caribbean Currency Authority) A regional organization that monitors the integrity of the monetary unit for the area and sets policies for revaluation and devaluation.

ECLA (Economic Commission for Latin America) Established on February 28, 1948, to develop and strengthen economic relations among Latin American countries.

FAO (Food and Agricultural Organization of the United Nations) Established on October 16, 1945, to oversee good nutrition and agricultural development.

FSLN (Frente Sandinista de Liberación Nacionál) Organized in the early 1960s with the object of ousting the Somoza family from its control of Nicaragua. After 1979 it assumed control of the government. The election of Violeta Chamorro in 1990 marked the end of the FSLN.

Fuegians An Indian people of the most southern area of Argentina (Tierra del Fuego).

GATT (General Agreement on Tariffs and Trade) Established on January 1, 1948, to provide international trade and tariff standards.

GDP (Gross Domestic Product) The value of production attributable to the factors of production in a given country, regardless of their ownership. GDP equals GNP minus the product of a country's residents originating in the rest of the world.

GNP (Gross National Product) The sum of the values of all goods and services produced by a country's residents in any given year.

Group of 77 Established in 1964 by 77 developing countries. It functions as a caucus on economic matters for the developing countries.

Guerrilla Any member of a small force of "irregular" soldiers. Generally, guerrilla forces are made up of volunteers who make surprise raids against the incumbent military or political force.

IADB (Inter-American Defense Board) Established in 1942 at Rio de Janeiro to coordinate the efforts of all American countries in World War II. It is now an advisory defense committee on problems of military cooperation for the OAS.

IADB (Inter-American Development Bank) Established in 1959 to help accelerate economic and social development in Latin America.

IBA (International Bauxite Association) Established in 1974 to promote orderly and rational development of the bauxite industry. Membership is worldwide, with a number of Latin American members.

IBRD (International Bank for Reconstruction and Development) Established on December 27, 1945, to make loans to governments at conventional rates of interest for high-priority productive projects. There are many Latin American members.

ICAO (International Civil Aviation Organization) Established on December 7, 1944, to develop techniques of international air navigation and to ensure safe and orderly growth of international civil aviation. Membership is worldwide, with many Latin American members.

ICO (International Coffee Organization) Established in August 1963 to maintain cooperation between coffee producers and to control the world market prices. Membership is worldwide, with a number of Latin American members.

IDA (International Development Association) Established on September 24, 1960, to promote better and more flexible financing arrangements; it supplements the World Bank's activities.

ILO (International Labor Organization) Established on April 11, 1919, to improve labor conditions and living standards through international action.

IMCO (Inter-Governmental Maritime Consultative Organization) Established in 1948 to provide cooperation among governments on technical matters of international merchant shipping as well as to set safety standards. Membership is worldwide, with more than a dozen Latin American members.

IMF (International Monetary Fund) Established on December 27, 1945 to promote international monetary cooperation.

IPU (Inter-Parliamentary Union) Established on June 30, 1889, as a forum for personal contacts between members of the world parliamentary governments. Membership is worldwide, with the following Latin American members: Argentina, Brazil, Colombia, Costa Rica, Haiti, Mexico, Nicaragua, Paraguay, and Venezuela.

ISO (International Sugar Organization) Established on January 1, 1969, to administer the international sugar agreement and to compile data on the industry. Membership is worldwide, with the following Latin American members: Argentina, Brazil, Colombia, Cuba, Ecuador, Mexico, Uruguay, and Venezuela.

ITU (International Telecommunications Union) Established on May 17, 1895, to develop international regulations for telegraph, telephone, and radio services.

Junta A Spanish word meaning "assembly" or "council"; the legislative body of a country.

Ladino A Westernized Spanish-speaking Latin American, often of mixed Spanish and Indian blood.

LAFTA (Latin American Free Trade Association) Established on June 2, 1961, with headquarters in Montevideo, Uruguay.

Machismo Manliness. The male sense of honor; connotes the showy power of a "knight in shining armor."

Marianismo The feminine counterpart of machismo; the sense of strength that comes from controlling the family and the male.

Mennonite A strict Protestant denomination that derived from a sixteenth-century religious movement.

Mercosur Comprised of Argentina, Brazil, Paraguay, and Uraguay, this southern common market is the world's fourth largest integrated market. It was established in 1991.

Mestizo The offspring of a Spaniard or Portuguese and an American Indian.

Mulatto A person of mixed Caucasian and black ancestry.

Nahuatl The language of an Amerindian people of southern Mexico and Central America who are descended from the Aztec.

NAFTA (North American Free Trade Agreement) Established in 1993 between Mexico, Canada, and the United States, NAFTA went into effect January 1, 1994.

NAM (Non-Aligned Movement) A group of nations that chose not to be politically or militarily associated with either the West or the former Communist Bloc.

OAS (Organization of American States) (Formerly the Pan American Union) Established on December 31, 1951, with headquarters in Washington, DC.

ODECA (Central American Defense Organization) Established on October 14, 1951, to strengthen bonds among the Central American countries and to promote their economic, social, and cultural development through cooperation. Members: Costa Rica, El Salvador, Guatemala, Honduras, and Nicaragua.

OECS (Organization of Eastern Caribbean States) A Caribbean organization established on June 18, 1981, and headquartered in Castries, St. Lucia.

PAHO (Pan American Health Organization) Established in 1902 to promote and coordinate Western Hemisphere efforts to combat disease. All Latin American countries are members.

Patois A dialect other than the standard or literary dialect, such as some of the languages used in the Caribbean that are offshoots of French.

Peon Historically, a person forced to work off a debt or to perform penal servitude. It has come to mean a member of the working class.

PRI (Institutional Revolutionary Party) The dominant political party in Mexico.

Quechua The language of the Inca. It is still widely spoken in Peru.

Rastafarian A religious sect in the West Indies whose members believe in the deity of Haile Selassie, the deposed emperor of Ethiopia who died in 1975.

Rio Pact (Inter-American Treaty of Reciprocal Assistance) Established in 1947 at the Rio Conference to set up a policy of joint defense of Western Hemisphere countries. In case of aggression against any American state, all member countries will come to its aid.

Sandinistas The popular name for the government of Nicaragua from 1979 to 1990, following the ouster of President Anastasio Somoza. The name derives from César Augusto Sandino, a Nicaraguan guerrilla fighter of the 1920s.

SELA (Latin American Economic System) Established on October 18, 1975, as an economic forum for all Latin American countries.

Suffrage The right to vote in political matters.

UN (United Nations) Established on June 26, 1945, through official approval of the charter by delegates of 50 nations at an international conference in San Francisco. The charter went into effect on October 24, 1945.

UNESCO (United Nations Educational, Scientific, and Cultural Organization) Established on November 4, 1946, to promote international collaboration in education, science, and culture.

Unicameral A political structure with a single legislative branch.

UPU (Universal Postal Union) Established on July 1, 1875, to promote cooperation in international postal services.

World Bank A closely integrated group of international institutions providing financial and technical assistance to developing countries.

Bibliography

GENERAL WORKS

Mark A. Burkholder and Lyman L. Johnson, *Colonial Latin America,* 3rd ed. (New York: Oxford University Press, 1998).

E. Bradford Burns, *Latin America: A Concise Interpretive History,* 6th ed. (New Brunswick, NJ: Prentice-Hall, 1994).

David Bushnell and Neill Macaulay, *The Emergence of Latin America in the Nineteenth Century,* 2nd ed. (New York: Oxford University Press, 1994).

Franklin W. Knight, *Race, Ethnicity and Class: Forging the Plural Society in Latin America and the Caribbean* (Waco, TX: Baylor University Press, 1998).

Thomas E. Skidmore and Peter Smith, *Modern Latin America,* 4th ed. (New York: Oxford University Press, 1997).

Barbara A. Tenenbaum, ed., *Encyclopedia of Latin American History,* 5 vols. (New York: Charles Scribner's Sons, 1996).

Claudio Veliz, *The Centralist Tradition of Latin America* (Princeton, NJ: Princeton University Press, 1980).

NATIONAL HISTORIES

The following studies provide keen insights into the particular characteristics of individual Latin American nations.

Argentina

Leslie Bethell, *Argentina Since Independence* (New York: Cambridge University Press, 1994).

Nicholas Shumway, *The Invention of Argentina* (Berkeley, CA: University of California Press, 1991).

Bolivia

Herbert S. Klein, *Bolivia: The Evolution of a Multi-Ethnic Society,* 2nd ed. (New York: Oxford University Press, 1992).

Brazil

E. Bradford Burns, *A History of Brazil,* 3rd ed. (New York: Columbia University Press, 1993).

Caribbean Nations

Franklin W. Knight, *The Caribbean: The Genesis of a Fragmented Nationalism,* 2nd ed. (New York: Oxford University Press, 1990).

David Lowenthal, *West Indian Societies* (New York: Oxford University Press, 1972).

Louis A. Perez Jr., *Cuba: Between Reform and Revolution,* 2nd ed. (New York: Oxford University Press, 1995).

Central America

Ralph Lee Woodward Jr., *Central America: A Nation Divided,* 2nd ed. (New York: Oxford University Press, 1985).

Chile

Brian Loveman, *Chile: The Legacy of Hispanic Capitalism,* 2nd ed. (New York: Oxford University Press, 1988).

Mexico

Michael C. Meyer and William L. Sherman, *The Course of Mexican History,* 5th ed. (New York: Oxford University Press, 1995).

Eric Wolf, *Sons of the Shaking Earth: The Peoples of Mexico and Guatemala; Their Land, History, and Culture* (Chicago: University of Chicago Press, 1970).

Ricardo Pozas Arciniega, *Juan Chamula: An Ethnolographical Recreation of the Life of a Mexican Indian* (Berkeley, CA: University of California Press, 1962).

Peru

José Carlos Mariategui, *Seven Interpretive Essays on Peruvian Reality* (Austin, TX: University of Texas Press, 1974).

David P. Werlich, *Peru: A Short History* (Carbondale, IL: Southern Illinois University Press, 1978).

Venezuela

John V. Lombardi, *Venezuela: The Search for Order, The Dream of Progress* (New York: Oxford University Press, 1982).

NOVELS IN TRANSLATION

The Latin American novel is perhaps one of the best windows on the cultures of the region. The following are just a few of many highly recommended novels.

Jorge Amado, *Clove and Cinnamon* (Avon, 1988).

Manlio Argueta, *One Day of Life* (Vintage, 1990).

Miguel Ángel Asturias, *El Señor Presidenté* (Macmillan, 1975).

Mariano Azuela, *The Underdogs* (Buccaneer Books, 1986).

Alejo Carpentier, *Reasons of State* (Writers & Readers, 1981).

Carlos Fuentes, *The Death of Artemio Cruz* (FS&G, 1964).

Jorge Icaza, *Huasipungo: The Villagers* (Arcturus Books, 1973).

Gabriel García Márquez, *One Hundred Years of Solitude* (Penguin, 1971).

Mario Vargas Llosa, *The Green House* (FS&G, 1985).

Victor Montejo, *Testimony: Death of a Guatemalan Village* (Curbstone Press, 1987).

Rachel de Queiroz, *The Three Marias* (University of Texas Press, 1991).

Graham Greene's novels about Latin America, such as *The Comedians* (1966), and V. S. Naipaul's study of Trinidad, *The Loss of El Dorado: A History* (1969), offer profound insights into the region.

CURRENT EVENTS

To keep up to date on the unfolding drama of Latin American events, the following are especially useful.

Current History: A World Affairs Journal
The Latin American issue usually appears in February.

Latin America Press

A newsletter (48 issues per year) that focuses on human rights and the role of the Catholic Church in Latin America. Available in Spanish as *Noticias Aliadas*.

Latin America Weekly Report

An excellent weekly review of economic and political developments in Latin America.

Latin American Regional Report

The Regional Reports are published monthly on Brazil, Mexico and Central America, the Caribbean, the Andean Group, and the Southern Cone.

Update Latin America

This bimonthly news analysis, published by the Washington Office on Latin America, pays particular attention to human rights problems in Latin America.

PERIODICALS

Americas

Organization of American States
17th and Constitution Avenues, NW
Washington, D.C. 20006
This periodical by the OAS is published 10 times per year in English, Spanish, and Portuguese.

The Christian Science Monitor

One Norway Street
Boston, MA 02115
This newspaper is published 5 days per week, with news coverage, articles, and specific features on world events.

Commonweal

Commonweal Publishing Co., Inc.
232 Madison Avenue
New York, NY 10016
This biweekly publication reviews literature, current events, religion, and the arts.

Dollars and Sense

Economics Affairs Bureau, Inc.
38 Union Square, Room 14
Somerville, MA 02143
Published monthly (except June and August), this magazine offers interpretations of current economic events from the perspective of social change.

The Economist

25 St. James's Street
London, England
This periodical presents world events from a British perspective.

Multinational Monitor

Ralph Nader's Corporate Accountability Research Group
1346 Connecticut Avenue, NW

Washington, D.C. 20006
This monthly periodical offers editorials and articles on world events and current issues.

The Nation

Nation Enterprises/Nation Associates, Inc.
72 Fifth Avenue
New York, NY 10011
Published 47 times during the year, this magazine presents editorials and articles dealing with areas of public interest—with special attention given to American politics and foreign policy, social problems, and education. Also covers literature and the arts.

The New Republic

The New Republic, Inc.
1220 19th Street, NW, Suite 200
Washington, D.C. 20036
Weekly coverage of politics, literature, and world events.

The New York Times

The New York Times Co.
229 West 43rd Street
New York, NY 10036
A daily newspaper that covers world news through articles and editorials.

Science News

Science Service
1719 N Street, NW
Washington, D.C. 20036
For those interested in science, this weekly publication gives an overview of worldwide scientific developments.

UNESCO Courier

7 Place de Fontenoy
Paris, France
Published by the UN, the magazine presents extensive treatment of world events by devoting each monthly issue to a specific topic.

The Wall Street Journal

Dow Jones Books
Box 300
Princeton, NJ 08540
Presents broad daily coverage of world news through articles and editorials.

World Press Review

The Stanley Foundation
230 Park Avenue
New York, NY 10169
Each month, this publication presents foreign magazine and newspaper stories on political, social, and economic affairs.

Index